Software Testing Foundation Level

Guide for ISTQB® certification

ISTQB® Certified Tester Foundation Level (CTFL)

Syllabus v4.0.1

November 2026

Catherine Newbould BSc. (Hons.), AKC

Software Testing
Certified Tester Foundation Level Syllabus v4.0.1
Guide for ISTQB® Certification

November 2023 and November 2026 (revised)

Catherine Newbould BSc. (Hons.), AKC
Website: revisionary.co.uk

This book can be ordered online at www.revisionary.co.uk
contact@revisionary.co.uk

Note for Librarians: A cataloging record for this book is available from
Nielsen Booknet: bookorders.nielsenbooknet.com

ISBN 978-0-9536056-6-8

AiFlex Publishing UK
publish@aiflex.com

About the Author: Catherine Newbould BSc. (Hons.), AKC.
With over 25 years in software and systems engineering, Catherine Newbould has extensive experience in software testing. Having held senior positions in systems support, computer systems education and management in the United Kingdom, Europe, South Africa and the United States, Catherine's experience ranges from operating systems to general systems testing, detailed assessments, defining processes and recommending fixes.

Involvement with exam preparation for ISTQB® Foundation, Advanced Test Analyst and Test Manager identified a need for a book aligned to the ISTQB® Syllabus v4.0.1 for Certified Tester Foundation Level (CTFL). In writing this guide, the author has used her experience gained from explaining concepts and setting practice exam questions on topics in previous guides for Advanced Test Analyst, Test Manager and Security Tester. She has drawn on her own extensive systems and software testing background. Based on this wealth of experience, the book includes over 200 relevant practice questions with detailed answers, hints on areas of potential difficulty and three complete practice exams aligned to the Syllabus and ISTQB® exam specification. Each practice exam has forty original questions with answers and full explanations. The book also includes examples and practice questions in each sub-section, advice on how to approach the exam, terms used detailed information on the ISTQB® specified exam format, question types and importantly where marks can be gained or lost. The practice exams, together with the in-depth descriptions and questions written by the author cover all specified learning objectives. Being aligned with the ISTQB® Syllabus and exam specifications, this guide provides the essential preparation for those wishing to achieve certification at Foundation Level.

Design and Production Editor
Nigel Powell BSc (Hons) Eng. has an extensive portfolio and a wide range of skills, including IT services, finance, project management, technical documentation and graphic design.

Consultant Editor
Elizabeth Powell, BA (Hons), CTAL-TA, CTAL-TM, CTAL-TTA, CT-AI, is a UK-based Senior Consultant Software Tester for general applications and mobile enterprise apps across various platforms. With internationally recognized certifications in Test Management, Test Analyst, and Technical Test Analyst at Advanced Level, and AI Testing Specialist, she has provided invaluable input across many areas of this book.

Keywords: Software Testing, ISTQB, ASTQB, Foundation, CTFL, Analyst, Manager, Self-study, Exam, Certification, Study Guide, Syllabus, v4.0, Learning Objective, Knowledge Level, Software Development, Test Case, Objective, Quality, Assurance, Control, Test Process, Test technique, Risk, Analysis, Test Automation, Impact, Lifecycle, SDLC.

Disclaimer

Many designations used by organizations to distinguish their products are claimed as trademarks of their respective companies. Where these designations appear in this book and AiFlex™ Publishing is aware of a trademark claim, designations are acknowledged. All product names and services identified in this book are used in an editorial way only and for the benefit of companies, with no intention of infringement of trademarks or other rights. Furthermore, by naming products and services it is not intended to convey endorsement or other affiliation with the company or trademark owner and the book publisher or its author.

Of particular mention, this book has been written with reference to the International Software Testing Qualifications Board ISTQB® Foundation Level (CTFL) materials. These materials are identified in *References*. The contents of this book and study materials have been created and produced independently. The contents have not been authorized, sponsored or approved by ISTQB or any of its National or International Member Boards or subsidiaries, training providers or their affiliates. There is no endorsement or affiliation, expressed or implied, between this book and any organization that prepares or provides training or software testing either in the United Kingdom or internationally.

Certain phrases, themes and context may have been used to align or adhere to the ISTQB® Syllabus. Every effort has been made to ensure the accuracy of the contents of this book. However, 100% accuracy of the information contained herein cannot be guaranteed. Later versions of ISTQB® documents may result in changes required. While no person can guarantee with certainty that working through any published materials will result in success in an exam, a studious approach using this book will provide a firm foundation of knowledge on the road to success and achieving the recognized international certification goal and greater potential for career advancement.

Additional materials and updates to the contents may be made available from time to time.
Please check the resource website revisionary.co.uk or email contact@revisionary.co.uk.

PREFACE

This book is for software testers and those with career paths in software testing and test management. The extensive content will help build knowledge, consolidate and extend understanding to the required level for success in the ISTQB® exam for CTFL certification. The guide is based on the ISTQB® Syllabus. It assumes some background knowledge of software testing and terminology. This guide can be used for self-study, to support e-learning and instructor-led training courses as well as being a practical reference for software testing.

This guide provides comprehensive coverage of the ISTQB® Foundation Level Syllabus and covers all learning objectives to the required knowledge level. It provides over 200 practice questions for consolidating knowledge and understanding, advice on how to approach the exam, sixteen exercises, and three Practice Exams, each with 40 original questions with answers and explanations.

The book is relevant for individuals in roles such as software tester, test analyst, test engineer, test consultant, test manager, user acceptance tester, and software developer. It can also be used by an individual who needs to gain a basic understanding of software testing, including project managers, business analysts, quality managers, software development managers, consultants and others.

Learning objectives are considered individually with key information focused directly on the learning objective and where appropriate, diagrams and tables to aid understanding. The format allows for an individual to work at their own pace, by either studying and practising questions for just one learning objective, a subgroup of learning objectives or a whole Syllabus section. Working methodically through the practice questions, answers and explanations builds on your skills in software testing in preparation for the three included Practice Exams.

Every software application needs to work as intended and be as reliable and stable as possible. Your skills in software testing are as important as those of the designers, software developers and others who contribute to a combined team effort. I wish you the very best for your exam preparation, taking the exam and your future career. Once successful in achieving the ISTQB® Certified Tester Foundation Level (CTFL) certification, the door opens to greater opportunities to further a career in software testing and beyond. This level of certification is a significant career milestone for any software tester. Those with ISTQB® tester certification may use CTFL after their name. This official certification is internationally recognized, see the 'successful candidate register' at scr.istqb.org.

Resource Website - revisionary.co.uk

Relevant materials and updates may be added periodically to the resource website revisionary.co.uk
To provide feedback or report inaccuracies, please email: contact@revisionary.co.uk
We welcome hearing from you.

Acknowledgements

This book follows the publication of guides for Advanced Test Analyst, Advanced Test Management, Advanced Technical Test Analyst, Specialist Security Tester and AI Testing ISTQB® certifications. The book is the result of several months of creative work to produce a high-quality resource aligned to the ISTQB® Syllabus v4.0 (2023) and revised for v4.0.1. It complements the reader's experience in software testing and can be used for self-study, to support training courses in instructor-led environments virtual settings and as a reference.

My sincere thanks go to Nigel and Elizabeth Powell for their invaluable contributions and support with ideas, proofreading, design, and production, as well as encouragement. My thanks go to all the students pursuing ISTQB certifications.
To all students of software testing aiming for the Foundation Level and other certifications, thank you for your support, and good luck with your studies.

Design and Production Editor
Nigel Powell BSc (Hons) Eng. has an extensive portfolio and a wide range of skills, including IT services, finance, project management, technical documentation and graphic design.

Consultant Editor
Elizabeth Powell, BA (Hons), CTFL, CTAL-TA, CTAL-TM, CTAL-TTA, CT-AI, is a UK-based Senior Consultant Software Tester for general applications and mobile enterprise apps across various platforms. With internationally recognized certifications in Test Management, Test Analyst, and Technical Test Analyst at Advanced Level, and AI Testing Specialist, she has provided invaluable input across many areas of this book.

I acknowledge this book relies on the ISTQB® Foundation Level CTFL Syllabus and the other documents listed in *References*. Portions of this publication reference ISTQB® copyright materials by ISTQB® and author contributors to publications. Copyright and specific citations to these and other publications and materials are acknowledged and also detailed in *References*.

This book has been written to comply with these documents (unless otherwise stated). The Syllabus has been used in accordance with the ISTQB® 2023 Foundation Level Syllabus v4.0 section 0.1 *'Purpose of this Syllabus'*, which states the ISTQB® Syllabus is provided, *'To the international software and systems engineering community, to advance the profession of software and systems testing, and as a basis for books and articles.'*
C. N.

About this Guide and Terms Used

This guide is based on the most up-to-date sources available at the time of publication. This includes the ISTQB® Foundation Syllabus v4.0.1 and other sources. Other referenced documents used are Exam Structures and Rules v1.2, Exam Structures & Rules Tables v1.19 and ISTQB® Glossary v4.8.

The three included practice exams cover all ISTQB learning objectives and adhere to ISTQB Exam structure and rules in the question format prescribed by ISTQB®. In addition, this guide has over 200 examples and questions with answers and explanations providing an opportunity to practice, consolidate learning and progress at the right pace to achieve certification.

The ISTQB® Glossary is regularly updated. ISTQB® aligns terminology with International Standards Organization ISO documents to reflect relevant changes. Some ISO standards have also been revised. Where appropriate, updates have been made in this book.

Syllabus

Where the term Syllabus is used without qualification, this refers to:
ISTQB® Certified Tester Foundation Level (CTFL) Syllabus version v4.0.1 (September 2024).

Release Notes

Unless otherwise specified, release notes refer to Syllabus v4.0.1 Appendix C.

Glossary

ISTQB® Standard Glossary of Terms used in Software Testing, version 4.8 and updates to the publication date of October 2026 where they are known.

Exam Structures and Rules

ISTQB® Certified Tester Exam Structures and Rules v1.2 (May 2025)
ISTQB® Exam Structures & Rules Tables v1.19 (Aug 2026)

These terms have, when it has been deemed useful to do so, been used together with other words from the expanded titles above.
Extracts from the above sources quoted in this guide are typically included in quotation marks and italics.
Locations and sources of the documents above are acknowledged here and given later in *References*.
Relevant materials and updates may be added periodically to the resource website revisionary.co.uk
To provide feedback or report inaccuracies, please email: contact@revisionary.co.uk

Other Books by C. Newbould

See later in this guide after the index pages for details on other books by the author.
See the resource website **revisionary.co.uk** for more information, sample pages as well as updates and details of new book releases and other media.

Notes on the Revised Edition of this Guide for Syllabus v4.0.1

The revised ISTQB Foundation Level (CTFL) Syllabus v4.0.1 incorporates minor corrections and updates to the earlier Syllabus v4.0 following the major rewrite of version 4.0 in April 2023. Syllabus v4.0.1 maintains the same core architecture and the same exam format as the earlier Syllabus. There are no structural changes. We made some readability improvements.

While this revised guide includes changes to align content with the specified Syllabus v4.0.1 Release Notes, many aspects were already covered correctly in the previous guide and therefore do not require modification.

The changes made to the wording of five Learning Objectives are minor and do not affect the text following the learning objectives, *see later*. These changes have been made in this revised guide and are: 'summarize' in FL-1.4.1 is changed to 'explain', the hyphen to 'shift-left' has been added in FL-2.1.5, 'static test techniques' is changed to 'static testing' FL-3.1.1, 'black-box, white-box and experience-based test techniques' is changed to 'black-box test techniques' FL-3.1.3, 'white-box test techniques' and 'experience-based test techniques' and 'scope of testing' is changed to 'test scope', FL-5.2.3. See Chapter *Required information, Learning Objectives.*

Three keywords have been added. These are: 'test process' and 'traceability' in Chapter 1 and 'test strategy' in Chapter three. The usage of these terms is covered in this guide.

Syllabus v4.0.1 recognizes the standard ISO/IEC 25010 was republished in 2023. The earlier guide already included details of both the 2011 and the 2023 versions of ISO/IEC 25010. Although it acknowledges that Syllabus v4.0.1 retains the original quality characteristics as specified in ISO/IEC 25010, the new names, 'interaction capability' (previously 'usability') and 'flexibility' (previously 'portability') are acknowledged as alternative names. Exams may contain either and the practice exam questions in this guide reflect this.

Syllabus v4.0.1 replaces 'quality control' with 'testing'. 'Testing' and 'quality control' QC are closely related, but they are not exactly the same. 'Testing' is a key activity within 'quality control'. While 'testing' focuses on evaluating software to identify defects and verify specified requirements, 'quality control' encompasses a broader range of activities used to assess whether the software product meets defined quality standards. This requires changes to the content of FL-1.1.2 and related questions to focus specifically on testing rather than the broader concept of quality control.

Minor corrections in Syllabus v4.0.1 include changes to better align with Glossary terms such as: 'types of tests' to 'test types', 'test monitoring and control' to 'test monitoring and test control'. Further minor corrections and clarifications in Syllabus v4.0.1 include changes such as: 'the perspective of testing' to 'the perspective of testers' and 'a reasonable coverage' to 'a reasonable level of coverage'.
Syllabus v4.0.1 has removed the use of 'post-project meeting' and 'completion criteria' as synonyms of 'retrospective' and 'exit criteria' respectively. These currently remain in the ISTQB Glossary so they could be used in some exams. For these types of minor corrections and clarifications, changes, where appropriate and not already in the earlier version of this guide have been made.

Some changes to the Syllabus v4.0.1 have not been made in this guide. For example, the ISQTB Release Notes specify that 'state transition diagram' is replaced by 'state diagram'. Both terms are correct. However, 'state transition diagram' is generally the more precise term used in software testing when describing how a system moves from one state to another in response to events or inputs and so continues to be used in this guide.

> 'State transition diagram' explicitly emphasizes the transitions between states triggered by events or inputs. It is particularly appropriate in the context of state transition testing.
> 'State diagram' is a shorter, broader term commonly used in software engineering and Unified Modeling Language UML. A UML state machine diagram shows states, transitions, events, and associated conditions or actions.

The general recommendation for a software testing textbook is to use 'state transition diagram when discussing state transition testing. The ISTQB Syllabus v4.0.1 and ISTQB Glossary v4.8 include 'state transition testing'.

Some changes in Syllabus v4.0.1 have been only partially implemented. For example, the Release Notes change 'goal', listed in the Glossary as a synonym of 'test objective', to 'test objective'. While this change is appropriate in some contexts, this has not been applied to business goals, personal career goals, etc. A further example is 'documentation' to be changed to 'testware'. 'Testware' is defined as work products and covers more than documentation. Some text is intended to specifically apply to 'documentation' and not to other work products.

This revised guide will continue to serve as a useful resource for anyone who needs to demonstrate practical knowledge of the fundamental concepts of software testing. It is relevant for individuals in a range of roles, including testers, test analysts, test engineers, test consultants, test managers, user acceptance testers, and software developers. It is also appropriate for those who require a basic understanding of software testing, including project managers, quality managers, software development managers, business analysts, IT directors, and management consultants.

Syllabus v4.0 to v4.0.1 Changes in Learning Objectives wording to align it with Glossary terms

FL-1.4.1: Summarize the different test activities and tasks →
Explain the different test activities and related tasks.

FL-2.1.5: Explain the shift-left approach →
Explain shift left.

FL-3.1.1: Recognize types of products that can be examined by the different static test techniques →
Recognize types of work products that can be examined by static testing.

FL-3.1.3: Compare and contrast static and dynamic testing →
Compare and contrast static testing and dynamic testing.

FL-4.1.1: Distinguish black-box, white-box and experience-based test techniques →
Distinguish black-box test techniques, white-box test techniques and experience-based test techniques.

FL-5.2.3: Explain how product risk analysis may influence thoroughness and scope of testing →
Explain how product risk analysis may influence thoroughness and test scope.

Table of Contents

INTRODUCTION

This guide can be used as a resource for independent study, to support a training course and for reference.

The structure of this guide is closely aligned to the six sections in ISTQB® Syllabus. The sections are divided into smaller sections and subsections for each learning objective. This enables learners to progress at their own pace and gives flexibility on the number of learning objectives covered in a study period. Each learning objective has a specified knowledge level of K1, K2 or K3.
The following are included:

- Information and explanations for all 64 learning objectives
- Over 200 practice questions covering all K1, K2 and K3 learning objectives
- Two to seven practice questions for each learning objective
- 16 exercises for the eight K3 level learning objectives
- Three original Practice Exams, each of 40 questions
- Answers and explanations for all practice questions, exercises and exam questions
- Hints and advice on how to approach the exam

Organize your Study Time

Organizing your study time allows you to allocate sufficient time to cover each learning objective, ensuring that you cover all the material you need to learn. With this guide being structured on learning objectives, it provides a flexible and convenient way to acquire knowledge and skills.

Organizing study time allows you to pace yourself. Focus on as many or as few learning objectives in any session as appropriate for your study schedule. Avoid overloading with too much material in a short amount of time as it can lead to decreased retention.

Recognize Terms and Learn Keywords

Knowing and understanding terms is important. A keyword is a word, group of words or concept of particular importance. Keywords are given at the start of each chapter and should be remembered. For more information, see Chapter *Required Knowledge - Terminology, Keywords and the Glossary*.

Focus on Learning Objectives, LOs

The Exam Structures and Rules states, *'Learning Objectives describe the gain on cognitive competence to be achieved in relation to a given content.'* For every learning objective, study the information provided in this guide. Questions in the exam are directly linked to learning objectives. For further details, see Chapter *Required Knowledge – Learning Objectives*.

Understand the Knowledge Levels, K-levels

Each learning objective has an assigned knowledge level. Understand and work to the K-levels required. An exam question may be based on one or more learning objectives. The highest K-level and its associated learning objective are typically assigned to the exam question. For a more detailed explanation of the K-levels, see Chapter *Required Knowledge.*

Practice questions and consolidate knowledge

Allow time to consolidate your knowledge. Everyone learns differently.

Study the exercises for the K3 level learning objectives. These will allow you to check your understanding of the eight K3 level concepts and techniques before practicing the questions.

Work through practice questions that cover all learning objectives to gauge your understanding and identify gaps in your knowledge. For every learning objective, there are between two and seven practice questions at the end of each sub-section. Check the answers and study the explanations. Practice questions follow the specified ISTQB format and meet the required knowledge levels. Information in the Chapter *About the exam – how to approach Exam questions* gives details that will also be useful for approaching the practice questions.

Use self-study clean page testing. Decide on a topic. Take a sheet of paper and write down or draw what you know. This guide includes lists, tables and diagrams of key points for many topics that support clean page practice.

Prepare for the Exam

For those intending to take the exam, understanding the layout of the exam, the format of questions and the marking scheme will boost confidence. This guide provides advice on how to approach the exam and details on where marks can be gained or lost. See Chapter *About the Exam – Where marks can be gained or lost.*

Exam Practice

This guide includes three practice exams, each containing 40 original questions. The questions adhere to the formats given in ISTQB® Exam Structures and Rules to simulate an exam. The three exams (plus an additional question) cover all learning objectives. Answers to the practice exam questions are included, together with detailed explanations. The order of questions in the practice exams follows the order given in the Exam Structures & Rules Tables document. However, with formal exams now being taken online, the order of questions may be randomized. There is advice on how to assess your practice exam result and identify learning objectives you should focus on to improve your understanding. See Chapter *Using the Practice Exams.*

REQUIRED KNOWLEDGE

The required knowledge is defined and guided through the use of Knowledge Levels (K-levels), and learning objectives (LOs). Knowledge levels indicate the depth of understanding and proficiency that should be achieved. Learning objectives are statements defining the specific, measurable outcomes expected from the attainment of that knowledge.

Knowledge Levels, K-levels

K-levels used at Foundation Level are as below. The levels originate from Bloom's taxonomy, see *References*. At Foundation Level, all exam questions carry one mark, irrespective of K-level.

K1 Remember Terms and concepts should be remembered, recognized and recalled. Definitions of keywords listed at the start of each section should be learned as all keywords in the Syllabus are examinable for their definition. K1 level learning objectives in the Syllabus begin with one of the following action verbs: identify, recall, recognize. In the Syllabus, there are 14 learning objectives at the K1 level. Questions at higher K-levels may also require K1 level understanding.

K2 Understand K2 level learning objectives require the understanding of facts, standards and techniques and how they interrelate. This level does not generally require the skills to apply the techniques. Learning objectives at this level may use one of the following action verbs: 'classify, compare, contrast, differentiate, distinguish, exemplify, explain, give examples or summarize'. In the Syllabus, there are 42 learning objectives at the K2 level.

K3 Apply K3 level learning objectives require the ability to apply facts, techniques and standards but not necessarily how to adapt them or select the most appropriate. Learning objectives in this Syllabus all start with 'apply, prepare, use'. In the Syllabus, there are 8 learning objectives at the K3 level.

Syllabus Section	**Number of Learning Objectives**			
	K1	**K2**	**K3**	**Total**
5. Managing the Test Activities	4	9	3	**16**
4. Test Analysis and Design	0	9	5	**14**
1. Fundamentals of Testing	3	11	0	**14**
2. Testing Throughout the SDLC	2	8	0	**10**
3. Static Testing	4	4	0	**8**
6. Test Tools	1	1	0	**2**
Total	**14**	**42**	**8**	**64**

Note: Several questions included in this guide are shown as 'consolidation' in place of K3 level. These questions relate to topics associated with K3 level learning objectives but may be at a lower knowledge level than K3. They have been included to help build understanding of the K3 level learning objective. In addition, there are exercises and a minimum of two practice questions for all K3 learning objectives. All exercises and questions have answers and explanations.

Terminology, Keywords and the Glossary

To be able to recognize what is meant by the learning objectives and to answer exam questions, terms need to be known, as defined in the Glossary. For example, answer options in the exam often include an option that may seem plausible but is incorrect when the strict definitions of terms are applied. The Glossary explains the differences between terms you may consider to be similar in meaning, for example, 'test specification', 'test process', 'test procedure', 'test script' and 'test execution schedule'.

A **Keyword** is a word, group of words or concept of particular importance. The Syllabus states, *'All terms listed as keywords .... shall be remembered (K1), even if not explicitly mentioned in the learning objectives.'* Keywords used in this guide are included at the start of each chapter 1 to 6. Several terms have been suggested where appropriate to the lists.

The **Glossary** can be accessed via the ISTQB® website home page. Access is also available at the App Store for Apple mobile devices and the Google Play Store for Android mobile devices. Both are provided by ISTQB® free of charge and without advertising.

Keyword mind maps are included on the ISTQB website, accessed via the Glossary help button. These show the areas where keywords are used and how keywords are connected. At the time of publication of this guide, there are some variations between which keywords are included in the Syllabus and which are in the mind maps. These and other variations may be resolved in later versions.

Abbreviations when used are typically also given in full. Abbreviations and acronyms are listed in Appendix A. This can be used as a checklist for making sure you are aware of the context of a relevant abbreviation.

Terminology evolves over time and with closer alignment to standards and naming conventions. The online Glossary and mobile app are subject to change. Definitions are from the current Glossary v4.8. The Glossary definitions quoted in this guide are typically included in quotation marks in italics. Definitions from other sources are also in quotation marks, but these are not typically in italics unless otherwise stated. ISTQB® Glossary Release Notes are not readily available. However, the history of terms can be viewed on the ISTQB website Glossary page using the search with history filters.

It is important to recognize when synonyms of terms are used. Keywords with the synonyms that are given in the Glossary include:

Keyword	**Synonyms in the ISTQB Glossary**
black-box test technique	black-box test design technique, specification-based test technique
black-box testing	specification-based testing
component integration testing	module integration testing
component testing	module testing
confirmation testing	re-testing
coverage	test coverage
defect	bug, fault, flaw
defect report	bug report
equivalence partitioning	partition testing
error	mistake
exit criteria	test completion criteria, completion criteria†
experience-based test technique	experience-based test design technique, experience-based technique
risk level	risk exposure
state transition testing	finite state testing
test completion	test closure
test completion report	test summary report
test condition	test situation, test requirement
test data	test dataset
testing	quality control††
test level	test stage
test objective	test goal
test progress report	test status report
test result	test outcome, result
test technique	test design technique
walkthrough	structured walkthrough
white-box test technique	white-box test design technique, structure-based test technique
white-box testing	clear-box testing, code-based testing, glass-box testing, logic-driven testing and structural testing, structure-based testing

† In Syllabus v4.0.1 'completion criteria' is removed as equivalent to 'exit criteria', see *Release Notes*.

†† In Syllabus v4.0.1 'testing' is specified as a part of 'quality control', and is not fully equivalent to 'quality control', see FL-1.2.2.

Other terms that are not keywords may also have synonyms, for example, false-negative (false-pass), false positive (false fail), test environment (test bed, test rig).

'retrospective' is recommended as an additional keyword. The Glossary lists synonyms: 'project retrospective', 'retrospective meeting', 'post-project meeting'. Syllabus v4.0.1 specifically removes 'post project meeting' as a synonym of 'retrospective', see *Release Notes*.

This guide refers to ISO/IEE definitions of terms where it is useful to do so. ISO/IEE definitions can be accessed online by a 'search' for the relevant standard, and then using the 'preview' button, see *References, ISO/IEE Standards*.

ISO/IEC 25010:2023 includes some updated quality characteristics and subcharacteristics. For example, the term 'Interaction capability' replaces 'usability'. 'Operational constraint' refers to the capability of the product to constrain its operation. For further details, see *Appendix E, ISO/IEC 25010:2023* and FL-2.2.2 page 84.

Learning Objectives

Learning Objectives, LOs serve to define the scope of the Syllabus. Learning objectives are assigned a Foundation Level FL- number specifying the section, sub-section and number within the sub-section.

This guide covers all learning objectives specified in the Syllabus and expands on concepts where appropriate. Diagrams and tables are included to aid understanding. Thoroughly studying the content of this guide and working through the practice questions to consolidate knowledge, will support success in the Foundation Level exam. Not all learning objectives will be included in any one exam.

The ISTQB® Exam Structures and Rules v1.2 specifies, '*All questions shall assess at least one Learning Objective from the syllabus under Examination. Questions may include supporting material at the K1 level from the rest of the syllabus*' and '*Where questions address more than one LO, then the question should primarily address the highest K-level LO*'.

The following table shows the relationship between Foundation Level (FL-) learning objective, knowledge level and exam question number as specified in the ISTQB® Exam Structures & Rules Tables v1.19 and the practice exams in this guide.

For example, there is one primary learning objective FL-1.3.1 listed for exam Question #4, this means the exam should contain one question based on FL-1.3.1, Testing Principles.
Alternatively, Question #1 could be based on one of two learning objectives, FL-1.1.1 or FL-1.2.2, so only one of these learning objectives may be examined. In addition to practice questions at the end of each sub-section, questions for specific learning objectives can be found in the practice exams as shown in the following table.

Exam Q#	FL-	K	Learning Objective	Practice Exam
1	1.1.1	K1	**What is Testing?** Identify typical test objectives	1
	1.2.2		**Why is Testing Necessary?** Recall the relationship between testing and quality assurance	2, 3
2	1.5.2	K1	**Essential Skills and Good Practices in Testing** Recall the advantages of the whole team approach	1, 2, 3
3	1.1.2	K2	**What is Testing?** Differentiate testing from debugging	1
	1.2.1		**Why is Testing Necessary?** Exemplify why testing is necessary	2
	1.2.3		**Why is Testing Necessary?** Distinguish between root cause, error, defect, and failure	3
4	1.3.1	K2	**Testing Principles** Explain the seven testing principles	1, 2, 3
5 - 7*	1.4.1	K2	**Test Activities, Testware and Test Roles** Explain the different test activities and related tasks	1, 2, 3
	1.4.2		**Test Activities, Testware and Test Roles** Explain the impact of context on the test process	2
	1.4.3		**Test Activities, Testware and Test Roles** Differentiate the testware that supports test activities	1
	1.4.4		**Test activities, Testware and Test Roles** Explain the value of maintaining traceability	1, 3
	1.4.5		**Test Activities, Testware and Test Roles** Compare the different roles in testing	2, 3
8	1.5.1	K2	**Essential Skills and Good Practices in Testing** Give examples of the generic skills required for testing	1
	1.5.3		**Essential Skills and Good Practices in Testing** Distinguish the benefits and drawbacks of independence of testing	2, 3
9	2.1.2	K1	**Testing in the Context of a Software Development Lifecycle** Recall good testing practices that apply to all SDLC	1, 2, 3
10	2.1.3	K1	**Testing in the Context of a Software Development Lifecycle** Recall the examples of test-first approaches to development	1, 2, 3
11	2.2.1	K2	**Test Levels and Test Types** Distinguish the different test levels	1
	2.2.2		**Test Levels and Test Types** Distinguish the different test types	2, 3
12	2.2.3	K2	**Test Levels and Test Types** Distinguish confirmation testing from regression testing	1, 3
	2.3.1		**Maintenance Testing** Summarize maintenance testing and its triggers	2

13	2.1.1	K2	**Testing in the Context of a Software Development Lifecycle** Explain the impact of the chosen software development lifecycle on testing	1
	2.1.6		**Testing in the Context of a Software Development Lifecycle** Explain how retrospectives can be used as a mechanism for process improvement	2, 3
14	2.1.4	K2	**Testing in the Context of a Software Development Lifecycle** Summarize how DevOps might have an impact on testing	1, 3
	2.1.5		**Testing in the Context of a Software Development Lifecycle** Explain shift left	2
15-16*	3.1.1	K1	**Static Testing Basics** Recognize types of work products that can be examined by static testing	1
	3.2.1		**Feedback and Review Process** Identify the benefits of early and frequent stakeholder feedback	2, 3
	3.2.3		**Feedback and Review Process** Recall which responsibilities are assigned to the principal roles when performing reviews	2, 3
	3.2.5		**Feedback and Review Process** Recall the factors that contribute to a successful review	1
17	3.1.2	K2	**Static Testing Basics** Explain the value of static testing	1, 3
	3.1.3		**Static Testing Basics** Compare and contrast static testing and dynamic testing	2
18	3.2.2	K2	**Feedback and Review Process** Summarize the activities of the review process	1, 3
	3.2.4		**Feedback and Review Process** Compare and contrast the different review types	2
19	4.1.1	K2	**Test Techniques Overview** Distinguish black-box test techniques, white-box test techniques and experience-based test techniques	1, 2, 3
20-21*	4.3.1	K2	**White-box Test Techniques** Explain statement testing	1
	4.3.2		**White-box Test Techniques** Explain branch testing	1, 2, 3
	4.3.3		**White-box Test Techniques** Explain the value of white-box testing	2, 3
22-23*	4.4.1	K2	**Experience-based Test Techniques** Explain error guessing	1, 2, 3
	4.4,2		**Experience-based Test Techniques** Explain exploratory testing	2, 3
	4.4.3		**Experience-based Test Techniques** Explain checklist-based testing	1

Exam Q#	FL-	K	Learning Objective	Practice Exam
24	4.5.1	K2	**Collaboration-based Test Approaches** Explain how to write user stories in collaboration with developers and business representatives	1, 3
	4.5.2		**Collaboration-based Test Approaches** Classify the different options for writing acceptance criteria	2
25-29	4.2.1	K3	**Black-box Test Techniques** Use equivalence partitioning to derive test cases	1, 2, 3
	4.2.2		**Black-box Test Techniques** Use boundary value analysis to derive test cases	1, 2, 3
	4.2.3		**Black-box Test Techniques** Use decision table testing to derive test cases	1, 2, 3
	4.2.4		**Black-box Test Techniques** Use state transition testing to derive test cases	1, 2, 3
	4.5.3		**Collaboration-based Test Approaches** Use acceptance test-driven development (ATDD) to derive test cases	1, 2, 3
30	5.1.2	K1	**Test Planning** Recognize how a tester adds value to iteration and release planning	1
	5.1.6		**Test Planning** Recall the concepts of the test pyramid	2
	5.2.1		**Risk Management** Identify risk level by using risk likelihood and risk impact	3
	5.3.1		**Test Monitoring, Test Control and Test Completion** Recall metrics used for testing	Additional
31	5.1.1	K2	**Test Planning** Exemplify the purpose and content of a test plan	1, 3
	5.1.3		**Test Planning** Compare and contrast entry criteria and exit criteria	2
32	5.1.7	K2	**Test Planning** Summarize the testing quadrants and their relationships with test levels and test types	1, 2, 3
33	5.2.2	K2	**Risk Management** Distinguish between project risks and product risks	1
	5.2.3		**Risk Management** Explain how product risk analysis may influence thoroughness and test scope	2
	5.2.4		**Risk Management** Explain what measures can be taken in response to analyzed product risks	3

Exam Q#	FL-	K	Learning Objective	Practice Exam
34	5.3.2	K2	**Test Monitoring, Test Control and Test Completion** Summarize the purposes, content, and audiences for test reports	1, 2
	5.3.3		**Test Monitoring, Test Control and Test Completion** Exemplify how to communicate the status of testing	3
35	5.4.1	K2	**Configuration Management** Summarize how configuration management supports testing	1, 2, 3
36-38	5.1.4	K3	**Test Planning** Use estimation techniques to calculate the required test effort	1, 2, 3
	5.1.5		**Test Planning** Apply test case prioritization	1, 2, 3
	5.5.1		**Defect Management** Prepare a defect report	1, 2, 3
39	6.1.1	K2	**Tool Support for Testing** Explain how different types of test tools support testing	1, 2, 3
40	6.2.1	K1	**Benefits and Risks of Test Automation** Recall the benefits and risks of test automation	1, 2, 3

* Note: From the ISTQB Exam Structures & Rules Tables v1.19, some questions are marked with an asterisk. *'If there are more questions to distribute between LOs in a group of LOs, then at least one question must be based on each LO. If there are less questions to distribute between LOs in a group of LOs then each question must cover a different LO.'*

In addition to the three practice papers of 40 questions each, this guide includes two to six practice questions for each learning objective. These practice questions are in the format of exam questions and provide practice opportunities at the required knowledge levels. Answers and explanations are included. This is summarized in the table below:

Syllabus Section	Learning Objectives	Practice Questions
1. Fundamentals of Testing	14	38
2. Testing Throughout the Software Development Lifecycle	10	29
3. Static Testing	8	21
4. Test Analysis and Design	14	56
5. Managing the Test Activities	16	58
6. Test Tools	2	4
Total	**64**	**206**

Also included are exercises for all K3 learning objectives.

ABOUT THE EXAM

The exam duration is 60 minutes. There are 40 questions, each worth one mark. To achieve a pass requires 26 marks (65%).

When you have the level of knowledge and understanding needed for the exam, go through the five-point plan below:

1	Understand the exam format
2	Understand the format of exam questions
3	Identify where marks in the exam can be gained or lost
4	Consider how to approach questions
5	Practice the questions

The basis for all exam information and questions is derived from the relevant documents available at the time of publication, see *References*.

Keep in mind, the ISTQB® statement from the Advanced Level Test Analyst Sample Exam – Questions Introduction, states '*The sample questions and answers and associated justifications in this sample exam set have been created by a team of subject matter experts and experienced question writers with the aim of assisting ISTQB® Member Boards and Exam Boards in their question writing activities*'. Member Boards have available to them the ISTQB Exam Structures and Rules and the specification of question formats. Member Boards may publish their own sample questions. The details in this chapter are based on the ISTQB documents.

Overall Exam Format

The exam consists of forty multiple-choice questions. You are asked to select one option from a list of four or for a few questions two options from a list of five. Not all 64 learning objectives will be examined, see *Required Knowledge*. The order of questions in the exam has not been specified.

In the practice papers here and the ISTQB sample, questions are ordered by the learning objective they target, except Q#15/16 in practice exam three. In an online exam, computer randomization results in questions or blocks of questions, that may be in a different order.

Format of Practice Questions and Exam Questions

All practice exams in this guide follow the specified exam format to cover the required knowledge levels.

Stem	A question phrase and sufficient information to select the correct response option(s).
Optional Problem Statement/Scenario	Questions include a problem statement or scenario when needed by the question stem. Problem statements and scenarios can be used to support any question type.
Response Options	For Type A and Matching Type, four options are given, one option is the correct response. For Pick-N questions five options are given, two of which are correct.

Types of Exam Questions

The three typical types of exam questions are:

ISTQB® Specified Format	Details	Answer
Type A	Stem and optionally a problem statement/scenario.	Four response options a) to d). One option is correct and should be selected.
Pick-N Type	Similar to Type A but with an additional answer option.	Five response options a) to e). Two options are correct and both should be selected. Scoring follows the rule, if both options selected are correct, the point is awarded, otherwise no mark is given.
Matching Type	Used to measure the ability to identify the relationship or association between related items. Items in the first list of four are labelled with numbers (1-4), and items in the second list of four are labelled with letters (A-D).	Four response options a) to d) may look like: a) 1B, 2D, 3A, 4C b) 1C, 2D, 3A, 4B c) 1C, 2A, 3B, 4D d) 1A, 2B, 3C, 4D One option is correct and should be selected.
Roman Type	Stem and optionally a problem statement/scenario. Five statements, each preceded by a Roman numeral i. to v.	Four options for a question such as '*Which statements are true?*', the options could be: a) i, ii, iii, v b) i, ii, iv c) iv, v d) All of the tasks Each numeral will appear in at least two options and not more than three, in its correct truth value.

There is no specification that all formats or a specific number of any of the specified formats must be included in the exam. Member boards will use Type A and may or may not use the other types. Some variation in the formats may be allowed.

Where Marks Can Be Gained or Lost

The following table shows the weighted distribution of questions by the chapters in the Syllabus.

Syllabus Section	**Number of Questions**			
	K1	**K2**	**K3**	**Total**
4. Test Analysis and Design	0	6	5	**11**
5. Managing the Test Activities	1	5	3	**9**
1. Fundamentals of Testing	2	6	0	**8**
2. Testing Throughout the SDLC	2	4	0	**6**
3. Static Testing	2	2	0	**4**
6. Test Tools	1	1	0	**2**
Total	**8**	**24**	**8**	**40**

The ISTQB® Structure and Rules v1.2 - Timing of Questions states,

'6.1.1. Exam takers are expected to allocate 1 minute to K1 level questions
6.1.2. Exam takers are expected to allocate 1 to 2 minutes to K2 level questions
6.1.3. Exam takers are expected to allocate 3 minutes to K3 level questions.'

At Foundation Level, all exam questions carry one mark, irrespective of their knowledge level. The above timings should be considered as maximum times, not average or typical times. With an hour for the exam and eight out of the forty questions at K3, allocating the full three minutes per K3 question will account for 24 minutes. This is just under half the exam time for only a possible 8 out of 40 marks. In the exam time remaining, 32 questions and 32 marks will be available, meaning just over a minute each to answer the remaining K1 and K2 level questions which significantly increases time pressure.

How to Approach Practice and Exam Questions

Use steps one to three below and if this is not adequate, continue with steps four and five.

1	Read the question carefully
2	Read all the answer options
3	Select the best answer option(s)
4	Use a process of elimination
5	When you do not know the answer

1 Read the question carefully This will help you focus on the question and not be distracted by incorrect options.

Look for short phrases embedded in the question that may have a significant bearing on the answer. Also, look for words such as 'all' or 'every' in the question as these may also have a significant bearing on the answer. Other words and phrases to look out for include, 'most appropriate', 'except for which', 'most correct', 'best', 'most likely', 'best approach', 'best action to take', 'best strategy', 'main', 'least' and 'usually'.

Look for the inclusion of negative words such as 'not', 'never', 'untrue', 'incorrect' that will affect the answer. Negative words can be prefixes such as 'in-' as in infeasible or 'un-' as in unimportant.
Notice negatives because they can reverse meaning.

The use of double negatives varies between different languages. When two negatives are used, one in the question and one an option, in standard English the negatives are understood to cancel one another and produce a weakened affirmative. Double negatives are handled differently in some languages other than English and are typically avoided in question and answer options.

Longer questions may contain more information than is required, for example in describing a scenario. This extra information can be a distraction. Identify and focus on the key information.

2 Read all the answer options An answer option that includes words such as 'all', 'always' or 'every' must be irrefutable. If you can think of a counter-example or situation, then the answer is not correct. For example, 'Every defect should be fixed', is an incorrect statement but, 'Defects should be fixed' is more correct and might be the right choice, depending on the wording of the rest of the question.
If an answer option includes words like 'may' or 'can be' this might be true in some, but not all cases.
If the answer option contains words such as 'sometimes', 'some' or 'most', the answer option does not have to be completely irrefutable.
If an answer option includes a word such as *'never'* a single counter-example will indicate the answer is not correct.

It is important to look carefully at the terms used. For example, ISTQB® Sample Exam Set A Question #18 based on learning objective FL-3.2.5 (Feedback and Review Process) asks *'Which of these statements is NOT a factor that contributes to successful reviews?'* The statements include, d) *'Failures found should be acknowledged appreciated and handled objectively',* which should be selected as the answer.
Reviews can find defects, not failures. The distinction between failure and defect is covered in learning objective FL-1.2.3 *(Why is Testing Necessary?).*

Carefully check the answer options against your first answer. Adjust your answer only when you are sure you should do this.

3 Select the best answer option(s) It is important to select the best answer, not just an answer option that appears to be correct. Often many answers will appear to be correct, but there will be a best answer.

Questions that require an answer that is 'best/most appropriate/most correct' may have options that are partly true and partly untrue or not true for all situations. Make sure you read all the options before selecting an answer. For example, if there is an option:

a) High-level tests make use of the Test Analyst's experience and the level of detail enables independent verification of the tests

This is not all correct, only the first part is, the second part applies to low-level tests.

For a question asking, 'Which of the statements are true?', if an answer option is, 'All of the above', do not select this if you know one of the options above is not correct. Similarly where an answer option is, 'None of the above', if you are confident at least one of the options is true.

Remember for 'Pick-N Type' format questions, two correct options are required.

4 Use a process of elimination If you are not sure which is the correct answer, rule out all the answer options you know are incorrect. Focus on the remaining answers. This greatly increases the chance you will select the correct answer.

5 When you do not know the answer After consideration of the question and all of the above points, if you are still unsure about the options, make a guess. It will not count against your exam score. It can be counterproductive to continue to spend more time on one particular question. Use your first answer choice. This does not mean your first answer is necessarily the correct answer option but is likely to be your best approach. While the multiple-choice questions are not intentionally designed to trick or confuse, they are designed to test 'knowledge and understanding'. The options will often include the most common wrong answer or answers that seem plausible but are ultimately incorrect.

Practice Exams

After studying the examples and working through the practice questions in this book, approach the practice exams with appropriate time constraints. If you are not attempting a complete practice exam, look at the K-levels and how long to spend on a question to work out a maximum time. Only use reliable sources for practice questions. Be aware that some questions from online sources may still be relevant, others may no longer be valid for Syllabus v4.0.1 and later updates.

Hints on Preparing for the Exam

Understand where to allocate your time when preparing to take the exam.

Beware of using sources, books and study materials based on an outdated Syllabus, such as the ISTQB® Syllabus 2018 v3.1.1 (sunset 9 May 2024) and earlier versions.

Keep in mind the points about the Glossary and definitions of terms raised in this guide.

Know the keywords but do not be limited to these only.

Ensure you are aware of synonyms of terms that may be used.

Use the learning objectives to check you have the correct level of knowledge and understanding.

Understand what is meant by the Knowledge levels (K-levels) and work to achieve the required level of knowledge.

Do not rely on just completing sample questions, your focus should be on the learning objectives.

Work through the K3 level exercises in this guide. K3 level questions at Foundation Level are: equivalence partitioning, boundary value analysis, defect Decision table, state transition testing, acceptance test-driven development, estimation techniques, test case prioritization and defect report preparation.

Practice using the test techniques associated with K3 level learning objectives.

Work through the practice questions methodically and study the answer explanations.

Assess where you need to do more study and review the relevant information in this guide.

Practice exam questions with appropriate time constraints (associated with the K-levels) or the full practice exams within the allotted time.

You will be under time pressure during the exam and you will not have time to go back and review questions. A good method of approaching a multiple choice format exam is therefore:
Read carefully, Understand, Answer and Move on quickly.

1. FUNDAMENTALS OF TESTING

The ISTQB Exam Structures & Rules Tables v1.19 specifies eight exam questions for this section. There are three K1 and eleven K2 level learning objectives.

Keywords given in the Syllabus
†coverage, debugging, defect, error, failure, quality, quality assurance, root cause, test analysis, test basis, test case, test completion, test condition, †test control, test data, test design, test execution, test implementation, †test monitoring, †test object, test objective, test planning, test procedure, test process, test result, testing, testware, traceability, validation, verification.

Not identified as keywords in Glossary or Syllabus: test environment, test management, test suite. Other suggested keyword not in Glossary: stakeholder.

†Test object included in the Syllabus in chapters 1 and 2. Coverage is included in the Syllabus in chapters 1 and 4. Test control and test monitoring are also included in the Syllabus in chapters 1 and 5.

1.1 What is Testing?

Software testing is a process that validates, verifies and acts to evaluate the quality of the system and assesses the level to which the test object fulfills its intended purpose. This includes reviewing any related work products such as requirements specification documentation. Software testing contributes to the successful delivery of a high-quality product, reduces the likelihood of post-release issues, and supports the overall success of software development projects.

FL-1.1.1 (K1) Identify typical test objectives

Test objective is defined in the Glossary as, *'The purpose for testing.'*

Test objectives can vary depending on factors such as risks, the software development lifecycle being followed and factors related to the business context such as corporate structure, competitive considerations and time to market. A specialist tester may be required for performing some of the test objectives, such as for performance efficiency or security testing.

Typical test objectives include:

Build confidence in the quality of the test object
Trigger failures and finding defects
Ensure the required coverage of a test object is achieved
Verify the specified requirements have been fulfilled
Verify the test object complies with contractual, legal, and regulatory requirements
Provide information to stakeholders to allow them to make informed decisions
Validate whether the test object is complete and works as expected by the stakeholders*
Validate compatibility and the specified implementation environment(s), devices, or operating systems and specified portability
Evaluate usability and accessibility
Verify performance efficiency, load capability and security as far as is possible
Contribute to reducing the risk level of inadequate software quality
Ensure the software adheres to regulatory, compliance and contractual requirements

*A stakeholder is an individual, group or organization that has a concern or is impacted by the outcome of a project. Stakeholders have varying degrees of influence on a project. Stakeholders may include:

Individuals or organizations requesting the software solution or product owners
End users
Project managers
Business analysts
Developers
Testers
Support and maintenance staff
Regulatory bodies, compliance officers
Marketing and sales representatives

Test objectives that are not valid and the reasons include:

Ensure no defects remain in the test object - testing shows the presence, not the absence of defects. (See FL-1.3.1 *Testing Principles*)
Undertake complete testing of all possible valid and invalid inputs - exhaustive testing is not possible. (See FL-1.3.1)
Test only fully developed products – testing can include, for example, examining draft documents, testing modules with code harnesses or test-driven development.
Automate all tests - some tests are better performed manually, such as when tests only have occasional use, before automated testing can be started or code where automated testing is difficult to implement, exploratory testing etc. (See FL-6.2.1 *Test Automation*)
Analyze all failures - this is part of debugging.

FL-1.1.2 (K2) Differentiate testing from debugging

	Testing	Debugging
Definition	The exploration of the test object to find defects.	The process used to analyze failures in order to identify defects and remove the causes of the failures.
Focus	Systematically executing various test cases, scenarios, and conditions to determine whether the software behaves as intended.	Investigating defects, analyzing error messages and incorrect behavior and making necessary code changes to eliminate the defects.
Primary objective	To find defects in the software and ensure that it functions correctly, performs well, and meets quality standards before it is released to users.	To locate the specific source of a defect, understand why it occurred, and correct the code to eliminate the defect.
When performed	Typically, throughout the software development lifecycle, starting from the early stages of development and continuing until the software is ready for release.	Typically, after a failure has been identified through testing or other means.
Outcome	Understanding of the software's behavior, its adherence to requirements and the identification of defects that need to be addressed.	Typically, an updated version of the software in which identified defects have been fixed.

With dynamic testing, the tester first triggers a failure and then reports it. Then defect debugging is undertaken. The developer investigates, identifies the defect that caused the failure and provides a fix. The tester retests to ensure that the defect no longer exists.

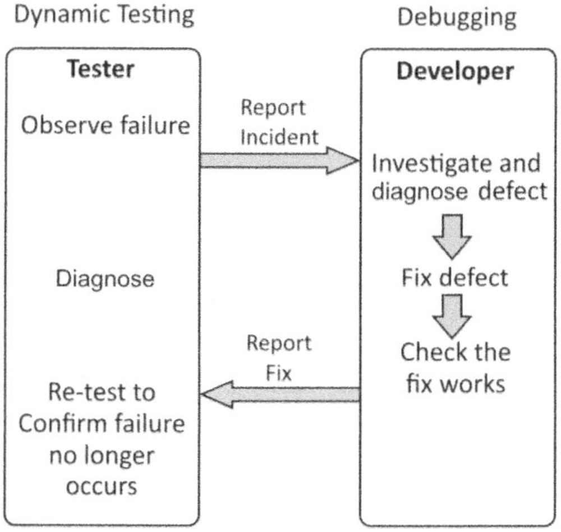

With static testing, a failure is not triggered. The area of the code is identified by static testing. The developer debugs the code without the need to investigate a failure.

	Testing	Debugging / Defect fixing
Objective	The purpose of testing is to find failures that arise from defects in the software	The purpose of debugging is to identify and correct the defects arising from failures found during the test process
Performed by	The tester or sometimes the developer, performs the testing	Undertaken by developer
Knowledge	Most testing requires no or little source code knowledge	Debugging needs good source code knowledge

1.1 Questions 1 to 5 FL-1.1.1, 1.1.2

Question 1 FL-1.1.1 (K1) Which of the following is not a valid objective for software testing?

a) Verify the test object complies with relevant regulatory requirements
b) Provide frequent information to stakeholders
c) Ensure the software meets user requirements.
d) Automate all test cases

Select ONE option

Question 2 FL-1.1.1 (K1) Which of the following is a valid objective for software testing?

a) Uncover all defects in the test object
b) Build confidence in the quality of the test object
c) Create as many defect reports as possible.
d) Create as many test cases as possible

Select ONE option

Question 3 FL-1.1.2 (K2) Which of the following statements best describes the distinction or link between debugging and testing?

a) Testing reduces the risk level of inadequate software, debugging identifies the risk level of inadequate software
b) Testing triggers failures, debugging analyzes and removes the causes of failures
c) Testing finds failures that indicate the presence of defects, and debugging confirms that a developer has fixed a defect
d) Debugging is an essential skill for all testers and a part of testing as it establishes crucial information required for fixing a defect

Select ONE option

Question 4 FL-1.1.2 (K2) Which of the following best describes the task of analyzing and fixing the cause of failures in a software system?

a) Debugging
b) Impact analysis
c) Alpha testing
d) System testing

Select ONE option

Question 5 FL-1.1.2 (K2) When dynamic testing is being used, which of the following are part of software testing and which are primarily part of debugging?

i. Diagnosing the failure
ii. Uncovering the failure
iii. Raising an incident report
iv. Fixing defect
v. Checking the failure no longer occurs

a) i, ii, iii and v are debugging, iv is testing
b) ii, iii and iv are debugging, i and v are testing
c) ii, iv and v are debugging, i and iii are testing
d) i and iv are debugging, ii, iii and v are testing

Select ONE option

1.1 Answers and Explanations 1 to 5 FL-1.1.1, 1.1.2

Answer 1 FL-1.1.1 K1

d) is the correct option. There are situations when manual testing is needed such as with test scenarios that are only to be validated once or occasionally, exploratory testing, some usability testing and complex test scenarios where it is not a feasible or efficient use of resources to automate.
a) is not the correct option as verifying compliance with relevant regulatory requirements is a valid test objective. b) is not the correct option. Providing information to stakeholders allows them to make informed decisions. c) is not the correct option. Ensuring user requirements are met is a valid test objective.

Answer 2 FL-1.1.1 K1

b) is the correct option. A valid objective is to perform testing to increase confidence in the quality of the test object.
a) is not the correct option While finding defects is an objective of testing, it's practically impossible to uncover all defects except possibly in small trivial test objects. c) is not the correct option. An objective based on the number of defect reports encourages duplicate reports, reports without full details and testing for failures that are easiest to trigger but not necessarily failures that may be high risk with high impact but take longer to find. d) is not the correct option. The objective is not to create as many test cases as possible but to create effective test cases.

Answer 3 FL-1.1.2 K2

b) is the correct option. Debugging is the process of analyzing and removing defects which are the causes of failures.
a) is not the correct option. Testing can help identify the risk level of inadequate software but by itself does not reduce it. Debugging does not identify the risk level of inadequate software.
c) is not the correct option. Confirmation testing, not debugging, confirms a defect has been fixed.
d) is not the correct option. Developers undertake debugging.

Answer 4 FL-1.1.2 K2

a) is the correct option. Debugging involves analyzing and fixing the cause of failures in a new software system. b) is not the correct option. Impact analysis shows which parts of the software could be affected. c) is not the correct option. Alpha testing is the first end-to-end testing of a product to ensure it meets the business requirements and functions correctly. d) is not the correct option. System testing identifies failures and does not involve fixing the cause of defects.

Answer 5 FL-1.1.2 K2

d) is the correct option. Dynamic testing uncovers failures and the tester raises an incident report. Debugging analyzes the defects and provides fixes for them. Confirmation testing checks the failure no longer occurs.
a), b) and c) are not correct options for the reasons given for d).

1.2 Why is testing necessary?

Software testing is a crucial phase in the software development life cycle that contributes to the quality, reliability, and correctness of the software being developed.

FL-1.2.1 (K2) Exemplify why testing is necessary

Testing contributes to the success of a project with:

- Cost-effective means of detecting defects
- Means of directly evaluating the quality of a test object at various stages in the software development lifecycle, providing input to management and stakeholder decisions, such as readiness for deployment
- Means of ensuring users' needs are considered throughout the development lifecycle
- May be to meet contractual, legal requirements or to comply with regulatory standards

Note: For this learning objective, the Syllabus highlights the high-level contributions to how testing contributes to success and why it is necessary. These are described above and used in the practice questions in this guide. ISTQB Sample Exam B, Question #1 focuses on specific test techniques, namely static testing, dynamic testing, static analysis and reviews. Detailed information about the benefits of test techniques is included later under the sections covering the learning objectives for these.

FL-1.2.2 (K1) Recall the relationship between testing and quality assurance

There is a common misconception that testing and quality assurance are interchangeable terms. This is not the case.

Quality Term	**Definition**
Testing	*'The process within the software development lifecycle that evaluates the quality of a component or system and related work products*
Quality Assurance, QA	*'Activities focused on providing confidence that quality requirements will be fulfilled'*

Quality Term	**Characteristics**
Testing	Product-orientated Corrective approach Focuses on activities that verify the product works as expected and supports the achievement of appropriate levels of quality Testing includes manual testing, automated testing and inspections of the product Testing is a major part of quality control Test results used to fix defects
Quality Assurance, QA	Process-orientated Preventative approach Focuses on implementation of standards and improvement of processes Test results provide feedback on how development and test processes are performing Can include audits of processes

Quality assurance and quality control are two parts of quality management (the other two parts are quality planning and quality improvement). Test results are used in both quality control and quality assurance but for different purposes.

FL-1.2.3 (K2) Distinguish between root cause, error, defect and failure

Term	Definition	Synonym
Root cause	*'A source of a defect such that if it is removed, the occurrence of the defect type is decreased or removed'*	
Error	*'A human action that produces an incorrect result'*	Mistake
Defect	*'An imperfection or deficiency in a work product where it does not meet its requirements or specifications'*	Fault or Bug
Failure	*'An event in which a component or system does not perform a required function within specified limits'*	

A coding mistake made by a person is an 'error' and results in a 'defect' existing in the software. The effect of an error on the system's operation or use can be found by triggering and observing a 'failure'. The diagram below shows the interrelation between error, defect and failure. The root cause is the underlying reason for the developer making the coding mistake, such as skill level or time pressure.

The diagram shows the sequence and relationships between error, mistake, defect, fault and failure.

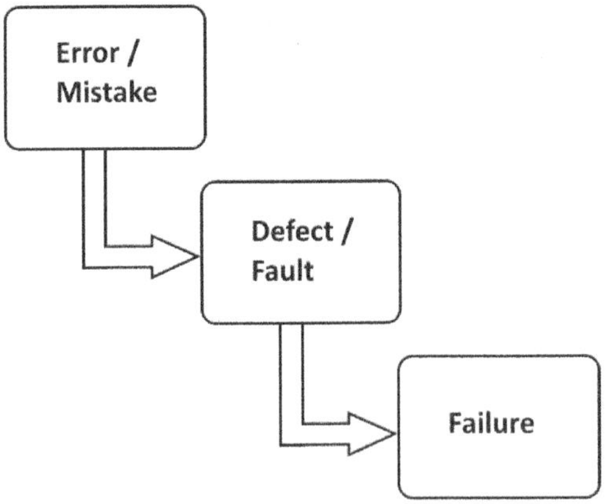

Root cause A root cause can be due to the absence of best practice, lack of applying knowledge or an environmental or external issue. Examples of root causes include:

- Procedures (inadequate, ambiguous, missing test step, lack of updates)
- Employee unable to perform a task (training, resources, time, budget, new or unfamiliar technology)
- Inadequate quality control or management systems
- Communications, unaware a procedure exists, inadequate or incorrectly communicated
- Lack of employee motivation, engagement or collaboration
- Internal or external pressures or distractions
- Complexity of the code, design, architecture, or the technology to be used
- Inclusion of unreliable third-party libraries
- Not considering conditions from the end user's perspective when testing

A root cause may occur due to an error. For example, lack of budget is considered to be a root cause and could be the result of an inadequate planning or estimation error. Identifying the root cause is crucial for effective quality assurance and process improvement because it allows teams to address the source of problems.

Error Errors result in failures and are of the following types:

- Slips coming from factors such as carelessness, misapplication of procedures or rules, time pressure
- Lapses coming from factors such as distractions, interruptions and forgetfulness, such as not saving the latest code updates or changes
- Mistakes coming from factors such as unawareness, taking shortcuts or other risks, incorrectly interpreting requirements, insufficient knowledge

Defect Most defects occur as a result of errors or oversights made by developers and are typically identified during dynamic testing by incurring a failure being triggered or as a direct result of static testing. Examples of defects include:

- Syntax errors such as misuse of parentheses
- Logic errors and, incorrect ordering of arithmetic operators, incorrect use of signs, boundary value errors
- Calculation errors or precision loss.
- Comparing inappropriate data types or incorrectly converting one data type to another
- Buffer overflows
- Use of an uninitialized variable
- Access violations

The following are methods for developers to prevent or limit the number of defects introduced:

- Coding techniques adopted and enforced by compilers
- Appropriate software development methodologies used
- Peer Review
- Code Analysis

Failure A failure is a consequence of a defect. If the test object does not perform as expected due to the occurrence of any defect, it is termed a failure. Not all defects result in failures, some may remain inactive in the code and may never be noticed.
Failures also occur due to the following reasons: hardware malfunction, incompatibility with different platforms, configuration errors, environmental issues such as electronic fields, power interruption during inclement weather, required satellite inputs etc.

Examples of types of failures include:

Sequencing or timing failures, such as with multi-core or multi-threaded software a response within the code is not obtained within the expected time interval with multi-core or multi-threaded software, incorrect or missing consideration of timeouts and improper sequencing

Performance failures where the software sends or receives a response outside of the required time interval

Omission failures where the software fails to send a request or receive an incoming response and does not deliver the expected outcome

Freeze or crash failures, the software completely fails to respond or exits unexpectedly

Arbitrary failures such as the software returning incorrect information

1.2 Questions 1 to 9 FL-1.2.1, 1.2.2, 1.2.3

Question 1 FL-1.2.1 (K2) Which of the following illustrates why testing is necessary?

a) To eliminate the need for collaboration between developers and stakeholders as testers will do this
b) To ensure the software is defect-free and reliable
c) To verify the software meets specified requirements and functions correctly
d) To replace the role of developers in identifying defects, giving more time for development work

Select ONE option

Question 2 FL-1.2.1 (K2) Which of the following illustrates why testing is necessary?

a) To reduce the time interval between when a correctly reported failure is submitted and when a fix is provided for confirmation testing
b) To eliminate the need for maintenance updates after deployment into production
c) To remove the need for quality assurance
d) To contribute to reducing the cost of development

Select ONE option

Question 3 FL-1.2.1 (K2) Which of the following is the best example of how test activities can contribute to the success of a project?

a) Spending time and effort involved in software development lifecycle activities
b) Targeting test effort on areas of high usage by making assumptions about how the software works
c) Keeping to the test plan created at the start at all time
d) Having a fresh approach and not taking into consideration testing conducted on previous projects

Select ONE option

Question 4 FL-1.2.2 (K1) Which of the following best describes the primary focus of quality assurance?

a) Identifying defects in the test object and ensuring they are resolved
b) Ensuring the software meets user requirements
c) Implementing processes to improve and maintain quality throughout the software development lifecycle
d) Executing test cases to evaluate both functionality and non-functionality

Select ONE option

Question 5 FL-1.2.2 (K1) The following are statements that apply to either testing or quality Assurance. Identify those that apply to testing.

a) Test results provide feedback on how development and testing processes are performing
b) Focus is on activities that verify the product works as expected and support the achievement of appropriate levels of quality
c) Works on the basis that if a good process is followed correctly, then it will generate a good product
d) Is a major form of quality control, while others include simulation and prototyping
e) Is a preventative, process-oriented approach

Select TWO options

Question 6 FL-1.2.3 (K2) Which of the following statements best describes a defect?

a) An imperfection or deficiency in a work product where it does not meet requirements or specifications
b) A human action that produces an incorrect result
c) An event in which a component or system does not perform a required function within specified limits
d) The unintended termination of the execution of a component or system before completion

Select ONE option

Question 7 FL-1.2.3 (K2) Which of the following best describes the key difference between a root cause and a fault in the context of software development and testing?

a) A fault is the result of user error, a root cause is a result of coding errors
b) A root cause is a specific instance of a defect, a fault is the underlying reason for the defect
c) A fault is a defect, while a root cause is the underlying reason for the defect
d) A root cause and a fault are synonymous terms and can be used interchangeably

Select ONE option

Question 8 FL-1.2.3 (K2) Which of the following best describes a failure in the context of software development and testing?

a) A coding error that does not affect the software's functionality
b) An event that prevents the software from functioning as intended
c) A defect that is discovered and fixed during quality control
d) A documentation error that doesn't affect software operation

Select ONE option

Question 9 FL-1.2.3 (K2) Which of the following statements is true?

a) Decisions made by a team member, but subsequently found to be wrong, are failures
b) Triggering the software to freeze and accept no further inputs is an example of inducing a failure
c) Failures can be triggered by both dynamic and static testing
d) The absence of best practices documentation is an example of a failure

Select ONE option

1.2 Answers and Explanations 1 to 9 FL-1.2.1, 1.2.2, 1.2.3

Answer 1 FL-1.2.1 K2

c) is the correct option. The primary purpose of testing is to verify that the software aligns with specified requirements, functions correctly, and identifies defects.

a) is not the correct option. Testing contributes to informing stakeholders and ensuring the software meets stakeholder expectations but it does not mean that collaboration between developers and stakeholders is eliminated.

b) is not the correct option. While testing improves software quality, it does not ensure the software is 100% defect-free software due to the inherent complexity of software systems.

d) is not the correct option. Developers and testers share responsibility for quality software. Early testing at the component level typically complements developer efforts.

Answer 2 FL-1.2.1 K2

d) is the correct option. Effective testing reduces the cost of development by catching defects early, reducing rework, and preventing issues in production.

a) is not the correct option. Testing does not reduce the time interval between failure report submission and when a fix is provided if the failure is reported with all the required and correct information.

b) is not the correct option. Software often requires maintenance updates due to changing requirements and environments. c) is not the correct option. Testing complements quality assurance efforts by identifying failures. Quality Assurance focuses on the implementation and improvement of processes.

Answer 3 FL-1.2.1 K2

a) is the correct option. It is important testers are involved from the start of the software development lifecycle as this helps in understanding. Defects will be uncovered early.

b) is not the correct option. Making assumptions about how the software works without proper validation can lead to overlooked issues and is not the best option. c) is not the correct option. Failing to adjust test efforts when software requirements change can result in testing the wrong functionalities or missing new ones. d) is not the correct option. Ignoring previous test experiences and not incorporating lessons learned can lead to repeated errors.

Answer 4 FL-1.2.2 K1

c) is the correct option. Quality assurance is focused on establishing guidelines, standards, and practices that enhance the overall development and test processes to produce high-quality software.

a) is not the correct option. The focus of quality assurance is to prevent defects through process improvements. Actual defect identification is part of quality control activities.

b) is not the correct option. While quality assurance does contribute to ensuring that software meets user requirements, this is not its primary focus. The setup and maintenance of processes that lead to consistent quality is the primary focus of quality assurance.

d) is not the correct option. Executing test cases to evaluate non-functionality is a test activity that is part of testing.

Answer 5 FL-1.2.2 K1

b) and d) are the correct options. b) Testing involves checking a product or system to identify defects and verify that it works as expected. Quality assurance QA focuses on improving processes to prevent defects and ensure quality. d) Quality control QC aims to identify defects by examining and testing the actual product. Testing verifies whether a product meets its requirements and is a quality control activity. Quality assurance aims to prevent defects by improving the processes used to create a product and is not part of quality control.
a) is not a correct option. The focus of quality assurance is on the implementation and improvement of processes. Testing is distinct from but supports quality assurance. c) is not a correct option. Quality assurance is based on the idea that following a good process correctly will produce a good product. e) is not the correct option. Testing is product-oriented and quality assurance is process-oriented.

Answer 6 FL-1.2.3 K2

a) is the correct option. This is the Glossary definition of a defect.
b) is not the correct option. This is the Glossary definition of an error. c) is not the correct option. This is the Glossary definition of a failure. d) is not the correct option. This is the Glossary definition of a risk. A defect applies to a wider range of issues than just unexpected termination of execution of a component or system before completion.

Answer 7 FL-1.2.3 K2

c) is the correct option. Fault is a synonym for 'defect', the root cause is the underlying condition that caused the defect. a) is not the correct option. A root cause can be the result of an error or mistake that is caused by a coding error. For example, the developer being distracted, an ambiguous requirement and other reasons. b) is not the correct option. A fault and a defect are the same and can be used interchangeably. d) is not the correct option. A root cause is the underlying reason for a fault.

Answer 8 FL-1.2.3 K2

b) is the correct option. A failure is an event in which a component or system does not perform a required function within specified limits.
a) Is not the correct option. A coding error that does not affect the software's functionality is a defect or issue in the code that may or may not lead to a failure depending on its impact.
c) is not the correct option. A defect that is discovered and fixed does not necessarily indicate a failure will occur if it has been fixed. For example, a defect was found during static testing and fixed. does not result in a failure when the system is in use.
d) is not the correct option. The error does not affect the functionality.

Answer 9 FL-1.2.3 K2

b) is the correct option. A failure is an event in which a component or system does not perform a required function within specified limits.
a) is not the correct option. Incorrect human decisions made are errors. c) is not the correct option. Failures are not triggered by static testing. d) is not correct. The lack of best practices documentation is an example of an error.

1.3 Testing Principles

Testing principles provide a set of guidelines and best practices that help guide and shape the test process to be effective, efficient, and aligned with the goals of producing high-quality software. The Syllabus includes seven testing principles.

FL-1.3.1 (K2) Explain the seven testing principles

#	Testing Principle	Summary
1	Testing shows the presence of defects, not their absence	Testing can show defects are present but cannot prove there are no defects remaining
2	Exhaustive testing is impossible	Testing all combinations of inputs and conditions is not feasible except in trivial cases
3	Early testing saves time and money	Testing early reduces or eliminates costly later changes
4	Defects cluster together	Defects are not uniformly distributed throughout the software or system
5	Tests wear out (previously referred to as the *Pesticide Paradox*)	Repeating test cases over and over again no longer finds new defects. Repeating tests can paradoxically be beneficial for some automated regression testing
6	Testing is context dependent	Testing is done differently in different contexts
7	Absence-of-defects is a fallacy	Finding and fixing a large number of defects does not ensure the success of the software or system

See *References*.

Principle 1: Testing shows the presence of defects, not their absence
Testing is a process that finds defects and reduces the probability of undiscovered defects remaining in the product under test, leading to improvement in the quality of the software. Testing does not prove that there are no defects. Even when no defects are found during testing, the product cannot be said to be 100% defect-free. Understanding this principle essential for correctly setting and managing stakeholders' expectations.

This principle is illustrated by Deming's red bead experiment. Deming set up a closed container of beads. Using a paddle, workers were invited to take out 50 beads to establish the color of the beads in the container. When a worker had all red beads. Deming cautioned against making the assumption assume all the beads in the container were red. In fact, in his container, Deming had 3,200 red beads and 800 white beads. See *References*.

There could be any number of reasons for not uncovering every defect including:

- Test cases did not cover every scenario
- The defect only happens in the production system (see testing in context)
- Testing for all combinations of inputs is not feasible (see Exhaustive testing principle)
- Race conditions† (see below)
- Pointers not cleared after first use of software
- Costs, resources or time are limited

†A race condition is an undesirable situation that occurs when a device or system attempts to perform two or more operations at the same time, but because of the nature of the device or system, the operations must be executed in the proper sequence to be done correctly. With a race condition, the software could be executed successfully many times with identical inputs and then only fail once. An example of a race condition is in multi-threaded software where two or more threads in a single process access the same memory location concurrently with at least one of the accesses for writing, and the threads do not use any exclusive locks to control the access to that memory location.

Principle 2: Exhaustive testing is impossible

For most systems, it is not possible to perform exhaustive (complete) testing of all possible inputs and conditions except for trivial cases. The domain of possible inputs and conditions is typically too large. Attempting to test all possible combinations wastes time and effort and is unlikely to affect the overall quality of the software.

For example, consider a password of six characters which can be alphabetic (both lowercase and uppercase) or numbers (0 to 9). Repetition of a character is allowed.

The total possible combinations is $(26 + 26 + 10) = 62^6$. This equates to 56,800,235,584 variations. The mandatory requirement to include at least one special character or use a computer-generated strong password extends this even further. It would take years to check every combination. As the number of possibilities becomes more complex, the possible combinations increase exponentially.

Factors that can affect the number of possible combinations that exist in the software and make exhaustive testing not possible include:

A large number of inputs or combinations of inputs
The software may have a large number of states
There may be timing constraints on the inputs. For example, an input may be valid at a certain time and invalid at other times
A global variable may be used, such as satellite data, GPS positioning or weather
It may not be possible to create all possible execution environments of the system

Test techniques such as equivalence partitioning and boundary value analysis can build confidence. Understanding this principle is essential when considering the balance needed between testing, time, resources, costs and product release.

Principle 3: Early testing saves time and money

Early testing in the software development lifecycle, often referred to as *'shift left'*, aims to identify and resolve defects as early as possible in the development process. Identifying defects early such as in the requirements or design phase, it is easier and less costly to resolve them compared to later on when the defects may have proliferated and entire areas of functionality may need to be rewritten. Defects discovered in the later stages of the development lifecycle can result in hastily written code fixes that may not be of high quality, higher costs or missed deadlines and budget overrun.

Finding defects before deployment significantly reduces costs by cutting down on the following that may otherwise be incurred after deployment:

Expenses incurred due to increased support costs
Unexpected expenses due to developing and distributing patches
High costs associated with service outages
Lawsuits associated with damages resulting from software failures
Increased penalties and insurance costs associated with unreliable software systems
Regulations that stipulate criminal prosecution for companies that develop software with missing or incomplete information
Lost sales due to damage to reputation

The increase in the cost of finding and fixing a defect over time is shown in the following graphic.

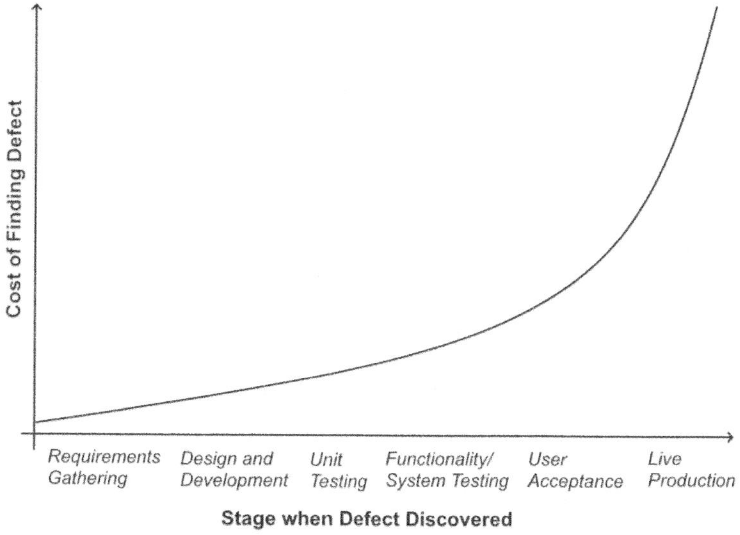

Principle 4: Defects cluster together

Defect clustering in software testing refers to the non-uniform distribution of defects. A small number of modules or components may contain most of the defects discovered. The basis for this is the Pareto principle, which states that approximately 20% of the modules or components account for approximately 80% of defects. A defect cluster is sometimes referred to as a defect hotspot.

Reasons for why a module may have a higher number of defects than another module include:

Size of module
New features being added that are going through updates
Complexity of design and coding
Older code is prone to breaking
Number of third-party integrations, use of libraries etc.
Number of modules, components or code dependencies

Example of a Pareto diagram, using sample data showing the relative frequency of causes for defects on websites. 20% of defects, broken links and missing are causing 80% of the reported defects.

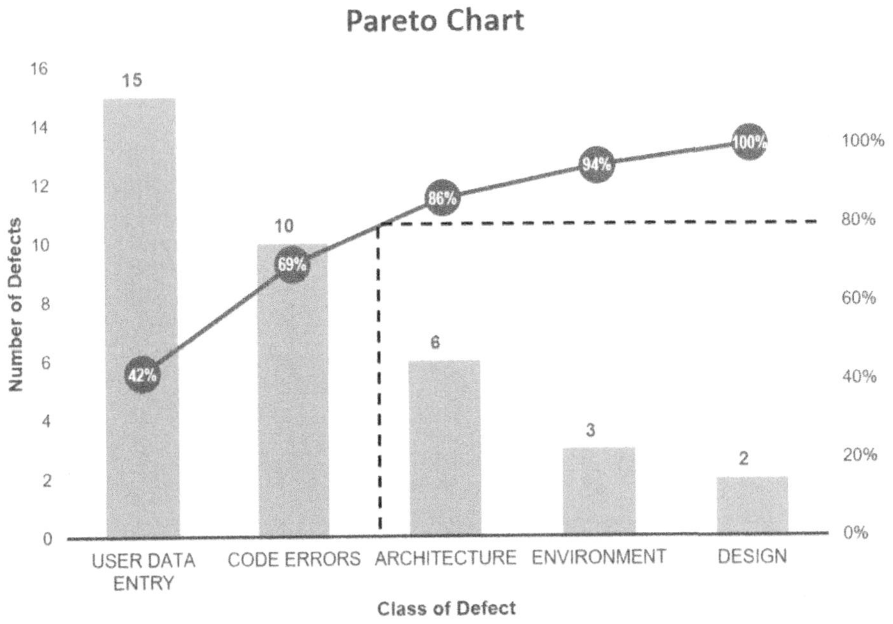

Predicted defect clusters and the actual observed defect clusters are important inputs for ongoing risk analysis and assigning test case priorities which can then be used to focus the test effort.

Principle 5: Tests wear out

This principle is that if the same set of test cases are executed again and again over a period of time then these set of tests are not likely to identify new defects.

Beizer wrote, *'Programmers and designers, given feedback on their bugs, do modify their programming habits and style in an attempt to reduce the incidence of bugs they know about. Furthermore, the better the feedback, the better the QA, the more responsive the programmers are, the faster those suites wear out.'* See *References*.

The principle is part of the pesticide paradox which is based on the idea that if a particular pesticide is used on a crop to kill or repel unwanted insects, the pests will eventually become immune to the pesticide and it will no longer be effective. Different pests may emerge. Likewise, continuously executing the same test cases with the same data will eventually fail to find new defects. Consequently, test cases and test data should be reviewed and modified over time to prevent this from happening.

Although Beizer wrote: *'Every method you use to prevent or find bugs leaves a residue of subtler bugs against which those methods are ineffectual.'* He did not say 'tests completely wear out' or 'tests no longer have any use'.

In reality, most organizations while developing new and updated tests, also continue to use existing tests in situations where repeating tests is beneficial, such as for:

- Regression testing after a code change is made, a new feature is added or a fix applied confirms that a code change in the software does not impact the existing functionality of the component or system
- Performance efficiency tests that need to be run repeatedly over a long period
- Build verification tests or sanity tests that need to be run every time there is a new build
- Scenarios where certain tests are important. The tests verify some critical functionalities of the system and these tests must be run periodically to make sure the functionalities continue to work without issues

Principle 6: Testing is context dependent

The test strategy and the test techniques used depend on the context of the systems or the software. For example, the testing of an iOS™ application is different from the testing of an e-commerce website and safety and finance systems need more extensive testing than other applications. Also, the test approach varies with the software development life cycle in use.

Consider an application for use by truck drivers. A screen, activated by touch, brings up a menu that includes options for radio, media, air-conditioning, lights, window wipers, parking cameras and more which in turn take the user to additional screens. For air-conditioning, there are options for temperature settings. Following release, there has been very little take-up. When used in moving vehicles, feedback suggests drivers found touch screen operation to be a distraction to driving mainly due to menu navigation and lack of familiarity.

Fully testing systems in context may not always be possible. In such scenarios, this information should be known and risk analysis undertaken. Reasons full context testing may not be feasible include:

- A system requires a managed cloud service that the test environment does not have access to
- Access to data is restricted due to its sensitivity or confidentiality
- High or specific levels of traffic or other factors in production cannot easily be replicated in the test environment
- Availability or costs of providing all types of hardware in the test environment

Principle 7: Absence-of-defects is a fallacy

Software testing involves more than merely finding defects. Thoroughly testing all specified requirements, executing all possible test cases, finding and resolving the defects identified may not ensure the success of the system. Validating requirements is also critical.

Reasons the software may not be successful include:

May be difficult to use
Does not meet the business requirements
Does not meet the users' expectations
Is inferior compared to other competing systems

The following scenario is an example of where the absence-of-defects fallacy applies:

Thorough testing of updated stock inventory management software has been completed and the defects identified have been resolved. This report has been submitted to management and has given them confidence about the product quality. However, when a demonstration of the software was given to the customer, the feedback was, *'although a large number of defects have been resolved, this is not what I require in the update as I want a simple user interface that warehouse operatives can easily use.'*

1.3 Questions 1 to 4 FL-1.3.1

Question 1 FL-1.3.1 (K2) Consider the following testing principles and statements:

1. Defects cluster together
2. Absence-of-defects fallacy
3. Tests wear out
4. Testing shows the presence of defects

A. Testing reduces the probability of defects remaining undiscovered in the software
B. This is an illustration of the Pareto principle
C. Finding and fixing a large number of defects does not ensure the success of a system
D. Test cases and test data should be regularly reviewed and revised

Which of the following best links the two lists above?

a) 1C, 2A, 3D, 4B
b) 1A, 2B, 3D, 4C
c) 1C, 2A, 3B, 4D
d) 1B, 2C, 3D, 4A

Select ONE option

Question 2 FL-1.3.1 (K2) Early testing is a testing principle. Which of the following is least true for early testing?

a) Identifies defects when they are less costly to fix
b) Can contribute to shorter development lifecycles
c) Is focused on finding defects regardless of their criticality
d) Can increase test resource demands

Select ONE option

Question 3 FL-1.3.1 (K2) Which of the following statements best supports one of the seven testing principles?

a) Test activities should start immediately after the completion of key development activities
b) Testing should adopt shift left
c) There is no beneficial outcome for the same tests to be run repeatedly over time
d) Testing should be independent of context and follow standard practices

Select ONE option

Question 4 FL-1.3.1 (K2) In the context of software development and testing, what does the Pareto Principle highlight?

a) A non-uniform distribution of defects occurs throughout the software
b) The importance of using different test cases over time to discover new defects
c) Use of automated testing tools for all types of testing
d) The need for software testing to focus exclusively on functional defects

Select ONE option

1.3 Answers and Explanations 1 to 4 FL-1.3.1

Answer 1 FL-1.3.1 K2

d) is the correct option. 1B - A small number of modules usually contains most of the defects discovered during pre-release testing or is responsible for most of the operational failures. 2B - It is a misconception to expect software verification to ensure the success of a system. In addition to verification, validation should be carried out. 3D - As stated in the Syllabus, if the same tests are run over time, they become increasingly ineffective in detecting new defects. Using the same tests in regression testing provides benefits. 4A - Testing shows the presence, not the absence of defects. a), b) and c) are not correct options for the reasons given for d).

Answer 2 FL-1.3.1 K2

c) is the correct option. Criticality based on, for example, requirements priority or risk analysis, can be assessed before testing starts and can then influence the focus of early testing

a) is not the correct option. Early testing aims to find defects when it is most likely they will cost less to fix. Finding Generally, it is significantly more expensive to fix defects found later in the development process, particularly after the software has been fully integrated or deployed.

b) is not the correct option. Early testing can contribute to shorter development cycles. By identifying and addressing defects early, there is less likelihood of delays caused by the need for extensive rework and defect fixing in later stages of the project.

d) is not the correct option. Testing early may require testers to adapt to changing code, leading to additional time and resource demands. This can affect the overall efficiency of the test process. Also, early in development with the software evolving, with frequent code changes, refactoring and updates, a greater amount of repeat testing of the same features is likely.

Answer 3 FL-1.3.1 K2

b) is the correct option. Shift left implements the principle of early testing. In some test approaches, the test basis can be reviewed early or test cases can be designed before development starts when testing is a driver for software development.

a) is not the correct option for the reasons given for b). c) is not the correct option. Although tests may become increasingly ineffective at finding new defects as the software is developed, repeating tests can be useful for regression testing to verify existing functionality has not altered.

d) is not the correct option. There is no singularly or universally acceptable approach to testing.

Answer 4 FL-1.3.1 K2

a) is the correct option. The software testing principle that defects cluster together is based on the Pareto principle. This states that for many outcomes, roughly 80% of consequences come from 20% of causes. b) is not the correct option. The 'tests wear out' or Pesticide Paradox principle states that using the same test cases for testing the software will not over time be useful for finding any new defects. To overcome this, test cases should be regularly reviewed and revised. c) is not the correct option. No testing principle recommends all tests should be automated. d) is not the correct option. Software testing should include testing of both functionality and non-functional characteristics.

1.4 Test Activities, Testware and Test Roles

Test activities represent the tasks and actions performed throughout the test process. Although testing is context-dependent, at a high level there are common sets of test activities. These activities form the test process.

Testware is defined as work products produced during the test process for use in planning, designing, executing, evaluating and reporting on testing. This includes test documentation.

Test roles define the responsibilities and roles of individuals involved in testing.

These three concepts work together to ensure successful software testing and the delivery of high-quality software products. They can be tailored to a given situation, for example how test activities are implemented, when test activities occur, the level of formality required in testware and the division of tasks are typically decided during test planning.

FL-1.4.1 (K2) Explain the different test activities and related tasks

The typical order of test activities that make up the test process is shown below. Depending on the software development lifecycle being used, there can be a degree of overlap from one activity with the next activity.

Test Activity	Summary of Tasks
Planning	Defining test objectives Selecting an approach that best achieves the objectives within the constraints imposed by the overall context Producing the test plan
Monitoring and Control	Monitoring: Ongoing checking of all test activities Comparing actual progress against plan Control: Taking the actions necessary to meet the test objectives
Analysis	Identifying testable features from the test basis Defining and prioritizing test conditions, (also referred to as test situations or test requirements) together with related risks and risk levels May be supported by the use of test techniques, see *Chapter 4* Answers the question 'What to test'
Design	Using the test conditions from analysis to produce test cases and other testware, such as test charters Identification of coverage items which serve as a guide to specify test case inputs Supported by the use of test techniques Defining test data requirements Designing the test environment and other required infrastructure and tools Answers the question, 'How to test'
Implementation	Creating or acquiring the testware, such as test data for test execution Organizing tests into test procedures and often into test suites Creating manual and automated test scripts as required Prioritizing test procedures and arranging within the test schedule Building the test environment and verifying it is set up correctly
Execution	Running tests according to a test execution schedule Comparing actual results with expected results Logging test results Analyzing anomalies to identify likely or possible causes to allow reporting based on failures observed
Completion	Usually occurs at milestones such as the end of an iteration, release, test level completion Identifying unresolved defects, change requests or product backlog items Identifying, archiving or handing over to appropriate teams any testware that may be useful in the future Shutting down the test environment to an agreed state Analyzing test activities to identify lessons learned and improvements for the future Producing a test completion report

Order of test activities (some overlap may occur) :

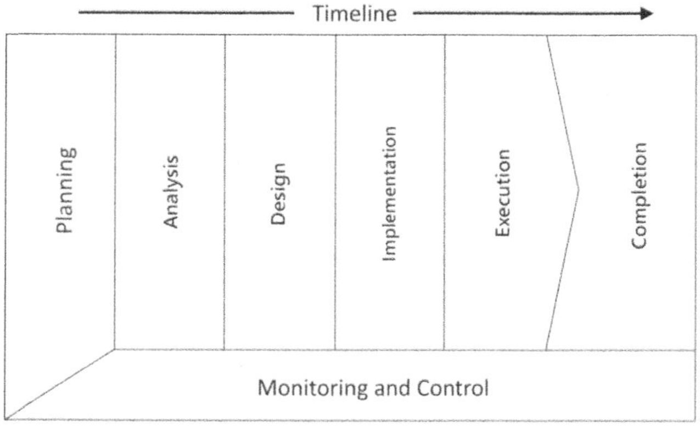

FL-1.4.2 (K2) Explain the impact of context on the test process

Context has an impact on software testing, shaping everything from test objectives and strategies to resource allocation and tool selection. Contextual factors affect testing as shown below:

Factor	Detail
Project size and complexity	Larger, more complex projects may require more extensive and detailed testing
Stakeholder involvement	Needs, expectations, willingness to participate, and motivation can all affect testing
Team members	Size of the test team and availability of testers, the testers' skills, knowledge and level of experience, training needs
Business domain	Market needs, legal regulations and standards compliance Industries such as healthcare, finance, and aerospace have stringent regulations that impact testing activities
Risk levels	Criticality of the test object, number of risks, identified risk levels
Technical	Type of software, product architecture, and technology used
Third party integration	Compatibility testing, API testing, and data interchange testing may be required
Project constraints	Scope, time, budget, resources, contractual obligations
Organizational	Organizational structure, communication, existing policies, and practices used
Software development lifecycle SDLC	Development methodology, the frequency of testing, and the roles and responsibilities of testers. Agile projects embrace change, while traditional projects may have more rigorous change control processes
Tools	Applicability, level updated, availability, usability (interaction capability), compliance, manual, automated
Test level	Including component testing, integration testing, system testing, acceptance testing

These factors have an impact on many test-related issues, including the test strategy, test techniques used, degree of test automation, required level of coverage, and level of detail of testware documentation and reporting. Contextual factors are interrelated and careful consideration is required to adapt test strategies and practices to the context of a project.

The following shows the same test cases, but a different order of execution based on different contexts.

Example: Test case prioritization

In this simple example, test cases have assessed risk levels and these are to be used for determining test execution order.

Test Case	Risk Level
TC1	High
TC2	Low
TC3	Medium

Based on risk level, the execution order of the test cases is TC1, TC3, TC2.
Adding essential mandatory regulatory requirements alters the execution order of test cases.

Test Case	Risk Level	Regulatory Requirements
TC1	High	No
TC2	Low	No
TC3	Medium	Yes

The order of test case execution now becomes TC3, TC1, TC2.

FL-1.4.3 (K2) Differentiate the testware that supports the test activities

Test Activity	Work Products produced during the Test Activity
Planning	Test plan Test schedule Risk register Entry and exit criteria
Monitoring and Control	Test progress reports Documentation of control directives Risk information
Analysis	(Prioritized) test conditions Defect reports for defects in a test basis
Design	(Prioritized) test cases Test charters Coverage items Test data requirements Test environment requirements
Implementation	Test procedures, manual and automated test scripts Test suites Test data Test execution schedule Test environment items including stubs, drivers, simulators, service virtualizations
Execution	Test logs Defect reports
Completion	Test completion report Action items for improvements of subsequent projects or iterations Documented lessons learned and change requests such as product backlog items Handover / Archive

FL-1.4.4 (K2) Explain the value of maintaining traceability

Traceability provides the ability to link work products such as requirements, test conditions, test cases and, test results forward(s) and backward(s) through the software development lifecycle. Traceability involves creating a traceability matrix, table or grid.

The main purpose of a requirements traceability matrix is to provide test traceability that shows all valid requirements are checked via test cases.

In the example below, business requirements can be traced through functional requirements to test case documentation.

Requirements Test Matrix (Three documents)
Project Name: Online Travel Booking System

Business Requirements Document BRD			Functional Requirements Document FRD		Test Case Document
Business Requirement ID#	**Business Requirement / Use Case**	**Priority**	**Functional Requirement ID#**	**Functional Requirement / Use Case**	**Test Case ID#**
BR1	Reserve seat	High	FR1.1	Single ticket	TC01, TC02
			FR1.2	Return ticket	TC01, TC03
			FR1.3	Season ticket	TC01, TC04
BR2	Payment	High	FR2.4	Debit card	TC05, TC06
			FR2.5	Credit card	TC07
BR3	Reward	Medium	FR2.6	Reward points	TC08

The test matrix above can be expanded with test conditions identified, test results etc.

Good traceability makes it possible to:

- Verify that requirements are covered by the test cases
- Have information on the status of the test activities such as being able to identify when test cases have been created, if test execution results are available and which requirements are therefore fulfilled
- Assess the impact and make decisions when changes. or unexpected events occur, such as which test cases need changing or rerun
- Where requirements, their risk and priority are traced through to test results, evaluate the level of outstanding risk and potentially accelerate release cycles
- Prove compliance
- Facilitate test audits
- Improve triage of defects, e.g. by linking them to requirements and their risk and priority
- Make test progress reports and test completion reports more easily understandable
- Assist in communicating technical aspects of testing to stakeholders in an understandable way
- Assess product quality, process capability and project progress against business goals
- Support coverage evaluation
- Help meet IT governance criteria

Note: **Test case** is defined as, *'A set of preconditions, inputs and actions (where applicable) expected results and post-test conditions developed based on test conditions.'*
From a test case, it is therefore possible to determine the inputs or test data. **Test data** is defined as, *'Data needed for test execution.'* **Test metric** is a test measurement scale and the method used for measurement. The coverage of the requirements is a test metric, not test data.

FL-1.4.5 (K2) Compare the different roles in testing
The Syllabus identifies two principal roles in testing, test manager and tester.

Role	Activities
Test Manager	Responsibility for the test process, test team and leadership of test activities Mainly focuses on the activities of test planning, test monitoring and test control and test completion. The role varies depending on the context, for example, in Agile software development, some test management tasks are handled by the Agile team. Tasks that span multiple teams or the entire organization may be performed by test managers outside of the development team
Tester	Responsible for the technical/engineering aspect of testing. Mainly focused on the activities of test analysis, test design, test implementation and test execution

Both roles are critical for delivering high-quality software, with the test management role providing leadership and strategic guidance and the testing role creating and executing tests and providing detailed feedback.

1.4 Questions 1 to 14 FL-1.4.1, 1.4.2, 1.4.3, 1.4.4, 1.4.5

Question 1 FL-1.4.1 (K2) Test cases are created during which test process activity?

a) Test design
b) Test planning
c) Test analysis
d) Test implementation

Select ONE option

Question 2 FL-1.4.1 (K2) Which two of the testing activities are most likely to be required for creating black-box test cases?

a) Test analysis
b) Test design
c) Test implementation
d) Test execution
e) Test monitoring

Select TWO options

Question 3 FL-1.4.1 (K2) Consider the following test process activities.

1. Test design
2. Test analysis
3. Test completion
4. Test execution
5. Test implementation
6. Test planning

Which is the correct sequence of the given activities?

a) 2, 1, 5, 6, 4, 3
b) 6, 2, 1, 5, 4, 3
c) 6, 1, 5, 4, 2, 3
d) 1, 6, 5, 4, 3, 2

Select ONE option

Question 4 FL-1.4.1 (K2) Identifying the expected test case result is part of test design. If the expected result is not identified, which of the following is true?

a) It may be difficult to repeat the test case
b) The test case cannot be implemented and then executed
c) It may be difficult to determine if the test case result is passed or failed
d) Automating the test case will not be possible

Select ONE option

Question 5 FL-1.4.1 (K2) Which of the following is a task undertaken during test Implementation?

a) Verifying the test environment is set up correctly
b) Specifying test implementation entry criteria
c) Setting up traceability between test cases and results
d) Evaluating the testability of the test basis

Select ONE option

Question 6 FL-1.4.2 (K2) Which of the following factors is likely to have the least influence on the way testing is performed?

a) Backing up test logs to the archive
b) Software development model being used
c) Usability of required test automation tools
d) The software architecture

Select ONE option

Question 7 FL-1.4.2 (K2) Context can impact the test process in the following ways except for which?

a) Shapes the test approach, scope, and priorities
b) Affects the frequency of automated testing
c) Level of formality of documentation and frequency of test reporting
d) Removes the need for any manual testing

Select ONE option

Question 8 FL-1.4.3 (K2) The following are created as work outputs from test design except for which?

a) Prioritized test cases
b) Test data requirements
c) Automated test scripts
d) Test environment requirements

Select ONE option

Question 9 FL-1.4.3 (K2) Consider the list of work products and the test activities:

1. Test log
2. Test charter
3. Stub or driver
4. Defect reports for defects in the test basis (if not fixed)

A. Test analysis
B. Test design
C. Test implementation
D. Test execution

Which of the following correctly links the two lists?

a) 1A, 2D, 3C, 4B
b) 1D, 2C, 3A, 4B
c) 1A, 2C, 3D, 4B
d) 1D, 2B, 3C, 4A

Select ONE option

Question 10 FL-1.4.4 (K2) A senior stakeholder asks for a copy of the document containing the information used for test analysis and test design and the link to test cases.
Which of the following should be provided?

a) Work Breakdown Structure (WBS)
b) The test plan
c) Requirements traceability matrix
d) Project management plan

Select ONE option

Question 11 FL-1.4.4 (K2) Good traceability does the following except for which?

a) Makes it possible to determine the impact of changes
b) Assists in communication of the technical aspects of testing to stakeholders in an understandable way
c) Describes the test objectives, the means and the schedule for achieving the objectives
d) Helps optimize the number of test cases necessary, eliminating duplication and identifying omissions

Select ONE option

Question 12 FL-1.4.4 (K2) Which one of the following is the primary reason for maintaining traceability throughout the test process?

a) To identify the value of the requirements
b) To map the requirements across the software development lifecycle
c) To determine the testability of the requirements
d) To determine who owns the requirements in the software development lifecycle

Select ONE option

Question 13 FL-1.4.5 (K2) Which of the following tasks belong primarily to the test manager's role?

a) Verifying the test environment is ready for use
b) Maintaining product backlog
c) Creating the test execution schedule
d) Producing the test progress report
e) Reprioritizing test efforts as needed

Select TWO options

Question 14 FL-1.4.5 (K2) The test team is working on a new mobile banking application. Which of the following tasks are primarily part of the tester's role?

a) Developing a test plan outlining the objectives and test scope
b) Ensuring a variety of mobile devices and operating systems for testing purposes will be available
c) Evaluating the user interface, navigation flow, and overall user experience to ensure ease of use and accessibility
d) Verifying transactions are processed accurately and that user data is protected
e) Determining control measures where needed to meet test objectives

Select TWO options

1.4 Answers and Explanations 1 to 14 FL-1.4.1, 1.4.2, 1.4.3, 1.4.4, 1.4.5

Answer 1 FL-1.4.1 K2

a) is the correct option. Test design is, *'The activity that derives and specifies test cases from test conditions.'* b) is not the correct option. Test planning is, *'The activity of establishing or updating a test plan.'* c) is not the correct option. Test Analysis is, *'The activity that identifies test conditions by analyzing the test basis.'* d) is not the correct option. Test implementation is, *'The activity that prepares the testware needed for test execution based on test analysis and design.'*

Answer 2 FL-1.4.1 K2

a) and b) are the correct options. The application or employment of test techniques is undertaken when creating test cases. c), d) and e) are not correct options for the reasons given for a) and b).

Answer 3 FL-1.4.1 K2

b) is the correct option. The order of the activities is Test planning, analysis, design, implementation, execution and completion. a), c) and d) are not correct options for the reasons given for b).

Answer 4 FL-1.4.1 K2

c) is the correct option. It may be difficult to determine if the test case result is passed or failed. Software testing is the process of evaluating and verifying that a software product does what is expected. After testing the particular software, if the expected result is not identified then, it is difficult to conclude whether the test case result is passed or failed.

a) is not the correct option. The test may be repeatable, but it still may be difficult to determine if the test case result is passed or failed. b) is not the correct option. Implementing and executing the test case does not result in knowing if the expected result has been achieved. d) is not the correct option. The test case may be automated, but it still may be difficult to determine if the test case result is passed or failed.

Answer 5 FL-1.4.1 K2

a) is the correct option. Ensuring the test environment is built and verified to be set up correctly are test implementation tasks.

b) is not the correct option. Specifying and meeting the test implementation entry criteria should be done before starting test implementation.

c) is not the correct option. Setting up traceability should start before test implementation.

d) is not the correct option. Evaluating the testability of the test basis is part of test analysis.

Answer 6 FL-1.4.2 K2

a) is the correct option. Backups of test logs to the archive are likely to have only a very low influence on the way testing is performed.

b) is not the correct option. Testing should fit with the software development model being used, for example, testing should be part of each iteration when an iterative development model is being used.

c) is not the correct option. If test automation tools are required, the tools should be both available and usable. Without this, testing may be incomplete or exceed the schedule if testing has to revert to all manual testing. d) is not the correct option. Software architecture refers to the organization of a system and this influences the way testing is performed. The architecture includes all units, components, how they interact with each other, the environment in which they operate, and the principles used to design the software.

Answer 7 FL-1.4.2 K2

d) is the correct option. Manual testing, for example, exploratory or usability testing, is always recommended irrespective of the context.

a) is not the correct option. Contexts, such as project goals, user needs, and regulatory requirements influence test process decisions.

b) is not the correct option. Context can affect the frequency of automated testing. Projects with rapid development cycles may emphasize frequent automated tests, while other projects may focus more on manual testing. c) is not the correct option. Some projects, where Agile methodology is being used, may use lightweight documentation. Other projects may involve a higher level of documentation. The frequency of test reporting varies depending on factors such as the test level, how long an iteration lasts or the requirements of stakeholders.

Answer 8 FL-1.4.3 K2

c) is the correct option. Automated test scripts are an output from test implementation.

a), b) and d) are not correct options. Prioritized test cases, test data requirements and test environment requirements are outputs from test design.

Answer 9 FL-1.4.3 K2

d) is the correct option.

1D - The test log is an output from test execution.

2B - A test charter, documentation of the test objective for a test execution session, is an output from test design.

3C - A stub is, 'a skeletal or special-purpose implementation of a software component, used to develop or test a component that calls or is otherwise dependent on it. It replaces a called component.' A driver is 'A component or tool that temporarily replaces another component and controls or calls a test item in isolation'. Stubs and drivers are outputs from test implementation.

4A - Defect reports regarding defects in the test basis (if not fixed) are outputs from the review of requirements which is part of test analysis.

a), b) and c) are not correct options for the reasons given for d).

Answer 10 FL-1.4.4 K2
c) is the correct option The requirements traceability matrix shows traceability.
a) is not the correct option. With a Work Breakdown Structure (WBS) work is broken into smaller tasks to make the work more manageable and approachable. b) is not the correct option The test plan describes the test objectives, the means and the schedule for achieving the objectives. d) is not the correct option. The project plan describes the project objectives, the means and the schedule for achieving the objectives.

Answer 11 FL-1.4.4 K2
c) is the correct option. The test plan describes the test objectives, the means and the schedule for achieving the objectives.
a), b) and d) are not correct options. These are part of test case management and good test case management relies heavily on traceability.

Answer 12 FL-1.4.4 K2
b) is the correct option. Dependencies and relationships between requirements should be recorded so they can be traced across the project life cycle. Creating and maintaining traceability facilitates verification that requirements are covered by the test cases (test cases to requirements and also provides other benefits during the software development lifecycle.
a) is not the correct option. Requirements are defined when creating a new product or modifying or making changes to an existing product. The value of the requirements is assessed at this time. c) is not the correct option. Assessment of the testability of requirements is part of the review and analysis of the test basis. d) is not the correct option. The project manager owns the requirements specification documentation.

Answer 13 FL-1.4.5 K2
d) and e) are the correct options. The test progress report (also referred to as the test status report) is produced by the test manager with input from testers. Reprioritizing test efforts is part of test control and the test manager's role.
a) is not a correct option. Verifying the test environment is ready for use is part of test implementation and is undertaken by the tester.
b) is not a correct option. Maintaining the product backlog is a task undertaken by the product owner.
c) is not a correct option. Creating the test schedule is part of test implementation and is undertaken by the tester.

Answer 14 FL-1.4.5 K2
c) and d) are correct options. The tester's focus is primarily on test analysis, test design, test implementation and test execution. a), b) and e) are not correct options. The test manager's focus is primarily on test planning, test monitoring and test control, and test completion.

1.5 Essential Skills and Good Practices in Testing

Skills refer to the specific abilities, knowledge, and expertise that individuals or teams possess and can apply to perform tasks effectively. Skills can be both technical and non-technical.

Good practices, often referred to as best practices, are established methods, approaches, or techniques that have been proven to produce good outcomes.

FL-1.5.1 (K2) Give examples of the generic skills required for testing

Generic skills required for testing include:

- Being an effective team member and being able to perform testing on different levels of test independence
- Testing knowledge to increase the effectiveness of testing, such as use of the various test techniques
- Attention to detail, thoroughness, carefulness and being methodical
- Curiosity and creativity in devising new tests and being able to think from different perspectives such as the operations staff and end users
- Analytical thinking with the ability to identify, define and extract crucial information
- Adaptability to new situations and challenges such as dealing with frequent software updates and new features
- Technical knowledge such as the applicability of test tools
- Domain knowledge to be able to understand and communicate with end users and business representatives
- Good communication skills, active listening, understanding, reporting and discussing defects
- Presenting test results in a constructive, not critical way
- Basic number skills to present and interpret test metrics such as percentages and cumulative numbers and to understand the ways metrics can be presented such as in graphs, tables or matrices

FL-1.5.2 (K2) Recall the advantages of the whole team approach

Whole team approach also called the team-based approach, is a project management style based on individual team members working closely together and sharing responsibility for the quality and success of the project.

The emergence of the team concept can be traced back to the late 1920s and early 1930s with the Hawthorne Studies, see *References*. In the 1960s there was a move towards having open office spaces with the benefit of encouraging collaboration between employees. Also in the 1960s, the saying, 'there is no I in team' which first emerged in sports reporting was adopted in many organizations. The meaning of the saying is not to work alone, but together with others to achieve a goal.

Key aspects of the whole team approach are:

- **Collaboration with team members** sharing their expertise and perspectives to collectively solve problems and make informed decisions. The collaborative discussions aim to identify the three perspectives of customer (what the problem is), development (how the problem may be solved), and testing (what about...).
- **Shared Responsibility**: Rather than assigning development and testing tasks separately, the whole team is collectively responsible for ensuring the quality and success of the project.
- **Cross-Functional Teams**: Teams are typically cross-functional, meaning they have all the necessary skills and roles within the team to complete a feature or deliverable, reducing dependencies on external teams.
- **Frequent Communication**: Open and transparent communication is encouraged, allowing team members to understand each other's work and progress.

The whole team approach encompasses the ability of individuals to work effectively in a team context and contribute positively to the team's goals. The whole team approach promotes robust communication and collaboration between the team members. This approach is an important consideration in software development methods, for example in Extreme Programming, XP.

With a whole team approach, there are opportunities for any team member with the requisite knowledge and skills to undertake any task. This does not mean that team members can take on any role at any time. They should only take on roles in which they are competent and where there is a need. The whole team shares a workspace which can be physical or virtual, as co-location enhances communication and collaboration within the team.

Different experts recommend the size of a whole team from their own experience. While there is no specific guidance on the optimum size, there is no suggestion larger teams are always better. Larger teams are more likely to have coordination and greater communication issues. The collaborative discussions aim to identify the three perspectives; the customer (what the problem is), development (how the problem may be solved), and testing (what about?).

While the whole team approach prioritizes collective accountability for quality, each team member is still equally accountable for quality.

Benefits from the whole team approach include:

- Improves team dynamics and promotes a positive workplace environment
- Enhances communication
- Enhances collaboration
- Creates synergy by allowing the various skill sets within the team to be leveraged for the benefit of the project
- Faster production on complex tasks
- Expands professional skills
- Fosters new opportunities
- Promotes sustained change

When team members from different backgrounds contribute their ideas and insights, an organization benefits from a more well-rounded perspective.
The whole team approach applies to how a single team works. It does not imply only one whole team is needed for a complete project. It also does not cover how multiple teams work on larger projects. The approach does not expect every team member to be involved in every decision. For example, the business representative does not need to be involved in every technical decision that does not affect the business outcome. Implementing such an approach would unnecessarily slow down the team's progress with little advantage. The approach is about how the team works together, with the aim of higher quality deliverables, but it does not necessarily result in faster deployment to end users.

Examples of whole team approach include:

- Testers help business representatives create suitable acceptance tests
- Testers provide input to the test manager to determine the schedule and budget
- The test automation approach is defined by testers with the help of development
- The test strategy is decided by testers in collaboration with developers
- Testers can provide developers with input on the impact of a failure

Adopting the whole team approach, teams can improve communication, adapt to changing requirements, and deliver higher-quality products with greater efficiency.

In some contexts, the whole team approach may not be appropriate. Examples of this include:

- Safety-critical software where a high level of independence of testing may be needed
- Areas of sensitive software or data use where a high level of confidentiality is needed
- New product where certain features need to be kept confidential before release in the marketplace

FL-1.5.3 (K2) Distinguish the benefits and drawbacks of independence of testing

The degree of testing independence varies widely between organizations, projects and test levels. For most projects, multiple levels of independence are used. Unit and component testing is typically undertaken by developers while later stages in the project are undertaken by more independent testers. External specialists may be brought in for highly specialized testing in a specific area, such as security or internationalization.

Independence is not a replacement for familiarity. The benefits and drawbacks can depend to some extent on the level of independence.

Level of independence

Organization of Testing	Independence
1 Authors/Developers testing their own work products	Least
2 Testing by other developers in the development team	↓
3 Tester as part of the development team	
4 Internal testing team as part of the project team	
5 Some external specialist testers with the internal test team	
6 External third-party testing	Most

No independent tester (developer)

The only testing undertaken is by developers who test their own code.

Benefits include:

If developers find any defects in the code, then it is comparatively easy to fix, as the code is known to them. This avoids any delay that might occur from receiving the defect report from another person at a later stage.

Drawbacks include the developer may:

Be focused on positive test cases

Lack an end-to-end user perspective

Have misunderstood requirements, in which case no matter how much testing is undertaken based on this misunderstanding, the defect will not be found. The developer may determine the code works as intended when written, which may or may not match the requirements

Be taken away from writing code and thus cause delay

Be overconfident and feel that, as they wrote the code, they can assume if it is working properly for one path, and there is little need to test all paths

Lose a sense of responsibility for quality

Testing performed by developers other than the developer writing the code

This arrangement provides little independence and still potentially has many of the drawbacks of the developer testing their own code. A developer testing another developer's code may be reluctant to report the defects or even consider a defect does not exist. The tester's mindset is usually focused on positive test cases.

Testing performed by a tester (or test team) as part of the development team

With this arrangement, a tester is part of the development team with the benefits that come from teamwork.

Drawbacks include:

- Testing may be given a lower status than software development
- The tester may have limited authority to influence quality goals or adherence to requirements
- The tester's mindset is focused more on positive adherence to requirements
- Being part of development, the tester may have development responsibilities in addition to testing

Internal independent tester

With this arrangement, a tester or test team is not part of development but is internal to the organization and reports through the test manager to project management. Testers may be specialists or non-development technical staff from the organization. They may be brought in for the reasons given below for external independent testers.

Benefits of having internal independent testers include:

- An impartial view of the software leads to efficient, assumption-free and uninfluenced testing
- Typically, more defects are found compared to testing performed by the development team as testers are likely to recognize different types of defects because of their diverse backgrounds and skills
- Testing may have and benefit from using separate facilities, tools, training, etc.
- Less likely to be compromised due to lack of time or budget
- Greater adherence to the customer goals and objectives
- Defects are only accepted as fixed when fixes are independently verified
- Testing is recognized by the organization as a career path

Drawbacks include:

- Not having the full benefits to be gained from working closely as a cross-functional team

Independent external testers

External testers can be brought in to supplement internal testing. The benefits can include cover for:

- Areas where generalized testing is likely to be insufficient
- Where specialization is necessary, such as security or performance
- Particular test technique expertise is required, such as automation

In addition to the possible drawbacks of an independent tester, while specialist testers should focus on overall software quality, their views may be limited to their area of expertise and may not be aligned with those of the organization.

Independent external testing

This model provides maximum independence between the tester and the developer. The quality of the external organization should be audited regularly.

Testing performed by an external organization may:

- Lack a broader view of business objectives and test objectives
- Have separate facilities, tools, training, etc.
- Bring a different set of assumptions to testing
- Need clear test requirements and a well-defined communication structure
- Need appropriate knowledge transfer
- Have ongoing communication problems
- Have an obsessive focus on finding defects
- Not leverage benefits from working closely as a cross-functional team within the organization

Summary of benefits

Independent testers are likely to recognize different kinds of failures compared to developers because of their different backgrounds, technical perspectives, and biases.

- An independent tester can verify, challenge, or disprove assumptions made by stakeholders during the specification and implementation of the system
- Independent testers can report in a more objective manner

Summary of drawbacks

- Over-reliance on the independent team
- Developers have less opportunity to gain testing experience
- Developers may lose a sense of responsibility for quality
- Independent testing may be seen as a bottleneck
- Independent testers may lack some important information about the test object

Note: There can be a cost benefit or cost increase from any of the arrangements, depending on the availability of resources, skills and context. For example, it may be less or more costly to use external testing compared to setting up internal testing.

1.5 Questions 1 to 6 FL-1.5.1, 1.5.2, 1.5.3

Question 1 FL-1.5.1 (K2) Which of the following is the best example of a generic skill testers should have?

a) Design and optimization of database skills
b) Strong debugging skills
c) Ability to accurately gather requirements
d) Attention to detail and a methodical approach

Select ONE option

Question 2 FL-1.5.1 (K2) Which of the following are generic skills typically required by a software tester?

a) Ability to design complex user interfaces
b) Strong mathematical skills for complex calculations
c) Excellent interpersonal and communication skills
d) Critical thinking and analytical abilities
e) Artistic creativity for graphic design tasks

Select TWO options

Question 3 FL-1.5.2 (K1) Which of the following is not necessarily true for whole team working?

a) The team works together from the same physical location
b) Team members recognize they cannot operate in isolation for the team to be successful
c) Team business representatives, managers, developers and testers all have some responsibility for the quality of the product
d) Team members collaborate in decision-making

Select ONE option

Question 4 FL-1.5.2 K2 Which of the following are most true with a whole team approach?

a) Responsibility for the quality of the product is shared by business representatives, developers and testers
b) Testers are responsible for developing all test cases including component test cases which they then give to the developers for testing as developers create stubs or drivers as necessary
c) User stories are written by business representatives and testers together in everyday or business language, these are then given to developers
d) Project costs are lower with a whole team approach as collaboration and sharing of skills eliminate the need for specialists
e) Role barriers are removed as team members contribute to project success based on their unique skills and perspectives

Select TWO options

Question 5 FL-1.5.3 (K2) Which of the following best illustrates a benefit of independent testing?

a) Independent testing reduces the need for communication between developers and testers
b) Independent testers have a different perspective and bias than developers
c) Independent testing always removes bottlenecks in the software development lifecycle
d) Developers do not need to understand how test cases have been designed

Select ONE option

Question 6 FL-1.5.3 (K2) Which of the following is the best justification for independent testing that is separate from the development team?

a) Independent testing will always use fewer resources than in-house testing
b) Independent testers determine the processes and methodologies used
c) Independent testing can be more effective at finding defects
d) Independent testers are not concerned about whether the project succeeds or fails

Select ONE option

1.5 Answers and Explanations 1 to 6 FL-1.5.1, 1.5.2, 1.5.3

Answer 1 FL-1.5.1 K2

d) is the correct option. Testers need to pay attention to detail and be methodical in covering the required testing.
a) is not the correct option. Developers design and optimize databases.
b) is not the correct option. Debugging is typically done by developers.
c) is not the correct option. Business Analysts are responsible for gathering requirements.

Answer 2 FL-1.5.1 K2

c) and d) are the correct options. c) Testers need strong interpersonal skills to collaborate effectively with developers and other stakeholders. Clear and concise communication is crucial for reporting test results and issues. d) Testers should be able to analyze software requirements, identify potential issues, and design effective test cases. Critical thinking helps in troubleshooting and root cause analysis. a), b) and e) are not correct options. Testers do not need to be experts in advanced mathematics, artistic creativity for graphic design or able to design complex user interfaces in their core testing roles. These skills might be beneficial in some specific contexts, but they are not typically required for testing software.

Answer 3 FL-1.5.2 K1

a) is the correct option. Although a whole team may be located in the same physical location, this is not always true as the team can collaborate in a virtual workspace.

b), c) and d) are not correct options as they are true for whole team working.

Answer 4 FL-1.5.2 K1

a) and e) are the correct options. a) Shared responsibility is a key aspect of a whole team approach.

e) A whole team approach encourages collaboration and contributions based on team members' skills and perspectives.

b) is not a correct option. Developers typically create unit tests. c) is not a correct option. In a whole team approach, user stories are written by business representatives, developers and testers together. d) is not a correct option. There may still be a need for specialist testers such as security or other specialists.

Answer 5 FL-1.5.3 K2

b) is the correct option. This is a benefit as independent testers are likely to recognize different kinds of failures compared to developers because of their different backgrounds and perspectives.

a) is not the correct option. In independent testing, communication with developers on the failures found is still needed. c) is not the correct option. Although in some circumstances, this may be true, independent testing can itself be perceived by developers as a bottleneck. The inclusion of 'always' makes this option incorrect. d) is not the correct option. As part of analyzing and fixing defects, developers need to understand how test cases were designed.

Answer 6 FL-1.5.3 K2

c) is the correct option. Independent testers can be more effective than in-house testers, depending on skills, location, environment and influences.

a) is not the best option. Independent testers may or may not use fewer resources than in-house testing.

b) is not the correct option. The organization should be involved in determining the processes and methodologies used. The aim of using independent testers is not to dictate how things should be done.

d) is not the best option. Testing effort should be aligned to achieve a successful outcome.

2. TESTING THROUGHOUT THE SOFTWARE DEVELOPMENT LIFECYCLE

The ISTQB Exam Structures & Rules Tables v1.19 specifies six exam questions for this section. There are four K1 and four K2 level learning objectives.

Keywords given in the Syllabus
acceptance testing, black-box testing, component integration testing, component testing, confirmation testing, functional testing, integration testing, maintenance testing, non-functional testing, regression testing, shift left, system integration testing, system testing, test level, †test object, test type, white-box testing.

Not identified as keywords in Glossary or Syllabus: retrospective, user story.
†Test object included in the Syllabus in sections 1 and 2.

2.1 Testing in the context of a Software Development Lifecycle

A software development lifecycle SLDC model is a structured framework used to guide the planning, design, development and testing of software systems. SDLC models help to streamline and organize the software development and test processes, providing a roadmap for the team to follow. Each model has its own set of phases, activities, and deliverables.

FL-2.1.1 (K2) Explain the impact of the chosen software development lifecycle on testing

Types of software development lifecycle models include:

SDLC	Examples	Details
Sequential	Waterfall, V-model	A system developed linearly with several discrete and successive phases and no overlap between them.
Iterative	Spiral, Prototype	A component or system developed through a series of iterations. Iterative development focus is on repeating the full development cycle with feedback and flexibility.
Incremental	Rational Unified Process RUP	A component or system developed through a series of increments. Incremental development builds on previously developed increments sequentially.
Big Bang	Small projects or proof-of-concept	This informal model has no specific planning or phases. Development happens without a structured process. All components and parts are integrated into the final version of the software.
Agile	Acceptance test-driven development ATDD, Behavior-driven development BDD, Crystal, Domain-driven design DDD, Extreme programming XP, Feature-driven development FDD, Kanban, Lean IT, Scrum, Test-driven development TDD	A group of software methodologies based on iterative/incremental development, where requirements and solutions evolve through collaboration with self-organizing cross-functional teams.
More than one type	Hybrid Agile Blended Agile	Hybrid Agile combines Agile with non-agile methods. Blended Agile is a combination of two or more established methods.

The choice of the software development lifecycle model impacts the following:

Scope and timing of test activities such as test levels and test types to be used
Role and responsibilities of the testers
Level of detail of testware documentation to be delivered
Test approach and choice of test techniques to be used
The use of and extent of test automation

SDLC	Testing Considerations
Sequential	In the initial phases testers typically participate in requirement reviews, test analysis and test design. The detailed study of the work product at the outset can raise concerns about the product content and act as a useful quality review. The executable code is usually created in the later phases, so typically dynamic testing cannot be performed in the early stages.
Iterative and Incremental	Each iteration may deliver a working prototype or product increment. This means that in each iteration both static testing and dynamic testing may be performed at several levels. Frequent delivery of iterations or increments requires fast test feedback. Regression testing is increasingly important at the end of all iterations with the number of regression tests and the time required for regression testing increasing. Regression testing may be increasingly automated. Full functionality is not available for testing until the final increment is available, but some functionality has been provided earlier than would have happened with a sequential SDLC.
Agile	Changes may occur throughout the project more frequently than with other SDLC models. Lightweight work product documentation is typical. Extensive test automation to make regression testing easier is common with the number of regression tests increasing. Most of the manual testing tends to be done using experience-based test techniques that do not require extensive prior test analysis and design. As with iterative and incremental SDLCs, full functionality is not available until the end of the final sprint but some functionality has been provided earlier than would have occurred with a sequential SDLC. Testers are part of a cross-functional team and typically have closer collaboration than with other SDLCs.

Summary: Sequential SDLC models are more structured and may be preferred for projects with stable and well-defined requirements.
Iterative/incremental/Agile SDLC models promote early and continuous testing, adaptability to changing requirements, and iterative/incremental delivery, making them well-suited for projects where flexibility and collaboration are essential.

FL-2.1.2 (K1) Recall good testing practices that apply to all software development lifecycles
Characteristics of good testing with all types of software development lifecycles include:

For every development activity, there is a corresponding test activity

Different test levels have different objectives specific to the particular level so that testing is efficient and effective, comprehensive and avoids redundancy

Testers should be involved in reviewing documents as soon as drafts are available

Test analysis and design for a given test level should begin before code implementation when testing is a driver for software development or during the corresponding development phase in the software development lifecycle

Developers may find and fix defects at an early stage. When testers are involved, failures should be reported effectively

FL-2.1.3 (K1) Recall examples of test-first approaches to development
The Syllabus includes three test-first approaches, where tests are defined before the code is written and act as a means of directing development. These are; Test-Driven Development, (TDD) is developer-focused, Acceptance Test-Driven Development (ATDD) and Behavior-Driven Development (BDD) are customer-focused.

Test-Driven Development, TDD

'A software development technique where test cases are developed, automated and then the software is developed incrementally to pass those test cases.'

Test-driven development is a process where the developer creates tests based on the specified requirements before producing code. The focus is on the implementation of a feature and component tests. Tests are typically in the same coding language as the test object. As developers are already familiar with their coding language, creating tests should be relatively easy. These tests tend to be technical and may be difficult for non-developers to fully understand. Test-Driven Development can be done by a single developer or a development team producing both tests and application code side by side to complete a feature. A potential disadvantage of test-driven development is that the process can be inappropriate for large or medium-scale designs.

Acceptance Test-Driven Development, ATDD

'A collaboration test-first approach that defines acceptance tests in the stakeholders' domain language.'

Acceptance criteria are used to define specific conditions or requirements. Acceptance criteria are objective measures that must be met for the component or system to be considered complete and satisfy the user, customer or other authorized entity. Acceptance-test-driven development guides software development with a customer focus on meeting acceptance criteria. The test cases are written at a higher level than those with test-driven development in language understandable to non-developers. Collaboration is promoted between business representatives, developers, and other stakeholders which serves to achieve a consensus and a shared understanding.

Acceptance criteria cover different aspects, positive and negative, functionality and non-functionality to ensure comprehensive testing. Acceptance criteria also provide input to the planning and estimation of development and testing effort.

Acceptance test-driven development can be used in the same project with test-driven development which typically involves early component tests.

Behavior-Driven Development, BDD

'A collaboration test-first approach to development in which the team is focusing on delivering expected behaviour from a component or system for the customer which forms the basis for testing.'

A cross-functional team focuses on ensuring tests are based on the desired behavior of the software product. This reduces the risk of incorrect assumptions, miscommunications or the need to re-write large portions of the software Test cases are written in a simple form of language that is easily understood by stakeholders. This is typically using a distinct sentence structure, Gherkin, with a 'Given/When/Then' format. For example:

Given username of 'user' and password of 'password',
When the login button is pressed,
Then the user is sent to the home screen.

When tests are written in this way, they should then be automatically translated by software into an outline for developers in their coding language. Developers then replace that outline with the code needed as appropriate.

Behavior-driven development can minimize the waste of development effort by implementing only the product behaviors that contribute to desired business outcomes.

FL-2.1.4 (K2) Summarize how DevOps might have an impact on testing
DevOps is an approach that aims to create synergy with development, testing and operations teams working together to achieve a set of common goals.

DevOps and Agile are not the same. Agile is a software development methodology that focuses on iterative, incremental, small, and rapid releases of software, together with customer feedback and addresses gaps and conflicts between the customer and developers. DevOps involves a cultural shift within an organization with continuous development, testing, integration, deployment, and monitoring of the software throughout the lifecycle. Any modification to the code may be tested immediately with continuous testing. This prevents concerns such as quality issues and release delays that might otherwise occur when testing is constrained or delayed until an iteration or increment of the software product is available.

Technical benefits of DevOps include:
- Early detection and faster correction of defects
- Continuous testing which allows for high-quality and more frequent releases
- Less complex problems to manage

Business benefits of DevOps include:
- Faster delivery of features
- Stable operating environments
- Improved communication and collaboration between the teams

Disadvantages of DevOps include:
- Infrastructure costs can be high for setting up the DevOps environment
- If DevOps is not properly configured, it can be costly due to the significant investment in automation and infrastructure
- If DevOps is not implemented correctly, it can lead to increased risks and possibly limited availability of people with DevOps skills

FL-2.1.5 (K2) Explain shift left
Shift left refers to the principle of early testing. Actions that can be taken to achieve a shift left include:
- Increasing the focus on requirements review, component testing and component integration testing, particularly in sequential software development models
- Within an incremental or iterative software development lifecycle, implementing a series of shorter iterations or increments to provide frequent and faster feedback
- Using model-based testing to reduce defects introduced during the requirements definition, architecture, and design phases to generate test design and test cases
- Adopting a DevOps approach with continuous integration, continuous testing and continuous deployment

A shift left can help find both functional and non-functional issues earlier than might otherwise be the case. The opposite of a shift left is a shift right. This is when test activities move towards the later stages of the software development cycle when a full production-like test environment is used or post-deployment.

A shift left may not always be advisable or the extent of the shift may be limited. In a few scenarios, some test cases defined early may require continuous and resource-intensive updating or become obsolete. This may happen, for example, with an iterative software development lifecycle when the software undergoes significant changes and rework between consecutive iterations.

When adopting a shift left, consideration should be given to:

- The software development lifecycle model in use
- The likelihood of changes in business requirements and when these may occur
- Features to be tested
- The possibility of code being rewritten or refactored between iterations

FL-2.1.6 (K2) Explain how retrospectives can be used as a mechanism for process improvement

A **Retrospective** is, *'A regular event in which team members discuss results, review their practices, and identify ways to improve.'*

The Glossary lists synonyms as 'project retrospective', 'retrospective meeting' and 'post-project meeting'. Syllabus v4.0.1 specifically removes 'post-project meeting' as an alternative to retrospective.

A retrospective provides a focused time for teams to learn from the past and each other so they can constantly improve the development process. The aims of a retrospective include:

- Allowing participants to express ideas, thoughts, and experiences in a safe environment
- Encouraging a continuous improvement mindset
- Documenting feedback
- Exposing issues from the previous sprint, iteration or software version that are holding the product or team back
- Aligning the team around the most important issues
- Informing leadership of potential roadblocks
- Helping make improved decisions for the next sprint, iteration or project
- Assigning responsibility for actions decided on during the retrospective and following up on these

Values that guide retrospectives are:

1. Focus on **Improvement**: This value encourages the team to reflect on what went well and what could have been done better to improve future performance, the primary objective of a retrospective.
2. Respect for **People**: This value ensures that every team member's perspective is valued, contributing to open and honest discussions.
3. **Engagement** of the team: This value promotes collaboration and recognizes that inputs from all team members, regardless of their roles, are important for driving improvements.
4. **Empowerment** of the team: This value encourages the team to collectively decide on actionable improvements that they can implement, fostering a sense of responsibility and autonomy.
5. Delivery of **Value**: This value ensures that the insights gained during the retrospective translate into practical improvements that positively impact the team's work and overall project success.

Benefits of retrospectives include:

- Improved productivity
- Improved team dynamics and team trust with better cooperation between development and testing
- Team learning
- Added customer value
- Improved test effectiveness, test efficiency and overall process

2.1 Questions 1 to 13 FL-2.1.1, 2.1.2, 2.1.3, 2.1.4, 2.1.5, 2.1.6

Question 1 FL-2.1.1 (K2) Which of the following best describes an impact on testing when a sequential software development model is being used in preference to other types of software development lifecycle models?

a) Limited documentation can lead to challenges in testing
b) Most of the manual testing tends to be done using experience-based test techniques
c) Testing has to be more adaptable and flexible
d) Dynamic testing starts later than it does with SDLCs

Select ONE option

Question 2 FL-2.1.1 (K2) How does testing vary with different software development life cycle models SDLCs?

a) Testing is a distinct phase that follows development in all SDLCs
b) Testing practices remain consistent across all SDLCs
c) Testing is not required in Continuous Integration/Continuous Delivery environments
d) Testing is a continuous and integrated process throughout development in Agile SDLCs

Select ONE option

Question 3 FL-2.1.2 (K1) Which of the following best describes good testing practice?

a) Design of test cases should always start as soon as the relevant development is complete
b) All test levels should have the same objectives to ensure testing is efficient throughout
c) For every software development activity, there is a corresponding test activity
d) Testers should review all development documentation

Select ONE option

Question 4 FL-2.1.2 (K1) Which of the following is a good testing practice that applies to all software development lifecycles?

a) Testers should delay performance efficiency testing until the final development stage
b) Testers should review documentation as soon as drafts are available
c) Testers should start test design as soon as relevant documentation drafts are available
d) Testers should review the test basis as part of test implementation

Select ONE option

Question 5 FL-2.1.3 (K1) Which of the following is true for Test-Driven Development (TDD)?

a) Test cases are designed and created before code is created
b) Starts with extensive software design followed by targeted function testing
c) Separates intent of tests from test implementation so that they are understood by stakeholders
d) Particularly useful when code must run under stringent real-time, memory, network, or performance constraints

Select ONE option

Question 6 FL-2.1.3 (K1) Which of the following is a development approach in which test cases are defined based on the expected behavior of the software?

a) BSD
b) SCM
c) BDD
d) FDD

Select ONE option

Question 7 FL-2.1.3 (K1) Which of the following statements is not true for Test-Driven Development, TDD?

a) Drives coding through test cases
b) Provides fast and frequent feedback from test results
c) Can be combined with Acceptance Test-Driven Development, ATDD
d) Is a collaborative approach in which developers, testers, and business representatives work together to analyze the requirements of a software system

Select ONE option

Question 8 FL-2.1.4 (K2) The following summarize how DevOps might impact testing except for which?

a) With its automated testing, DevOps removes the need for manual testing
b) Increases early visibility of functional and non-functional defects
c) Promotes automated processes that facilitate establishing stable test environments
d) Promotes shift left

Select ONE option

Question 9 FL-2.1.4 (K2) Which of the following best describes the goal of DevOps?

a) Having an environment where change management does not control software releases
b) Implementing an environment to release more reliable software faster than might otherwise be possible
c) Creating an environment where development and testers have responsibility for all development and operation tasks
d) Making greater use of automation to reduce the number of people required to deliver software products

Select ONE option

Question 10 FL-2.1.5 (K2) Which of the following best supports shift left?

a) Increasing focus on and shift toward beta testing
b) Establishing a feedback loop directly with the development team to report and prioritize issues identified by the customer in production
c) Reviewing the requirements specification from the perspective of testers to identify ambiguities, incompleteness and inconsistencies
d) Continuing testing in the production test environment after deployment to identify real/run-time failures before the customer encounters them

Select ONE option

Question 11 FL-2.1.5 (K2) Which of the following does not support shift left?

a) Continuous integration and continuous delivery with automated component testing
b) Component testing that is run with a test harness when appropriate
c) Dynamic testing starting before static code testing
d) Commitment from stakeholders for changes in development and test approach

Select ONE option

Question 12 FL-2.1.6 (K2) Which of the following statements is true for team retrospectives?

a) Retrospectives can lead to improved cooperation between development and testing
b) The team as a whole accepts agreed action items with no one person alone being given responsibility for an action
c) Minutes are not taken so attendees do not feel inhibited about raising issues that did not go well or risk blame being attributed to a person
d) Repeating the same agenda and pattern as a previously successful retrospective encourages the success of later retrospectives

Select ONE option

Question 13 FL-2.1.6 (K2) Which values are typically embraced during a retrospective?

a) Competition and Individual achievements recognized
b) Hierarchy and centralized decision-making
c) Continuous learning and improvement
d) Adherence to the original plan

Select ONE option

2.1 Answers and Explanations 1 to 13 FL-2.1.1, 2.1.2, 2.1.3, 2.1.4, 2.1.5, 2.1.6

Answer 1 FL-2.1.1 K2

d) is the correct option. The executable code is usually created in the later phases, so typically dynamic testing cannot be performed in the early stages.
a) is not the correct option. Limited documentation with omissions, discrepancies or ambiguities can lead to challenges in testing.
b) is not the correct option. Using experience-based test techniques does not require extensive prior test analysis and design and is, therefore, more typical in Agile software development lifecycles.
c) is not the correct option. Testing has to be more adaptable and flexible in Agile software development, providing fast feedback, as well as changes in the product and the marketplace.

Answer 2 FL-2.1.1 K2

d) is the correct option. In Agile methodologies, testing is a continuous and integrated process throughout development.
a) is not the correct option. The timing of testing activities and the level of integration with development can vary significantly between these different SDLCs.
b) is not the correct option. Testing practices vary widely across different SDLCs, as the test approach is heavily influenced by the chosen SDLC model.
c) is not the correct option. Testing is a crucial part of CI/CD. It is automated and integrated into the deployment pipeline to ensure that software changes are reliable.

Answer 3 FL-2.1.2 K1

c) is the correct option. For every software development activity, there is a corresponding test activity.
a) is not the correct option for the reasons given for c).
b) is not the correct option. Different test levels have specific and different objectives specific to that level so that testing is efficient and effective, comprehensive and avoids redundancy.
d) is not the correct option Testers should be involved in reviewing relevant documents as soon as drafts are available. This does not mean <u>all</u> development documents need to be reviewed as some may not be relevant.

Answer 4 FL-2.1.2 K1

b) is the correct option. Testers should review work products as soon as drafts are available to support shift left.
a) is not the correct option. Performance efficiency testing should be part of a comprehensive testing strategy from the early stages of the SDLC. This allows for early identification and resolution of performance issues. c) is not the correct option. Test design (test case creation) should be based on approved documentation, not on early drafts as test effort may be wasted if software design changes following amendments to draft documentation. d) is not the correct option. The test basis should be reviewed as part of test analysis.

Answer 5 FL-2.1.3 K1
a) is the correct option. TDD is a test-first approach to development.
b) is not the correct option. TDD is a test-driven development approach.
c) is not the correct option. With TDD, tests are written by developers and are not in a plain text format understandable by other stakeholders.
d) is not the correct option. TDD does not focus on expected behavior.

Answer 6 FL-2.1.3 K1
c) is the correct option. BDD is Behavior-Driven Development.
a) is not the correct option. BSD is Berkeley Software Distribution.
b) is not the correct option. SCM is Software Configuration Management.
d) is not the correct option. FDD is Feature-Driven Development.

Answer 7 FL-2.1.3 K1
d) is the correct option. Test cases are written by developers with no or little participation from stakeholders.
a) is not the correct option. TDD adopts a prescriptive test-first approach of creating tests that express the intended functionality of the code at the unit level.
b) is not the correct option. A key aspect of TDD is to provide fast and frequent feedback.
c) is not the correct option. A user story requirement determined in ATDD can be split by a developer into a set of tasks needed to implement that functionality. Developers can then implement these tasks using TDD.

Answer 8 FL-2.1.4 K2
a) is the correct option. DevOps does not remove the need for manual testing. For example, testing some usability features from a user's perspective may be better done manually.
b) is not the correct option. A benefit of DevOps is faster delivery and earlier detection of defects, functional and non-functional. c) is not the correct option. Automation is a key part of DevOps.
d) is not the correct option for the reasons given for b).

Answer 9 FL-2.1.4 K2
b) is the correct option. Implementing an environment to release more reliable software faster than might otherwise be possible is the goal of DevOps.
a) is not the correct option. Change management involves the controlled identification and implementation of required changes. Organizations need to embrace change management.
c) is not the correct option. Stakeholders, business representatives and others have responsibility for some tasks. d) is not the correct option. DevOps does not necessarily mean the number of people required, changes. It does mean different skill sets may be needed.

Answer 10 FL-2.1.5 K2

c) is the correct option. Shift left is based on finding defects early in the software development lifecycle. Reviewing specifications can find potential defects before they are introduced into the code. a) is not the correct option. Beta testing is a form of acceptance testing, which is typically carried out late in the software development lifecycle at an external site to the developer's test environment. b) is not the correct option. Shift left aims to find defects before the software is deployed into production. d) is not the correct option for the reasons given for b).

Answer 11 FL-2.1.5 K2

c) is the correct option. Static code testing does not require the code to be running and can be started before dynamic testing, which requires the code to be running.

a) is not the correct option. The use of continuous integration and continuous delivery supports shift left. b) is not the correct option. With a test harness, a component can be tested before other components that call or are called by it are available and thus supports shift left.

d) is not the correct option. It is important to have stakeholders' commitment as shift left may result in extra training, effort and costs earlier in the project.

Answer 12 FL-2.1.6 K2

a) is the correct option. Better cooperation is achieved through collaboration in retrospective reviews and optimized regularly.

b) is not the correct option. Actions must be followed up and should therefore have assigned responsibility. Having accountability is important.

c) is not the correct option. Minutes should be taken at retrospectives to record actions agreed. The minutes should not apportion blame to any individuals.

d) is not the correct option. The agenda and pattern of retrospectives should vary to promote creativity and new ideas for improving the test process. With the same format and agenda, there is a tendency for this team to revisit the same issues repeatedly which may not be beneficial.

Answer 13 FL-2.1.6 K2

c) is the correct option. Retrospectives emphasize continuous learning and improvement. The purpose of a retrospective is to reflect on what went well, what could be improved and how the team can enhance its processes and collaboration.

a) is not the correct option. Retrospectives encourage collaboration and teamwork. There are other opportunities for recognizing the contributions of an individual.

b) is not the correct option. Team members discuss and review their practices.

d) is not the correct option. Retrospectives focus on evolving practices for better outcomes.

2.2 Test Levels and Test Types

Test levels refer to distinct stages or phases of testing in the test process. Each test level serves a specific purpose and targets different aspects of the software under test. The reason for having test levels is to make the software test process more systematic and to prevent overlap and repetition of test activities between the software development lifecycle phases.

Note: The ISTQB Glossary defines test level as, *'A specific instantiation of a test process'* and gives 'test stage' as a synonym. The ISO definition of 'test level' is, 'one of a sequence of test stages, each of which is typically associated with the achievement of particular objectives and used to treat particular risks.' See *References ISO 29119-2 2021*.

Test types categorize testing activities based on the specific objectives and characteristics of the tests. They define the focus and purpose of the test effort. Common test types include functional, non-functional, black-box and white-box testing.

Note: The ISTQB Glossary defines test type as, *'A group of test activities based on specific test objectives aimed at specific characteristics of a component or system.'* This applies to functional and non-functional test types. The Syllabus also includes both black-box and white-box testing as test types.

FL-2.2.1 (K2) Distinguish the different test levels

Test levels covered in the Syllabus are unit/component testing, integration testing, system testing, system integration testing and acceptance testing.

To accommodate specific test levels, a test environment may contain multiple environments such as a unit test environment or a system test environment.

Test levels are distinguished by the following non-exhaustive list of attributes:

Test object	Each test level has a defined test object(s) to test.
Test objectives	These vary depending on the test level.
Test basis†	The documents from which the requirements of the test object(s) can be obtained. In addition to the requirements specification, documents or diagrams relevant to the test level.
Defects/Failures	As the focus area for each test level is different, the failures and defects will also differ.
Approach	The way of working for designing and executing tests varies with test level.
Responsibilities	Responsibility for testing varies according to the skills, knowledge and experience required for the test level.

† Each of the test levels may have additional documents in the test basis relevant to the test level. Testing at all levels should take into account the requirements specification and if applicable regulations, standards, contracts and other relevant documents.

The choice of test level and the extent to which each level is applied depends on the project's objectives, context and requirements.

Test Level	Attributes
Component Testing	**Test object**: a component / module / unit **Test objectives**: finding and fixing defects early **Additional test basis**: code or component specifications **Defects/failures**: related to incorrect code and logic **Approach**: test components in isolation. Static testing is particularly useful. Fix defects as and when found without a formal defect management process **Responsibility**: normally performed by developers
Component Integration Testing, CIT	**Test object**: two or more interacting components **Test objectives**: testing interfaces and interactions between components **Additional test basis**: sequence diagrams, component level architecture, interface and communication protocol specifications **Defects/failures**: related to interface mismatches, and incorrect parameters or structures for passing data between components, API related **Approach:** heavily dependent on the specific integration testing adopted (bottom-up, top-down, big-bang, sandwich/hybrid, incremental) † May need test harnesses, stubs or drivers **Responsibility**: Developers or testers
System Testing	**Test object**: system **Test objectives**: verifying the behavior of the system meets the specified requirements functionally and non-functionally **Additional test basis**: architecture diagram, workflow diagram **Defects/failures**: related to meeting specified requirements both functionally and non-functionally **Approach**: typically conducted in a dedicated environment that closely mimics the production environment in terms of both hardware and software **Responsibility**: undertaken by the testing team. In some scenarios, can be an independent test team
System Integration Testing, SIT	**Test object**: underlying integration of systems and external services that are intended to work together **Test objectives**: testing the interfaces between the system under test and other systems and external services to evaluate interoperability capability between the system elements and other systems **Additional test basis**: external interface definitions, system interface and communication protocol specifications, architecture diagram for the overall system, workflows, data flows **Defects/failures**: related to interfaces and interactions with other systems and external services **Approach**: has a prerequisite in which multiple underlying integrated systems have already undergone and passed system testing. Tests the required interactions between these systems and external services as a whole **Responsibility**: undertaken by the testing team, which can be an independent test team or a test team of the existing system(s) and/or services which are to be integrated

Acceptance Testing	**Test object**: complete system, the test environment can be that of the organization developing the software (e.g. alpha testing) or that of the customer (e.g. beta testing) **Test objectives**: testing the whole system from an end-user perspective, and also check the usability aspects of the system along with functional aspects. validating and demonstrating readiness for deployment **Additional test basis**: acceptance criteria, user documents, regulations, standards, contract **Defects/failures**: related to acceptance criteria not being met **Approach**: depends on the type of users, these can be for example, clients, agents, operational staff, managers, administrators etc. and if applicable also depends on regulations, standards and contract **Responsibility**: ideally performed by the intended users. May be performed by the product owner, customer or in some scenarios by the test team

† A **Harness** is a collection of stubs and drivers needed to execute a test suite.
Stubs are used in bottom-up integration testing to simulate lower-level components that have not been developed yet or are not yet available for testing.
Drivers are used in top-down integration testing to simulate higher-level components that call lower-level components, which may not have been developed yet or are not yet available for testing.

Test Level Examples

Component testing: A restaurant needs an app that allows customers to order at their tables without a server. A component has been designed and coded for the 'Add to order' function. The component can be tested in isolation. Other components for submitting the order and obtaining confirmation that the order can be satisfied, can be tested separately.

Note: The Glossary defines 'component' as, *'A part of the system that can be tested in isolation'* and lists 'module' and 'unit' as synonyms. Other sources make a distinction, identifying a unit as the smallest piece of code that can be tested. In the example above, 'Add to order' and 'Remove from order' could be considered as two units of code. The ISO definition for 'component' includes the following in a note to the entry, 'The terms module, component, and unit are often used interchangeably or defined to be sub-elements of one another in different ways depending upon the context. The relationship of these terms is not standardized.' See *References, ISO Standards ISO 24765:2010(en).*

Component integration testing, CIT: A banking app has a function where users can set up a savings account. It includes a money-transferring capability from a user's main account to the user's savings account. These are separate components. Integration testing focuses on the interfaces to ensure that passing information between components functions smoothly and correctly.

System testing: A fitness app has been created with capabilities such as setting up and tracking monthly fitness goals, consolidating fitness and wellness metrics building personalized exercise sessions and providing users with a fitness report. This will be assessed in system testing.

System integration testing, SIT: An accounting application, human resources information, inventory management and enterprise resource planning need to interoperate. Testing includes verifying systems can exchange data and share documents electronically.

Acceptance testing: The Syllabus identifies the following as the main forms of acceptance testing:

Alpha testing: This is carried out by the internal testers of the software development organization immediately before software completion and is conducted at the developers' site.

Beta testing: This is undertaken by customers, is conducted at the customer's site and is usually performed when alpha testing has been completed successfully.

Contractual acceptance testing: In some projects, the criteria for accepting a product are defined in the contract. Testing should verify the software complies with legal requirements.

Operational acceptance testing, OAT: This evaluates the system as a whole to establish if the operations and system administrators can accept the system. This may include testing administrator functions, load, reliability, maintainability, backup and restore, and other relevant software characteristics and functions.

Regulatory acceptance testing: The software must meet industry or national regulatory standards. For example, some countries have strict laws that a website should adhere to accessibility standards.

User acceptance testing, UAT: This is mainly carried out by end-users. There may be different user groups who will use the software, and the testing should ensure all users are represented. For example, a logistics scheduling application may be used by administrators, delivery drivers, customers tracking orders and managers. All these will have a different perspective on how the software should work for them and should be included in the user acceptance testing.

FL-2.2.2 (K2) Distinguish the different test types
The Syllabus identifies four test types, functional, non-functional, black-box and white-box testing.

Functional testing seeks to evaluate whether each function of the test object works as specified in the software requirements. Functional testing deals with 'what' the test object should do. Each function is compared to the corresponding requirement to establish if its output is consistent with expectations. The objective of functional testing is to check functional appropriateness, functional completeness and functional correctness. Functional testing can start early in the software development lifecycle as part of reviews or as soon as the function is available.

Functional testing answers questions such as:

Can I set up an account?
Can I add items to my shopping cart?
Can I view frequently asked questions?
Can I check out my order?
Is the amount I am being charged, correct?

The answers should typically be a simple 'Yes' or 'No'.

Non-functional testing seeks to evaluate attributes other than the functional characteristics of a test object. Non-functional testing deals with 'how well the system behaves.' The Quality Characteristics model, (*Reference ISO/IEC 25010:2011 / 2023*).
The main categories for non-functional testing are:

Performance efficiency
Compatibility
Usability – Interaction capability in ISO/IEC 25010:2023
Reliability
Security
Maintainability
Portability – Flexibility in ISO/IEC 25010:2023
Safety (Added in ISO/IEC 25010:2023)

For changes to the categories since publication of the Syllabus, see *Appendix E – ISO/IEC 25010:2023*

Non-functional testing answers questions such as:

How fast does this page load?
What happens if 10,000 people are logged in at the same time?
Is the web page laid out intuitively?
How adaptable is the software to other environments?

Not all non-functional testing questions can be answered with a simple Yes/No response.

While non-functional defects are often associated with runtime behavior, some aspects of non-functional quality can be identified by examining code structure or the code itself without executing it. For example:

- Poor performance efficiency from inefficient algorithms or data structures, excessive resource consumption, such as memory leaks, high processor usage, or lack of optimization in critical sections of code.
- Maintainability issues from code with poor naming conventions, inconsistent coding styles, hard to understand, or code duplication that can lead to inconsistencies.

It is necessary to uncover non-functional defects that are context-dependent with dynamic testing.
In Agile software development, some non-functional test cases may span more than one iteration in a software development lifecycle.

ISO 25010:2011 Quality Characteristics Model

Functional suitability	**Performance efficiency**	**Compatibility**	**Usability**	**Reliability**	**Security**	**Maintain-ability**	**Portability**
Functional correctness	Time-behaviour	Interoperability	Appropriateness recognizability	Maturity	Confidentiality	Modularity	Adapability
Functional appropriateness	Resource utilization	Co-existence	Learnability	Availability	Integrity	Reusability	Installability
Functional completeness	Capacity		Operability	Fault tolerance	Non-repudiation	Analysability	Replaceability
			User error protection	Recoverability	Accountability	Modifiability	
			User interface aesthetics		Authenticity	Testability	
			Accessibility				

Note: For updates and changes to the model, see *Appendix E – ISO/IEC 25010:2023.*

The Syllabus v4.0.1 continues to use the original names of characteristics, but adds 'Interaction capability' and 'Flexibility' as alternatives to 'Usability' and 'Portability'. These may be used in exam questions. 'Safety' is a new additional characteristic included in the ISO/IEC 25010 model and referenced in the Syllabus as part of non-functional testing.

Black-box testing involves testing a system with no prior knowledge of its internal workings. It is specification-based and derives tests from documentation not related to the internal structure of the test object. The system's behavior is checked against its specifications.

Functionality and non-functionality can be tested. Testers do not require coding skills.

Examples of black-box testing techniques include equivalence partitioning, boundary value analysis, decision tables and state transition testing. These are explained in sections FL-4.2.1 to FL-4.2.4.
A synonym of black-box testing given in the ISTQB Glossary is *'Specification-based testing.'*

White-box testing is structure-based and derives tests from the system's implementation or internal structure, using the code, knowledge of the architecture, workflows and data flows. Testers to inspect and verify the inner workings of the software, the code, infrastructure, and integrations with external systems to uncover underlying structure issues. White-box testing is typically easy to automate and is an essential part of the automated build processes in Continuous Integration/Continuous Delivery (CI/CD) development. White-box testing can achieve complete code coverage.

Examples of white-box testing techniques include statement testing and branch testing, these are explained in sections FL-4.3.1 and FL-4.3.2.

Synonyms of white-box testing listed in the ISTQB Glossary are clear-box testing, code-based testing, glass-box testing, logic-coverage testing, logic-driven testing, structural testing, and structure-based testing.

FL-2.2.3 (K2) Distinguish confirmation testing from regression testing

Confirmation testing and regression testing are both change-related testing and are used during the software development lifecycle, before deployment into production of the software product or system. (Testing after deployment into production is referred to as maintenance testing).

Confirmation testing is performed to check that modifications made to correct a defect have successfully removed the failure(s) caused by that defect. Confirmation testing has a defined scope and is performed until the defect reported from a failed test case result is shown to have been fixed. Confirmation testing may also be used after changes connected with a non-functional software characteristic such as a performance target or acceptance criteria.

Depending on the risk, confirmation testing tests the fixed version of the test object and can include either or both:

- Executing all test cases that have previously had failed results due to the defect
- Adding new test cases to cover the changes that were needed to fix the defect

Confirmation testing is needed on any test level where a defect is fixed or when changes are made to that level. Confirmation testing is performed before regression testing.

Regression testing aims to verify that changes have not caused unintended effects and that the test object still complies with its specifications. Regression testing checks that the modifications have not adversely affected functionality, reliability, performance efficiency or another software characteristic and have not introduced additional defects. Regression testing may not be restricted to the test object itself but can be related to the test environment or other test objects.

The extent of regression testing can be optimized by first conducting an impact analysis which will show the parts of the software that could be affected. Impact analysis is defined as, *'A software testing approach that helps define all risks associated with any change(s) made to the test object.'*

Regression tests may be repeated many times and typically the number of regression test cases increases with each iteration or release. There is a strong case for automating regression test cases, starting early in the project. Regression testing is needed at all test levels where changes have been made.

Passed is defined as, *'The status of a test result if the actual result matches the expected result.'*
Failed is defined as, *'The status of a test result if the actual result does not match the expected result.'*

Example: Confirmation and regression testing
The table below shows all possible results that could be obtained from three consecutive test runs. Execution 1 is the initial testing of the test object. When a test case result is determined as failed, a fix is applied to the source code and is available in the next version of the software product.
Executions 2 and 3 are where fixes have been applied. The table uses:

(C) for confirmation test results, where a previous failed test case result and a fix is being tested.
(R) for regression test results, where a previous passed test case result is being tested to ensure the test case result is still passed.

A regression test case result of failed in Execution 3 indicates a new fix is required and a fourth execution round with a confirmation test is needed.

	Test Case Result		
Test Case	**Execution 1**	**Execution 2**	**Execution 3**
TC01	Passed	Failed (R)	Passed (C)
TC02	Passed	Failed (R)	Failed (C)
TC03	Passed	Passed (R)	Passed (R)
TC04	Passed	Passed (R)	Failed (R)
TC05	Failed	Failed (C)	Passed (C)
TC06	Failed	Failed (C)	Failed (C)
TC07	Failed	Passed (C)	Passed (R)
TC08	Failed	Passed (C)	Failed (R)

2.2 Questions 1 to 12 FL-2.2.1, 2.2.2, 2.2.3

Question 1 FL-2.2.1 (K2) Which of the following is not a test level?

a) System testing
b) Acceptance testing
c) Security testing
d) Integration testing

Select ONE option

Question 2 FL-2.2.1 (K2) Which of the following best distinguishes system testing and acceptance testing?

a) System testing focuses on validating the system as a whole for user satisfaction, acceptance testing assesses the overall system's functionality
b) System testing focuses on validating business rules are correctly implemented, acceptance testing focuses on the system's non-functional characteristics such as performance efficiency and security
c) System testing focuses on verifying all interactions between components work correctly, acceptance testing focuses on validating user satisfaction
d) System testing focuses on verifying the whole system meets the specified requirements, acceptance testing focuses on whether the software aligns with needs and expectations

Select ONE option

Question 3 FL-2.2.1 (K2) Alpha testing is a type of testing at which test level?

a) Component
b) Acceptance
c) Integration
d) System

Select ONE option

Question 4 FL-2.2.1 (K2) When a software component under test calls another component that is not yet available, for testing to proceed, a skeletal implementation of the missing component can be used. The skeletal implementation of such a component is called which of the following?

a) Stub
b) Module
c) Driver
d) Domain

Select ONE option

Question 5 FL-2.2.2 (K2) Which of the following statements best describes a functional test?

a) For an online inquiry system, checking the effect of high volumes of traffic in an online inquiry system
b) For a delivery collection system, checking and displaying the location of the nearest collection points to the user's location using GPS
c) Measuring the response time of an online airline booking system
d) For an online information system, checking the user interface does not require an unacceptable number of mouse clicks to view required information

Select ONE option

Question 6 FL-2.2.2 (K2) Which of the following is a test type as defined in the Syllabus?

a) Functional testing
b) System testing
c) Statement testing
d) Performance efficiency testing

Select ONE option

Question 7 FL-2.2.2 (K2) Non-functional testing is which of the following?

a) Test technique
b) Test type
c) Test level
d) Test process

Select ONE option

Question 8 FL-2.2.2 (K2) White-box testing is which of the following?

a) Experience-based testing
b) Design-based testing
c) Structure-based testing
d) Exploratory testing

Select ONE option

Question 9 FL-2.2.2 (K2) Which of the following is not an alternative name for white-box testing?

a) Translucent-box testing
b) Logic-coverage testing
c) Logic-driven testing
d) Glass-box testing

Select ONE option

Question 10 FL-2.2.2 (K2) Black-box tests are derived from which of the following?

a) Source code
b) Structural model of the architecture
c) Requirements specification
d) Results from white-box testing

Select ONE option

Question 11 FL-2.2.3 (K2) Which of the following is a correct statement for regression testing?

a) Is performed before or after confirmation testing depending on circumstances
b) Test cases need to be repeated so are always automated
c) Only run during the later stages of system and acceptance testing
d) Checks unchanged areas of the software have not been affected by a defect fix

Select ONE option

Question 12 FL-2.2.3 (K2) The table below shows the results obtained from three consecutive test runs. Execution 1 is the initial testing of the test object. When a test case result is determined as failed, a fix is applied to the source code and available in the next version of the software product. Executions 2 and 3 are where fixes have been applied and test cases are repeated.

	Test Case Result		
Test Case	**Execution 1**	**Execution 2**	**Execution 3**
TC02	Passed (1)	Failed (5)	Failed (9)
TC03	Passed (2)	Passed (6)	Passed (10)
TC06	Failed (3)	Failed (7)	Failed (11)
TC07	Failed (4)	Passed (8)	Passed (12)

Which of the above tests are executed as regression tests?

a) 6, 8, 10, 12
b) 5, 6, 10, 12
c) 5, 6, 7, 8, 9, 10, 11, 12
d) 10, 12

Select ONE option

2.2 Answers and Explanations 1 to 12 FL-2.2.1, 2.2.2, 2.2.3

Answer 1 FL-2.2.1 K2

c) is the correct option. Security testing is a test type and can be conducted at any test level. a), b) and d) are not correct options as they are test levels.

Answer 2 FL-2.2.1 K2

d) is the correct option. System testing is defined as, *'A test level that focuses on verifying that a system as a whole meets specified requirements.'* Acceptance testing is defined as, *'A test level that focuses on determining whether to accept the system.'*

a), b) and c) are not correct options for the reasons given for d).

Answer 3 FL-2.2.1 K2

b) is the correct option. Alpha testing is a type of acceptance testing performed in the developer's test environment by roles outside the development organization.

a), c) and d) are not correct options for the reason given for b).

Answer 4 FL-2.2.1 K2

a) is the correct option. A stub is, *'A skeletal or special purpose implementation of a software component used to develop or test a component that calls or is otherwise dependent on it. It replaces a called component.'*

b) is not the correct option. Module is a synonym of 'component'.

c) is not the correct option. A driver is, *'A tool or component that temporarily replaces another component and controls or calls a test item in isolation.'* d) is not the correct option. A domain in computing is a distinct subset of the internet whose addresses share a common suffix or are controlled by a particular organization or individual.

Answer 5 FL-2.2.2 K2

b) is the correct option. Displaying the location of the nearest collection points is a functional requirement.

a) is not the correct option. Checking the effect of high volumes of traffic is performance efficiency or load testing, both are non-functional. c) is not the correct option. Measuring response time is non-functional performance efficiency testing. d) is not the correct option. Testing the User Interface for acceptable behavior is part of usability testing, which is non-functional.

Answer 6 FL-2.2.2 K2

a) is the correct option. Functional testing is a test type.

b) is not the correct option. System testing is a test level. c) is not the correct option. Statement testing is a test technique and part of white-box testing. d) is not the correct option. Performance efficiency testing is part of non-functional testing.

Answer 7 FL-2.2.2 K2

b) is the correct option. Non-functional testing is a test type used to verify non-functional software characteristics.

a) is not the correct option. A test technique is, *'A procedure used to define test conditions, design test cases, and specify test data.'*

c) is not the correct option. A test level is, *'A specific instantiation of a test process.'*

d) is not the correct option. A test process is, *'A set of test activities performed to achieve a test objective'*. Test activities are; test planning, test monitoring and test control, test analysis, test design, test implementation, test execution, test completion and test closure.

Answer 8 FL-2.2.2 K2

c) is the correct option. Structure-based testing is given in the Glossary as a synonym for white-box testing. a), b) and d) are not correct options. Experience-based testing, design-based testing and exploratory testing are not synonyms of white-box testing.

Answer 9 FL-2.2.2 K2

a) is the correct answer. Translucent-box testing is an alternative name for grey-box testing and is not part of the Syllabus. b), c), and d) are not correct options as glass-box testing, logic-coverage testing, and logic-driven testing are listed as synonyms in the ISTQB Glossary for white-box testing which is part of the Syllabus.

Answer 10 FL-2.2.2 K2

c) is the correct option. Black-box testing is specification-based.

a) and b) are not correct options. White-box tests are derived from the internal structure (code, architecture, workflows and data flows). d) is not the correct option. Black-box and white-box testing are separate test types.

Answer 11 FL-2.2.3 K2

d) is the correct option. Regression testing detects whether defects have been introduced or uncovered in unchanged areas of the software after a defect fix.

a) is not the correct option. Regression testing is performed after confirmation testing. b) is not the correct option. Although there is a strong case for automating regression testing, some regression testing may be done manually.

c) is not the correct option. Regression testing is needed at all levels if the defects are fixed and/or changes are made on these levels.

Answer 12 FL-2.2.3 K2
b) is the correct option. When a test case passes and is rerun in a later execution round, it is regression testing. The purpose is to check the original defect has not returned, see the table below.
If it is the first time a test case is run, or if the test case result failed in the previous execution run and then the test case is repeated, this is confirmation testing. a), c) and d) are not correct options.

	Test Case Result		
Test Case	**Execution 1**	**Execution 2**	**Execution 3**
TC02	Passed (1)	**Failed (5)**	Failed (9)
TC03	Passed (2)	**Passed (6)**	**Passed (10)**
TC06	Failed (3)	Failed (7)	Failed (11)
TC07	Failed (4)	Passed (8)	**Passed (12)**

2.3 Maintenance Testing

Maintenance testing is defined by the ISTQB Glossary as, *'Testing the changes to an operational system or the impact of a changed environment to an operational system.'*

FL-2.3.1 (K2) Summarize maintenance testing and its triggers

Maintenance testing of a modification made to an operational system involves evaluating the success of implementation of the modification and checking for possible regression in parts of the system that remain unchanged. Impact analysis may be done before a modification is made, to help decide if the modification should be made. There are different types of maintenance testing, depending on the reason for the modification or retirement of the software. These types, together with the reason or trigger, include: (See *References ISO 14764:2022 definitions*).

Adaptive maintenance 'Modification of an operational software product or system to keep the software product usable in a changed or changing environment.' For example, the changes can be upgrades to the operating system or environment.

Additive maintenance 'Modification of an operational software production system performed to add functionality or features to enhance the usage of the product.' Not all additions or enhancements can be handled through the maintenance process, larger changes may involve a new development effort.'

Corrective maintenance 'Modification of a software product performed after delivery to correct discovered problems.

Note 1 to entry: The modification repairs the software product to satisfy defined system requirements.'

Emergency maintenance 'Unscheduled modification (hotfix) performed to temporarily keep a system operational, pending corrective maintenance.

Note 1 to entry: Emergency maintenance may be performed to make a software system partially operational such as modification to the software or its parameters to limit operations, functionalities, inputs, outputs, interfaces, usability, etc. Emergency maintenance can be regarded as a type of corrective maintenance.'

Perfective maintenance Recoding or refactoring a software product, for example, to improve software performance efficiency, maintainability or other software attributes.

Preventive maintenance 'Modification of a software product after delivery to correct latent faults in the software product before they occur in the live system. Preventive maintenance can be regarded as a type of corrective maintenance.'

Retirement maintenance Retiring software at the end of the software lifecycle. For example, this can involve testing data archiving if long data retention periods are required. Testing the restore and retrieval procedures after archiving may also be needed if archived data is required during the retention period.

The scope of maintenance testing depends on:

Degree of risk of the modification (likelihood and occurrence)
Size of the existing system
Size of the modification made

2.3 Questions 1 to 4 FL-2.3.1

Question 1 FL-2.3.1 (K2) A modification of a software product has been made to an operational system to correct recently discovered defects. You are tasked with assessing if any detectable unexpected side effects may have occurred in the operational system. Which type of testing should be undertaken?

a) Regression testing
b) Maintenance testing
c) Confirmation testing
d) Negative testing

Select ONE option

Question 2 FL-2.3.1 (K2) Which type of maintenance testing is triggered by the recoding or refactoring of a software product for maintainability?

a) Corrective
b) Preventative
c) Perfective
d) Adaptive

Select ONE option

Question 3 FL-2.3.1 (K2) Which of the following is not a potential trigger for maintenance testing?

a) An unscheduled modification made temporarily to a production system to keep it operational
b) Migration of an operational system to a different platform
c) Planned backups of the database used by the production system
d) An operational product reaching its end of life and due to be archived

Select ONE option

Question 4 FL-2.3.1 (K2) Which of the following in an operational system would not typically trigger maintenance testing?

a) Enhancements are made to the software or the environment
b) Obsolete capabilities are deleted from the software
c) Code refactoring is made to improve performance efficiency
d) Monitoring of the system availability is required

Select ONE option

2.3 Answers and Explanations 1 to 4 FL-2.3.1

Answer 1 FL-2.3.1 K2

b) is the correct option. Maintenance testing is undertaken when an operational software product is subject to modification.

a) is not the correct option. Regression testing is used in the test environment, not with a software product after delivery in software. c) is not the correct option. Confirmation testing is performed after fixing a defect to confirm that a failure caused by that defect does not reoccur.

d) is not the correct option. Negative testing is testing a component or system in a way for which it was not intended to be used.

Answer 2 FL-2.3.1 K2

c) is the correct option. Perfective maintenance is performed when recoding or refactoring software, is undertaken. For example, to improve performance efficiency, maintainability or other software attributes.

a) is not the correct option. Corrective maintenance is performed to correct discovered failures in the operational system. b) is not the correct option. Preventative maintenance is when there is a modification of an operational software product to correct latent faults before they occur in the operational system.

d) is not the correct option. Adaptive maintenance is when a modification of an operational software production system is performed to add functionality or features to enhance the usage of the product.

Answer 3 FL-2.3.1 K2

c) is the correct option. Maintenance testing is, *'Testing the changes to an operational system or the impact of a changed environment to an operational system and would not be required after planned backups.* a), b) and d) are not correct options as they are potential triggers for maintenance testing.

Answer 4 FL-2.3.1 K2

d) is the correct option. Maintenance testing is required after modifications are made to the software product, system or environment. Monitoring is not typically a trigger for maintenance.

a), b) and c) are not correct options as they all involve modifications that trigger maintenance testing.

3. STATIC TESTING

The ISTQB Exam Structures & Rules Tables v1.19 specify four exam questions for this section. There are three K1 and five K2 level learning objectives.

Keywords given in the Syllabus
anomaly, dynamic testing, formal review, informal review, inspection, review, static analysis, static testing, technical review, walkthrough.

3.1 Static Testing Basics

Static testing is testing that does not involve the execution of the test item. A wide range of types of documentation or code can be examined. Testers, business representatives (including Product Owners, business analysts), and developers collaborate in example mapping, collaborative user story writing, and backlog refinement sessions to make sure user stories and their associated work products satisfy the agreed acceptance criteria and quality standards. The main objective of static testing is to identify defects, errors and vulnerabilities in the test object at an early stage of the development process before the code is actually executed. Static testing can be performed using manual or automated methods. Manual methods include human inspection and review, while tools that automate testing use algorithms and predefined rules to analyze the test object. Static analysis can be applied for verification and validation.

The types of defects found by static testing include:

- Ambiguities or inconsistencies in documentation
- Deviation from coding standards including naming conventions
- Syntax errors
- Unreachable code or subroutines not called
- Logic errors
- Design errors such as miscoding of control or data flow compared to diagram/model
- Mismatched parameters for type order or number, between calling and called code
- Infinite loops
- Simple cases of memory leaks
- Duplicate code that may affect maintainability
- Inefficient code
- Excessive code complexity
- Some code constructs that may affect non-functional quality characteristics

FL-3.1.1 (K1) Recognize types of work products that can be examined by static testing

Almost any work product can be examined using static testing. Examples include; specification documents, design documents, source code, test plans, test cases, product backlogs, test charters, project documentation, installation procedures, models and contracts. A work product that is difficult for humans to interpret may not be appropriate for static testing, such as third-party executable code due to legal protection.

For automated static testing, the work products need a machine-readable structure against which they can be checked, such as models, code or text with formal syntax. Static analysis tools include code checkers, control flow analyzers, data flow analyzers, spelling and grammar checkers, readability tools and more.

FL-3.1.2 (K2) Explain the value of static testing

Static testing can provide value by:

- Finding certain defects at the earliest stage of the software development lifecycle
- Involving less test effort as test cases are not required
- Identifying defects that dynamic testing cannot
- Improving development productivity. Although static testing requires an upfront investment of time, it can result in increased productivity by reducing the need for extensive debugging and rework later in the development process
- Identifying and resolving issues early reduces project delays caused by defects. This can lead to shorter development cycles and faster time-to-market
- Leading to reduced maintenance over time by identifying and addressing issues early in the software development lifecycle
- Identifying missing requirements that could impact the success of the project
- Discovering security vulnerabilities and coding patterns that might lead to security risks
- Detecting potential reliability issues in code and design, such as error-handling strategies and failover mechanisms, help ensure the software operates reliably and is available when needed
- Checking compliance with regulatory and industry-specific requirements. Systematically reviewing documentation against the specified requirements. Checking the code and design adhere to specific standards, such as security protocols, data privacy regulations, and other compliance-related aspects
- Identifying code constructs that could lead to performance bottlenecks, such as inefficient algorithms or resource leaks. While it does address these aspects during development, leading to better performance efficiency, static testing is not a replacement for dedicated performance efficiency test techniques
- Analyzing code and architectural design to assess how well the software can scale to handle increased loads or user demands
- Higher return on investment and costs as it is significantly less costly to fix problems early
- Code reviews and inspections promote collaboration among team members, knowledge sharing and a collective understanding of the codebase and project requirements

FL-3.1.3 (K2) Compare and contrast static testing and dynamic testing

Static testing is applied to non-executing work products. Dynamic testing is applied to executing work products. Static testing and dynamic testing complement each other. They share similar objectives, namely to support the detection of defects in the test object. Both can be conducted manually, with the use of tools that automate tests or a combination of both. However, there are differences between them.

Differences include:

	Static Testing	Dynamic Testing
Timing	Performed early in the software development process, typically during the design and coding phases before the code is executed. Allows for early resolution of defects.	Performed during the execution of the software, usually after the code is compiled or interpreted, which may lead to late-stage defect fixing.
Purpose	Focuses on reviewing and analyzing the code, design, and documentation.	Involves executing the software and observing its behavior.
Types of Defects	Typically defects related to coding standards, design flaws, documentation inconsistencies and errors, syntax and logic issues.	Functional and non-functional defects related to the runtime behavior.
Tools and Techniques	Can involve manual, automated and/or static analysis tools.	Involves running the software with test cases using testing frameworks and tools.
Execution	Does not involve executing the code and is typically non-intrusive.	Involves the execution of the code, and can be intrusive, as may modify data or change system states.
Test Cases	Test cases are not executed, instead, code is reviewed and defects in it are identified based on examination.	Test cases are executed, and the behavior of the software is observed.
Cost	Generally cost-effective as catch issues are caught early, reducing the extent and cost of fixing defects later in the development process.	Can be resource-intensive, requiring hardware and a software environment, to be set up and available. When defects are discovered late in the development cycle, costs increase.

Limitations of static testing include:

- If coding standards or static analysis rules are overly strict, static testing may identify code constructs that are technically acceptable but do not conform to those specific rules.
- Some static analysis tools may not be sufficiently context-sensitive to understand the specific use case of a code segment and may miss certain issues that require deep domain knowledge or extensive analysis
- If custom code patterns or libraries that deviate from standard conventions are used, static analysis tools may not recognize them as valid, potentially leading to false-negative results
- Issues related to external dependencies or third-party libraries may not always be identified by static testing
- Consideration of environmental factors such as network conditions, load, or the presence of other applications running concurrently on the same system
- Highly obfuscated or intentionally obfuscated code, which is often used in malware or cybersecurity-related scenarios

Limitations of dynamic testing include:

- If the test cases do not cover all possible paths, scenarios, or edge cases in the test object, defects in untested areas may be missed, resulting in false-negative results
- Dynamic testing relies on appropriate and accurate test data to stimulate software operation. If the test data does not include certain conditions or inputs that trigger defects, those defects may remain undiscovered. Also, specific test data may trigger false-positive results that do not occur in real-world scenarios
- Differences between the test environment and the production environment can lead to false negatives. Some defects may only manifest under specific production conditions
- Some defects may occur infrequently or under rare conditions. Dynamic testing may not always reproduce these conditions, resulting in false-negative results
- Certain defects such as those related to timing or race conditions may be challenging to reproduce consistently during testing, leading to false-negative results

3.1 Questions 1 to 9 FL-3.1.1, 3.1.2, 3.1.3

Question 1 FL-3.1.1 (K1) In your organization, which of the following can typically be reviewed using static testing?

i. Real-time performance response times
ii. Third-party chatbot plugins
iii. External vendor's proprietary geolocation data production method
iv. The organization's distributed source code repository
v. The organization's centralized code repository

a) All of these
b) An option not listed here
c) v only
d) iii, iv and v only

Select ONE option

Question 2 FL-3.1.1 (K1) Which of the following is the best example of what can be examined effectively using static testing?

a) Code that has been obfuscated
b) Hardware devices that will be part of the test environment
c) Complex multimedia files or moving images generated in real time
d) Network configuration files

Select ONE option

Question 3 FL-3.1.2 (K2) Which of the following is true for static testing?

a) Finding certain code defects is less efficient compared to using dynamic testing
b) Can be used to examine a work product
c) Can include manual and automated testing
d) Cannot be used with Continuous Integration CI

Select ONE option

Question 4 FL-3.1.2 (K2) Which of the following is a capability of static testing?

a) Identifies issues related to security vulnerabilities
b) Observes how the software responds to inputs and interacts with users in a real-time
c) Considers environmental factors such as network conditions, load, or the presence of other applications running concurrently on the same system
d) Analyzes data values or variables at runtime

Select ONE option

Question 5 FL-3.1.2 (K2)
The following can potentially be found by static testing and some can potentially be confirmed by dynamic testing. Which cannot be found using dynamic testing?

a) Infinite loops
b) Logic errors
c) Unused variables that impair the readability of the code
d) The exact location in the code of a defect
e) Missing characters in error messages

Select TWO options

Question 6 FL-3.1.2 (K2) Which of the following is not found using static testing of code?

a) Defect
b) Failure
c) Bug
d) Fault

Select ONE option

Question 7 FL-3.1.2 (K2) Which of the following best describes a primary objective of static testing?

a) Identifying syntax errors
b) Ensuring code runs at maximum speed
c) Testing code with real user data
d) User acceptance testing

Select ONE option

Question 8 FL-3.1.3 (K2) Which of the following statements differentiates static testing from dynamic testing?

a) Static testing focuses on functional issues, dynamic testing focuses on code and documentation issues
b) Static testing is used for functional testing, dynamic testing is used for non-functional testing
c) Static testing is performed early in the software development process, dynamic testing is performed during code execution
d) Static testing is more costly compared to dynamic testing due to the need for specialized tools
e) Static testing is not directly intrusive on system data and state changes, dynamic testing may modify input data and change system states

Select TWO options

Question 9 FL-3.1.3 (K2) For which of the following should dynamic test techniques be used?

a) Assessing real-time response times
b) Reviewing design documents
c) Enforcing coding standards
d) Identifying unreachable code

Select ONE option

3.1 Answers and Explanations 1 to 9 FL-3.1.1, 3.1.2, 3.1.3

Answer 1 FL-3.1.1 K1

b) is the correct option. iv and v can be examined by static testing. i requires the code to be directly executed and so cannot be examined using static testing. Static testing is not a replacement for dedicated performance efficiency test techniques. ii and iii typically cannot be examined as they are the property of third parties. a), c) and d) are not correct options for the reasons given for b).

Answer 2 FL-3.1.1 K1

d) is the correct option. Static testing can be used to examine configuration files.
a) is not the correct option. Static testing may face limitations when dealing with highly obfuscated or intentionally obfuscated code, which is often used in malware or cybersecurity-related scenarios.
b) is not the correct option. Static testing is used for examining software-related artifacts, such as source code, configuration files, and documentation. It is not suitable for analyzing physical or non-software products, such as hardware devices or mechanical systems.
c) is not the correct option. Static testing is done on textual or code-based artifacts and not on multimedia files generated in real time.

Answer 3 FL-3.1.2 K2

c) is the correct option. Static testing can include manual or automated testing on documents or code that is not being executed.
a) is not the correct option. Certain code defects can be found early using static testing and more efficiently than dynamic testing, typically resulting in lower overall effort. Creating test cases is not required.
b) is not the correct option. A work product that is difficult for humans to interpret may not be appropriate for static testing, such as third-party executable code due to legal reasons. d) is not the correct option. Static testing finds code defects early and is often incorporated into continuous integration frameworks.

Answer 4 FL-3.1.2 K2
a) is the correct option. Static testing can discover security vulnerabilities by identifying coding patterns that might lead to security risks b),c) and d) are not correct options as they are capabilities of dynamic testing.

Answer 5 FL-3.1.2 K2
c) and d) are the correct options. c) Static testing should identify unused variables that can impair the readability of the code. d) Dynamic testing triggers failures and does not identify the exact location of the defect in the code.
a) is not a correct option. An infinite loop can result in a lockout from the code so could be confirmed by appropriate dynamic testing. b) is not a correct option. Logic errors that result in incorrect calculations of other functions could be confirmed by appropriate dynamic testing. e) is not a correct option. Missing characters could be identified in the code seen during dynamic testing.

Answer 6 FL-3.1.2 K2
b) is the correct option. Static testing cannot trigger a failure as the code is not being run.
a) is not the correct option. Static testing identifies and locates defects in the code.
c) and d) are not correct options for the reasons given for a). Bug and fault are synonyms of 'defect'.

Answer 7 FL-3.1.2 K2
a) is the correct option. Syntax errors can be found from inspection of the code, without the code being executed. b), c) and d) are not correct options. When the code is running, the type of testing undertaken is testing is dynamic, not static. User acceptance testing involves end-users testing the software to ensure it meets their specific needs and is a dynamic testing phase.

Answer 8 FL-3.1.3 K2
c) and e) are the correct options. c) Static testing is performed early in the software development process as it includes a review of documentation and code that does not need to be running. e) Dynamic testing requires the code to be executable and is performed during code execution so may modify data and change system states. With static testing, code is not executed and is not intrusive on data and system states. a) is not a correct option. Static testing is primarily concerned with code review and identifying issues related to code quality, design, and documentation, while dynamic testing focuses on validating functional and non-functional requirements. b) is not a correct option for the reasons given for a). d) is not a correct option. The cost of testing can vary depending on several factors, and it is not necessarily true that static testing is more expensive. The costs of static testing and dynamic testing depend on the specific project and the tools used.

Answer 9 FL-3.1.3 K2
a) is the correct option. Response times are best evaluated when the code is executed. b), c), and d) are not correct options. These can be evaluated using static testing, without the test object being executed.

3.2 Feedback and Review Process

A feedback and review process involves collecting input, suggestions, opinions and evaluations from stakeholders, peers, experts, or users regarding the test process, product, documents or any other deliverable or process. Feedback and review are crucial for identifying issues and making informed decisions.

FL-3.2.1 (K1) Identify the benefits of early and frequent stakeholder feedback

The benefits of early and frequent stakeholder feedback include:

- Early communication of potential quality issues
- Helps the development team to improve their understanding of what they are building
- Allows the development team to focus on the features that deliver the most value to stakeholders
- Allows the development team to focus on the features that have the most positive impact on identified risks
- Provides stakeholders with information they can use when making decisions
- Helps avoid misunderstandings about requirements
- Helps avoid changes to requirements not being understood or not being implemented early
- Removes the risk of failure to deliver what stakeholders want
- Removes or reduces costly rework
- Can avoid missed deadlines
- Removes a tendency for 'blame games'

FL-3.2.2 (K2) Summarize the activities of the review process

Different review types have some common characteristics which include:

- Uncovering defects in the work product, documents, function, logic, implementation etc.
- Verifying the work product meets expectations or requirements
- Establishing the work product adheres to applicable standards
- Making software development and later testing management
- Helping software development productivity efficiency and effectiveness

Differences in characteristics between review types depend on factors which include:

- The level of formality (see below)
- Purpose and scope
- The review entry and exit criteria
- Roles and responsibilities of participants
- Individual preparation required
- Level of documentation required and reporting
- Training that may be required
- Planned number of reviews, (for example an informal review might be conducted before a later more formal review or the size of work products may be too large to be covered in a single review so the review process may be invoked multiple times to cover the whole work product)

ISO 20246:2017 establishes, 'A generic framework for work product reviews that can be referenced and used by all organizations involved in the management, development, test and maintenance of systems and software. It contains a generic process, activities, tasks, review techniques and documentation templates that are applied during the review of a work product.'

The framework is structured yet flexible and can be tailored to a particular situation. The extent of the activities in the review process is determined by the level of formality and the type of review being undertaken, see later FL-3.2.4 Reviews.

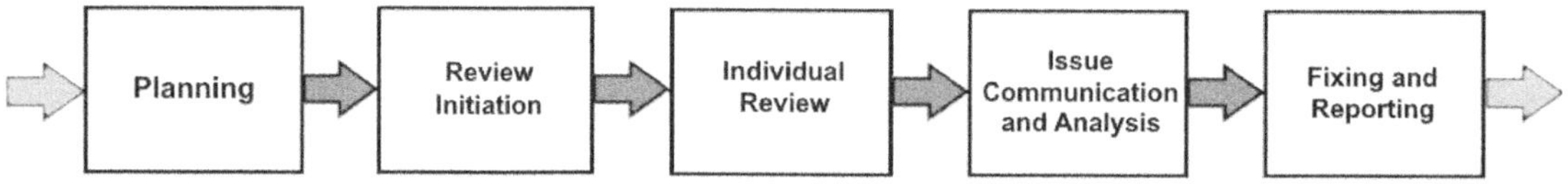

Work Product Review Process

The level of formality of a review depends on factors such as:

- The software development lifecycle being used
- The maturity of the development process
- The criticality and complexity of the work product being reviewed
- Legal, regulatory or contractual requirements
- The need for an audit trail

For more formal reviews, more of the tasks described in the review activities will be required. For informal reviews, some of the tasks described below will not be needed.

Review Activity	Details
Planning	The scope of the review, which comprises the purpose, the work product to be reviewed, quality characteristics to be evaluated, areas to focus on, the review exit criteria, supporting information such as standards, effort and the timeframes for the review, is defined.
Review Initiation (Kick-off)	The objective is to ensure all participants and everything involved are prepared to start the review. This includes making sure every participant has access to the work product under review, is aware of the scope and characteristics of the review type to be undertaken, understands the roles, focus and responsibilities and receives everything needed to perform the review. Training of reviewers may be arranged.
Individual Review (Preparation)	For some types of reviews, every reviewer performs an individual review to assess the quality of the work product under review, identify anomalies, recommendations, and questions by applying one or more review techniques (e.g. checklist-based reviewing, scenario-based reviewing). The ISO/IEC 20246 standard provides more depth on different review techniques. The reviewers can log all their identified anomalies, recommendations, and questions.
Issue Communication and Analysis	Since the anomalies identified during a review are not necessarily defects, all these anomalies need to be analyzed and discussed. For every anomaly, a decision should be made on its status, ownership and required actions. If a review meeting is held, issues can be sent for collation and prioritization before the meeting or raised at the meeting. If a review meeting is not held, then issues are typically sent to the individual performing the analysis. Participants can decide what the quality level of the reviewed work product is and what follow-up actions are required. A follow-up review may be required to complete actions.
Fixing (rework) and Reporting	Unless the review is very informal, for every defect a defect report should be created so that corrective actions can be followed up. Once the exit criteria are reached, the work product can be accepted. The review results are reported.

FL-3.2.3 (K1) Recall which responsibilities are assigned to the principal roles when performing reviews

A variety of different stakeholders take part in reviews and these stakeholders may take on several different roles. (Note: Not all the roles are used in all review types). The roles and responsibilities can be tailored to suit the specific needs of an organization or a particular software development project The objective is to promote collaboration, identify and address issues and improve the overall quality of the software product.

Manager:

- Decides on what is to be reviewed, provides resources such as staff and allocates time for the review

Moderator: (also known as Facilitator)

- Ensures the effective running of review meetings
- Is responsible for time management.
- Facilitates communication and collaboration among participants in an environment in which everyone can speak freely
- Ensures that the review process follows the defined objectives and guidelines
- Manages any conflicts or disagreements during the review

Review leader:

- Takes overall responsibility for the review
- Organizes when and where the review will take place
- Decides who will be involved
- Coordinates the review activities
- Assigns specific tasks to reviewers
- Monitors progress and guides reviewers
- Consolidates feedback and ensures that it has been properly documented
- Reports the review findings to the relevant stakeholders

Reviewers:

- Evaluate the work product being reviewed
- Identify defects, issues, and areas for improvement
- Provide constructive feedback and suggestions
- Verify compliance with relevant standards, guidelines, and requirements
- Follow the review process and guidelines defined by the moderator
- A reviewer may be someone working on the project, a subject matter expert or any other stakeholder

Scribe: (also known as Recorder)
- Documents the review proceedings, decisions, and actions
- Collates anomalies from reviewers and records identified defects, issues, and improvement suggestions
- Maintains accurate records of review findings and recommendations
- Prepares a review report summarizing the results and outcomes

Author:
- Participates in the review process as the creator of the work product
- Provides clarifications and explanations on the design, implementation, or functionality
- Collaborates with reviewers to address identified issues or concerns
- Implements agreed-upon changes or fixes based on review feedback
- In an Inspection, cannot also act as the review leader or scribe

Other, more detailed roles are possible, as described in the ISO/IEC 20246 standard, see *References*.

FL-3.2.4 (K2) Compare and contrast the different review types

There are many different types of reviews. The Syllabus focuses on the following four commonly used types. Details of other types of reviews are included in the ISO/IEE 20246 standard, see *References*.

Informal Review

An Informal review does not follow a defined process and does not have a formal or documented procedure. The review can find potential defects, anomalies, errors or process issues while minimizing the cost and resources. It can also generate ideas and solutions to quickly solve problems and provide some familiarization for participants. The team of reviewers checks the work product and gives comments. An informal review compared to other types of reviews does not require the same level of preparation by participants. There is little or no formal documentation of the outputs.

Walkthrough Review

A walkthrough is a review led by an author who takes participants through the work product or process under review. It is common for the product or process under review to be presented by scenarios, dummy runs or simulations. Participants ask questions and make comments about possible issues. The review can find defects, facilitate the exchange of ideas, provide training for the participants on the work product or process under review and achieve consensus.

With a small company, where development and testing teams work well together and the customer is very engaged, a walkthrough review, with some lightweight documentation, may be the appropriate type of review.

Technical Review
A technical review is undertaken by technical experts who examine the quality of a work product or process and identify variances from the specifications, product design and standards. In addition to finding potential defects, the review can seek consensus on technical issues, evaluation of the quality and build confidence in the work product or process. It may also generate new ideas, motivate and support authors to improve and consider alternative options.

Inspection
An inspection is a formal type of review that is prescribed and systematic. The aims of the review include detecting potential defects, evaluating quality and building confidence in the work product or process, preventing future similar defects through author learning root cause analysis, achieving consensus and motivating and enabling authors to improve future work products and processes. Participants should receive information in advance. This can be by attending an orientation meeting or other means. They should examine the work product or process in advance. Issues and defects are documented at the review and the technical status of the work product or process is determined. If the work product or process needs rework, another inspection may be needed to verify the changes. Checklists are commonly used.

For any project where detailed formal output documentation is required, an inspection is appropriate. In a large company where developers and testers work independently of each other and there is formal communication with the customer, an inspection should be undertaken.

FL-3.2.5 (K2) Recall the factors that contribute to a successful review
A review can be determined to be successful if it achieves outcomes including:

- Defects/issues in the work product are identified
- Quality characteristics of the work product are evaluated
- Reviewers have gained knowledge about the work product
- Consensus on decisions made has been reached
- New ideas have been generated
- Updates to the work product are made
- Participants have identified potential improvements in their working practices

Factors that contribute to a successful review include:

- Support from management for the review process
- Defining clear objectives and measurable exit criteria
- Providing adequate time for participants to prepare for the review
- Choosing the appropriate review type to achieve the given objectives, and suit the type of work product, the review participants, the project needs and context
- Adopting a systematic approach appropriate to the review type

- Review focusing on the different needs, for example, a team member reading requirements from the perspective of the tester would design a set of tests for a potential test plan and answer questions arising from the activities being performed, a team member reading from the perspective of the developer would generate a high-level design
- Scenario-based review
- Performing reviews in small portions, so that reviewers do not lose concentration during an individual review and/or the review meeting (when held)
- Providing feedback from reviews to stakeholders and authors so they can improve the work product or process under review and their activities
- Making reviews part of the organization's culture, to promote learning and process improvement
- Providing adequate training for all participants so they know how to fulfill their role
- Facilitating meetings

To successfully assess a requirements specification, questions a tester could ask include:

- Are the requirements understandable without gaps, consistent with each other and unambiguous?
- Are the requirements consistent with what is specified in the general description of the software or system?
- Are the requirements testable? Is all the information necessary to identify the inputs to the requirement given?
- Have any of the necessary inputs been omitted?
- Are any inputs specified that are not needed for this requirement?

Note: Evaluation of participants should never be an objective of a review.

3.2 Questions 1 to 12 FL-3.2.1, 3.2.2, 3.2.3, 3.2.4, 3.2.5

Question 1 FL-3.2.1 (K1) Which of the following best describes a benefit of early and frequent feedback during the test process?

a) Transfers project risk to stakeholders
b) Increases overall project costs
c) Enhances collaboration and communication with stakeholders
d) Obtains stakeholders' approval for the test approach

Select ONE option

Question 2 FL-3.2.1 (K1) Early and frequent feedback can lead to which of the following:

a) Limiting stakeholder involvement to save time and meet deadlines
b) Increasing project complexity
c) Rushing development
d) Reducing the likelihood of rework being extensive

Select ONE option

Question 3 FL-3.2.2 (K2) Which of the following is part of the activities for all reviews?

a) The roles of the scribe and the author are clearly defined and differentiated
b) Every reviewer performs an individual review before a meeting to assess the quality of the work product under review
c) A review meeting is scheduled so that issues with the quality of the work product can be raised and discussed
d) If anomalies are identified during a review, a decision should be made for each on its status, ownership and required actions

Select ONE option

Question 4 FL-3.2.2 (K2) What is the typical order of the formal review process activities?

a) Individual review, planning, review initiation
b) Planning, review initiation, individual review
c) Review initiation, planning, individual review
d) Review initiation, individual review, planning

Select ONE option

Question 5 FL-3.2.3 (K1) In a formal review, which of the following statements on roles and responsibilities are correct?

a) The manager organizes when and where the review will take place
b) The reviewer fixes the work product under review
c) The scribe collates the anomalies raised and records review information
d) The facilitator provides the resources, such as staff and time for the review
e) The review leader decides who will be involved in the review

Select TWO options

Question 6 FL-3.2.3 (K1) Which of the following is not true for the roles and responsibilities in formal reviews?

a) Reviews include stakeholders who, in some types of reviews, can take on several roles
b) A reviewer needs to be a person working on the project
c) The review leader is responsible for mediation between participants should it be required
d) The author fixes the work product under review

Select ONE option

Question 7 FL-3.2.3 (K1) For a formal review, who decides what is to be reviewed?

a) Manager
b) Facilitator
c) Reviewer
d) Review leader

Select ONE option

Question 8 FL-3.2.3 (K1) Consider the following tasks in an inspection of an essential document.

1. Producing the document under review
2. Checking the document under review
3. Documenting the review meeting
4. Updating the document under review

a) The author is responsible for 1 and 4, the reviewer is responsible for 2, and the scribe is responsible for 3
b) The author is responsible for 1, 2 and 3, the scribe is responsible for 4
c) The scribe is responsible for 1 and 3, the reviewer is responsible for 2 and 4
d) The author is responsible for 1, the scribe is responsible for 2 and 3, and the reviewer is responsible for 4

Select ONE option

Question 9 FL-3.2.4 (K2) Which of the following is true for reviews?

a) Technical walkthroughs are the most formal type of reviews
b) Any work product that can be reviewed can be inspected
c) To be useful, all types of reviews should have formal, documented output
d) In any review, a participant can take on any two or more roles

Select ONE option

Question 10 FL-3.2.4 (K2) Which of the following is a review led by a person in the role and with the responsibilities of the author?

a) Informal review
b) Walkthrough
c) Technical review
d) Inspection

Select ONE option

Question 11 FL-3.2.5 (K1) The following are factors that contribute to the success of review meetings except for which?

a) Finding and acknowledging failures, then handling them objectively
b) Guiding the meeting to make sure everyone participates and reaches the agreed-upon meeting goals
c) Providing feedback from reviews to stakeholders and authors so they can improve the product and their activities
d) Choosing the review type to suit the type of work product, review participants, project needs and context

Select ONE option

Question 12 FL-3.2.5 (K1)

Which of the following best describes an action that contributes to a successful review meeting?

a) Allowing for all comments by having a free format with no predefined agenda
b) Having a large number of participants without specific responsibilities, with input from participants having equal importance
c) Having clear objectives, well-defined roles and encouraging constructive feedback
d) Ensuring the meeting is not time-limited so that all inputs can be fully considered

Select ONE option

3.2 Answers and Explanations 1 to 12 FL-3.2.1, 3.2.2, 3.2.3, 3.2.4, 3.2.5

Answer 1 FL-3.2.1 K1

c) is the correct option. Early and frequent feedback aids collaboration and communication which leads to improved common understanding of requirements.

a) is not the correct option. All members of the project team share risk responsibility. b) is not the correct option. Early and frequent feedback can contribute to defects being fixed at an early stage and this reduces overall costs. d) is not the correct option. The test approach should have been agreed upon as part of planning.

Answer 2 FL-3.2.1 K1
d) is the correct option. Early and frequent feedback helps in identifying issues sooner, reducing the need for extensive rework.
a) is not the correct option. Early and frequent feedback materially enhances stakeholder involvement. It ensures that stakeholders have opportunities to provide input, review progress, and make suggestions throughout the development process. This involvement promotes collaboration and results in better alignment with stakeholder expectations. b) is not the correct option. Early and frequent feedback can help prevent complexity from accumulating by addressing issues before they become more intricate and harder to resolve. c) is not the correct option. Rushed development is more likely when there's a delay or lack of feedback.

Answer 3 FL-3.2.2 K2
d) is the correct option. If anomalies are identified during a review, the decision should be made on its status, ownership and required actions.
a) is not the correct option. Informal reviews may not have scribes in which case there is no need to define the scribe's role. b) is not the correct option. In informal and some walkthrough reviews, reviewers do not need to perform an individual review before the review meeting if a meeting is held.
c) is not the correct option. A review typically involves a meeting, but it is not essential. The results of individual reviews can be collated and communicated appropriately by other means.

Answer 4 FL-3.2.2 K2
b) is the correct option. A review should be planned and then initiated. Reviewers should then undertake some preparation with individual reviews. a), c) and d) are not correct options for the reasons given for b).

Answer 5 FL-3.2.3 K1
c) and e) are the correct options. The scribe collates the anomalies raised and records review information. The review leader decides who will be involved in the review.
a) is not a correct option. The review leader organizes when and where the review will take place.
b) is not a correct option. The author fixes the work product under review.
d) is not a correct option. The facilitator provides the resources, such as staff and time for the review.

Answer 6 FL-3.2.3 K1
c) is the correct option. A moderator ensures the effective running of the review meeting, including mediation. The review leader has overall responsibility for the review, deciding who should be involved.
a) is not the correct option. Reviews include various stakeholders who, in some types of reviews, take on several roles. In inspections, the author cannot act as the review leader or scribe.
b) is not the correct option. A reviewer can be a person on the project, a subject matter expert or any other stakeholder. d) is not the correct option. An author creates and fixes the work product under review.

Answer 7 FL-3.2.3 K1

a) is the correct option. A manager decides what is to be reviewed and provides appropriate resources.
b) is not the correct option. A facilitator or moderator ensures the effective running of the review meeting. c) is not the correct option. A reviewer performs the actual review.
d) is not the correct option. A review leader has overall responsibility for the review, deciding who should be involved.

Answer 8 FL-3.2.3 K1

a) is the correct option. The responsibilities are:
1. Producing the document under review – Author.
2. Checking the document under review – Reviewers.
3. Documenting the meeting – Scribe.
4. Updating the document under review – Author.
b), c) and d) are not correct options for the reasons given for a).

Answer 9 FL-3.2.4 K2

b) is the correct option. Any work product that can be reviewed can be inspected.
a) is not the correct option. Inspections are the most formal of reviews.
c) is not the correct option. Informal reviews have little or no formal output documentation.
d) is not the correct option. In inspections, the author cannot act as the review leader or scribe.

Answer 10 10 FL-3.2.4 K2

b) is the correct option. A walkthrough is led by the author.
a) is not the correct option. There is no defined procedure for an informal review.
c) is not the correct option. The Syllabus states, *'A technical review is performed by technically qualified reviewers and led by a moderator.'*
d) is not the correct option. In an inspection, the author cannot act as the review leader.

Answer 11 FL-3.2.5 K1

a) is the correct option. Reviews find defects not failures.
b) is not the correct option. Facilitating meetings contributes to their success.
c) is not the correct option. The objective of a review is to improve the product.
d) is not the correct option. The appropriate type of review should be chosen.

Answer 12 FL-3.2.5 K1

c) is the correct option. Having clear objectives, well-defined roles and encouraging constructive feedback contribute to having a successful review. a) is not the correct option. The review meeting needs to have focus. b) is not the correct option. Participants with well-defined roles and not merely a large number of participants contribute to successful reviews. d) is not the correct option. Having unlimited time can result in reviewers losing concentration or frustration that they are kept away from their other tasks. If necessary, reviews should be split into several smaller ones.

4. TEST ANALYSIS AND DESIGN

The ISTQB Exam Structures & Rules Tables v1.19 specifies eleven exam questions for this section. There are nine K2 and five K3 level learning objectives. Those at K3 level are in FL-4.2.1 to FL-4.2.4 Black-box techniques and FL-4.5.3 Acceptance test-driven development ATDD.

Keywords given in the Syllabus

acceptance criteria, acceptance test-driven development, black-box test technique, boundary value analysis, branch coverage, checklist-based testing, collaboration-based test approach, †coverage, coverage item, decision table testing, equivalence partitioning, error guessing, experience-based test technique, exploratory testing, state transition testing, statement coverage, test technique, white-box test technique.

Not identified as keywords in Glossary or Syllabus: test-driven development (TDD), behavior-driven development (BDD). †Coverage included in the Syllabus in sections 1 and 4.

4.1 Test Techniques Overview

Software test techniques are methods and strategies used to systematically evaluate the functionality and quality of software or systems. These techniques are crucial for identifying errors, failures and defects, ensuring the software meets its intended requirements, and assessing its reliability.

The choice of test technique depends on factors such as the project requirements, the software's complexity, the availability of resources, and the required level of test coverage. A comprehensive strategy typically combines multiple test techniques to achieve the required test coverage.

FL-4.1.1 (K2) Distinguish black-box test techniques, white-box test techniques and experience-based test techniques

The Syllabus identifies three distinct types of test techniques: white-box testing, black-box testing, and exploratory testing. Combining techniques from white-box testing, black-box testing and exploratory testing provides a more comprehensive and balanced test approach compared to using techniques from just one of the types.

White-box test techniques are based on the internal structure of a component or system. This type of testing may be carried out by the developer or a tester who has knowledge of and access to the design, internal structure, algorithms, system architecture or code implementation of the test object. It is not possible to create white-box test cases before the design, structure or code is available.

Synonyms of white-box test technique are white-box test design technique and structure-based test technique. Techniques used in white-box testing include statement testing and branch testing. Synonyms of white-box testing are clear-box testing, code-based testing, glass-box testing, logic-coverage testing, logic-driven testing, structural testing, and structure-based testing.

Black-box test techniques are based on the specification of a component or system where the tester does not have knowledge or access to the internal workings of the software being tested. With black-box testing:

- The focus is on the externally visible behavior and functionality of the test object.
- Test cases are based on the system's functional requirements, specifications, and expected behavior
- Does not require the tester to have code-reading skills
- Test cases are independent of how the software is implemented. If the implementation changes, but the required behavior stays the same, then the test cases are still useful
- Uncovers defects from a user's perspective
- Relies heavily on specifications, requirements and user documentation to guide testing

Potential disadvantages include:

- With the focus on external behaviors, there is a risk of missing certain paths, conditions or code segments that may contain errors
- Can require significant effort and detailed documentation

Techniques used in black-box testing include equivalence partitioning, boundary value analysis, decision table testing and state transition testing.

Synonyms of black-box testing are specification-based testing and closed-box testing (ISO 29119-1:2022). Synonyms of black-box test technique are black-box test design technique and specification-based test technique.

Experience-based test techniques use the knowledge, intuition, and expertise of the testers, insights gained from similar projects and known industry best practices. Experience-based test techniques can uncover errors, failures and defects that may be missed using the white-box and black-box test techniques.

Experience-based test techniques are particularly useful in situations such as:

- Non-availability or inadequate requirements specification
- Limited knowledge of the software product
- Limited time to perform testing
- With a test object involving few risks

Potential disadvantages include:

- Lack of consistency and reproducibility, as it can depend heavily on the tester's skills and/or checklist accuracy and completeness
- No or limited objective code coverage metrics
- 100% code coverage is not likely to be achieved
- Test objects with high risks need to also be tested with other formal test techniques

Experience-based test techniques include error guessing, exploratory testing, and checklist-based testing.

4.1 Questions 1 to 6 FL-4.1.1

Question #1 FL-4.1.1 (K1) Which of the following correctly distinguishes experience-based, white-box and black-box test techniques?

a) Experience-based testing is synonymous with requirements-based testing, white-box testing is based on predefined requirements, black-box testing requires knowledge of the internal code
b) Experience-based testing involves testers who have domain and testing expertise, white-box testing evaluates the test object without knowledge of internal workings, black-box testing is based on predefined requirements
c) Experience-based testing requires domain expertise, white-box testing is synonymous with static testing, black-box testing focuses on usability testing and performance efficiency
d) Experience-based testing involves testers with appropriate domain and testing expertise, white-box testing evaluates software with knowledge of the internal workings of the test object, black-box testing assesses the behavior of the test object based on the requirements specification

Select ONE option

Question #2 FL-4.1.1 (K1) Which of the following is not an alternative term for white-box testing?

a) Closed-box testing
b) Clear-box testing
c) Glass-box testing
d) Logic-driven testing

Select ONE option

Question #3 FL-4.1.1 (K1) Boundary value analysis is which type of test technique?

a) Experience-based
b) White-box
c) Black-box
d) All combinations

Select ONE option

Question #4 FL-4.1.1 (K1) Which test techniques are most appropriate if the specifications are outdated?

a) White-box and black-box
b) White-box and experience-based
c) Experience-based and black-box
d) Black-box only

Select ONE option

Question #5 FL-4.1.1 (K1) Which of the following is a structure-based test technique?

a) Decision table testing
b) State transition testing
c) Boundary value analysis
d) Branch testing

Select ONE option

Question #6 FL-4.1.1 (K1) Which of the following is the best example of a requirements specification-based test technique?

a) State transition testing
b) Branch testing
c) Statement testing
d) Exploratory testing

Select ONE option

4.1 Answers and Explanations 1 to 6 FL-4.1.1

Answer #1 FL-4.1.1

d) is the correct option. Experience-based test techniques use the knowledge and experience of testers. White-box test techniques are based on analysis of the internal structure or code of the test object. Black-box test techniques are based on an analysis of the specified behavior of the test object without reference to its internal structure.

a), b) and c) are not correct options for the reasons given for d).

Answer #2 FL-4.1.1

a) is the correct option. Closed-box testing is a synonym of 'black-box' testing (ISO 29119-1).

b), c) and d) are not correct options. Clear-box testing, glass-box testing and logic-driven testing are listed in the Glossary as synonyms of white-box testing (ISTQB Glossary).

Answer #3 FL-4.1.1

c) is the correct option. Boundary value analysis is a specification-based test technique based on the analysis of behavior around partition boundaries and is a black-box test technique. a) is not the correct option. Experience-based test techniques are based on the tester's experience, knowledge and intuition. b) is not the correct option for the reasons given for c). d) is not the correct option. All combinations testing is a combinatorial test technique.

Answer #4 FL 4.1.1

b) is the correct option. White-box test techniques are based on the internal structure of the software and experience-based test techniques rely on the tester's skills and knowledge.

a), c) and d) are not correct options as they include black-box test techniques. Black-box testing is specification-based testing.

Answer #5 FL-4.1.1

d) is the correct option. Branch testing is a white-box testing technique also termed a structure-based test technique.

a), b) and c) are not correct options. Decision table testing, state transition testing and boundary value analysis are black-box, also termed specification-based test techniques.

Answer #6 FL-4.1.1

a) is the correct option. State transition testing is a black-box test technique, also termed specification-based. b) and c) are not correct options. Branch testing and statement testing are white-box test techniques, also termed structure-based test techniques. d) is not the correct option. Exploratory testing is an experience-based test technique that can be useful when there are few or inadequate requirements specifications or when time is limited.

4.2 Black-box Test Techniques

Four commonly used black-box test techniques are included in the Foundation Syllabus: Equivalence Partitioning, Boundary Value Analysis, Decision Table Testing and State Transition Testing.

As all 4.2 learning objectives, one for each test technique, are all K3 level you need to both understand and also be able to apply the test technique. For these four learning objectives plus learning objective FL-4.5.3, there are five questions specified in the ISTQB Exam Structures & Rules Tables v1.19. In the practice exams provided in this guide, the five questions cover the five different learning objectives required.

FL-4.2.1 (K3) Use equivalence partitioning to derive test cases

Equivalence Partitioning (EP) is a software test technique that divides data elements into groups or sets that are expected to exhibit similar behavior. These groups or sets are called equivalence partitions or equivalence classes. A partition may be a set of discreet values or a set of continuous values within a range. All entries in a partition are handled in the same way. For equivalence partition testing, values within a partition do not need to be ordered.

Partitions should not overlap and typically have more than one element to justify considering elements as equivalent and the use of equivalence partitioning. However, if using combinatorial techniques to combine multiple sets of partitions, a partition (but not all) may in a few circumstances have just one element, for example when combinatorial techniques are to be used or a value such as zero is to be considered by itself.

Examples of Partitions

Partition 1	Partition 2	Partition 3
Customers with loyalty cards	Customers without loyalty cards	
Daily activities	Monthly activities	
After 00:00 to 09:00 hours	After 09:00 to 18:00 hours	After 18:00 to 24:00 hours
Integers 1 - 9	Integers 10 - 99	Integers 100 - 1,999
First letter A - J	First letter K - R	First letter S - Z
Command 'Query'	Command 'Deposit'	Command 'Pay'
Blue color items	Red color items	Other color items

A valid equivalence partition includes values that should be accepted by the software under test.

An invalid equivalence partition includes values that should be rejected by the software. A more appropriate term would be 'equivalence partitions for invalid values'. The equivalence partition itself is not invalid, only the values within the partition. An invalid input partition does not necessarily mean the values it contains cannot be input by a user. It means that an input is not one of the expected inputs for a particular field. Invalid equivalence partitions should be tested in isolation to avoid defect masking.

If an input condition specifies one defined range, one valid and two invalid equivalence classes are defined: within the range is valid, too large or too small are invalid. For example: the age range for insurance is specified as the number of years from 17 - 99. The valid equivalence class is [17 - 99]. Invalid equivalence classes are [less than 17] and [more than 99]. A further possible invalid equivalence class might be for non-numeric inputs to the age field.

Invalid values can be those:

Defined in the test object specification and should be rejected by the test object with appropriate response

Where no processing is specifically given in the test object specification. For example, if a specification states that a user can make a ticket reservation by entering the required date and an invalid input, that may not be specifically included in the specification, would be a date earlier than the time of booking

Software should behave appropriately and acceptably with invalid inputs, for example with one or more of the following: an error message, request for clarification or reentry of input, blocking of certain inputs, disabling forward or next button, termination of current processing. Unhandled invalid inputs, such as failure to terminate, runtime exceptions, and more can result in operational failures of the system, user dissatisfaction or security vulnerabilities that might be able to be maliciously exploited.

Equivalence partition testing reduces the total number of possible test cases. For 100% minimum test case coverage, one test case is designed and executed for each partition. The testing is based on the assumption that the one test case for a specific partition is representative of all possible test cases for the set of entries in that partition. Additional test cases for a partition do not increase coverage.

Example: Equivalence partitioning
A savings account in a bank earns a different rate of interest depending on the balance in the account. An account can be opened with $50 or more. All values are in whole integers. If the balance is in the range of $50 up to $200, the interest rate is 1%. If a balance is over $200 and up to $1,000, the interest rate is 2% and balances of over $1,000 up to a $Max value have a 3% interest rate.
Equivalence partitions in this example can be seen in the line diagram below:

Invalid | Valid (for 1% interest) | Valid (for 2%) | Valid (for 3%) | Invalid
$49 | $50 $200 | $201 $1,000 | $1,001 $Max | $Max + 1

Selecting a random set of test cases based on balances, without consideration of the partitions, for example: $50, $150, $300, $400, $500, would not guarantee testing all interest outcomes.

Selecting $48, $58, $250, $Max and $Max+1 would test each equivalence partition once.

When to use equivalence partitioning

Equivalence partitioning is a test technique that can be used at any test level. Equivalence partitioning coverage is expressed as a percentage, the number of partitions determined or exercised divided by the total number of partitions identified and multiplied by 100.

Deciding which partitions to exercise depends on the risk analysis and test objectives. For a thorough test approach all valid and then all invalid partitions should be tested. However, if a particular input that is not expected by the specification could be entered by a user and has been assessed to have a high-risk impact if it occurs, this may indicate testing an invalid partition first. If there is time pressure and the test objective is to gain user confidence of typical transactions with a minimum number of tests, testing only valid transactions may be the best approach. Risk analysis and time pressures may indicate only a particular subset of partitions are tested.

Equivalence partitioning is particularly effective when used in combination with boundary value analysis.

Common pitfalls with equivalence partitioning

Particular care is required with some exam questions. Look out for:

1. When the partitions cover a range of number sizes that have significantly different degrees of magnitude, care is needed to correctly identify the partitions. For example, in a property tax scenario, the first £4,000 is tax-free, the next £250,000 is subject to 5% tax, followed by the next £10,000 being taxed at 10%. Any value greater than this incurs a 12% tax. For the highest boundary, do not be tempted to add (4 + 25 +10) = £39 then add zeros (£39,000 or £390,000). The valid partitions are up to and including £4,000, greater than £4,000 and up to and including £254,000, greater than £254,000, up to and including £264,000 and the highest boundary, greater than £264,000.
2. A question may require consideration of both valid and invalid partitions. Beware, invalid partitions may be embedded in the question. For example, an online trading company sells goods up to $500.You have been tasked with testing a new release that includes a new and simplified delivery rate scheme. Orders must be for $5 or above. You will be using equivalence partitioning. The new delivery rates are as follows:

    $5 to $50, basic delivery rate
    $51 to $100, high delivery rate
    Above $100, free delivery

    Three partitions are shown above. Embedded in the question is a minimum order value of $5 and a maximum of $500. Two additional partitions are required for invalid partitions:

    $1 to $5
    Above $500
3. Zero may need to be considered in its own partition. Historically, problems could occur when a program tried to divide by zero, this is now typically picked up when entering code in the development phase. However, in some scenarios, zero may be viewed as an exception with a different output to all other values, so should be in its own partition.

4. A partition spanning negative and positive numbers might be best split into two partitions, one for negative numbers, one for positive numbers, or possibly three partitions with zero in its own partition. The decision to do this is based on the scenario, the resources available and the risk factors. If an exam question has a scenario where having these extra partitions may be an advantage and the question asks for the minimum number of partitions but such a division is not allowed for in the answer options, assume the extra partitions are not required.
5. A question asking, *'Which answer option has numbers in different partitions?'*, is not necessarily asking for an answer option that has a number in each or every partition. When checking the option values, always continue to the end of each list. Do not abandon the answer option for being wrong merely because there is a missing value for a particular partition. For example, with partitions 1-9, 10-50, 51-80, 81-105, 106-150 and the question asks, *'Which answer option has numbers in different partitions?'*, an answer option 7, 17, 57, 117 would be correct. It would not be correct if the question asks for a value in each partition as there is no number for the partition 81-105.

Combining multiple sets of partitions

Software often has more than one set of equivalence partitions when it handles complex data that can be split into multiple distinct sets based on different criteria or conditions.

Examples include software for or with:

- Multiple input parameters
- Complex business rules
- Multi-mode or multi-state systems
- User roles and permissions
- Localization and internationalization

A test case may need to cover values from several different sets of partitions. This requires the use of combinatorial techniques for the selection of values for a test case from different equivalence partitions. ISTQB defines combinatorial testing as, *'A black-box test technique in which test conditions are specific combinations of values of several parameters.'* Combinatorial testing (ISO 29119-4) includes as examples all combinations testing, pairwise testing, Each Choice (EC) testing and base choice testing. The Glossary does not indicate combinatorial testing is a required term for Foundation Level. However, Syllabus v4.0.1 includes mention of Each Choice coverage and the ISTQB sample exam v1.0 question #20 assumes knowledge of pairwise testing.

The simplest combinatorial technique of Each Choice is included in the Syllabus v4.0.1 text. Each Choice is explained in the example 1 below.

For other combinatorial test techniques, there is no ISTQB learning objective and hence no exam question is mandated on pairwise, N-wise or all combinations testing. However, an understanding of pairwise testing is assumed for ISTQB Sample Exam Set A v1.2 2023-11-06 Question #20, specified as an example for learning objective *'FL-4.2.1 (K3) Use equivalence partitions to derive test cases.'* See Appendix B, Pairwise and N-wise Testing for details on the systematic approach to use for ISTQB Sample Exam Set A v1.2 2023-11-06 Question #20 and additional examples.

Examples: Equivalence partitioning - Combinatorial approaches

Scenario: A car manufacturer supplies three models; Saloon, Hatchback and SUV (partition 1). Each can be supplied with exterior finishes, simplified here to either metallic or solid paint colors (partition 2) and different interior finishes, simplified here to Cloth or Leather interior.

Example 1: Each Choice (EC) coverage

Each Choice coverage is the simplest coverage criterion in the case of multiple sets of partitions. One value from each partition for each characteristic must be used in at least one test case. This is a subset of pairwise or all-pairs testing.

Test Case	Model	Exterior Finish	Interior Finish
1	Saloon	Metallic	Cloth
2	Hatchback	Solid	Leather
3	SUV	-	-

Each input value is included in a test case. Dash '-' indicates either value can be chosen.

As Ammann states, *"EC leaves a lot of flexibility to the tester in terms of how to combine the test values so only can be called a relatively weak criterion"*, see *References*. Ammann also points out, *"EC may be too simplistic and ineffective"*, compared to other combinatorial techniques.

To strengthen Each Choice, domain knowledge of the program should be incorporated. Testers may recognize that selection of certain parameter-value pairs is more important than random selection.

Feasible and infeasible options may be missed. For example:
A vehicle manufacturer is launching a new range that includes saloon, hatchback and SUV models. The engine options are; petrol, electric and hybrid. A saloon can have any of the three types of engine as can a hatchback. An SUV can only have petrol or hybrid. Using Each Choice, the following test cases cover all parameter-value pairs:

Test Case 1: Saloon / Petrol
Test Case 2: Hatchback / Electric
Test Case 3: SUV / Hybrid

However, there is no test case confirming a choice of SUV / Electric will be rejected.

Example 2: All Combinations
All unique combinations are tested, in this example all triples and 12 test cases are required:

Test Case	Model	Exterior Finish	Interior Finish
1	Saloon	Metallic	Cloth
2	Saloon	Metallic	Leather
3	Saloon	Solid	Cloth
4	Saloon	Solid	Leather
5	Hatchback	Metallic	Cloth
6	Hatchback	Metallic	Leather
7	Hatchback	Solid	Cloth
8	Hatchback	Solid	Leather
9	SUV	Metallic	Cloth
10	SUV	Metallic	Leather
11	SUV	Solid	Cloth
12	SUV	Solid	Leather

Example 3: Pairwise / All-Pairs Testing
Pairwise (or all-pairs testing) is a combinatorial technique in which test cases are designed in such a way that every possible combination of pairs of input values is covered. Six test cases are required.

Test Case	Model	Exterior Finish	Interior Finish	Pairs tested
1	Saloon	Metallic	Cloth	Saloon/Metallic, Saloon/Cloth, Metallic/Cloth
2	Saloon	Solid	Leather	Saloon/solid, Saloon/Leather, Solid/Leather
3	Hatchback	Metallic	Cloth	Hatchback/Metallic, Hatchback/Cloth
4	Hatchback	Solid	Leather	Hatchback/solid, Hatchback/Leather
5	SUV	Metallic	Cloth	SUV/Cloth, SUV/Cloth
6	SUV	Metallic	Leather	SUV/Solid, SUV/Leather

Metallic/Cloth is covered in Test Case 1 as shown, (also covered in Test Cases 3 and 5 not shown). Solid/Leather is covered in Test Case 2 as shown and also in Test Cases 4 and 6.

Pairwise testing is explained in detail in Software Testing Advanced Test Analyst Complete Guide for ISTQB Exam, C. Newbould, published 2022, see *References*. There are ways to calculate the minimum number of test cases required which can be complex when there are large numbers of inputs or input values to a test case or some pairs may not be feasible so can be removed.

FL-4.2.1 (K3) Exercises: Equivalence Partitioning

FL-4.2.1 (K3) Exercise 1 Using two sets of partitions

You are testing an application for an airline company that gives incentives to frequent flyers. Regular (up to and including 10 sectors flown) entitles the passenger to free onboard beverages. Gold (11 or more sectors flown up to and including 19) entitles the passenger to the use of a lounge. Platinum (20 or more sectors flown up to and including 29) entitles the passenger to an additional free cabin bag. Executive Platinum (30 or more sectors flown) entitles the passenger to priority boarding. The incentives are additive. For example, a platinum level passenger would have free beverages onboard, use of a lounge and an additional free cabin bag. Zero and negative sectors are invalid. Sectors are always integer values. Depending on the fare paid, bonus miles are awarded. Coach = 1.5 x miles, Business = 2 x miles, First = 4 x miles. Standby tickets attract no bonus, only the number of miles flown.

Part 1: From the information given above, draw an equivalence partitions line diagram for sectors flown and indicate values for the sectors flown to test each partition. How many valid equivalence partitions for sectors flown are there?

Part 2: From the information given above, draw an equivalence partitions line diagram for fare paid bonuses. How many valid equivalence partitions for Fare type Bonus miles are there?

Part 3: From the information given above, derive the minimum number of test cases for 100% minimum coverage for one value from every valid sector flown partition with all fare types.

Part 4: From the information given above, derive the minimum number of test cases for 100% minimum coverage for one value from every valid sector flown partition with all fare types and an Each Choice value for Fare type Bonus partitions.

FL-4.2.1 (K3) Exercise 2 Using one set of partitions

You are planning testing for an application for collecting Stamp Duty Land Tax (SDLT) on the purchase of properties in the United Kingdom. The requirements specify the following: Various percentages of tax apply depending on the purchase price. Integer £ figures only are to be used. A purchase price of zero or less than £0 is invalid and should return an error. For £1 to £125,000, the rate is 0%. Between £125,00 and £250,00 inclusive the rate is 2%. For more than £250,00 but less than or equal to £82,500 the rate increases by an additional 3%. For £825,001 to £1 million, there is an additional 2%. For the highest partition of above £1 million, there is a further increase by an additional 2%, taking the top rate to 10%. (Values are integers and no decimals).

When considering the use of equivalence partitioning, what mistake(s) in the given information will hamper the testing, assuming the partition £1 to £125,000 is correct?

FL-4.2.1 Exercise 1 Answer

Part 1 Answer

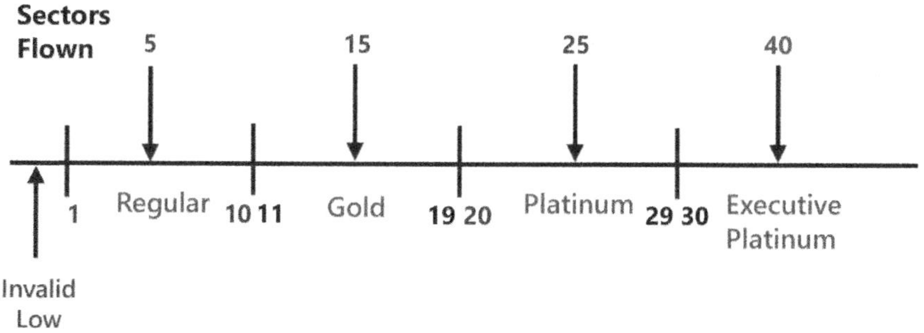

Values of sectors flown 5, 15, 25 and 40 are values in each partition. Other values can be chosen.

There are 4 Valid Sector partitions:

- Regular ≥1 and ≤10 sectors
- Gold ≥11 and ≤ 19
- Platinum ≥20 and <30 sectors
- Executive Platinum ≥30

Part 2 Answer

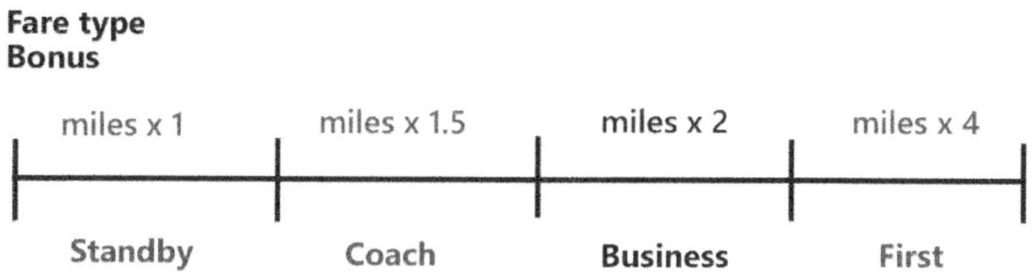

There are 4 Fare type bonus partitions:

Standby / Coach / Business / First

Part 3 Answer

There are 4 x 4 = 16 test cases required.

Part 4 Answer

There are 4 test cases required when Each Choice (EC) is used.

Test Case	Sectors	Fare type
TC01	Any value [1-10]	Standby
TC02	Any Value [11 – 19]	Coach
TC03	Any Value [20 – 29]	Business
TC05	Any value ≥30	First

FL-4.2.1 Exercise 2 Answer

Six mistakes hamper valid equivalence partition testing as highlighted below:

Partition number	Band	Rate Percentage
1	£1 to £125,000	0%
2	**£125,00** to **£250,00**	2%
3	**£250,00** to **£82,500**	5%
4	£825,001 to £1,000,000	7%
5	**£1,000,000** and above	**10%**

Zero is missing in four places: £125,00 partition 2, £250,00 partitions 2 and 3, and £82,500 partition 3. £1,000,000 should be in one partition only. Partition 5 should start at £1,000,001.
The additional interest of 2% for partition 4 should have increased the rate to 9%.

The correct table is:

Partition number	Band	Rate Percentage
1	£1 to £125,000	0%
2	£125,001 to £250,000	2%
3	£250,001 to £825,000	5%
4	£825,001 to £1,000,000	7%
5	£1,000,001 and above	9%

FL-4.2.2 (K3) Use boundary value analysis to derive test cases

Boundary value analysis (BVA) involves testing the boundaries of ordered equivalence partitions. An understanding of equivalence partitioning is therefore required as a prerequisite for boundary value analysis. Examples of partitions (ordered by increasing or decreasing values) to which boundary value analysis can be applied include:

- Numbers
- Text strings lexicographically ordered
- Numeric attributes of non-numeric variables (e.g. length, weight, physical size, etc.)
- Number of loop execution cycles, including loops in state transition diagrams or tables
- Number of iteration elements in stored data structures such as arrays
- Duration of activities (time)

If the ordering of a partition is not relevant from the business point of view, then boundary value analysis should not be used.

There are many reasons why defects may occur on boundaries including:

- Boundaries may be points of discontinuity in the behavior of the code
- The requirements specification may not specifically define exact boundaries leading to different interpretations
- An input may increase up to a certain specified number and above the value, unpredictable action may occur.
- There may be off-by-one mistakes such as using '<=' or '≤' instead of '<' or initializing a counter to 0 instead of 1, (loop control)
- Some boundaries that may need to be handled as special cases in the code may go unnoticed

Partitions based on numerical values should have boundary values based on the smallest possible precision, see later in this chapter.
The Syllabus includes both two-value and three-value boundary value analysis.

Two-Value Boundary Testing

Two-value boundary testing uses the boundary value and the value of its closest neighbor in the adjacent partition which is just outside the boundary by the smallest possible increment. For example, if a partition includes numbers from 1 to 10 in increments of 0.1, the values to test are 0.9, 1, 10.0 and 10.1. Using two-value boundary testing, a sequence of consecutive partitions adds two further tests at each subsequent boundary. Two-value boundary analysis is typically shown by a number line model.

```
Partitions:    ______| 1.0 to 10.0 |  10.1 to 100.0  |______
Test values:   0.9 | 1.0     10.0 | 10.1      100.0 | 100.1
```

To achieve 100% coverage with two-value boundary testing, test cases must be created to cover all identified boundary values. Coverage is measured as the number of boundary values exercised divided by the total number of boundary values and expressed as a percentage. For the example above, six test cases are indicated for 100% minimum coverage.

Three-Value Boundary Testing

Three-value boundary analysis uses values as in two-value boundary analysis plus an additional value just off the boundary. Some of the coverage items may not be actual boundary values, but just off a boundary. To achieve 100% coverage with three-value boundary testing, test cases must cover all coverage boundary values and their neighbors. Coverage is measured as the number of boundary values and their neighbors exercised divided by the total number of boundary values and their neighbors and expressed as a percentage. In the example above, three-value boundary testing might test (0.9, 1.0, 1.1), (9.0, 10.1, 10,2) and (100, 100.1, 100.2). In this situation, nine test cases would provide 100% minimum three-value boundary coverage.

Selecting Two-Value or Three-Value Boundary Testing

Consider the following: A customer is given loyalty points. When the customer has accumulated 10 loyalty points, future purchases are discounted by 10%. As a Test Analyst, you are tasked with testing the upper boundary of 'No discount' and the lower boundary of '10% discount'.

Two-value boundary testing, number line model:

```
      | No discount  | 10% discount |
 0 | 1             9 | 10         99 | 100
```

Testing the lower boundary for a 10% discount (using two values) requires a test case for 9 (where No discount = passed) and a test case for 10 (where 10% discount = passed).

Three-value boundary analysis, inequality model:

1 ≤ loyalty points ≤ 9		10 ≤ loyalty points ≤ 99	
0 1 2	8 9 10	9 10 11	98 99 100
Lower boundary	Upper boundary	Lower boundary	Upper boundary

Three-value boundary analysis is more rigorous than two-value boundary analysis as it may detect defects not identified by two-value boundary analysis. Comparing two-value and three-value boundary analysis for the given loyalty points scenario:

Discount	**Loyalty Points**	**Two-value Lower Boundary**	**Two-value Upper Boundary**
None	1 ≤ points ≤ 9	0, 1	9, 10
10%	10 ≤ points ≤ 99	10, 11	99, 100

Discount	**Loyalty Points**	**Three-value Lower Boundary**	**Three-value Upper Boundary**
None	1 ≤ points ≤ 9	0, 1, 2	8, 9, 10
10%	10 ≤ points ≤ 99	9, 10, 11	98, 99, 100

If the outcome for the test case with 9 points incorrectly results in 10% discount (failed result) and the test case for 10 points results in 10% discount (passed result), with three-value boundary testing there is an additional test for 8 points. If this additional test correctly results in 8 points giving no discount, the defect can be identified as 'points < 9' has been implemented. Arguably, if two-value testing is used when a boundary defect is found, additional test(s) can be added as required. For example, in the scenario above, another test case would have been required if the defect was 'points < 8'.

The decision to use two-value or three-value boundary analysis will depend on the criticality, risks, budget, testers' experience, time available and how many partitions are to be tested. If the boundaries of only one partition are to be tested, such as in a scenario where an updated version of the software is required for a partition boundary change, three-value testing may be advisable. The best strategy is likely to be using two-value analysis and if there are failed test case results, then consider using three-values for the specific boundary the failed where test case results occurred. Further test cases may help in identifying the defect that is shown in the two-value analysis results.

FL-4.2.2 (K3) Exercise: Boundary Value Testing

In the login system under test, users must provide a username and a password to log in. The system has a password length requirement, which specifies that passwords must be between 8 and 16 characters in length (inclusive).

Part 1: Using two-value boundary testing, what tests are required and what are the expected results for two-value testing of the password input?

Part 2: Using three-value boundary testing, what tests are required and what are the expected results for two-value testing of the password input?

Part 3: Give one advantage and one disadvantage three-boundary value testing has when compared to two-value boundary testing?

FL-4.2.2 Exercise Answer

Part 1 Answer

Two-value boundary testing	**Test Case Input**	**Expected result**
One below Minimum boundary	Password with exactly 7 characters	Login refused
Minimum boundary	Password with exactly 8 characters	Login allowed
Maximum boundary	Password with exactly 16 characters	Login allowed
One above Maximum boundary	Password with exactly 17 characters	Login refused

Part 2 Answer

Three-value boundary testing	**Test Case Input**	**Expected result**
One below Minimum boundary	Password with exactly 7 characters	Login refused
Minimum boundary	Password with exactly 8 characters	Login allowed
One over Minimum boundary	Password with exactly 9 characters	Login allowed
One under Maximum boundary	Password with exactly 15 characters	Login allowed
Maximum boundary	Password with exactly 16 characters	Login allowed
One above Maximum boundary	Password with exactly 17 characters	Login refused

Part 3 Answer

Advantages include:

Three-value boundary testing provides more comprehensive testing by examining values below, at, and above the boundaries. This helps identify potential off-by-one errors and subtle issues. This is particularly important when testing over a range of boundaries, that is more than the two boundaries of just one partition.

Three-value boundary testing is more robust in detecting defects related to boundary conditions and handling values that are slightly outside both sides of specified boundaries.

Possible answers for disadvantages include:

Three-value boundary testing requires the creation of more test cases, which can be more time-consuming and complex to manage.

Three-value boundary testing may require additional testing resources and time compared to two-value boundary testing.

4.2 Questions 1 to 8 FL-4.2.1, 4.2.2

Question 1 FL-4.2.1 (Consolidation)

The primary reason for using equivalence partitioning is to uncover which of the following types of defects?

a) Incorrect handling of sequences of events
b) Incorrect handling of classes of inputs
c) Incorrect handling of the combination of two or more inputs
d) Incorrect handling of logic combinations

Select ONE option

Question 2 FL-4.2.1 (K3) You are working on an application for registering users on a membership program and are using equivalence partitioning. Users less than 18 years old are too young to be registered for the program. Between 18 and 50 years inclusive, the user can register with a 20% discount. Users over 50 can register as seniors but are not eligible for a discount.

Which of the following values for age are in the same equivalence partition?

a) 16, 17, 18
b) 50, 51, 52
c) 18, 49, 50
d) 17, 49, 51

Select ONE option

Question 3 FL-4.2.1 (K3) A supermarket provides home deliveries to customers who place orders for between €25.00 and €250.99 of goods. The order total is calculated from the items selected and is not a direct user input. Orders over €50.99 are not charged for delivery. All other orders are subject to the standard delivery charge. Using equivalence partitioning, how many partitions are required?

a) 6
b) 3
c) 2
d) 4

Select ONE option

Question 4 FL-4.2.1 (K3) In an examination, a student can be awarded between 0 and 200 marks. Students must achieve 50% of marks for an examination 'Pass'. A 'C' grade is awarded for 150 marks or below but above the pass mark. A 'B' grade for 151 to 180 marks. For above 180 marks an 'A' grade is awarded.

Which of the following show marks that are each in different partitions?

a) 50, 120, 170, 180
b) 100, 160, 180, 190
c) 50, 100, 160, 180
d) 100, 140, 180, 190

Select ONE option

Question 5 FL-4.2.1 (K3) A shirt manufacturer supplies the following options which are grouped in equivalence partitions:

Collars: Point, Cutaway, Button-down
Cuffs: Single with one button, Double with cufflinks
Color: White, Cream, Light blue

Using the equivalence partitions and the combinatorial technique Each Choice (EC), a minimum of how many test cases are required?

a) 2
b) 3
c) 7
d) 9

Select ONE option

Question 6 FL-4.2.2 (K3) In an examination, a student can receive between 0 to 200 marks. Students must achieve 50% of the marks to pass the examination. Grade C is awarded for 150 marks or below but above the pass mark, a grade B for 150-180 marks and above 180 marks a grade A.

Using two-value boundary value analysis which of the following tests the grade C boundaries?

a) 100, 150
b) 99, 100, 150, 151
c) 99, 100, 149, 150
d) 100, 101, 150, 151

Select ONE option

Question 7 FL-4.2.2 (K3)

You are testing an application that calculates tax to be paid on income (in whole £s) based on low, middle and high rates. A middle rate tax is to be paid on incomes above £45,000 and up to £140,000. Test cases have already been executed for income values of £11,850, £11,851, £25,001, £44,999, £45,000, £47,001, £140,000, £150,000 and £150,001.

What level of minimum coverage for three-value boundary testing of the middle rate partition has already been completed?

a) 100%
b) 66%
c) 83.3%
d) 33%

Select ONE Option

Question 8 FL-4.2.2 (K3)

When an automated driver insurance system for a vehicle is installed, it functions as follows:

If the vehicle is driven at 30 mph or less, the system operates in a normal condition
If the speed increases to over 30 mph, but not over 33 mph, an over-speed reminder sounds
If the speed increases to over 33 mph, but not more than 40 mph, an alert sounds to slow down
If the speed increases to over 40 mph, an alert sounds and a driver penalty is recorded

The speed in mph is recorded in integer numbers by the system and only values on the boundaries of the equivalence classes are selected. Which of the following is a correct set of values identified by applying two-value boundary value analysis?

a) 0, 29, 30, 32, 39, 40, 41
b) 29, 30, 33, 40, 41
c) 30, 31, 33, 34, 40, 41
d) 29, 30, 32, 33, 40, 45

Select ONE option

4.2 Answers and Explanations 1 to 8 FL-4.2.1, 4.2.2

Answer 1 FL-4.2.1

b) is the correct option. a) is not the correct option. The use of state transition is appropriate. c) is not the correct option. After equivalence partitions, a combinatorial technique such as Each Choice can be used. d) is not the correct option. The use of a decision table would be appropriate for logic combinations.

Answer 2 FL-4.2.1

c) is the correct option. The values 18, 49 and 50 are all in the partition for users eligible to register with a 20% discount. a) is not the correct option. The values 16 and 17 are in the partition for users not eligible to register. The value 18 is in the partition users can register with a 20% discount.
b) is not the correct option. The value 50 is in the partition for users eligible to register with a 20% discount, 51 and 52 are in the partition for seniors. d) is not the correct option. 17, 49 and 51 are all in different partitions.

Answer 3 FL-4.2.1

d) is the correct option. There are four partitions and a test case value for each partition is required.

Partition 1: €0.01 to €24.99 Partition 2: €25.00 to €50.99
Partition 3: €51.00 to €250.99 Partition 4: €251.00 and over

As the order total is calculated from the items selected and is not a direct user input, a partition for non-numeric totals is not needed. a), b) and c) are not correct options for the reasons given for d).

Answer 4 FL-4.2.1

d) is the correct option. A 'Pass' is 100 marks, 140 is a 'C' grade, 180 is a 'B' grade and 190 is an 'A' grade.

Fail	Pass	C grade	B grade	A grade
0 99	100	101 150	151 180	181 200

a) is not the correct option. 170 and 180 are both 'B' grade.
b) is not the correct option. 160 and 180 are both 'B' grade.
c) is not the correct option. 160 and 180 are both 'B' grade.

Answer 5 FL-4.2.1

b) is the correct option. Three partitions are required for Each Choice equivalence partitioning:

Collar: 3 options | Cuff: 2 options | Color: 3 options

Selecting one element from each partition and covering all elements, can be achieved with three test cases. For example, TC1 Collar Point, Cuff single with one button, Color White.
TC2 Collar Cutaway, double with cufflinks/Color White. TC3 Collar Button-down, cuff either, color Cream. a), c) and d) are not correct options for the reasons given for b).

Answer 6 FL-4.2.2
d) is the correct option. The pass mark is 100. A 'C' grade is awarded for marks of 101 to 150 inclusive. These boundary values should be tested to confirm a 'C' grade is awarded together with values just outside to confirm that a 'C' grade is not awarded outside the valid limits.
a) is not the correct option. Two values are required at each boundary. b) and c) are not the correct options, for the reasons given for d).

Answer 7 FL-4.2.2
d) is the correct option.

Band	Taxable Income	Tax Rate	3-value Lower Boundary	3-value Upper Boundary
Higher Rate	£45,001 to £140,000	40%	£45,000/£45,001/£45,002	£139,999/£140,000/£140,001

£45,000 and £140,000 have already been tested. This leaves four out of the six values still to be tested as 2/6 is equal to 33% minimum coverage. a, b) and c) are not correct for the reasons given for d).

Answer 8 FL-4.2.2
c) is the correct option. The boundaries are 30/31, 33/34, 40/41. a) is not the correct option. 33 is not included. b) is not the correct option. There are not two values for the 33/34 boundary. d) is not the correct option as 41 should be included, not 45.

FL-4.2.3 (K3) Use decision table testing to derive test cases
Decision table representation is used to show that a given combination of conditions or input values leads to a specific set of actions or outputs. The basic structure of a decision table is based on rows and columns that intersect in a matrix creating cells. Decision tables can be an effective way of recording complex logic, such as business rules. The value of a decision table is that it shows combinations of conditions that might not otherwise have been identified during test design or exercised during testing.

There are two sorts of decision table representation, one is classic or traditional, and the second, which is now commonly used by many organizations is based on OMG-DMN® notation (Object Management Group Decision Model Notation).

The ISTQB Foundation Syllabus focuses on the 'classic' full decision table representation with its use of columns corresponding to rules, no variation in orientation 'conditions' and 'actions' and inclusion initially of all possible combinations including infeasible ones. Combinations of conditions that are infeasible can be removed from a decision table to simplify it. Reducing or minimizing the full table by considering infeasible combinations and merging redundant columns is outside of the scope of the Foundation Syllabus.

Many testers in their work will commonly encounter OMG-DMN® decision tables. These differ from the classic full decision tables included in the Foundation Syllabus. The ISTQB Advanced Test Analyst Syllabus includes OMG-DMN® and states, *'A decision table is a tabular representation of a set of conditions and related actions, expressed as rules indicating which action shall occur for which set of condition values [OMG-DMN]'.* The OMG-DMN® notation allows different orientations of the tables. OMG-DMN® based decision tables are not limited as classic tables are by the number of values a condition may have and can accommodate overlapping rules. They also optionally include comments / annotation, line style and more. Although outside of the scope of the Foundation Syllabus, OMG-DMN® is an important and useful notation. See Appendix C Decision Tables OMG-DMN® for examples and more detail on OMG-DMN® decision tables, and the book Software Testing Advanced Test Analyst Complete Guide for ISTQB Exam by C. Newbould ISBN 978-0-9536056-3-7.

For the exam, the ability to read, understand and use a decision table is required. Knowing how a 'classic' decision table is created is beneficial for achieving the required K3 knowledge level.

Full Decision Table Layout and Creation

A full classic decision table is divided into the following sections.

	Rule							
	R1	R2	R3	R4	R5	R6	R7	R8
Conditions to test	Condition entries							
Actions to take	Actions/Outcomes							

The **Conditions to test** section lists all the conditions (inputs). A condition can be values that are:

- Boolean (having one of two values, true or false)
- Binary (having a base-2 numeral system, which uses only two symbols, such as 0 and 1)
- Categorical (such as low/medium/high)
- Numeric (such as less than 10, between 10 and 20 inclusive, greater than 20)

Classic decision tables focus on the use of conditions with two values or possibly three values. They become difficult to handle when more condition values need to be considered and OMG-DMN notation should then be considered.

Where conditions are Boolean, having two simple values such as 'True' or 'False', these can be considered as aligned to the 'IF … THEN … ELSE statement in programming languages.

Where conditions have multiple values, such as 'high', 'medium', low', these can be considered aligned to a programming CASE statement which occurs in most modern programming languages and allows a selection to be made between a set of values.

Note: Conditions with only two possible values are most likely to be used in the Foundation Level exam.

Each condition has a row.

The **Actions to take** section lists the possible actions, outcomes or results that can occur as a result of the decision. Each action has a row.

The **Condition entries** section sets out the possible combinations of condition values. Each column represents a unique combination of condition values and maps it to a corresponding action by continuing the column through the action outputs section.

The Foundation Syllabus gives the common notation for condition entries as:

> ' 'T' *(true) meaning the condition is satisfied,* 'F' *(false) the condition is not satisfied.'* *
> ' '-' *dash for the value of a condition when it is irrelevant for the action outcome.'* See later.
> ' 'N/A' *means that the condition is infeasible for the given rule.'*

* Other variations such as 'Y' (Yes) and 'N' (No), 'H' (High), 'M' (Medium), 'L' (Low) may be used.

The **Rule** number heading to each column assigns a unique identifier or number to each rule. The rule heading is not always included, but it can help in referencing specific rules or for documentation purposes.

The **Actions/Outcomes** section identifies the specific action(s) to be taken for the combination in the column.

The Foundation Syllabus gives the common notation for Actions/Outcomes as:

> *"X" means that the action should occur. "Blank" means that the action should not occur.'*

Other notations that may be used include, 'Y' (Yes), or 'N' (No), 1, (other numerical value such as the actual value for a discount total).

Number of Columns

The number of columns required in a full table is equal to the product of the numbers of the values of each condition. In a scenario with three Boolean conditions, the full limited-entry decision table has (2 x 2 x 2) = 8 columns. In a scenario with one condition having one of three possible values and two further Boolean conditions, the number of columns needed is (3 x 2 x 2) = 12. In a scenario with one condition having one of four possible values and two further Boolean conditions, the number of columns needed is (4 x 2 x 2) = 16.

Number of Rows

The number of rows required is equal to the number of actions. Where actions are additive, for example, discounts, an additional row may be added to show the additive results of the actions such as, 'Total discount'.

Steps required to construct a full decision table covering all combinations of conditions:

Step 1: Define the decision

The first step in creating a decision table is to clearly define the decision to be modeled.

Step 2: Identify the conditions

List all the conditions or factors that affect the decision. This determines the number of working rows needed in the top half of the table.

Step 3: Determine the number of possible combinations

The number of columns (rules) required is determined by multiplying the numbers of the possible values for each condition together. When n conditions have two possible values, the number of columns required is 2^n. For example, for three conditions each having two possible values $2^3 = 8$ columns are required. For four conditions each having two possible values, $2^4 = 16$ columns are required.

For three conditions, one of which has three options, such as low, medium or high (or three numerical ranges) and two other conditions each having two values, $3^1 \times 2^2 = 12$ columns are required.

Step 4: Identify the actions and outcomes

List the possible actions that can result from the combination of conditions.

This determines the number of rows required in the lower part of the table.

Step 5: Create and populate the table

Create a table structure with the required number of rows and columns. Use the notation as identified earlier/above to fill in the table.

Example 1: Three two-value conditions with two possible actions.

	Rule							
	R1	**R2**	**R3**	**R4**	**R5**	**R6**	**R7**	**R8**
Condition								
C1	T	T	T	T	F	F	F	F
C2	T	T	F	F	T	T	F	F
C3	T	F	T	F	T	F	T	F
Action*								
A1		X		X				
A2				X	X			

* Action outcomes shown as 'X' will vary according to the scenario.

Example 2: One condition having three possible values, two conditions having two possible values and two possible actions.

	Rule											
	R1	**R2**	**R3**	**R4**	**R5**	**R6**	**R7**	**R8**	**R9**	**R10**	**R11**	**R12**
Condition												
C1	H	H	H	H	M	M	M	M	L	L	L	L
C2	T	T	F	F	T	T	F	F	T	T	F	F
C3	T	F	T	F	T	F	T	F	T	F	T	F
Action*												
A1			X				X				X	
A2			X			X		X				

* Action outcomes shown as 'X' will vary according to the scenario.

Example 3: Two conditions each having three possible values and one action output.
C1 is High, Medium and Low and C2 is Red, White and Blue.

	Rule								
	R1	**R2**	**R3**	**R4**	**R5**	**R6**	**R7**	**R8**	**R9**
Condition									
C1	H	H	H	M	M	M	L	L	L
C2	R	W	B	R	W	B	R	W	B
Action									
A1	X		X					X	

Values other than H, M, L and R, W, B may be used. See Exercise 2.

Step 6: Review and validate

Review the decision table to ensure it accurately represents the decision logic. Verify that all possible combinations are accounted for and that the outcomes align with the business rules or requirements. Columns showing infeasible combinations of conditions can be deleted.

Use of Dash '-'

Using '–' dash for a 'Condition' being irrelevant to the outcome should be used with care.
Consider the following:

	Rule			
	R1	**R2**	**R3**	**R4**
Condition 1	T	T	F	F
Condition 2	T	F	T	F
Action 1	X	X		
Action 2	X		X	X

The value of Condition 2 does not affect the outcome action in Rules 3 and 4 and could be replaced in both these rules by '-'. This would reduce the number of distinct columns (test cases) to three for covering all output actions.

	Rule		
	R1	**R2**	**R3**
Condition 1	T	T	F
Condition 2	T	F	'–'
Action 1	X	X	
Action 2	X		X

However, it is possible a defect may be missed. If Condition 2 is chosen as T in Column 3 and the test case passes, it does not guarantee that if Condition 2 is F the combination with Condition 1 as F will also pass.

Decision Table Coverage

For 100% minimum coverage of a decision table, create cases for each rule (column). Test case coverage expressed as a percentage is the number of test cases determined or exercised, divided by the total number of possible test cases multiplied by 100.

$$\text{Coverage} = \frac{\text{Test cases determined or exercised}}{\text{Total possible test cases shown by test technique}} \times 100\%$$

FL-4.2.3 (K3) Exercises: Decision Tables

FL-4.2.3 (K3) Exercise 1: Classic full decision table

You are working on a payroll application. There are two categories of employees, salaried and contract. All employees are retained to work for 40 hours per week for which there is a standard pay amount. Salaried employees receive the standard pay every week regardless of hours worked. If a salaried employee works additional hours, their Hours Worked Record is updated with the additional number of hours. If a salaried employee works less than 40 hours, their Hours Worked Record is updated to reflect the reduced hours. Contract employees receive the standard pay for 40 hours of work. If the hours worked by a contract employee are less than 40, the weekly hourly wage is used to calculate pay and an Absence Report is produced. For additional hours worked over 40 hours in a week by a contract employee, the standard pay plus the agreed overtime rate is used to calculate pay.

Part 1: Create a full decision table, using Boolean values (True or False) for the three conditions, Salaried employee? (1), Work Hours <40? (2) and Work Hours = 40? (3). When both Work Hours conditions are false, assume the employee is working more than 40 hours.
How many columns can be removed as being impossible situations?
How many test cases then required for 100% minimum coverage of your table?

Part 2: Create a full decision table, using two conditions, Salaried employee? (1) and Work Hours? (2) where Salaried employee can have a value True or False and Work Hours can have one of three values, <40, =40 and >40.
How many columns can be removed as being impossible situations?
How many test cases then required for 100% minimum coverage of your table?

FL-4.2.3 Answer

Part 1 Answer

Test Case	**1**	**2**	**3**	**4**	**5**	**6**	**7**	**8**
Condition								
Salaried Employee	T	T	T	T	F	F	F	F
Work Hours <40	T	T	F	F	T	T	F	F
Work Hours =40	T	F	T	F	T	F	T	F
Action								
Standard Pay	X	X	X	X				
Calculate Hourly rate					X	X	X	X
Calculate overtime								X
Absence Report					X	X		
Hours Record addition	X	X						
Hours Record deduction				X				

Part 1 Answer *continued*

Two columns can be removed as being impossible situations.
Columns 1 and 5 are not possible as an employee cannot be working both =40 hours and <40 hours at the same time. This leaves 6 test cases (columns).

Test Case	**2**	**3**	**4**	**6**	**7**	**8**
Condition						
Salaried Employee	T	T	T	F	F	F
Work Hours <40	T	F	F	T	F	F
Work Hours =40	F	T	F	F	T	F
Action						
Standard Pay	X	X	X			
Calculate Hourly rate				X	X	X
Calculate overtime						X
Absence Report				X		
Hours Record addition	X					
Hours Record deduction			X			

Part 2 Answer
Full Decision Table with one condition having three values:

Test Case	**1**	**2**	**3**	**4**	**5**	**6**
Condition						
Salaried Employee	T	T	T	F	F	F
Hours worked	<40	=40	>40	<40	=40	>40
Action						
Standard Pay	X	X	X		X	X
Calculate hourly rate				X		
Calculate overtime						X
Produce absence report				X		
Hours record addition	X					
Hours record deduction			X			

There are no columns to remove for impossible situations. Six test cases (6 columns) are required for 100% minimum coverage of the table.

FL-4.2.3 (K3) Exercise 2: Reviewing a decision table

You are reviewing the following decision table. Dash '–' indicates where a condition value is irrelevant for the outcome action(s).

	Rule					
Conditions	**R1**	**R2**	**R3**	**R4**	**R5**	**R6**
Premium Customer	T	T	T	F	F	–
Active Member	–	T	F	–	F	F
Purchase ≥ $100	T	F	F	F	T	F
Actions						
Free shipping	X		X			
Points added	X	X				X
2% discount	X				X	

Part 1: From the given decision table, identify errors or contradictions.
Part 2: If one test case is executed to cover R1, give a reason why a defect could have been missed.

FL-4.2.3 Answer

Part 1 Answer

R3 and R6 are contradictory, R6 could have T, F, F, the same combination of conditions as R4 but the outcome actions are different.

Rules R4 and R6 are contradictory, R4 could be F, F, F and has no outcome action. R6 could also be F, F, F but has the outcome 'Points added'. Having no outcome is not itself an error. To check the actions are correctly input into the table requires more information about the scenario, unless it does not conform to the scenario.

Part 2 Answer

Using one test case covers the combination of conditions T, either T or F as represented by '–' and T. Assume T, T, T is chosen and the test passes with the correct outcome actions. It is possible the combination T, F, T could fail.

FL-4.2.3 Exercise 3 Decision table using values other than T and F

The following decision table assesses a customer's eligibility for a loan. Credit Rating and Debit to Income (DTI) are being used. CR has been obtained from a credit rating company. A higher credit rating is best. DTI has been calculated by adding monthly bills and dividing by gross monthly income, multiplied by 100 to give a percentage. The lower the DTI, the lower the risk of the customer to lenders. The decision table below is an example of where values can be used instead of True/False.

	Rule				
	R1	**R2**	**R3**	**R4**	**R5**
Condition					
Credit Rating, CR	< 610	610 to 709	610 to 709	≥ 710	≥ 710
Debt to Income, DTI	–	≥ 28%	< 28%	> 35%	≤ 35%
Action					
Risk determined	Declined	Declined	Approved	Referred*	Approved

*Referred means to be given further consideration before a decision is made.

TC1: Credit Rating = 700 Debt to Income = 20%
TC2: Credit Rating = 710 Debt to Income = 28%
TC3: Credit Rating = 650 Debt to Income = 35%
TC4: Credit Rating = 600 Debt to Income = 28%
TC5: Credit Rating = 709 Debt to Income = 28%

Part 1: How many test cases result in 'Declined'?
Part 2: What is the decision table coverage?

FL-4.2.3 Answer

Part 1: Three test cases result in Declined.
TC1 tests R3, Action Approved. TC2 tests R5, Action Approved. TC3 tests R2, Action Declined. TC4 tests R1, Action Declined. TC5 tests R2, Action Declined.

Part 2: Rule 4 is not covered by the test cases.
With 4 out of 5 rules, the decision table coverage is 80%.

This example adopts some notation based on OMG-DMN™. For examples, see *Appendix C OMG-DMN*.

FL-4.2.4 (K3) Use state transition testing to derive test cases

State transition testing, also referred to as finite state testing, is a test technique that can be used when a system has a finite number of states and a change, event or input results in a change of state. A change between states is termed a transition. The change may depend on a condition being met. A condition may also be referred to as a transition condition or a transition guard.

A **state transition diagram** is a visual representation of all the states a system has and the possible transitions between these states. The diagram may show the conditions or events that cause a transition to occur and the outputs or actions carried out as a result of the transition.
State transition diagrams can be drawn in a number of ways according to the convention being used. But typically, states are represented as nodes with transitions as interconnecting directional arrows and events or conditions are optionally included as labels on the arrows. The initial state can be indicated by a line with a black dot.

Example: State transition diagram
Consider a vehicle that can be deactivated (engine off), stopped (engine on), accelerating, constant speed or decelerating. This is shown in the following diagram:

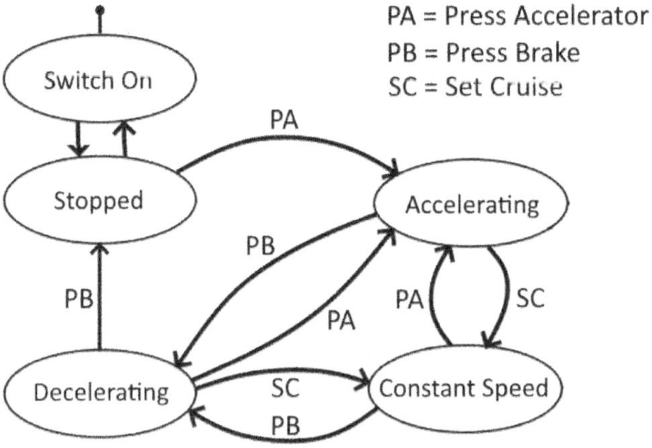

A **state transition table** is a visual or tabular representation used to describe the behavior of a state-transition system. The table is a grid showing each possible state and the valid transitions between states. Invalid transitions can optionally be included or if not then deduced.

Example: State transition table
A basic state transition table for all valid zero switches for the vehicle example above is below:

Initial State	End State
Deactivated	Stopped
Stopped	Deactivated
Stopped	Accelerating
Accelerating	Constant Speed
Accelerating	Decelerating
Constant Speed	Accelerating
Constant Speed	Decelerating
Decelerating	Constant Speed
Decelerating	Accelerating
Decelerating	Stopped

A more detailed state transition table can include additional columns for events, conditions and actions. The 0-switch table can be expanded as follows:

Initial State	Event	Guard Condition	Action	Next State
Deactivated	Journey planned	Starter pressed on	Engine on	Stopped idling
Stopped idling	Journey abandoned or stopped	Starter pressed off	Engine off	Deactivated
Stopped idling	Journey start	Accelerator pedal pressed	Move with speed increasing	Accelerating
Accelerating	Speed limit zone reached	Set cruise control	Move to constant speed	Constant speed
Accelerating	Approaching traffic lights	Brake pressed	Move with speed decreasing	Decelerating
Constant speed	Overtaking	Accelerator pedal pressed	Move with speed increasing	Accelerating
Constant speed	Approaching traffic lights	Brake pressed	Move with speed decreasing	Decelerating
Decelerating	Enter new speed limit zone	Set cruise control	Slow to constant speed	Constant speed
Decelerating	Exit speed limit zone	Accelerator pressed	Move with speed increasing	Accelerating
Decelerating	Traffic lights red	Brake pressed	Slow to no speed	Stopped

The order of the columns' next state and action can be swapped depending on which state is responsible for initiating the action. N-switch coverage where N is greater than zero is not included in the Foundation Syllabus v4.0.1. For higher levels of N-switch coverage. For more details, see Software Testing Advanced Test Analyst, Complete Guide for ISTQB Exam by C. Newbould.

As specified in the Syllabus, *'A test case based on a state transition diagram or state table is usually represented as a sequence of events, which results in a sequence of state changes (and actions, if needed). One test case may, and usually will, cover several transitions between states.'*

There are many possible coverage criteria for state transition testing. The Foundation Syllabus includes three; all states coverage, valid transitions coverage and all transitions coverage.

All States Coverage is:

$$\frac{\text{Number of states visited}}{\text{Total number of states}} \times 100$$

All states coverage can typically be achieved without exercising all transitions and so is a weaker coverage measure than all transitions coverage.

Valid Transitions Coverage (also called 0-switch coverage) is:

$$\frac{\text{Number of exercised single valid transitions}}{\text{Total number of single valid transitions}} \times 100$$

where a single transition is from one state to another adjacent state.

Note: Normal operation is defined by a valid transition between valid states.

An **invalid transition** can be interpreted as either:

An operation that is not the normal expected correct operation such as the specification states a user is required to enter a correct passcode (in request state) and also states an incorrect passcode or none should be rejected (in error state) as invalid. In some instances, the transition to rejecting the incorrect passcode may be considered a valid transaction in terms of being specified, or invalid in terms of not being the normal expected operation.

or

A transition occurs between states that are valid but the transition between them is not.
For example, UK traffic lights operation is specified as:

Red light: Stop → Red & Amber lights: Prepare to Go → Green light: Go, if the way is clear → Amber light: Stop, provided it is safe to do so. Then start again with Red light: Stop. The states of Green and Red are valid. A transition from Green to Red is not specified and is therefore invalid.

When using valid state coverage, it is important to qualify the measure with how invalid transitions should be interpreted, such as according to what invalid operations have been specified or what has not been included in the specification but needs to be addressed to prevent the software acting inappropriately such as going into a loop.
The interpretation of invalid transitions is similar to how infeasible combinations of conditions are interpreted when using decision tables.

All Transitions Coverage is:

$$\frac{\text{Number of single valid transitions exercised plus attempts to exercise invalid transitions}}{\text{Total number of single valid and invalid transitions}} \times 100$$

All transitions coverage can shift the emphasis away from valid transitions to invalid transitions, potentially overshadowing positive testing, where the application's expected behaviors are tested. Achieving complete invalid transition coverage can be challenging, especially in systems with complex state machines. The number of invalid state transitions can be vast, making it impractical to test all possible scenarios exhaustively. Due to the extensive nature of invalid transition testing, it may require a significant amount of time and resources. In practice, it might not be feasible to test all potential invalid transitions thoroughly, leading to prioritization and potential trade-offs. These considerations mean all transitions coverage is less regularly used than all valid transitions coverage.

Other Coverage

Includes N-switch where n is a positive number and round-trip coverage, including self-loop. These are explained in more detail in the book Software Testing Advanced Test Analyst Complete Guide for ISTQB Exam by C. Newbould ISBN 978-0-9536056-3-7.

FL-4.2.4 (K3) Exercise: State Transition Testing

You are working with an application that allows a user to book an exam. Exams are available at various levels. The initial state is 'Start'. By inputting the required subject, the user can initiate a transition to 'Exam Selection'. The software will display the availability of relevant exams. The user can then select an exam and transition to 'Booking'. The exam is reserved. If the user decides not to select an exam from those displayed, they can return to 'Start' to initiate a booking for an exam in a different subject. In 'Booking', the user is asked to provide the required data. If this data is accepted, the user transitions to 'Confirmation'. If the data is not accepted, the user does not fully complete the entry or cancels the booking, the transition returns to 'Exam Selection'. At 'Confirmation', the user is issued with a receipt and then moved to 'End'. 'End' can also be reached from 'Start' if the user decides to abandon the booking. The user can also move from 'Start' to 'End' if they have changed their mind about making a booking.

Part 1: From the details given, draw a state transition diagram showing the states, transitions and transition triggers.

Part 2: From the details given, create a state transition table showing the states, transition triggers and actions.

Part 3: From either the state transition diagram or the state transition table, determine how many test cases are required for all states transition coverage are required?

Part 4: From either the state transition diagram or the state transition table, determine how many test cases are required for all transitions coverage?

FL-4.2.4 Exercise Answers

Part 1 Answer

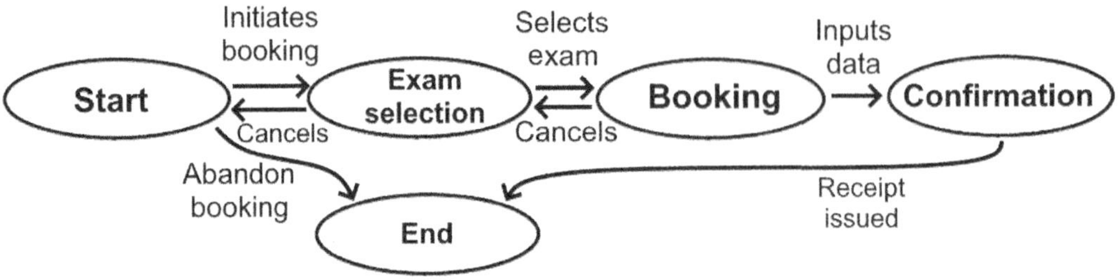

Part 2 Answer

State	Event	Next State	Action
Start	User initiates booking based on level of exam	Exam selection	Relevant exam availability displayed
Start	User abandons making a booking	End	
Exam selection	User selects exam	Booking	Exam reserved
Exam Selection	User decides not to book an exam	Start	Warning message
Booking	User provides required data	Confirmation	Booking confirmed
Booking	User cancels booking or fails to provide required data	Exam selection	Relevant exam availability displayed
Confirmation	User issued receipt	End	

Part 3 Answer

One test case is required. Test Case: Start → Exam Selection → Booking → Confirmation → End.

Part 4 Answer

Two test cases are required. These are:

Test Case 1: Start → Exam Selection → Booking → Confirmation → End.

Test Case 2: Start → Exam Selection → Booking → Exam Selection → Start → End.

4.2 Questions 9 to 23 FL-4.2.3, 4.2.4

Question 9 FL-4.2.3 (Consolidation)

Which of the following are true when using a decision table?

a) Is suitable for testing any software quality characteristic
b) Identifies missing logic rules
c) Useful for summarizing all outcomes for the specified input values
d) Can easily capture dynamic or time-dependent logic changes in a system
e) Cannot identify contradictory actions for the same set of conditions

Select TWO options

Question 10 FL-4.2.3 (K3) An e-retail company wishes to reward its customers with loyalty cards. For orders with a value greater than £50 a 3% discount applies. For orders less than or equal to £50, the discount is 1%. Customers without loyalty cards receive no discounts.

For a full classic decision table, how many columns/test cases are required for all possible combinations?

a) 4
b) 12
c) 8
d) 6

Select ONE option

Question 11 FL-4.2.3 (K3) You are using a decision table with 32 columns and 4 rows. You have derived cases based on 24 of the columns.

What percentage coverage of the full decision table is achieved with the 24 test cases?

a) $\frac{(32 \times 4)}{24} \times 100$

b) $\frac{24}{32} \times 100$

c) $\frac{24}{(32 + 4)} \times 100$

d) $\frac{32}{24} \times 100$

Select ONE option

Question 12 FL-4.2.3 (K3) Customers of a buyers club can order goods without being a premium customer or having active membership. Customers with an active membership are allocated points on all purchases which they can redeem for rewards. For active membership, customers must have placed two or more orders in the previous two months. Premium customers are customers who have collected 500 or more points in the previous year. Premium customers purchasing goods worth \$100 or more have free shipping. A customer can be an active member and a premium member. The decision table is for all valid purchases and does not need to check for \$0 or a negative purchase amount as these have previously been verified by the application.

	Rule							
Conditions	**R1**	**R2**	**R3**	**R4**	**R5**	**R6**	**R7**	**R8**
Premium Customer	T	T	T	T	F	F	F	F
Active Membership	T	T	F	F	T	T	F	F
Purchase ≥ \$100	T	F	T	F	T	F	T	F
Actions								
Free shipping	X		X	X				
Points	X	X	X		X	X		

Which of the following is true?

a) Columns R3 and R4 are incorrect
b) There are no infeasible columns
c) Columns R2 and R3 are incorrect
d) Column R5 is incorrect

Select ONE option

Question 13 FL-4.2.3 (K3) Customers of a buyers club can order goods without being a premium customer or having an active membership. Customers with active membership are allocated points on all purchases which they can redeem for rewards. For active membership, customers must have placed two or more orders in the previous two months. Premium customers are customers who have collected 500 or more points in the previous year and premium customers have free shipping on orders of $100 or more. An active member can also be a premium member. The decision table is for all purchases and does not need to check for $0 or a negative purchase amount as that has previously been verified by the application.

	Rule							
Conditions	**R1**	**R2**	**R3**	**R4**	**R5**	**R6**	**R7**	**R8**
Premium Customer	T	T	T	T	F	F	F	F
Active Membership	T	T	F	F	T	T	F	F
Purchase ≥ $100	T	F	T	F	T	F	T	F
Actions								
Free shipping	X		X					
Points	X	X			X	X		

The organization has now decided that customers who have either premium or active membership or both who pay with a bank transfer will receive a 1% discount. The only other option for paying is to use a credit card and this has no discount.

How many extra columns need to be added to the table above for a new full decision table that includes the 1% discount option?

a) The extra condition does not apply to customers who are not premium or active members, R7 and R8 do not need to be split into two columns so 6 extra columns are required
b) One extra condition with two values requires two extra columns
c) One extra condition is being added, one extra column is needed
d) All eight columns need to be split into two columns each so 16 columns are required

Select ONE option

Question 14 FL-4.2.3 (K3) You are working with a delivery application for deliveries to either Zone A, Zone B or Zone C. Input value and field validation have been done, with any zones other than A, B or C having been rejected. In the decision table conditions section below, if the Zone is not A or B, it is assumed to be C and if the delivery is not express, it is assumed to be standard. The action section is still to be completed with different delivery costs.
The conditions section of a full classic decision table based on the given information is shown below.

	Rule							
Conditions	**R1**	**R2**	**R3**	**R4**	**R5**	**R6**	**R7**	**R8**
Zone A?	T	T	T	T	F	F	F	F
Zone B?	T	T	F	F	T	T	F	F
Express?	T	F	T	F	T	F	T	F

Based on the given scenario, how many of the above rules describe impossible situations?

a) 1
b) 2
c) 3
d) 4

Select ONE option

Question 15 FL-4.2.3 (K3) The following decision table is for testing a delivery application. Goods can be dispatched from Zone A or Zone B, otherwise when neither Zone A nor Zone B, then Zone C. There are now three types of delivery, same day, express (next business day) otherwise standard delivery (up to 5 business days). If delivery is neither same day nor express, it can be assumed to be standard.

You have the following conditions part of a decision table. The actions (price costs) will be added at a future time when the conditions section is approved as representing feasible combinations of inputs.

	Rule															
Conditions	**R1**	**R2**	**R3**	**R4**	**R5**	**R6**	**R7**	**R8**	**R9**	**R10**	**R11**	**R12**	**R13**	**R14**	**R15**	**R16**
Zone A?	T	T	T	T	T	T	T	T	F	F	F	F	F	F	F	F
Zone B?	T	T	T	T	F	F	F	F	T	T	T	T	F	F	F	F
Same day?	T	T	F	F	T	T	F	F	T	T	F	F	T	T	F	F
Express?	T	F	T	F	T	F	T	F	T	F	T	F	T	F	T	F

Based on the given scenario, how many of the above rules describe impossible situations?

a) 7
b) 6
c) 8
d) 9

Select ONE option

Question 16 FL-4.2.3 (K3) Decision testing is being used for an e-retail site. Two test cases have already been generated and executed for the rules R1 and R2 shown below:

		Rule	
		R1	R2
Conditions	Order value ≥ $50	T	F
	Loyalty card	F	T
Actions	5% discount	F	F
	Free delivery	T	F

Which two of the test cases below would achieve full coverage of a complete decision table when combined with the test cases that have already been generated for rules R1 and R2?

		Test Cases			
		DT1	DT2	DT3	DT4
Inputs	Order value	$65	$51	$50	$49
	Loyalty card	Yes	No	Yes	No

a) DT1 and DT2
b) DT2 and DT4
c) DT1 and DT4
d) DT2 and DT3

Select ONE option

Question 17 FL-4.2.4 (Consolidation) When using state transition testing, which of the following is not true?

a) All states coverage is weaker than valid transitions coverage
b) Achieving full valid transitions coverage guarantees full all states coverage
c) Achieving full all transitions coverage guarantees both full all states coverage and full valid transitions coverage
d) Achieving full all states coverage guarantees full all transitions coverage

Select ONE option

Question 18 FL-4.2.4 (K3)

A real estate application allows property to be sold online. A property is listed, then the transition '*Publish to Web*' results in moving the property to the state 'Waiting for Offer'. When an offer is received, the state changes to 'Review Offer'. There are then two possible outcomes, '*Reject*' triggers a return to 'Waiting for Offer' or '*Accept Offer*' triggers a move to 'Sold Subject to Contract'. Transition from 'Sold Subject to Contract' to 'Property Sold' or if '*Failed*' return to 'Property Listing'.

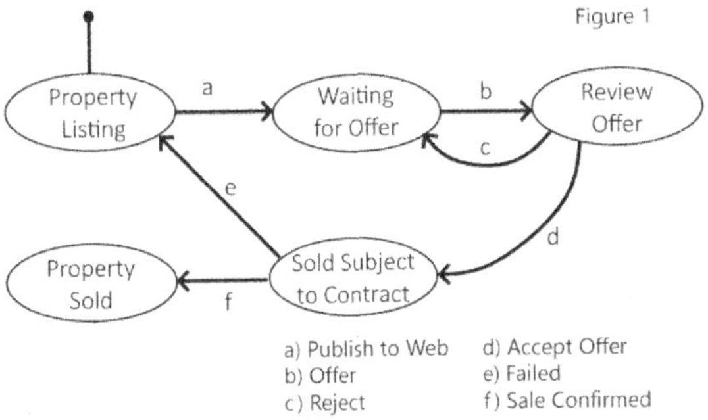

Figure 1

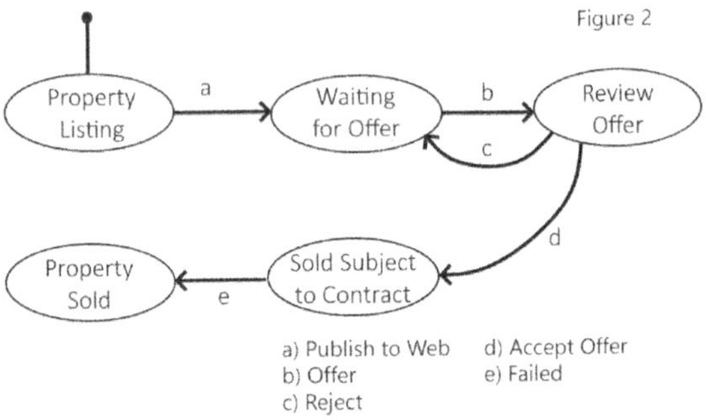

Figure 2

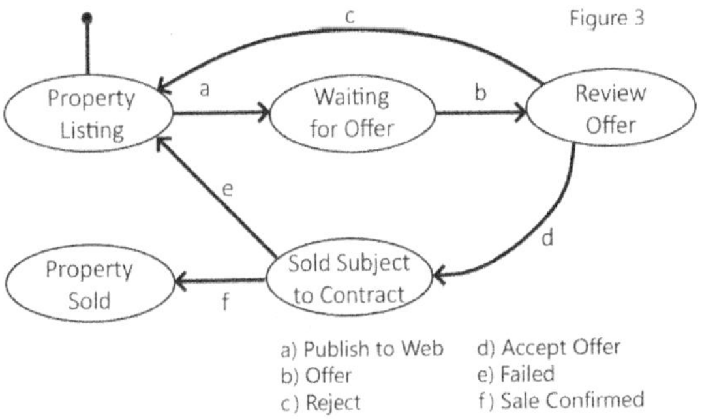

Figure 3

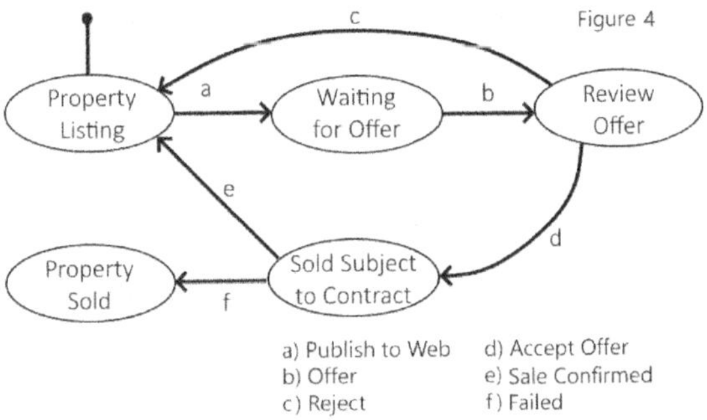

Figure 4

Which is the correct state transition diagram?

a) Figure 1
b) Figure 2
c) Figure 3
d) Figure 4

Select ONE option

Question 19 FL-4.2.4 (K3) The motion sensor system can only be switched from an off state to ready when the key is inserted. The key can be turned to the active state so that the action to sound the alarm when motion is detected is taken. When the alarm is sounding, the only valid option to stop the alarm is to turn the key back to the ready state. The key can also be turned from the active state to the ready state when the intention is to switch the system off. The key can be removed from the ready state and this puts the system in the off state.

How many valid 0-switch transitions should be tested?

a) 3
b) 4
c) 5
d) 6

Select ONE option

Question 20 FL-4.2.4 (K3) You are testing an application for an employee, who works part-time at home, and part-time in the office, to book a desk in the office. The application is modelled by the state transition table shown below.

Initial State	**Condition**	**Action**	**End State**
S1 Desk request	Desk available	Desk count reduced Desk reserved	S2 Desk confirmation
S1 Desk request	Desk not available	Request put on waitlist	S3 On waitlist
S2 Desk confirmation	User accepts desk reservation		S4 in Use
S2 Confirmation	User cancels request	Desk count increased	S5 End
S3 On waitlist	Desk becomes available	Desk reserved Desk count reduced	S2 Desk available confirmed
S3 On waitlist	User cancels request		S5 End
S4 In use	User ends use of desk	Desk count increased	S5 End

What is the minimum number of test cases starting with S1 and ending with S5 required to achieve all valid transitions coverage?

a) 5
b) 7
c) 3
d) 2

Select ONE option

Question 21 FL-4.2.4 (K3) Based on the state transition diagram below, how many test cases starting from 'Order Preparation' and ending at a terminal state are required for 100% all transitions coverage?

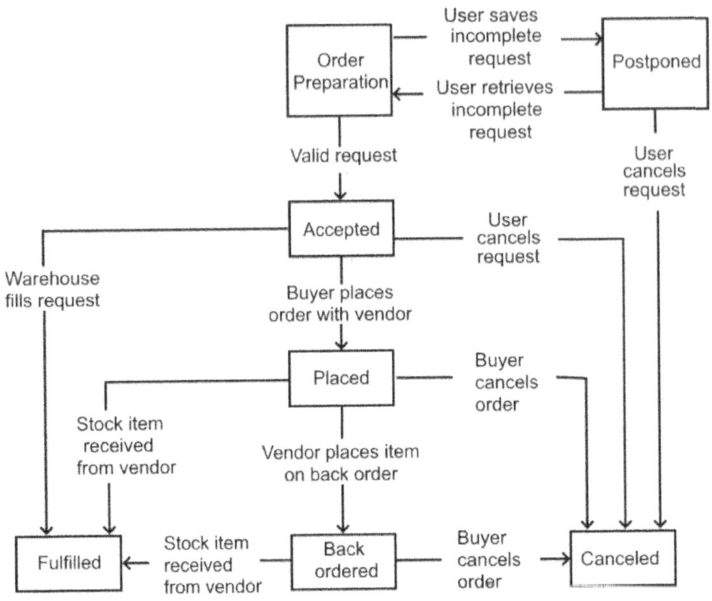

a) 5
b) 7
c) 6
d) 4

Select ONE option

Question 22 FL-4.2.4 (K3)

A computer system has five states: 'Power On', 'Booting', 'Running', 'Sleep', and 'Shut Down' where the computer is powered off. The possible state transitions are as follows: the system can go from 'Power On' to 'Booting', from 'Booting' to 'Running', from 'Running' to either 'Sleep' or 'Shut Down', from 'Sleep' to either 'Running' or 'Shut Down' and from 'Shut Down' back to 'Power On'.

Which of the following represents a sequence of valid transitions between the specified states?

a) Power on → Running → Sleep → Running → Shut Down
b) Power on → Booting → Running → Shut Down → Sleep
c) Power on → Booting → Running → Sleep → Running
d) Power on → Running → Booting → Sleep → Shut Down

Select ONE option

Question 23 FL-4.2.4 (K3) A greenhouse has a window that has three possible states: 'Closed', 'Half Open', and 'Fully Open'. The window is opened and closed by the test object depending on the internal temperature. If the temperature rises above 20°C, the window half opens. If the temperature rises above 30°C, the window fully opens and then if the temperature drops below 25°C, the window returns to being half open. If the temperature drops below 15°C, the window closes.

How many 0-switch transitions are there?

a) 2
b) 3
c) 4
d) 5

Select ONE option

4.2 Answers and Explanations 9 to 23 FL-4.2.3, 4.2.4

Answer 9 FL-4.2.3

b) and c) are the correct options. b) Decision tables can help identify missing logic rules. While reviewing the decision table, testers can look for patterns or gaps in the logic. For example, a certain combination of conditions may not be covered by any rule. c) Decision tables support summarizing all outcomes in a scenario for the specified input values.
a) is not a correct option. Decision tables are not used to test some quality characteristics, such as usability, user satisfaction or response times. Decision tables are useful when static logic is tested. d) is not a correct option. Decision tables test static logic and are not easily adaptable to handle changing the logic in real time. e) is not a correct option. Decision tables enable consistency checking. Testers can look for inconsistencies in the rules, such as contradictory actions for the same set of conditions.

Answer 10 FL-4.2.3

a) is the correct option.
Full decision table:

	Rule			
	R1	**R2**	**R3**	**R4**
Conditions				
Loyalty card?	T	T	F	F
Order > £50?	T	F	T	F
Actions				
3% discount	X			
1% discount		X		

b), c) and d) are not correct for the reasons given for a).

Answer 11 FL-4.2.3

b) is the correct option. In this scenario, Test Coverage = (24/32) x 100 = 75%.

a), c) and d) are not correct options for the reasons given for b).

Answer 12 FL-4.2.3

a) is the correct option. R3 should not have points as the member is not active. R4 should not have free shipping as the order is less than $100.The full decision table with all possible combinations is:

	Rule							
Conditions	**R1**	**R2**	**R3**	**R4**	**R5**	**R6**	**R7**	**R8**
Premium Customer	T	T	T	T	F	F	F	F
Active Membership	T	T	F	F	T	T	F	F
Purchase ≥ $100	T	F	T	F	T	F	T	F
Actions								
Free shipping	X		X					
Points	X	X			X	X		

b), c) and d) are not correct options for the reasons given for a). (Shading indicates a removed X).

Answer 13 FL-4.2.3

d) is the correct option. Adding a combination with two possible values increases the table size from 8 to 16 columns. For a full decision table, testing that 'bank transfer' does not trigger a discount in any situations where the customer is not a premium or active member, is required.

	Rule															
Conditions	**R1**	**R1#**	**R2**	**R2#**	**R3**	**R3#**	**R4**	**R4#**	**R5**	**R5#**	**R6**	**R6#**	**R7**	**R7#**	**R8**	**R8#**
Bank Transfer	T	F	T	F	T	F	T	F	T	F	T	F	T	F	T	F
Premium Customer	T	T	T	T	T	T	T	T	F	F	F	F	F	F	F	F
Active Membership	T	T	T	T	F	F	F	F	T	T	T	T	F	F	F	F
Purchase ≥ $100	T	T	F	F	T	T	F	F	T	T	F	F	T	T	F	F
Actions																
Free shipping	X	X			X	X										
Points	X	X	X	X					X	X	X	X				
1% Discount	X		X		X		X		X		X					

a), b) and d) are not correct options for the reasons given for d).

Answer 14 FL-4.2.3

b) is the correct option. R1 and R2 are infeasible as the delivery cannot be to both Zone A and Zone B at the same time. Columns R7 and R8 are assigned for delivery to Zone C so are feasible. All rules except R1 and R2 indicate one zone and one delivery option.

a), c and d) are not correct options for the reasons given for b).

Answer 15 FL-4.2.3

a) is the correct option. Any column with Zone A and Zone B with both 'T' is impossible, rules R1, R2, R3, R4. Any column with 'same day' and 'express' with both 'T' is impossible, rules R1, R5, R9, R13. Note rule R1 is in both of the above lists and should be counted once only.
It follows that 7 rules describe impossible situations.
Any column with Zone A or Zone B with both 'F' can be assumed to be Zone C.
Any column with same day and express with both 'F' can be assumed to be standard delivery.
b), c) and d) are not correct options for the reasons given for a).

Answer 16 FL-4.2.3

c) is the correct option. For DT1 and DT4, the following test cases have R1 matches DT2, R2 matches DT3.

		Test Cases / Rules			
		DT1	**DT2/R1**	**DT3/R2**	**DT4**
Conditions	Order value ≥ $50	T ($65)	T	F	F ($49)
	Loyalty card	T	F	T	F
Actions	5% discount	T	F	F	F
	Free delivery	T	T	F	F

a), b) and d) are not correct options for the reasons given for c).

Answer 17 FL-4.2.4

d) is the correct option as it is not true. As stated in the Syllabus, achieving full all transitions coverage guarantees both full all states coverage and full valid transition coverage, not vice versa.
a) is not the correct option as it is true. All states coverage can typically be achieved without exercising all the transitions and is therefore weaker. b) is not the correct option as it is true. Exercising all valid transitions typically guarantees full all states coverage.
c) is not the correct option as it is true. Achieving full all transitions coverage means all states, valid and invalid transitions are covered.

Answer 18 FL-4.2.4

a) is the correct option.
b) is not the correct option. There is no transition '*Sale Confirmed*' f shown and the transition '*Reject*' e should go to 'Property Listing'.
c) is not the correct option. 'Review Offer' with '*Reject*' transition c should go to 'Waiting for Offer'.
d) is not the correct option. Transitions '*Failed*' e and '*Sale Confirmed*' f are incorrectly swapped.

Answer 19 FL-4.2.4

b) is the correct option. The state transition table for valid transitions shows four transitions as follows:

Initial State	Event / Transition	End State
Off	Key inserted	Ready
Ready	Key removed	Off
Ready	Key turned to active	Active
Active	Key turned to ready	Ready

a), c) and d) are not correct options for the reasons given for b).

Answer 20 FL-4.2.4

c) is the correct option. The following test cases cover all valid transitions:

Test case 1: S1 (desk available) to S2 (user takes desk) to S4 (user ends use of desk) to S5.
Test case 2: S1 (desk not available) to S3 (desk request cancelled) to S5.
Test case 3: S1 (desk not available) to S3 (desk becomes available) to S2 (user takes desk) to S4 (user ends use of desk) to S5.

a) is not the correct option. There are five states. Coverage of the transitions is required.
b) is not the correct option. There are seven transitions, but more than one can be tested in the same test case. d) is not the correct option. Two test cases are needed for all states coverage but this does not test all valid transitions coverage.

Answer 21 FL-4.2.4

a) is the correct option. For all transitions coverage, the five test cases required are:

Order preparation → Postponed → Order preparation = Accepted → Fulfilled
Order preparation → Accepted → Placed → Fulfilled
Order preparation → Accepted → Placed → Canceled
Order preparation → Accepted → Placed → Back ordered → Canceled
Order preparation → Postponed → Canceled

b), c) and d) are not correct for the reasons given for a).

Answer 22 FL-4.2.4

c) is the correct option. All transitions are valid.
b) is not the correct option. There is no transition from 'Shut Down' to 'Sleep'. a) is not the correct option. From 'Power On', the only possible transition is to 'Booting'. d) is not the correct option. From 'Power On' there is no transition directly to 'Running' and no transition from 'Running' to 'Booting'.

Answer 23 FL-4.2.4

c) is the correct option. The sequence is: Closed ←→ Half Open ←→ Fully Open. If the window is, 'Fully Open', it always goes to 'Half Open' and then 'Closed'.
a) is not the correct option. 0-switch transitions exist in both directions between the three states
b) is not the correct option. There are three states, but this is not the number of valid transitions.
d) is not the correct option. If the temperature drops from 30°C to below 15°C it will have transitioned through 25°C, so there is no 0-switch transition from 'Fully open' to 'Closed'.

4.3 White-box Test Techniques

There are many different white-box test techniques, each with varying degrees of thoroughness. Two code-focused white-box test techniques are included in the Syllabus, statement testing and branch testing. There are three learning objectives, one for each of the two test techniques and one for the value of white-box testing, all at K2 level, requiring the ability to explain the technique or its value. Other techniques used in higher test levels, such as API testing or using coverage not related to code, such as neuron coverage in neural network testing are outside the scope of Foundation Level.

FL-4.3.1 (K2) Explain statement testing

A **statement** is any line of code that instructs the compiler to perform a specific task.
From the Glossary, **statement testing** is, *'a white-box test technique in which test cases are designed so as to execute statements.'* The coverage items in statement testing are executable statements in the code.

$$\text{Statement coverage} = \frac{\text{Number of executed statements}}{\text{Total number of executable statements}} \times 100\%$$

For 100% statement coverage, all executable statements in the code are exercised at least once.

Example: Statement coverage
Consider the following code:

```
START
READ X
READ Y
  IF "X > Y" THEN PRINT "X is greater than Y" ELSE PRINT "X is not greater than Y" ENDIF
EXIT
```

For 100% statement coverage of this pseudo code, one test case is sufficient, for example, X = 5, Y = 2 covers the three executable statements.

Advantages of statement testing include:

- Can exercise each line of code, ensuring that all statements are executed at least once, increasing the probability of detecting defects that might be in less frequently executed code paths
- Provides a metric for code coverage, which helps to assess the proportion of code exercised
- Is effective in finding syntax errors, logic errors, and other issues related to individual statements
- If a test case fails during statement testing, it can narrow down the location of the defect to a specific line of code, making debugging and fixing the issue more manageable
- Can often be automated, making it easier to rerun tests when code changes or updates are made, saving time and effort. The ease of automating statement testing depends on the complexity of the statements

Disadvantages of statement testing include:

- Does not guarantee all possible scenarios and specific combinations of statements have been tested. Certain business logic errors and integration issues may go undetected
- Lacks context: The testing is done at a low level, focusing on lines of code. It may not account for how different parts of the code interact with each other or how the test object behaves in real-world scenarios
- Achieving high statement coverage can be time-consuming, especially for large and complex code bases
- May provide a misleading low coverage value if the total number of statements in the source code has been calculated including dead, unused or unreachable code
- Does not detect design issues or incorrect business logic that may be present in the software

FL-4.3.2 (K2) Explain branch testing

The definition of **branch** from the Syllabus is, *'a transfer of control between two nodes in which source code statements are executed in the test object.'* Also from the Syllabus, *'Each transfer of control can be either unconditional (straight-line code) or conditional (a decision outcome) or unconditional (straight-line code)'.*

Conditional branches typically result from code statements such as:

- If .... then Action 1 Else Action 2
- Switch / Case
- Decision to Exit or Continue in a loop
- Guard clause
- Ternary operator

Branch coverage is defined as:

$$\text{Branch coverage} = \frac{\text{Number of branches exercised}}{\text{Total number of branches}} \times 100\%$$

To achieve 100% branch coverage, all branches must be exercised at least once, with the following met:

- All straight-line transfers of control must be covered
- All decision points must be covered for all outcomes (IF statements, Switch/Case statements).
- All logic operators must be covered for all outcomes.
- All decisions to exit or continue with loops must be covered.

Low branch coverage may indicate some scenarios have not been tested.
Note: 'Decision testing' is a subset of the ISTQB definition of branch testing. Decision testing tests outcomes when the transfer of control between two nodes is based on a decision (conditional branch). Decision testing does not therefore include testing unconditional transfers of control. Decision testing is distinct from decision table testing, which is a black-box test technique.

Example: Branch testing

Consider the following code:

```
START
READ X
READ Y
  IF "X > Y"  PRINT "X is greater than Y"  ELSE  PRINT "X is not greater than Y" ENDIF
EXIT
```

There are seven branches (A through G), as shown in the control flow diagram below.

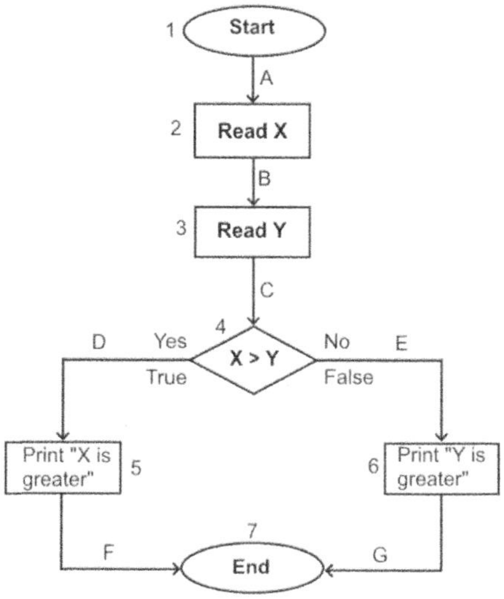

For 100% branch coverage of the pseudo-code two test cases are required, such as:

Test Case ONE, X=5, Y = 2

Test Case TWO, X=2, Y = 2

If only Test Case ONE is executed, 5 of the 7 branches are covered, (Branches are A, B, C, D, F), or 5/7 resulting in 71% coverage.

Advantages of branch testing include:

- Validates the control flow and the software behaves as intended
- Ensures all possible branches (true and false outcomes) of conditional statements, loops, and decision points are tested
- Can reveal logic errors in the code, such as incorrect conditions or unexpected outcomes
- More thorough testing compared to statement testing as it includes exercising code paths that may involve multiple statements and conditions
- Provides a clearer coverage metric than statement testing for assessing the code

Disadvantages of branch testing include:

- Does not cover all possible scenarios. While branch testing ensures that each branch of a conditional point is executed, it does not guarantee all combinations of conditions are tested when there are nested IF clauses and more complex conditional points that involve multiple conditions and dependencies that might be overlooked
- More costly than statement testing. In large and complex codebases, the number of test cases required to achieve high branch coverage can become prohibitively large, making the testing process time-consuming and resource-intensive
- May provide a misleading low coverage percentage if the total number of branches in the source code has been calculated including dead or unreachable code
- Should not be used with short-circuit programming. Short-circuit programming is where the compiler skips the execution or evaluation of some sub-expressions in a logical expression. The compiler stops evaluating the further sub-expressions as soon as the value of the expression is determined

FL-4.3.3 (K2) Explain the value of white-box testing

Advantages of white-box testing include:

- Can provide comprehensive coverage of the codebase. White-box testing helps test areas of the code that are not exercised by black-box or experienced-based testing
- Is useful when code is refactored. As software evolves, developers often need to refactor or modify code to improve performance efficiency, maintainability, or other aspects
- Can target specific areas of the code or simulate particular conditions, such as error handling or edge cases. This flexibility allows for precise testing of critical code segments
- In integration testing, helps to ensure interfaces are matched and components will work correctly together. This is especially valuable in complex systems
- Can serve as documentation for the codebase, making it easier for new developers to understand the internal workings of the software
- Helps with debugging as it uses the internal structure of the software to identify the defect more efficiently than may be possible by using other techniques
- Can be used in static testing. White-box test techniques are well-suited to review code that is not ready for execution, pseudo code and other high-level or top-down logic which can be modelled with a control flow graph

White-box testing has some limitations. These include:

Requires access to, good knowledge and understanding of the code and internal software structure.

May miss certain scenarios that could be uncovered by black-box testing, such as testing from a user perspective or missing requirements from the requirements specification.

Can provide insights into potential performance efficiency issues based on the use of certain code constructs, but is not a replacement for dedicated performance efficiency test techniques

Can identify some security vulnerabilities in the code such as such as code injection possibilities or buffer overflows, but should be backed up with other security test techniques

4.3 Questions 1 to 8 FL-4.3.1, 4.3.2, 4.3.3

Question 1 FL-4.3.1 (K2) How many test cases are required for 100% statement coverage of the pseudo-code?

```
Start
Read [Customer name]
Read [Record]
   If Age < 18  Then  Print “Reject” +[Customer name]  Else  Print “Accept” +[Customer name]
   Endif
Exit
```

a) 1
b) 2
c) 3
d) 4

Select ONE option

Question 2 FL-4.3.1 (K2) Consider the following control flow diagram.

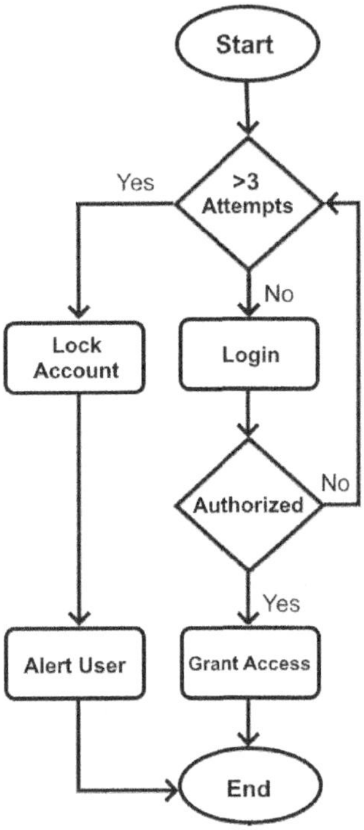

How many test cases are required for 100% statement coverage?

a) 3
b) 1
c) 2
d) 4

Select ONE option

Question 3 FL-4.3.1 / FL-4.3.2 (K2) Consider the control flow diagram with statements U to Z.

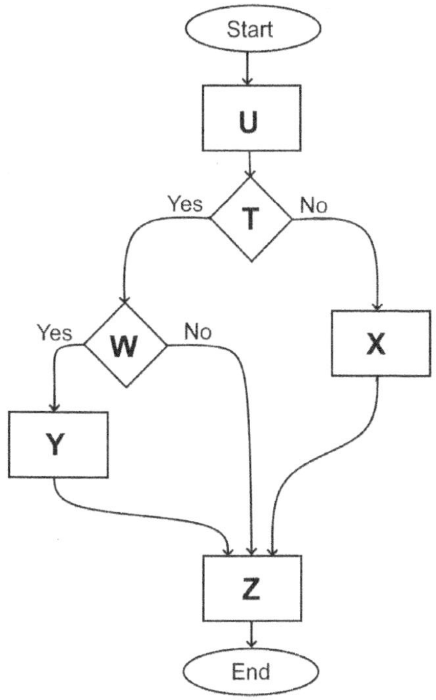

Which of the following is true for the test cases required?

a) Two for 100% statement coverage and three for 100% branch coverage
b) One for 100% statement coverage and two for 100% branch coverage
c) Three for 100% statement coverage and two for 100% branch coverage
d) Two for 100% statement coverage and two for 100% branch coverage

Select ONE option

Question 4 FL-4.3.1 / FL-4.3.2 (K2) Consider the control flow diagram with statements S to Z.

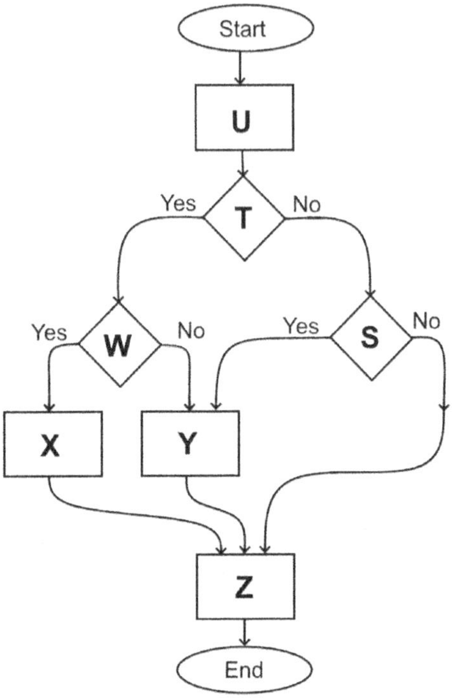

From 'Start' through to 'End', which of the following is true for the test cases required?

a) Two for 100% statement coverage and three for 100% branch coverage
b) Three for 100% statement coverage and four for 100% branch coverage
c) Four for 100% statement coverage and two for 100% branch coverage
d) Two for 100% statement coverage and four for 100% branch coverage

Select ONE option

Question 5 FL-4.3.2 (K2) Which of the following is false for branch testing?

a) All the different decision outcomes in the code are exercised
b) All transfers of control between two nodes are tested
c) Less costly in terms of time compared to statement testing
d) Subsumes statement coverage

Select ONE option

Question 6 FL-4.3.3 (K2) Which of the following best describes a value of white-box testing?

a) Ensures the software is user-friendly and intuitive
b) Identifies defects and vulnerabilities in the software's internal logic and structure
c) Validates the software's functionality against specified requirements
d) Assesses the software's response times under different load conditions

Select ONE option

Question 7 FL-4.3.3 (K2) Which of the following statements is not true for what white-box testing can achieve?

a) Ensure all of the code is exercised
b) Provide an objective assessment of code coverage
c) Target specific areas of the code
d) Identify gaps in the requirements specification

Select ONE option

Question 8 FL-4.3.3 (K2) Which of the following best describes when white-box testing can typically first start?

a) When a design model or the code is available
b) During the creation of software requirements specification
c) After the creation of the software requirements specification
d) During or after the installation of the software in the test environment

Select ONE option

4.3 Answers and Explanations 1 to 8 FL-4.3.1, 4.3.2, 4.3.3

Answer 1 FL-4.3.1

a) is the correct option. All statements are covered by one test case. All branches covered would require two test cases. b), c) and d) are not correct options for the reason given for a).

Answer 2 FL-4.3.1

c) is the correct option. Two test cases are required for 100% statement coverage.
Test case one: Start, successful Attempt, Login, Authorized, Access Granted, End.
Test case two: Start, unsuccessful fourth Attempt, Lock Account, Alert User, End.

Answer 3 FL-4.3.1 / FL-4.3.2

a) is the correct option. For 100% statement coverage – TC1: Start, U, T, W, Y, Z, End.
TC2: Start, U, T, X, Z, End. For branch coverage – TC1 and TC2 as for statement coveral plus TC3: Start, U, T, W, Z, End. b), c) and d) are not correct options for the reasons given for a).

Answer 4 FL-4.3.1 / FL-4.3.2

b) is the correct option. 100% statement coverage is achieved with, TC1: Start, U, T, S, Y, Z, End.
TC2: Start, U, T, W, Y, Z, End and TC3: Start, U, T, W, X, Z, End.
100% branch coverage is achieved with, TC1, TC2, TC3 as above plus TC4: Start, U, T, S, Z, End.
a), c) and d) are not correct options for the reasons given for b).

Answer 5 FL-4.3.2

c) is the correct option. Branch testing is more costly compared to statement testing.
a), b) and d) are not correct options as they are all true.

Answer 6 FL-4.3.3

b) is the correct option. With white-box testing, test cases evaluate the internal structure or code.
a) is not the correct option. White-box testing is structural testing. c) is not the correct option. White-box testing test cases are derived from the internal structure or code and not from the specified requirements. d) is not the correct option. Although white-box testing can identify code that may not be optimized for performance efficiency, it does not test response times under different loads.

Answer 7 FL-4.3.3

d) is the correct option. White-box testing is based on the internal structure of the software and not on the requirements specification. Therefore, white-box testing does not identify gaps in the requirements.
a) is not the correct option. White-box testing provides coverage metrics that show the amount of code that has been covered by testing. White-box testing can then identify additional tests to increase code coverage to 100%. b) is not the correct option. White-box testing can provide objective metrics on the amount of code checked. c) is not the correct option. White-box testing can target specific areas of the code, such as error handling.

Answer 8 FL-4.3.3
a) is the correct option. As the test cases are dependent on how the software is designed, they can be created as soon as design details or code is available.
b), c) and d) are not correct options for the reasons given for a).

4.4 Experience-based Test Techniques

Three commonly used experience techniques, error guessing, exploratory testing and checklist-based testing are covered by three learning objectives that are all at the K2 level. The ISTQB Exam Structures & Rules Tables v1.19 specify the exam questions on two out of the three learning objectives.

FL-4.4.1 (K2) Explain error guessing
Error guessing is a testing technique where testers use their skills, and knowledge of potential errors to guess and design test cases that target specific areas of the software where defects or vulnerabilities are likely to exist. Testers need to think creatively, use intuition and imagine how users will interact with the test object. This technique is an informal and ad hoc approach to testing that complements other testing techniques.

From the ISO 29119-1:2022 definition entry, 'The relevant knowledge [for error guessing] can be gained from personal experience, or can be encapsulated in, for example, a defects database or a "bug taxonomy".'

'Fault attack' is a methodical approach to the implementation of error guessing where the tester intentionally makes a directed and focused attempt to evaluate a specific characteristic of the test object by attempting to force specific failures to occur.

Error guessing provides value including:

- In situations where comprehensive requirements are lacking or time is limited, error guessing can help fill gaps in test coverage
- Enhancing overall test coverage by targeting areas not covered by other techniques

Disadvantages of error guessing include:

- Can lead to inconsistent test coverage if different testers make different assumptions about defect-prone areas
- May not effectively uncover potential defects, particularly in situations involving intricate business logic or complex algorithms
- Is typically not appropriate to rely solely on error guessing, particularly if the project requires a more systematic and documented test approach

FL-4.4.2 (K2) Explain exploratory testing

Exploratory testing is a technique where testers dynamically design, execute and evaluate tests based on their experience, skills, knowledge and exploration of the test item and the results of previous tests.

Exploratory testing does not eliminate the need for testers to prepare test ideas before test execution. Test charters can be created before execution which include test objectives and test ideas.

Key aspects of exploratory testing are:

- Involves the tester exploring the software and simultaneously designing and executing tests based on observations and insights gained during testing
- Often carried out without detailed test plans or scripts, allowing for flexibility and adaptability
- A highly interactive and iterative approach, where the tester's experience, intuition, and domain knowledge play a crucial role in uncovering defects and exploring the behavior of the test object
- Can uncover unexpected defects and scenarios not found by scripted techniques
- Can use a test charter containing test objectives to guide testing
- Test objectives may be used as high-level test conditions
- Coverage items are identified and executed during the test session
- Is sometimes performed using session-based testing or defined time-boxes to structure testing

Advantages of exploratory testing include:

- Testers can quickly gain increased familiarity with the test object
- Testers can make real-time decisions about where to focus their efforts and which areas to explore in more depth
- Allows for time and resource flexibility as testers can allocate time and resources based on the observed risks and priorities
- Complements other test approaches by adopting a different perspective, uncovering unexpected issues, and providing rapid feedback
- Particularly effective in scenarios where requirements are inadequate or out of date, the system is complex and time constraints limit test case development

Disadvantages of exploratory testing include:

- Possible lack of consistency as different testers perform the exploratory testing and this can lead to variations in testing coverage, priorities, and approaches. It may also result in inconsistent reporting of defects or observations
- Does not adhere to predetermined test cases so can be challenging to perform regression testing or ensuring that previously fixed defects have not resurfaced
- Relies heavily on testers' assumptions, possible biases and perspectives. Testers may inadvertently focus on areas they find interesting or assume the presence of defects without sufficient evidence. This can introduce biases and potentially overlook other critical areas that require testing

FL-4.4.3 (K2) Explain checklist-based testing

Checklist-based testing is a technique that uses predefined checklists to guide the test effort. The approach is systematic to ensure that specific criteria, requirements or best practices are checked. Checklists can be generic or more specific to various aspects of the software, such as functionality, usability, performance efficiency, security, compliance or even heuristics.

Checklists, in modern times, can be for manual use, automated if they contain items in an appropriate format or a combination of manual use and automated. Syllabus v4.0.1 states *'Checklists should not contain items that can be checked automatically, items better suited as entry criteria, exit criteria, or items that are too general (Brykczynski 1999)'*. This was not part of Syllabus 3.1. Many recent sources for some situations, advocate it is appropriate and effective to create checklists in a format that can then be used to automate the required checking to be done. As learning should primarily be aligned to the Syllabus, a checklist should be considered as a guide for a reviewer undertaking a software inspection process, and give guidance for finding defects during their examination of a work product.

Brykczynski made the following five points: (see *References*).

'1. Checklists should be regularly updated so that reviewers may be more likely to read and use them.'

'2. Checklists should not be longer than a single page. A reviewer is less inclined to flip through pages of a checklist while examining, say, a code listing. A single-page checklist can be placed on a desk and read in close proximity to the product being examined.'

'3. Checklist items should be phrased in the form of a question though question-based checklist items could be re-phrased as imperative sentences such as Verify.'

'4. Checklist items should not be too general, for example, 'Are all requirements complete, consistent, and unambiguous?' is too general.'

'5. Checklist items should not be used for conventions better enforced through other means such as the use of automated tools, entry criteria and exit criteria before the inspection meeting.'

In 1999, Brykczynski did not embrace a wider use of checklists with the possibility of automating checklists as part of testing. Automated checklist-based testing may not be suitable in all situations. However, it can help improve testing efficiency, reduce human error, and provide consistent and repeatable test execution.

If a checklist is automated, it may not need to be limited to one page as proposed by Brykczynski. However, care should be taken to ensure the checklist does not become too long as this will increase the effort needed to keep the checklist up to date or result in it becoming too unwieldy to be used.

Automating a checklist requires an appropriate, software-readable format. The evolution of Artificial Intelligence (AI) tools is improving the readability of different formats and natural language text.

Examples where automation of a checklist may be useful include:

Continuous Integration/Continuous Deployment (CI/CD) Pipelines: Checklist-based testing, can be integrated into the pipeline to ensure checks are performed automatically when code changes or deployments occur.

Pre-test setup: The checklist can include entries related to the setup of the test environment or the configuration of the test automation tools. This ensures that the necessary infrastructure and prerequisites are in place.

Test automation frameworks enable automation of the steps within a checklist by writing test scripts following the instructions.

Test case generation tools: Some tools offer test case generation capabilities, where the tool generates test cases automatically based on the checklist.

Spreadsheet automation: Checklists created in spreadsheet software can often be automated using built-in macro capabilities to automate tasks related to checklist items.
Test execution and monitoring: The checklist can include entries to verify that the automated tests are running as expected and producing the desired outcomes. This may involve checking test logs, reviewing test results, and monitoring the progress.

Post-test analysis: The checklist can include entries to analyze and evaluate results generated by automated tests. This can involve reviewing generated reports, identifying patterns or trends in test results, and comparing them with expected outcomes.

Advantages of checklist-based testing include:

- Created in advance an outline of items or criteria that need to be checked during testing. These checklists may be based on industry standards, best practices and generic or specific requirements.
- Can ensure critical areas of the software are thoroughly tested and no important items are missed.
- Can be useful for experienced testers to quickly and efficiently test.
- Can guide less experienced testers.
- Promotes consistency and standardization across the test process. Testers follow the same checklist, ensuring that all necessary aspects are addressed consistently.
- Can be tailored to fit the specific needs of the project. Testers can modify or extend the checklist based on the specific requirements, features, or risks associated with the software being tested.
- Can be reused across multiple testing cycles. As the project evolves, the checklist can be refined and expanded to incorporate new items or lessons learned from previous testing cycles.
- Supports the documentation of the test results and findings. Testers can track the status of each item on the checklist, note any deviations or issues found, and generate reports for stakeholders.
- Can be used in conjunction with other test techniques such as exploratory testing or scripted testing.

Disadvantages of checklist-based testing include:

- Testers may limit themselves to only considering entries on the checklist and ignore other potential problem areas.
- Checklist-based testing is not a substitute for critical thinking or exploratory testing.
- Over time, checklist entries may become outdated and fewer issues are found if the checklist is not regularly maintained.
- A checklist that is continually updated may become excessively long and therefore unusable.
- An organization may start with a well-defined test process but over time, reliance on and confidence in checklist-based testing may lead to parts of the defined test process being missed or ignored.

Including automated test-related items in a checklist can provide a holistic view of the test effort, combining both manual and automated aspects and help in capturing and addressing any additional considerations that may arise during testing.

4.4 Questions 1 to 8 FL-4.4.1, 4.4.2, 4.4.3

Question 1 FL-4.4.1 (K2) Which of the following statements is most true for error guessing?

a) A formal test technique that relies on the knowledge and skills of the tester
b) A test approach that Involves randomly selecting test cases without any specific focus
c) An informal test technique that can enhance overall test coverage
d) A test technique used to simulate user behavior by replicating actual usage patterns

Select ONE option

Question 2 FL-4.4.1 (K2) Error guessing is best explained by which of the following?

a) Uses the knowledge and experience testers have of defects identified in the past and typical errors made by developers
b) Tests the software at or beyond the limits of its specified requirements to determine its behavior
c) Imagines how a user will interact with the test object to guess the errors a user could make
d) Involves making assumptions about errors in the test object and eliminates the need for performing formal tests

Select ONE option

Question 3 FL-4.4.1 (K2) Error guessing on an updated release of an application includes the following, except for which?

a) Using the tester's experience of how the application has worked in the past
b) Creation of a comprehensive set of test scripts for use by test automation tools
c) Understanding of the types of errors the developers tend to make and the types of defects that result from these errors
d) Knowledge of the types of failures that have occurred in other, similar applications

Select ONE option

Question 4 FL-4.4.2 (K2) The technique of exploratory testing is which of the following?

a) Experience-based
b) White-box
c) Black-box
d) Glass-box

Select ONE option

Question 5 FL-4.4.2 (K2) Which best describes an informal test technique where a tester uses information gained while testing the software to design new and improved tests?

a) Decision table testing
b) Exploratory testing
c) Error guessing
d) Checklist-based testing

Select ONE option

Question 6 FL-4.4.2 (K2) Which of the following statements are least true for exploratory testing?

a) Makes it unnecessary for testers to prepare test ideas in advance of test execution
b) Can uncover unexpected problems that automated testing may miss
c) Supports gaining increased familiarity of the test object
d) Leverages the domain expertise and creativity of skilled testers
e) Testers do not need to have any understanding of the functioning of the test object

Select TWO options

Question 7 FL-4.4.3 (K2) Which of the following is least true for checklist-based testing?

a) Can result in more comprehensive testing compared to some other techniques
b) Can be quick and efficient for experienced testers to use
c) Is effective at finding defects in complex scenarios
d) When written in an appropriate format, can be easily automated

Select ONE option

Question 8 FL-4.4.3 (K2) Checklists should not include which of the following?

a) Graphical interface properties
b) Entry criteria and exit criteria
c) Functional testing elements
d) Non-functional testing elements

Select ONE option

4.4 Answers and Explanations 1 to 8 FL-4.4.1, 4.4.2, 4.4.3

Answer 1 FL-4.4.1

c) is the correct option. Error guessing can enhance overall test coverage by targeting areas not covered by other techniques. a) is not the correct option. Error guessing is a formal test technique, not a formal one. b) is not the correct option. The focus is to look for failures based on the experience and knowledge of testers. d) is not the correct option. Error guessing may include simulating user behavior but this is only part of the technique.

Answer 2 FL-4.4.1

a) is the correct option. Error guessing uses the knowledge and experience testers have of where defects and errors have occurred in the past. b) is not the correct option. Testing the software at or beyond the specified limits is primarily load and stress testing. c) is not the correct option. Imagining how a user will interact with the test object and guessing the errors a user could make is primarily part of usability testing. d) is not the correct option. Error guessing does not eliminate the need for performing tests.

Answer 3 FL-4.4.1

b) is the correct option. Error guessing is based on the experience of a tester and/or previous experience of other projects. The creation of new test scripts for use by automated test tools is outside the domain of error guessing.

a), c) and d) are not correct options as they are not within the error guessing technique.

Answer 4 FL-4.4.2

a) is the correct option. Exploratory testing is a test technique based on the tester's experience, knowledge and intuition. b), c) and d) are not correct options for the reasons given for a).

Answer 5 FL-4.4.2

b) is the correct option. Exploratory testing is a test technique where the tester gains knowledge of the test object while testing. a) is not the correct option. Decision table testing is a formal test technique. c) is not the correct option. Error guessing is based on using knowledge and experience from previous projects d) is not the correct option. Checklist-based testing uses a predefined list.

Answer 6 FL-4.4.2

a) and e) are the correct options as they are the least true. a) Test charters are created before execution which include test objectives and test ideas. e) While the tester may have limited familiarity with the test object, the tester needs to gain a good understanding of how the test object should function to be able to determine if what is found is, in fact, a failure.

b) is not a correct option. Exploratory testing is excellent at finding defects and issues that may not have been anticipated during the test planning phase and can uncover unexpected problems that automated tests may miss. c) is not a correct option. Exploratory testing supports concurrent learning. d) is not a correct option. Exploratory testing is an experience-based test technique.

Answer 7 FL-4.4.3

c) is the correct option. Checklist-based testing has a defined structure and may overlook complex, exploratory, or unscripted testing that often reveals defects.
a) is not the correct option. Checklist-based testing can help ensure comprehensive coverage by systematically checking off items on the checklist. Each item may represent a test case or condition that needs to be verified, contributing to thorough test coverage. b) is not the correct option. Experienced testers familiar with the test process can efficiently use checklists as they can quickly identify and execute the necessary related test cases. Thus, checklists provide a structured approach that can save time for testers. d) is not the correct option. A checklist in an appropriate format, can easily be automated by creating scripts or test cases that follow a checklist's instructions. Automated checklists help ensure consistent and repeatable test processes.

Answer 8 FL-4.4.3

b) is the correct option. Checklists should not include items better suited as entry criteria or exit criteria.
a), c) and d) are not correct options. Graphical interface properties, functional and non-functional testing can be included in checklist-based testing.

4.5 Collaboration-based Test Approaches

Each of the test techniques mentioned in the sections above on white-box, black-box and experience-based testing have particular objectives for defect detection. In comparison, collaborative-based approaches also focus on defect avoidance through collaboration, communication and teamwork. Involving a cross-functional team provides a broader skill set to support defect avoidance. This results in higher content quality and greater resilience, thus mitigating some risk.

The ISTQB Exam Structures & Rules Tables v1.19 specifies one question on either learning objective 4.5.1 or 4.5.2, both being K2 level. Learning objective 4.5.3, at K3 level is linked with the four learning objectives on black-box testing, for which five questions are specified on any of these. This may be revised in later versions of the ISTQB structure tables to have one question on each of the K3-linked learning objectives.

FL-4.5.1 (K2) Explain how to write user stories in collaboration with developers and business representatives

A user story, in collaborative approaches, comes from the team dividing up work into small functional increments. The aim of a user story is, once implemented, it yields a contribution to the value of the overall product, irrespective of the order of implementation.

A user story is commonly expressed in one sentence in the format:

As a **<role>**, I want to **<activity or capability>** so that **<some valuable outcome>**

This sentence must be clear and distinct. The goal must be an achievement aim and not an actor's task list. The actor can be:

Principle actor:	has user goals fulfilled by using the system.
Supporting actor:	provides a service to the system, for example the billing fulfillment component of an online ordering application.
Offstage actor:	has an interest in the behavior of the object under test, such as a regulatory body auditing the application

Examples:

As a new user of the website, I want to register so that I can buy listed products.

As an online bank customer, I want to access my bank statement so that I can keep track of my funds.

Key aspects of a collaborative approach to writing user stories include:

All team members are encouraged to participate in user story workshops and discussions

Team members provide diverse perspectives and contribute their expertise

All team members should have a common understanding of the user stories, and the expected value to end-users

User story content, prioritization, and scope should involve input from all appropriate stakeholders with collaborative decisions

Continuous feedback and refinement allow for enabling user stories to evolve as new information emerges

Team members actively listen to each other, and communicate effectively

Techniques such as story brainstorming, mapping, wireframes, mockups and whiteboarding can be used in a collaboration approach.

Note: In sequential development when requirements are not specified as user stories, a shared vision of the software is accomplished through formal reviews.

Several factors can hinder the collaboration of a team, making it less effective in achieving its objectives. Common issues that do not help collaboration include:

- Poor communication among team members can lead to misunderstandings, duplication of efforts, missed opportunities to share insights or findings, challenging to both understanding progress and contributing effectively
- If team members fail to share information with others, (knowledge siloing) it can make collaboration difficult and limit the collective understanding of the project
- An inappropriate competitive atmosphere or lack of trust can inhibit teamwork and result in suboptimal collaboration
- Inadequate documentation of test plans, test cases, and test results can make it challenging for team members to understand the testing progress and contribute effectively
- When team members have conflicting or unclear goals, it can result in different priorities
- If the test team lacks appropriate collaboration platforms or access to necessary resources, this can hinder their ability to work together efficiently
- Without strong support from leadership, team members may feel demotivated and undervalued, affecting their willingness to collaborate and contribute to the team
- Frequent turnover in a test team can disrupt team dynamics and make it challenging to build a strong and cohesive collaboration culture

For successful collaboration in creating user stories, participants need a clear understanding of the three 'Cs', essential aspects of user stories. These are:

Card: The card is the physical media that describes a user story, such as an index card or an entry on an electronic board. The card identifies the requirement, its priority and the acceptance criteria. It also includes expected development time and test duration.

Conversation/Communication: The requirements are communicated and understood between the business representatives, users, developers and testers. How the software will be used is explained and this can be documented or verbal. Conversation/communication should start during the release-planning stage and be ongoing.

Confirmation: The specified acceptance criteria for the user story should be tested and satisfied.

A team may use the INVEST technique to assess the quality of a user story. INVEST is an acronym for:

- Independent: Discrete or self-contained, does not rely on another user story based on order, overlap or containment
- Negotiable: Always can be subject to change
- Valuable: of value to the business or customer
- Estimable: Can be estimated
- Small: Small enough to be planned as part of an iteration
- Testable: Unambiguous, sufficient detail, has an identifiable expected result that can be compared with the actual result

Teams may vary the way they document user stories. Regardless of the approach taken, documentation should be concise, sufficient, and necessary.

The tester's role in user story conversations and creation includes identifying:

- Gaps or missing details, such as inputs, by asking open-ended questions to other members of the cross-functional team
- Missing functional and non-functional requirements in stories and helping the team to complete them
- Ambiguity or overlap
- Missing elements such as non-functional aspects and suggesting ways to test the story
- Dependencies on order
- Testability, such as it possible to set up the required circumstances
- Different ways to test a user story

FL-4.5.2 (K2) Classify the different options for writing acceptance criteria

Acceptance Criteria are specific conditions that must be met for a user story or specified requirement to be considered complete and ready for delivery. They provide details on how the test object should behave and what is expected to ensure the test object meets its intended purpose. Acceptance criteria help:

- Define and refine the scope of the user story or requirement to avoid ambiguity and provide a clear definition of done
- Reach consensus among the stakeholders
- Describe both positive and negative behavior
- Serve as a basis for Acceptance Test-driven Development, ATDD
- Help with better accuracy in planning and test estimation

Acceptance criteria can be classified, depending on the specific context, the project's needs and the level of detail required. The two most commonly used ways to write and classify acceptance criteria are scenario-oriented and rule-oriented.

Scenario-oriented acceptance criteria are characterized by a detailed description of how a software feature or user story should function in various situations with a focus on user value. The acceptance criteria can, for example, be written based on narrative statements or the Gherkin format of Given/When/Then used in Behavior-driven development (BDD).

Narrative statements describe the desired behavior or functionality of the software typically in plain, descriptive language. Gherkin format is based on the structured syntax of **'Given/When/Then'**. 'Given' describes the initial preconditions or setup, 'When' specifies the actions or inputs, and 'Then' states the expected outcomes. This format helps ensure the preconditions, actions, and expected outcomes of a scenario are included.

Rule-oriented acceptance criteria detail the behavior and requirements based on specific rules that must be met for the software to be considered acceptable or complete. Rules must be specific and measurable with constraints identified. The rules can be derived from business logic rules, standards or regulatory requirements. Rule-oriented acceptance criteria can be a bullet point verification checklist or a tabulated form of input-output mapping.

FL-4.5.3 (K3) Use Acceptance Test-driven Development (ATDD) to derive test cases

Acceptance test-driven development (ATDD) involves team members with different perspectives (customer, business, development, testing) collaborating to create acceptance tests before the implementation of the corresponding user story or requirement. While user stories are often used in ATDD, the principles and practices of ATDD can be applied to various types of requirements or specifications. This includes functional requirements, system specifications, business rules, regulatory compliance criteria and non-functional requirements such as performance efficiency and usability (interaction capability). The primary principle is to have acceptance criteria collaboratively defined and test cases then derived based on the requirements or specifications, regardless of the specific format or terminology used.

When acceptance criteria are in a format supported by a test automation framework, developers can automate the test cases by writing the supporting code as they implement the feature and then if required make modifications to improve the code. A major risk the team should be aware of is that an automation tool used by development may hinder rather than advance collaboration with other team members. Tools should be adapted to meet the team's needs rather than the other way around.

Key stages in ATDD are:

Step 1: Hold a specification workshop where user stories or requirements and (if not yet defined) acceptance criteria are analyzed, discussed, and written by the team members. Ensure there is a common understanding. Identify incompleteness, ambiguities, or defects in the user stories.

Step 2: Create the test cases based on the acceptance criteria. This can be done by the team as a whole or by an individual tester before coding the area covered by the test case starts. Tests are written in a natural language format that both technical and non-technical stakeholders can understand. No two test cases should describe the same characteristics, this avoids problems if test cases are allocated to different developers. Typically, the first test cases designed are positive, confirming the correct behavior without exceptions or error conditions, and comprising the sequence of activities executed if everything goes as expected. After the positive test cases are done, the team should perform negative testing.

Step 3: After minimum code has been written and test case results are determined as passed, typically there will be code refactoring. Acceptance test cases should be rerun to ensure that the changes made during refactoring did not break the desired functionality. Throughout the process, communication with stakeholders should be maintained, feedback gathered, and improvements based on the feedback received may be made to test cases.

Example: Writing acceptance criteria and deriving test cases from a user story.
User Story: As a registered user, I want to be able to reset my password so that I can maintain a higher level of security of access to my account.

Scenario Acceptance Criteria using Given/When/Then format for positive outcomes:

AC1: Given I am on the login page, When I tap the 'Reset Password' link,
Then a password reset page is displayed.

AC2: Given I am on the password reset page, When I enter my email address and submit it,
Then I receive an email with a link to reset my password.

AC3: Given I have received the password reset email, When I tap the reset link in the email,
Then I am taken to a page where I can enter a new password.

AC4: Given I have entered a new password and confirmed it, When I submit the form,
Then the system confirms that my password has been reset.

AC5: Given I have reset my password, When I try to log in with the new password,
Then I can successfully access my account.

Note: Acceptance criteria are also required for negative outcomes, detailing requirements for error messages and appropriate actions to be taken by the software.

Test Cases:

TC1: Verify tapping the "Reset Password" link on the login page displays the password reset page.
TC2: Verify submitting an email address on the password reset page sends a reset email.
TC3: Verify tapping the reset link in the email takes me to the password reset page.
TC4: Verify submitting a new password on the password reset page successfully changes my password.
TC5: Verify after resetting my password, I can successfully log in with the new password.

FL-4.5.3 (K3) Exercise: Acceptance Test-driven Development

Identify inaccuracies in the following description of an acceptance test-driven development approach.

1. Stakeholders collaborate to gather and define requirements, expressed as user stories. They work closely together to define clear and specific acceptance criteria for each user story.
2. A collaborative session is then held between the developer and the tester to discuss and clarify acceptance criteria and ensure a common understanding.
3. Test cases based on the acceptance criteria are created. These are written to be understandable to developers and aid automation but may not be understandable by others.
4. Developers use the test cases to guide code implementation of the user story requirement, with the aim of making the test cases pass.
5. Testers use different tests to independently verify the implemented requirement meets the defined acceptance criteria. Any discrepancies or defects are reported and addressed.
6. An implemented requirement, when developed and successfully tested, is demonstrated to stakeholders to ensure alignment with expectations.
7. Regression testing is now performed to check existing functionality has not been adversely affected.
8. Based on feedback from stakeholders, any necessary adjustments are made. This may involve refining the criteria or addressing new insights.
9. After incorporating feedback and making changes, code is incorporated into the continuous deployment pipeline

FL-4.5.2 Exercise Answer

There are four inaccuracies which are:

2 The collaborative session to discuss and identify acceptance criteria and ensure a common understanding should include a business representative or product owner. The collaborative session is often referred to as a specification workshop or the 'Three Amigos'.

3 Test cases should be written in a language format that both technical and non-technical stakeholders can understand.

5 Testers use the same acceptance test cases.

7 Regression testing should be performed after feedback and changes have been made and before incorporation into the deployment pipeline.

4.5 Questions 1 to 11 FL-4.5.1, 4.5.2, 4.5.3

Question 1 FL-4.5.1 (K2) Which of the following do not contribute to a successful collaborative approach to writing user stories?

a) Introducing a competitive atmosphere to encourage the development of individual team members
b) Encouraging frequent turnover in the test team to ensure different perspectives are considered
c) Ensuring goals are aligned for all team members and appropriate stakeholders and understood
d) Having input on user story content, prioritization, and scope from appropriate stakeholders
e) Ensuring there is a team focus on the end user's requirements

Select TWO options

Question 2 FL-4.5.1 (K2) When team members with different roles work collaboratively to write user stories, which of the following is least likely to be a factor that contributes to a successful outcome?

a) Frequent communication between the different roles
b) Small portions of the work identified and worked on concurrently to the extent possible
c) Shared responsibility for software quality
d) Team members build knowledge silos

Select ONE option

Question 3 FL-4.5.1 (K2) When adopting a collaborative approach to writing user stories, which of the following best describes an action that contributes to a successful outcome?

a) Limit input from cross-functional team members
b) Ensure frequent opportunities for conversations and other communication between team members
c) Ensure acceptance criteria are sufficiently broad to cover different interpretations by various stakeholders
d) Arrange for individual team members to write different user stories so that a comprehensive set of user stories is written by the team in the shortest and most resource-efficient way

Select ONE option

Question 4 FL-4.5.1 (K2) In collaborative writing of a user story, if a stakeholder, such as a developer or a tester, does not know how to test a user story this may indicate the following except for which?

a) The user story is not adequately clear
b) The user story does not reflect something of value to the stakeholder
c) The stakeholder has access to the test environment with the software installed
d) The stakeholder needs help with testing

Select ONE option

Question 5 FL-4.5.2 (K2) Which of the following is the correct format for writing scenario-oriented acceptance criteria for use with Behavior-driven Development?

a) Given/When/Then
b) When/Given/Then
c) Given/Then/When
d) When/Then/Given

Select ONE option

Question 6 FL-4.5.2 (K2) Which of the following are the two commonly used formats that most acceptance criteria can be classified by?

a) Scenarios
b) Implementation details
c) Technical specifications
d) Rules
e) Test execution procedures

Select TWO options

Question 7 FL-4.5.2 (K2) Using which of the following best describes a way of documenting scenario-oriented acceptance criteria?

a) Bullet point verification list
b) Given/When/Then format
c) Tabulated form of input-output mapping
d) Technical implementation specification

Select ONE option

Question 8 FL-4.5.2 (K2) When determining if acceptance criteria should be written as rule-oriented or scenario-oriented, which of the following are true?

a) When the primary focus is to validate data or calculations rigorously, rule-oriented acceptance criteria are appropriate, scenario-oriented acceptance criteria are typically used when the primary focus is on the user's experience and how they interact with the software
b) Rule-oriented acceptance criteria use the rule 'Given/Then/When' format, scenario-oriented acceptance criteria are always written in a free format
c) Rule-oriented acceptance can use a tabulated form of input-output mapping, scenario-oriented acceptance criteria are used when strict adherence to a standard is mandated
d) Rule-oriented acceptance criteria can be more precise for communicating exact conditions and actions, scenario-oriented acceptance criteria provide a broader context for a user story
e) Rule-oriented acceptance criteria describe positive and negative outcomes, scenario-oriented acceptance criteria describe only positive scenarios

Select TWO options

Question 9 FL-4.5.3 (K3) You have the following scenario acceptance criteria using narrative statements for an application that tracks task completions:

A tester can log into the project management tool and view their assigned projects and tasks

The tester should be able to select a task, add or update any relevant comments or attachments and then when the tester has completed the task, mark it as 'Completed', the system should send an email confirming this to the project manager

Using the narrative acceptance criteria above, which of the following would be an appropriate test case for positive behavior?

a) When relevant comments or attachments are made to a task record, the project manager is notified of these by email
b) After changing the status of an assigned task to 'Completed', relevant comments or attachments can be added
c) The tester can view all projects and tasks
d) When the status of an assigned task is changed to 'Completed', the project manager is notified of this by email

Select ONE option

Question 10 FL-4.5.3 (K3) You have the rule-oriented acceptance criteria for the 'Payment Process' part of the software:

Rule 1: User should be able to make a payment for the items selected.
Rule 2: User should receive an order confirmation and payment receipt.

You have the following test cases:

1. User can add and remove items from their shopping cart
2. User can select a specified payment method
3. Payment process securely collects payment information
4. Payment is successfully processed
5. User can indicate standard or premium delivery
6. User receives a payment confirmation message or email after a successful payment
7. The payment receipt contains accurate details of the order and payment amount
8. User can track delivery

Which of the following best describes test cases that have been derived from the given acceptance criteria?

a) 2, 4, 8
b) 1, 2, 3, 5, 6, 7
c) 2, 3, 4, 6, 7
d) 4, 5, 7, 8

Select ONE option

Question 11 FL-4.5.3 (K3) Consider the following user story.
As a manager, I want to be able to view employee leave requests so that I can approve or reject them.

Acceptance criteria have been determined as:

The manager should be able to view all already booked leave of all team members and all new leave requests submitted by employees.
The leave requests must display the leave type, employee's name, employee number and requested dates.
The manager should be able to approve or reject leave requests by clicking on the appropriate buttons.
After approving or rejecting a leave request, the employee should be notified on behalf of the manager of the decision.
Approved leave requests should be reflected in the booked leave of all team members and in the employee's leave balance.

Which of the following tests are not derived or are incorrectly derived from the given acceptance criteria?

a) An employee can check they have sufficient leave remaining to cover the leave request before submitting the request
b) The manager can view all pre-booked approved leave
c) The employee is notified on behalf of the manager if the leave is approved
d) The leave request is complete when it includes the employee's name, employee number and requested dates
e) A rejected leave request does not alter the employee's leave balance

Select TWO options

4.5 Answers and Explanations 1 to 11 FL-4.5.1, 4.5.2, 4.5.3

Answer 1 FL-4.5.1 K2

a) and b) are the correct options. a) A competitive atmosphere between team members does not aid team collaboration. b) High turnover in the test team can be disruptive to collaboration.
c) is not a correct option. Alignment of goals is a key requirement for collaboration to be successful.
d) is not a correct option. Input from appropriate stakeholders is part of a collaboration approach.
e) is not a correct option. A team focus on the end user's requirements ensures the stories deliver value to the intended users.

Answer 2 FL-4.5.1 K2

d) is the correct option. A knowledge silo is where someone has information or skills that are not shared.
a) is not the correct option. Frequent communication is essential for collaborative working roles.
b) is not the correct option. dividing the work is part of a collaborative approach.
c) is not the correct option.

Answer 3 FL-4.5.1 K2

b) is the correct option. Good communication is essential for a collaborative approach.

a) is not the correct option. A good outcome of a collaborative approach is achieved when cross-functional team members are included.

c) is not the correct approach. Acceptance criteria should be clean and well-defined so that all team members have a common understanding.

d) is not the correct option. Individuals working on different user stories is not a collaborative approach.

Answer 4 FL-4.5.1 K2

c) is the correct option. Having access to the test environment does not indicate anything about the stakeholder's ability to know how to test a user story. The other options, unclear user story, not of value to the stakeholder or help required could all be indications of why the stakeholder does not know how to test a user story. a), b) and d) are not correct options for the reasons given for c).

Answer 5 FL-4.5.2 K2

a) is the correct option. The correct format for writing acceptance criteria is "Given/When/Then". 'Given' describes the context and is first, 'When' describes some action to be carried out, and 'Then' specifies the observable consequence.

b), c and d) are not correct options for the reasons given for a).

Answer 6 FL-4.5.2 K2

a) and d) are the correct options. Most acceptance criteria can be documented in either a scenario-oriented or rule-based format.

b) is not a correct option. Acceptance criteria focus on the expected behavior and outcomes of the software and not on how the software implementation should be done. Implementation details are typically left to the discretion of the development team.

c) is not a correct option. Acceptance criteria typically do not include technical.

e) is not a correct option. Acceptance criteria do not provide explicit instructions on how to execute tests. Test execution details are typically documented in separate test plans and/or test scripts.

Answer 7 FL-4.5.2 K2

b) is the correct option. The Given/When/Then format is used with Behavior-Driven Development to describe the situation, action and outcome.

a) and c) are not correct options. Rule-oriented acceptance criteria may be based on a bullet point verification list or a tabulated form of input-output mapping.

d) is not the correct option. Technical implementation details are not typically part of the acceptance criteria.

Answer 8 FL-4.5.2 K2

a) and d) are the correct options. The classification of acceptance criteria as either rule-based or scenario-based is determined by the nature of the requirement, the desired level of detail, and the specific context of the software being developed.

c) is the correct option. Rule-oriented criteria explicitly state the condition and the resulting action based on that condition. Instead of specifying a strict rule, scenario-oriented criteria focus on how the system should respond to different customer actions.

b) is not the correct option. Scenario-oriented acceptance criteria can be written with the Given/Then/When format used with Behavior-driven Development. Rule-oriented acceptance criteria may be based on a bullet-point verification list, be in a tabular form or other precise format.

c) is not a correct option as rule-oriented acceptance criteria are typically written for situations where strict compliance with certain rules or standards is essential.

e) is not a correct option. Both scenario-oriented criteria and rule-oriented criteria can be written to describe either positive or negative outcomes.

Answer 9 FL-4.5.3 K3

d) is the correct option. Testing whether an email confirmation is sent to the project manager should be done after the status of the task is changed to 'Completed'.

a) is not the correct option. Email confirmation is not sent to the project manager until the tester sets the status to 'Completed'. b) is not the correct option. Relevant comments or attachments should be added before the status of the task is changed to 'Completed'.

c) is not the correct option. A tester should only be authorized to view tasks assigned to them.

Answer 10 FL-4.5.3 K3

c) is the correct option. Test cases 2, 3, 4, 6 and 7 all relate to the 'Payment Process' and are derived from the rule-oriented acceptance criteria.

a), b) and d) are not correct options.

Test case 1: User can add and remove items from their shopping cart. This is part of 'Selection of goods' and is not included in the rules.

Test case 5: User can indicate standard or premium delivery is not included as part of the rules given. This is part of the stage before payment.

Test case 8: User can track delivery is not a requirement that can be determined from the rules given.

Answer 11 FL-4.5.3 K3

a) and d) are the correct options. a) The user story focuses on the manager's perspective, The employee's requirements for submission are separate. d) The leave type, such as annual, compassionate or in place of overtime has been omitted.

b) is not a correct option. The manager should be able to view previously booked and approved leave.

c) is not a correct option. The test is derived from the acceptance criteria, which specify the employee should be notified on behalf of the manager. A missing test for notification of refusal does not invalidate the test for notification of acceptance. e) is not the correct option. A rejected leave request is a valid test.

5. MANAGING THE TEST ACTIVITIES

The ISTQB Exam Structures & Rules Tables v1.19 specifies nine exam questions for this section. There are four K1, nine K2 and three K3 level learning objectives. Those at K3 are FL-5.1.4, 5.1.5, 5.5.1.

Keywords given in the Syllabus

defect management, defect report, entry criteria, exit criteria, product risk, project risk, risk, risk analysis, risk assessment, risk control, *risk identification, risk level, risk management, risk mitigation, risk monitoring, risk-based testing, test approach, test completion report, †test control, †test monitoring, test plan, test planning, test progress report, test pyramid, testing quadrants, test strategy.

Not identified as a keyword in the Glossary or Syllabus: smoke test.

*Risk identification as defined in the Glossary is, *'The process of finding, recognizing and describing risks.'* ISO25010:2023 defines risk identification as, 'The capability of the product to identify a course of events or operations that can expose life, property or environment to unacceptable risk'.

†Test control and test monitoring are included in the Syllabus in sections 1 and 5.

5.1 Test Planning

Test planning is an important phase of the test process where a plan is developed to guide the test efforts for a particular project. Test planning ensures that testing is organized, structured, and aligned with the project's requirements.

FL-5.1.1 (K2) Exemplify the purpose and content of a test plan

The purpose of a test plan is that it serves to:

- Provide clear guidance and direction for the testing team by defining what needs to be tested, how it should be tested, and when testing activities will occur. This serves to focus test efforts and should ensure they are well-organized.
- Support ongoing comparisons of actual progress against planned progress.
- Ensure the testing objectives are aligned with the project's goals and requirements.
- Demonstrate testing will adhere to existing test policy and strategy or explain variation.
- Define the scope of what will be tested and this prevents misunderstandings and scope creep.
- Outline the required resources, including personnel, tools, equipment, and environments, to ensure the necessary resources are allocated appropriately.
- Identify the test approach, methodologies and techniques that will be used.
- Outline how different test types; functional, performance efficiency, security will be performed.
- Provide a timeline for different testing phases, ensuring that testing activities are integrated into the overall project schedule and deadlines.
- Act as a means of communication between team members and other stakeholders.
- Helps ensure stakeholders share a common understanding.
- Provide a record of how testing was planned and executed for future reference.

Contents of a test plan can include:

Section	Content
Introduction	Overview of the purpose and scope of the test plan. Identification of the software/application being tested. Brief description of the project's background and objectives.
Test Objectives	Clear statement of the test objectives. Explanation of what needs to be achieved through testing.
Testing Scope	Definition of what is included and excluded from the testing such as identification of the features, functions, and components to be tested. List of standards, regulatory, contractual requirements that must be adhered to.
Test Policy and Strategy	Confirmation of adherence to test policy and test strategy or details of and explanations for where testing will vary from test policy and test strategy
Test Approach	Details of the testing methodologies, and techniques to be used, such as where manual testing and where automated testing will be used. The levels of testing (component, integration, system, etc.). Overview of how different types of testing (functional, performance efficiency, security, etc.) will be performed. Overview of how testing will be determined complete for each phase.
Test Deliverables	List of work products that will be produced as a result of testing (test cases, test scripts, defect reports, etc.) Details on how deliverables will be organized and managed.
Test Environment	Description of the hardware, software, and network configurations required for testing. Information about tools and testing frameworks to be used.
Test Schedule	Timeline for different testing phases and activities. Dependencies on other project activities and milestones.
Test Resources	Testing roles and responsibilities. Identification of any external resources or third-party vendors involved in testing.
Test Risks and Mitigation	Identification of potential risks and challenges related to testing. Strategies and plans for mitigating and managing those risks.
Test Cases	Details about how tests will be executed, including test case prioritization and regression testing.
Defect Management	Process for reporting, tracking, and managing anomalies, defects or issues discovered during testing. Definition of severity and priority levels for defects.
Metrics and Reports	Metrics and measurements to track the progress and quality of testing. Reporting frequency and format for communicating testing status to stakeholders.
Approvals and Sign off	Names and roles of individuals who need to approve the test plan. Process for obtaining approval and sign-off on the test plan.
References	List of references, standards, and documents used in creating the test plan.

Each section of the test plan should, if relevant, also include details of any constraints or restrictions that may apply. A sample test plan structure and test plan template can be found in the standard ISO/IEC/IEEE 29119-3. See *References*.

FL-5.1.2 (K1) Recognize how a tester adds value to iteration and release planning
With iterative software development lifecycles, there are typically two kinds of planning, release planning and iteration planning.

Release planning looks ahead to the release of the product and serves as the basis for the test approach and test plan across all iterations.

Iteration planning looks ahead to the end of a single iteration.

Differences between release planning and iteration planning:

	Release planning	**Iteration planning**
Scope	Focuses on a broader scope, typically spanning multiple iterations or sprints. Involves high-level planning and mapping out the overall objectives and features for a product deployment.	Focuses on a smaller scope, usually one iteration or sprint. Involves more detailed planning.
Timeframe	Covers a longer timeframe, often several months to a year, depending on the size and complexity of the project.	Covers a shorter timeframe and is repeated at the beginning of each iteration/sprint. A sprint typically lasts one to four weeks.
Objectives	Defines the high-level objectives for the release. This involves identifying the key features, user stories, and functionalities that need to be delivered by the end of the release.	Breaks down the user stories into smaller, actionable items that can be completed within the iteration.
Prioritization	The team decides on the priority of features and user stories based on business value, customer feedback, and other strategic considerations.	The team selects a subset of user stories or tasks from the product backlog based on priority, complexity, and feasibility.
Backlog	Defines and redefines the product backlog.	Is concerned with the iteration backlog.
Team size / Resource allocation	Sets the overall team capacity with consideration of any constraints that might impact the delivery timeline.	Allocates resources based on the team's capacity for the upcoming iteration.

A tester can add value to release planning by:

- Contributing their expertise to ensure that the quality aspects of the release are considered during the planning phase. They advocate for sufficient time and resources dedicated to testing activities
- Participating in writing testable user stories that can be used as requirements
- Collaborating with stakeholders to define clear and meaningful acceptance criteria for user stories
- Participating in project and quality risk analysis
- Providing input on estimating the time required for testing tasks
- Collaborating with the team to define the overall testing strategies for the release
- Contributing to the creation of a high-level test plan that outlines the testing scope, objectives, approach, and resources required

A tester can add value to iteration planning by:

- Determining the testability of user stories
- Breaking down user stories into testing tasks
- Estimating the test effort for all testing tasks in the iteration
- Identifying and refining functional and non-functional aspects of the test object

FL-5.1.3 (K2) Compare and contrast entry criteria and exit criteria

Entry criteria specify the conditions that must be satisfied before a phase, process, or project can begin. Using entry criteria ensures the necessary prerequisites, budget, resources and information are available for a successful start. For example, entry criteria for the test execution phase for a flight ticket booking application could include the necessary backend services, such as database access and API endpoints for flight data / data retrieval, which are developed and available for use in testing.

Exit criteria given in the Glossary as having the synonym completion criteria, define the conditions that must be met before a particular phase, process, or project can be considered complete and satisfactory making it ready to move to the next stage or to be deployed into production. For example, exit criteria for the test execution phase for a flight ticket booking application could include functionality that has been verified to meet the approved design and requirements.

Entry and Exit criteria are both useful for promoting order, quality and efficiency in the test process, to ensure tasks progress smoothly. The exit criteria from one phase may be the entry criteria to the next phase. For example, the exit criteria from the test design phase may specify that 90% of test cases have been designed and are ready to be implemented. This could be the entry criteria for the test implementation phase.

Differences between entry and exit criteria include:

	Entry criteria	Exit criteria
Purpose	Focus is on ensuring preparedness for starting a task or phase	Focus is on evaluating completion and readiness for progressing
Timing	Evaluated before a phase or process begins	Assessed at the end of a phase or process
Validation	Validate the prerequisites for the next phase	Validate the outcomes of a phase
Summary	Relate to the requirements for starting the work	Relate to the outcome of the work

Note: The Definition of Ready (DoR) and Definition of Done (DoD) are two concepts primarily used in Agile software development that are sometimes incorrectly assumed to be the same as entry and exit criteria.

Definition of Ready (DOR) involves having clear criteria that a user story must meet before being accepted into an upcoming iteration. Definition of Ready ensures user stories are adequately prepared and defined.

Entry criteria ensure that the environment, resources, and prerequisites are met before initiating a task or process and are applied in various phases such as requirements gathering, test design and more.

Definition of Done (DoD) is an agreed-upon list of the activities deemed necessary to achieve a product increment, usually represented by a user story, to a 'Done' state by the end of a sprint. DoD ensures user stories are developed and tested to a specified quality level before being considered complete.

Exit criteria ensure specific conditions and requirements have been met before moving forward.

5.1 Questions 1 to 10 FL-5.1.1, 5.1.2, 5.1.3

Question 1 FL-5.1.1 (K2) Which of the following are most correct for the purpose or content of a test plan?

a) A document for use by testers, the test policy and test strategy documents are available for management and other stakeholders
b) Written at the start of the project and defines the scope, schedule and potential risks which then remain in place without change throughout the test process
c) Serves as a means of communication for team members and other stakeholders
d) Documents the sequence of test cases in execution order and any associated actions that may be required to set up the initial preconditions
e) Provides for a coordinated approach to the test process and demonstrates testing will adhere to existing test policy or explain why testing will deviate from it

Select TWO options

Question 2 FL-5.1.1 (K2) Which part of a test plan does the following belong to?

'Component testing and component integration testing will be undertaken with testing, as specified in the requirements, for 100% branch coverage for each component classified as critical.'

a) Test approach
b) Assumptions and constraints
c) Context of testing
d) Project and product risks

Select ONE option

Question 3 FL-5.1.2 (K2) During an iteration planning meeting, the team is considering a user story. The business representative advises that the customer should have two linked screens to enter the information. Developers state there are technical limitations with linked screens, particularly when switching between screens while entering data. Developers also raised further concerns about application response times.

Which of the following best represents advice a tester should give to the iteration planning meeting?

a) The user story needs to be a single page to reduce the test automation effort
b) Usability is more important than performance efficiency and response time
c) The user story needs acceptance criteria to be testable
d) The response time should be specified and be two seconds or less

Select ONE option

Question 4 FL-5.1.2 (K1) When planning an iteration or release, a tester typically contributes to the following except for which?

a) Detailed risk analysis of user stories
b) Determining the testability of user stories
c) Estimating the development time
d) Identifying non-functional aspects of the test object
e) Defining the regulatory requirements

Select TWO options

Question 5 FL-5.1.2 (K1) How do testers add value to release planning?

a) Ensure the release of stable, reliable and secure software
b) Make decisions on the project's budget
c) Focus only on the functional aspects of the system to be tested
d) Provide insights into potential risks

Select ONE option

Question 6 FL-5.1.3 (K2) A set of requirements that must be met before the test process can start are known as what?

a) Validation criteria
b) Acceptance criteria
c) Success criteria
d) Entry criteria

Select ONE option

Question 7 FL-5.1.3 (K2) Which of the following would not typically be considered to be entry criteria for test analysis to start?

a) The budget is in place
b) The test environment is available
c) The schedule for test phases is in place
d) The test basis has been reviewed and approved

Select ONE option

Question 8 FL-5.1.3 (K2) Which of the following could be included as test execution exit criteria?

a) 80% of the test cases created to cover the identified minimum test coverage have been executed
b) All defects are found and those assessed to be high or medium levels of concern have been confirmed as resolved by fixes or other mitigation
c) Testing has shown the system is secure
d) All test cases have been created for all test conditions identified

Select ONE option

Question 9 FL-5.1.3 (K2) Consider the following as exit criteria and the test process phases:

1. Test environment is available
2. Test data to support test conditions and test cases has been identified
3. Ambiguities in the test basis have been identified and resolved
4. Confirmation testing has been undertaken

A. Test implementation
B, Test analysis
C. Test execution
D. Test design

Which of the following best links the exit criteria to the test phase?

a) 1B, 2A, 3D, 4C
b) 1C, 2D, 3A, 4B
c) 1C, 2A, 3B, 4D
d) 1A, 2D, 3B, 4C

Select ONE option

Question 10 FL 5.1.3 (K2) Which of the following statements best describes entry and exit criteria?

a) Entry criteria are requirements defined by stakeholders at the start of the project, exit criteria are determined by the project manager at the close of the project
b) Entry criteria define requirements that must be met before a defined test phase can start, exit criteria define requirements that must be met before a defined test phase can be considered to have been completed
c) Entry criteria are the same as Definition of Ready (DOR), and exit criteria are the same as Definition of Done (DOD)
d) Entry criteria are readiness conditions for the test process or phase to start and are established by the test team, exit criteria serve the same purpose as acceptance criteria and are defined by the end-user

Select ONE option

5.1 Answers and Explanations 1 to 10 FL-5.1.1, 5.1.2, 5.1.3

Answer 1 FL-5.1.1 K2

c) and e) are correct options. c) The test plan serves as a means of communication.

e) The test plan describes the test objectives to be achieved and the means and the schedule for achieving them, organized to coordinate testing activities.

a) is not a correct option. The test plan should be available to managers and stakeholders who wish to monitor overall progress. b) is not a correct option. Test plans may need to be changed, for example, if the schedule changes. d) is not the correct option. This option describes the test procedure document, created during test implementation.

Answer 2 FL-5.1.1 K2

a) is the correct option. The test approach section includes the test levels, metrics to be collected, exit criteria and more. b) is not the correct option. Test levels and 100% branch coverage requirements are not assumptions or constraints. The test assumptions and constraints. c) is not the correct option. The context of testing includes reference to the test basis, test scope, test objectives and more.

d) is not the correct option. Project and product risks are part of the risk register section.

Answer 3 FL-5.1.2 K2

c) is the correct option. A tester can contribute to iteration planning by helping ensure the testability of user stories is feasible. a) is not the correct option. Test automation typically does not depend on the number of application input screens.

b) is not the correct option. The priority of quality characteristics, such as usability (interactive capability) and performance efficiency, are determined through a collaborative effort involving stakeholders who may not all be at the specific iteration planning meeting.

d) is not the correct option. Specifying the response time is not the responsibility of the tester.

Answer 4 FL-5.1.2 K1

c) and e) are the correct options. c) Estimating the development time is not part of the role of a tester.

e) There may be a requirement to test for regulatory compliance, but defining the regulatory requirements is not part of the role of a tester. a), b) and d) are not correct options. The tester can provide valuable inputs to risk analysis, testability and identification of non-functional aspects.

Answer 5 FL-5.1.2 K1

d) is the correct option. Testers can help identify and address high-risk areas before they become significant problems.

a) is not the correct option. Testing shows the presence of defects, not their absence so it cannot ensure the stability, reliability and security of the test object. b) is not the correct option. Managers, not testers make decisions on project budget. c) is not the correct option. Testers can focus on the functional and non-functional characteristics of the software.

Answer 6 FL-5.1.3 K2

d) is the correct option. Entry criteria refer to requirements that must be fulfilled before the test process can start.

a) is not the correct option. Validation criteria refer to confirmation by examination that a work product matches a stakeholder's needs.

b) is not the correct option. Acceptance criteria refer to the criteria that the test object must satisfy to be accepted by a user, customer, or other authorized entity.

c) is not the correct option. Success criteria are about determining whether the project has achieved its intended outcomes.

Answer 7 FL-5.1.3 K2

b) is the correct option. This is part of test implementation which occurs after test design. a), c) and d) are not correct options. They can all be entry criteria for test analysis.

Answer 8 FL-5.1.3 K2

a) is the correct option. The level of test execution coverage is a valid test execution exit criteria. Although 100% would be the optimal level, there has to be a balance between testing, resources, and release schedule making a percentage lower than 100% acceptable in some circumstances.

b) is not the correct option. One of the principles of testing is that it is not possible to say that all defects are found, testing shows the presence of defects, not the absence of any further defects.

c) is not the correct option. It is not possible to say that the system is secure, vulnerabilities and methods of attack evolve. Monitoring security is a continual requirement. Exit criteria can only state that specific known threats have been tested.

d) is not the correct option. Creating test cases is part of test analysis and design and this should be an entry criteria for test implementation.

Answer 9 FL-5.1.3 K2

d) is the correct option. 1A - Setting up the test environment is part of test implementation and is required before test execution can start.

2D - Test data to support test conditions and test cases should have been identified in test design so that data can be prepared as part of test implementation.

3B - In test analysis, the test basis should have been evaluated to identify ambiguities, omissions, inconsistencies, contradictions and superfluous statements.

4C - Test execution includes confirmation testing. Completing confirmation testing can be one of the exit criteria for test execution.

a), b) and c) are not correct options due to the links explained for d).

Answer 10 FL-5.1.3 K2

b) is the correct option. Entry criteria can be used at the start of a test phase or test process. Exit criteria can be used at the end of a test phase or test process.

a) is not a correct option. Stakeholders and project management can provide input to both entry criteria and exit criteria. The assessment of whether exit criteria are met is typically a collaborative effort involving stakeholders and team members.

c) While both entry criteria and the Definition of Ready (DOR) aim to ensure that work items are appropriately prepared, entry criteria apply to a broad range of tasks, phases, or processes in a project. DOR specifically focuses on user stories or backlog items in the context of Agile development. d) is not a correct option. Exit criteria determine when a phase or activity is ready to move to the next stage. Exit criteria for a test phase such as test implementation are not set by the end user.

Acceptance criteria define the specific requirements a deliverable must meet to be considered complete and accepted by the customer.

FL-5.1.4 (K3) Use estimation techniques to calculate the required test effort

Test effort estimation is the process of estimating the resources, time, and costs required to complete test activities for a project. It involves predicting the amount of effort needed to meet the test objectives, including analysis of the requirements, designing test cases, executing tests, considering results and reporting defects. Test effort estimation is important in project planning as it helps ensure that adequate testing can be undertaken and resources are available when required. Using any test estimation technique can result in an incorrect estimate due to incorrect assumptions. It is therefore important to identify and understand the assumptions made.

The Syllabus includes four test estimation techniques, two are metrics-based, ratio and extrapolation and two are expert-based, three-point and Wideband Delphi.

Metrics-based estimation techniques

Estimation based on ratios

Also known as heuristic or rule-of-thumb estimation, uses pre-established ratios to estimate the test effort. Estimates based on ratios of the historical data from the organization's own projects are generally the best sources to use. Estimation based on ratios is relatively simple for stakeholders to understand and can be useful for initial indicative estimates. However, many factors can have a significant impact on an estimation based on ratios, making them inaccurate.

The Syllabus refers only to duration ratio-based estimation. This involves estimation based on the amount of time for the development and the test effort in previous projects. For example, if in a previous project, the development-to-test effort ratio was 3:2 and in the current project the development effort is expected to be 600 person-days, the test effort can be estimated to be (600 x 2/3) = 400 person-days.

Duration ratio-based estimation works best in scenarios where there are routine and repetitive tasks, limited resource variability, simple projects, consistency in the level of complexity of code being developed, reliable historical data, standardized processes and no new challenges during the project. In other scenarios, estimation based on ratios should be combined with more accurate techniques, such as Work Breakdown Structure (WBS) and expert judgment. Duration estimation based on ratios is not recommended as the primary approach for critical projects or when high estimation accuracy is required.

Historically, Lines of Code (LOC) estimation based on ratios has been used. This involved estimating the test effort based on the amount of code created and previous test effort. For example, consider a situation where data from previous projects suggests that, on average, testing requires one hour of test effort per 1,000 lines of code and the software to be tested has been estimated to need approximately 60,000 lines of code. When completed, the LOC estimation based on ratios for test effort would be 60,000/1,000 hours = 60 hours. LOC is not recommended as it is more problematic than an estimate of duration based on ratios, see later.

Problems with the use of duration and other estimations based on ratios of test techniques include:

- The complexity of the code, the number of test cases or the skills of the testing team is not taken into account
- Testing tasks can vary widely in complexity and effort required. Some test cases may be straightforward and quick to execute, while others may be complex, requiring extensive analysis and execution time
- Estimations based on ratios often overlook the test objectives. Testing may have different objectives, such as verifying critical functionality, exploring edge cases, or performing comprehensive regression testing. Each objective may require a different level of effort
- A ratio-based estimate may assume that testing can be performed continuously without considering resource constraints, such as the availability of testers, test environments, and test data. Variations in resources can significantly impact testing timelines
- Projects are often subject to scope changes, the number of changes approved and implemented during the project can affect testing requirements
- Some ratios may be influenced by historical practices, bias, or subjective judgments, leading to estimates that are inaccurate for use in the current project
- Projects may involve changes in technology, tools, or resource skill sets that impact effort and productivity. Estimation based on ratios alone does not account for these
- Estimation based on ratios does not provide a structured way to collect and analyze data for continuous process improvement
- Dependency on the historical data being accurate
- Limited adaptability to Agile or iterative software development where requirements and features evolve continuously

Additional problems for LOC estimation based on ratios include:

It does not apply to elements that do not involve traditional code, such as databases or configuration files

Focus is on code quantity over quality

Factors such as use of different programming languages affect the number of lines of code and the estimate

Inconsistent with modern development practices such as practices like microservices, containerization and code generation may result in smaller, more efficient codebases

Code refactoring may affect the testing effort significantly and LOC estimation based on ratios does not easily accommodate such changes

Estimation based on extrapolation

Extrapolation is the process of making an estimate based on extending the pattern or trend of known values such as for test effort already completed. The estimate cannot be made before or at the start of a first iteration as actual values are needed. Measurements are made as early as possible in the software development lifecycle. Then, with enough measurements, the estimate can be made. The more values available, the more accurate the estimate.

Linear extrapolation involves extending a straight-line prediction beyond the known values. This type of extrapolation assumes the relationship between past and future values will continue to be linear in the future. In reality, software development and test processes are rarely linear, due to factors such as moving through different test levels, change requests, regression testing needs and release date. For example, as the release date approaches, there may be higher expectations from stakeholders for thorough testing including more testing on non-functional software characteristics such as performance efficiency, maintainability and more.

Polynomial, exponential or conic extrapolation may have greater accuracy than linear extrapolation. ISTQB Sample Exam Question set C, Question #31 uses a recursive formula, see later.

Extrapolating both higher and lower boundaries of an estimate provides upper and lower estimates, as shown in Example 1 (following page).

Syllabus 4.0 states extrapolation, *'is very suitable in iterative SDLCs. For example, the team may extrapolate the test effort in the forthcoming iteration as the averaged effort from the last three iterations.'* However, extrapolation and averaging are two distinct methods and can produce similar or different outcomes.

Consider a scenario with three values of tester hours in the first three iterations available. These are 26, 22 and 18. There is a decreasing by four trend. For the next iteration, using linear extrapolation results in an estimate of 14 tester hours. Averaging the three iterations gives an estimate of (26 + 22 + 18) / 3 = 22 tester hours. The two estimates here are different.

Example 1: Linear boundary extrapolation to estimate velocity
Velocity is a term used in Agile development for the total effort estimate of the team associated with user stories that were completed during an iteration. A user story point is a unit of measurement for a user story based on factors such as complexity, effort, uncertainty, and risk.

In the current project, during the first sprints, the completed story points vary significantly from eight to sixteen, with for example twice as much work performed in sprint 3 (eight story points) compared to sprint 12 (16 story points). As the project progresses and the team gains relevant experience with the software, the number of story points achieved converges. Extrapolating the upper and lower numbers of story points is shown below.

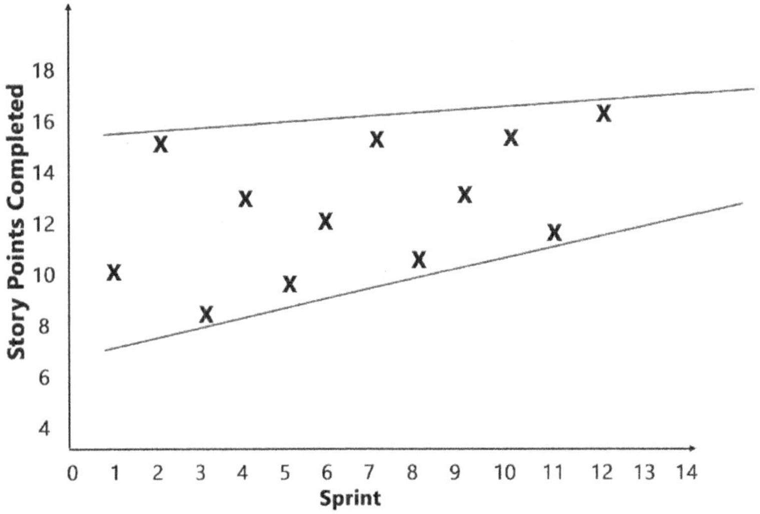

Based on the linear extrapolation, the range of the number of story points in sprint 13 can estimated to be between 11 and 16.

Estimation based on averaging
Averaging is the process of calculating the mean or average of a set of known values. It involves adding all the values and dividing by the number of values to obtain a single representative value.

The effectiveness of averaging test effort for estimation in an iteration depends on the consistency of the test process, the stability of the project, and the understanding of the factors that influence testing effort in each iteration. If one or more iterations significantly differ from the average, relying solely on the average can lead to overestimation or underestimation of the testing effort.

The use of rolling averages combined with extrapolation is sometimes used. This requires a minimum of two rolling averages but is more accurate if three or more rolling averages are used.

Example 2: Using rolling averages to estimate velocity
Using the same scenario as in Example 1, rolling averages can be calculated as follows:

Sprint	Story Points completed	Moving average	Next Sprint estimate
1	10		
2	15		
3	8	33	
4	13	32	11
5	9	30	10.7
6	12	34	10
7	15	36	11.3
8	10	37	12
9	13	38	12.3
10	14	37	12.7
11	11	38	12.3
12	15	40	12.7

In this example, the first three rolling averages (11, 10.7, 10) indicate a decreasing trend and an estimate lower than that which actually occurs. If the four rolling averages (11, 10.7, 10, 11.3) are used, the trend estimate would produce an approximately horizontal line. Only after five rolling averages (eight iterations), would the trends estimate be an increasing line. The estimate for sprint 13, rounded to a whole integer value is 13. This is now within the range given in Example 1.

Weighted averages in a recursive model

Extrapolation based on a recursive model involves using a recursive formula or relationship between known values to make predictions or estimate values beyond the known values. In this context, 'recursive' refers to a formula or equation that can be used to calculate an estimate using values from previous steps.

An example of a recursive model is to use the equation:

$$E(n) = \frac{(3 \times A(n-1) + A(n-2))}{4}$$

E(n) is the estimate for the nth step or iteration and depends on A(n-1), the actual result for the previous step or iteration and A(n-2), the actual result for the step or iteration two back. The equation serves to provide a weighted average based on the previous two steps or iterations. By using the weights of 3 and 1, more importance is attached to the value at n-1. The division by 4 normalizes the result so that E(n) is on a similar scale as the original values A(n-1) and A(n-2).

This recursive model assumes each step or iteration is of the same duration. If one step of iteration lasts longer than another, the estimate cannot be considered reliable. Also, the method is not reliable if the relationship between E and A is not well-defined and the actual values follow a varying trend. In reality, software testing and processes are subject to many influences over the software development lifecycle, such as different test levels and test types to be used in the different iterations, change requests, size and complexity of the latest version of the test object, external factors and more. It is rarely possible to have a well-defined relationship between E and A. Other estimation methods including expert judgement should be used to supplement the use of such models.

Problems with the use of extrapolation and averages for test effort estimation include:

- Estimates cannot be made before the start of the test process
- Assumes variables, such as the size, complexity of the software, availability of resources, and project-specific constraints remain constant
- The learning curve effect is not considered. Teams often become more efficient and effective as they gain experience
- The project may undergo significant change or the test process may evolve disrupting any trend
- Testing in iterations may be variable. There may be different testing objectives for particular iterations, such as functional testing, regression testing and performance efficiency testing, each of which may have different effort requirements
- Using a limited number of data values, or where the values may not be reliable, may give inaccurate outcomes
- The farther extrapolation is extended from the known values, the higher the likelihood of error, especially if the underlying conditions change

Because extrapolation cannot start before data values are available and assumes the relationship between past and future values will continue, which is rarely the case in software development and testing, extrapolation is generally not recommended for estimation.

Expert-based estimation techniques

Estimation using Wideband Delphi

Wideband Delphi is an estimation technique in which experts independently make estimates. The results are collected and if there are deviations that are out of range of the agreed-upon boundaries, the experts discuss their estimates. Each expert then independently makes a new estimate based on the feedback and discussion. The intent is that the process is repeated until consensus is reached. Wideband Delphi can be time-consuming, particularly if there are delays in reaching an agreement.

There are many reasons why Wideband Delphi may not reach a consensus and these include:

- External factors, such as time constraints, external pressures, or organizational politics may affect the experts' willingness to collaborate and reach a consensus
- The experts may have strong personal convictions or preconceived ideas that may be difficult to change
- Some experts may have individual agendas or interests that are not aligned with the group's goals. When the item to be estimated is uncertain, such as not having a well-defined scope or is highly complex, experts may have varying interpretations of the problem or may differ in their risk assessments
- The experts may have significantly different opinions or come from diverse backgrounds
- If the experts feel that they lack their own essential information or data to make informed estimates, they may be hesitant to reach a consensus
- If there are communication breakdowns and experts are unable to express their views and concerns clearly, it can impede the consensus-building process

In addition, Wideband Delphi assumes that expert opinions remain consistent and that the nature of the problem being estimated does not change throughout the estimation process.

Estimation using planning poker

This is also called scrum poker and is a variation of Wideband Delphi. It is commonly used in Agile software development, particularly in Scrum and Extreme Programming, XP. The approach is a consensus-based gamified method for making estimates. Team members individually make estimates by playing numbered cards face-down to the table, instead of speaking them aloud. The cards are then revealed, and the estimates are discussed by the team. If the estimates differ widely, the process is repeated.

Estimation using three-point estimation

Three estimates are made by experts. The most optimistic estimate (a), the most likely estimate (m) and the most pessimistic estimate (b). The final estimate (E) is a weighted arithmetic mean.
In the Syllabus, the version given for calculating the final estimate is:

$$\text{Estimate } E = \frac{(a + (4 \times m) + b)}{6}$$

The Syllabus refers to *'the measurement error: SD = (b – a) / 6'* where '*a*' is the most optimistic estimate and '*b*' the most pessimistic. SD generally is used for standard deviation and is not the same as measurement error. While standard deviation and measurement error are related concepts, they have distinct meanings and serve different purposes in data analysis and quality assurance.

Measurement error also known as measurement uncertainty, is an assessment of the inaccuracies and uncertainties associated with the estimation process, using the formula given in the Syllabus. For example, for three estimates of 48, 33, 24, the measurement of error is (48 – 24) / 6 = ±3.

Standard deviation SD is a statistical measure of the dispersion or variability of a set of data points and is used to assess the spread or distribution of data. Standard deviation is calculated by taking the square root of the variance. The variance is the average of the squared differences between each data point and the mean. To calculate the standard deviation, SD for the given data (48, 33, 24) work through the steps below:

1. The mean (average) = (48 + 33 + 24) / 3 = 105 / 3 = 35
2. The squared differences between each data point and the mean are:
   For 48: $(48 - 35)^2 = 169$ For 33: $(33 - 35)^2 = 4$ For 24: $(24 - 35)^2 = 121$
3. The mean of these squared differences (variance) = (169 + 4 + 121) / 3 = 294 / 3 ≈ 98 (rounded to the nearest whole number)
4. The standard deviation is the square root of the variance, $\sqrt{(98)} \approx 9.9$ (to one decimal place)

Standard deviation and measurement error are expressed as a '± value' when qualifying the weighted arithmetic mean. Standard deviation calculators are available online from several sources.

Three-point estimation may not result in an accurate estimate for similar reasons as given for Wideband Delphi not reaching a consensus. In addition, three-point estimation relies on the experts having a common understanding of what constitutes optimistic, most likely and pessimistic estimates.

FL-5.1.4 (K3) Exercises: Test Estimation

FL-5.1.4 (K3) Exercise 1: Ratios

Based on ISTQB Sample Exam Set C v1.0 Question #31, using the same historical data.
You are starting a new project P5 and are calculating an estimate for costs. From previous projects, the development and test effort costs were as shown below and the P5 development estimate is given:

Project	Development Effort ($)	Test Effort ($)
P1	800,000	40,000
P2	1,200,000	130,000
P3	600,000	70,000
P4	1,000,000	120,000

Part 1: The estimated development effort cost for the new project P5 is $800,000. Using the data from the four previous projects and cost ratio-based estimation, what is the estimate for test effort for P5?

Part 2: An initial estimate is from part one. When reviewing the historical values, why, based only on these values, might the estimate in part 1 be unreliable? Give three reasons specifically based on the numbers in the table.

FL-5.1.4 (K3) Exercise 2: Extrapolation and Averaging

Scenario: You are working on a project that involves multiple iterations of development and testing. This exercise is based on the Syllabus explaining only using three iterations.
From the first three iterations, the following has been recorded:

Iteration 1: 15 hours of testing effort
Iteration 2: 19 hours of testing effort
Iteration 3: 23 hours of testing effort

Part 1: Using linear extrapolation, estimate the testing effort required for iteration 4.

Part 2: Using averaging, estimate the testing effort required for iteration 4.

Part 3: In reality, the testing effort for iteration 4 may require much more time and resources than either of the estimates from parts 1 and 2 suggest. This can lead to missed deadlines, insufficient test coverage, and an increased risk of defects. Give at least five examples of factors that could make either or both of the estimates above inaccurate for iteration 4.

FL-5.1.4 (K3) Exercise 3: Extrapolation using Weighted Averages

Use the estimation formula:

$$E(n) = \frac{(3 \times A(n-1) + A(n-2))}{4}$$

Where E(n) is the estimate for the nth iteration. A(n-1) is the actual result for the previous iteration and A(n-2) is the actual result for the iteration that is two back.

Complete the table below. For the variance, give both the numerical and the % difference of the actual results over the estimation.

Iteration (n)	Actual Result A	Estimate E	Variance of A(n) and E(n)
1	7		
2	5		
3	9		
4	11		
5	7		
6			

FL-5.1.4 (K3) Exercise 4: 3-point Estimation

Using three-point estimation for test effort for a new high-risk feature, the following estimates have been made:

Most optimistic estimate	60 person-hours
Most likely estimate	75 person-hours
Most pessimistic estimate	96 person-hours

Part 1: What is the final estimate and the measurement error?

Part 2: Give three reasons why 'optimistic" may be misunderstood or misinterpreted.

Part 3: Give three reasons why 'pessimistic' may be misunderstood or misinterpreted.

FL-5.1.4 (K3) Exercise 5: Wideband Delphi

You have identified experts and obtained their support for participating. The experts may be internal team members, specialists or external consultants. You have prepared and distributed to the experts a document that outlines the specific parameters or variables related to the test effort that you want to estimate. What are the next steps to take to arrive at an estimate for the test effort?

FL-5.1.4 Exercise Answers: Test Estimation

FL-5.1.4 Exercise 1 Answer: Ratios

Part 1 Answer: The total development effort over the four previous projects is $3,600,000. The total test effort over the four projects is $360,000. This means the cost ratio of development effort to test effort is 10:1. For the new project P5 with a development estimate of $800,000, the test effort estimate is $800,000 x 1/10 = $80,000.

Part 2 Answer: Three possible reasons for the estimate from Part 1 being unreliable are:

1. Test effort as a percentage of development percentage shows an increasing trend (P1 to P4), as shown below. This is not reflected in the estimate of test effort for P5 and should trigger an investigation into why costs are increasing over time and whether this should be factored in.

Project	Development effort ($)	Test Effort ($)	Test Effort as a % of Development effort
P1	800,000	40,000	5%
P2	1,200,000	130,000	10.8%
P3	600,000	70,000	11.6%
P4	1,000,000	120,000	12%
P5	800,000	80,000	10%

2. Project P5 has the same development effort as Project P1, but the estimate from part 1 for the P5 test effort is double (5% to 10%). This should trigger an investigation into why there is a significant discrepancy.

3. The estimate depends on the number of previous projects considered. With P1 having a significantly different test effort as a percentage of development effort value, consideration could be given to not including this data as it might be unreliable. If only the three most recent projects are considered, the total development effort is $2,800,000 and the test effort is $320,000. The ratio is 70:8. So for project P5, the test effort estimate is $800,000 x 8/70 = $91,500 (or 11.4%).

Using ratio-based estimation should in such a scenario be supplemented with other estimation techniques and sense-checked.

FL-5.1.4 Exercise 2 Answer: Extrapolation and Averaging

Part 1: The trend is plus four hours for the next iteration. For iteration 4, extrapolation indicates 27hrs.
Part 2: Average Testing Effort = (15 hrs + 19 hrs + 23 hrs) / 3 = 19 hours.
Part 3: Any examples that refer to a new challenge or change in iteration 4 that has not been accounted for, or the unreliability of, the hours of testing effort from one or more of the previous iterations. Possible answers are:

Previous test-hours data are not reliable or three values are not sufficient. Greater accuracy is achieved with more data points for extrapolation or the use of rolling averages.

Iteration 4 involves particularly complex modules and components that require extensive testing. The increased complexity is not reflected in the estimate.

For iteration 4, the testing team faces resource constraints, with fewer experienced testers available. This affects productivity and efficiency and was not accounted for in the estimate.

The project scope significantly expands in iteration 4 due to the introduction of new features and functionality. The increased scope was not considered when estimating was undertaken.

Iteration 4 introduces stricter quality standards and regulatory requirements, necessitating more comprehensive testing activities and documentation. These requirements were not considered in the estimate.

In iteration 4, new or different technologies are adopted and there are an increased number of integration points that were not present in the previous iterations. Testing these new technologies and integration points requires additional effort that was not accounted for in the estimate

There are an increased number of integration points in iteration 4 that were not present in the previous iterations. Additional testing is required.

All iterations should be treated as variable, as in iteration 4, there may be different test techniques needed for different objectives such as load testing, accessibility testing, regression testing and performance efficiency testing, each of which may have test effort requirements different to what was required in the previous iterations.

The team becomes more efficient and effective as they gain experience from the previous iterations. The learning curve effect has not been considered in the estimates made with the project.

This exercise underscores the limitations of relying solely on extrapolation or averaging for test effort estimation, particularly when there are significant changes in project scope, complexity, resources, quality requirements, or technology. Extrapolation estimation, if used, should be supplemented with other estimation techniques that take into account the specific context and influences on the project.

FL-5.1.4 Exercise 3 Answer: Extrapolation using a recursive formula

Iteration (n)	Actual Result A	Estimate E	Variance of A(n) and E(n)
1	7		
2	5		
3	9	$\frac{((3 \times 5) + 7)}{4}$ = **5.5**	9 – 5.5 = **+3.5**
4	11	$\frac{((3 \times 9) + 5)}{4}$ = **8**	11 – 8 = **+3**
5	7	$\frac{((3 \times 11) + 9)}{4}$ = **10.5**	7 – 10.5 = **-3.5**
6		$\frac{((3 \times 7) + 11)}{4}$ = **8**	

Estimations for iterations 1 and 2 cannot be made as A(n-1) and A(n-2) are not available until the start of iteration 3. For iteration 3, the estimate is 5.5 and variance of 3.5, approximately a 61% discrepancy. For iteration 4, the estimate is 8 and variance of 3, approximately 37% discrepancy. For iteration 5 the estimate is 10.5 and variance of -3.5, or negative 33% discrepancy approximately.

This underscores why extrapolation using a recursive model may not be reliable.

FL-5.1.4 Exercise 4 Answer: 3-point Estimation

Part 1: The final estimate for test effort is (60 + (4 x 75) + 96) / 6 = 76 person-hours and the measurement error is (96 – 60) / 6 = ±6 hours.

Part 2: Possible reasons why 'optimistic" may be misunderstood or misinterpreted include:

- Over-confident in the success of the project
- Having a positive bias and tendency to focus on best-case scenarios
- Feeling pressure to meet the expectations of stakeholders or project deadlines
- May not have encountered challenges that could arise in the current project

Part 3: Possible reasons why 'pessimistic' may be misunderstood or misinterpreted include:

- Excessive risk-averse thinking
- Lack of thorough understanding of the task or project
- Caution in managing stakeholder expectations by presenting a conservative estimate
- Overestimate of challenges that might be encountered

FL-5.1.4 4 Exercise 5 Answer: Wideband Delphi

1. Each expert provides their estimates and assumptions independently, without being influenced by the opinions of others.
2. Collect the responses from the experts and consolidate the data. This can be done manually or with the help of specialized software.
3. Provide feedback and the opportunity for discussion. Arrange a meeting of the experts to discuss the aggregated results. Areas of agreement and disagreement can be identified. The meeting allows the experts the opportunity to review their own estimates and supporting assumptions.
4. After the feedback and discussion, ask the experts to revise their estimates individually based on the insights gained during the discussion. This aims to move to convergence towards a consensus estimate.
5. Continue repeating the collection of responses, consolidation and feedback sessions until a convergence of opinions is achieved and a consensus estimate is obtained or opinions converge within an agreed acceptable range.

5.1 Questions 11 to 19 FL-5.1.4

Question 11 FL-5.1.4 (Consolidation) Which of the following best describes the main reason for using the Wideband Delphi technique when planning test effort?

a) To facilitate open communication among stakeholders
b) To use metrics for determining the test effort
c) To estimate the test effort by seeking input from experts
d) To track progress using a visual representation of tasks

Select ONE option

Question 12 FL-5.1.4 (Consolidation) Which of the following is an example of the expert-based approach to test estimation?

a) Agile burndown chart
b) Estimation based on ratios
c) Wideband Delphi
d) Root cause analysis

Select ONE option

Question 13 FL-5.1.4 (Consolidation) Which of the following is an example of the metrics-based approach to test estimation?

a) Wideband Delphi
b) Heuristic evaluation
c) Agile planning poker
d) Extrapolation

Select ONE option

Question 14 FL-5.1.4 (K3) The test effort over the first three iterations of testing has been recorded as: Iteration 1: 6 hours, Iteration 2: 14 hours and Iteration 3: 16 hours.
Using the average of the three values, what is the estimate for iteration 4?

a) 18
b) 12
c) 14
d) Another value not listed

Select ONE option

Question 15 FL-5.1.4 (K3) In a previous project, the ratio of development days to test effort days was 4:3, and in the current project, the development effort is expected to be 48 person-days. Using estimation based on duration ratios, what is the expected test effort?

a) 32 person-days
b) 36 person-days
c) 44 person-days
d) 64 person-days

Select ONE option

Question 16 FL-5.1.4 (K3) Using three-point estimation to estimate test effort for a new feature added to an application feature, the following estimates have been made:

Most optimistic estimate	2 person-hours
Most likely estimate	6 person-hours
Most pessimistic estimate	10 person-hours

What is the final estimate of person-hours?

a) 6 person-hours
b) 7 person-hours
c) 8 person-hours
d) 10 person-hours

Select ONE option

Question 17 FL-5.1.4 (K3) Using three-point estimation to estimate test effort for an updated software application, the following estimates have been made:

Most optimistic estimate	20 person-hours
Most Likely estimate	70 person-hours
Most pessimistic estimate	90 person-hours

What is the final estimate of person-hours?

a) 50 person-hours
b) 60 person-hours
c) 65 person-hours
d) 70 person-hours

Select ONE option

Question 18 FL-5.1.4 (K3) Using three-point estimation to estimate test effort for a new feature added to an application feature, the following estimates have been made:

Most optimistic estimate	12 person-hours
Most likely estimate	13.5 person-hours
Most pessimistic estimate	18 person-hours

The final estimate has been calculated to be 14 person-hours. What is the measurement error?

a) 1.0 person-hour
b) 1.5 person-hours
c) 3.5 person-hours
d) 5.5 person-hours

Select ONE option

Question 19 FL-5.1.4 (K3) The following estimates have come from using Wideband Delphi to estimate the person-days required for testing an updated software application. The team has previously agreed that if consensus cannot be reached within the time available, and if the variation in the results is small, the number with the most experts agreeing can be used.

	Estimate by Expert					
	A	B	C	D	E	F
Round 1	31	25	18	28	14	18
Round 2	25	23	18	22	18	17
Round 3	18	18	18	19	18	17

There is no time available for a further round. Which of the following should now happen?

a) No further action is required as consensus has been achieved
b) The product owner decides what the estimate should be
c) The average of all the estimates made should be used
d) A final estimate of 18 person-days is accepted

Select ONE option

5.1 Answers and Explanations 11 to 19 FL-5.1.4

Answer 11 FL-5.1.4 Consolidation

c) is the correct option. Wideband Delphi is defined as, *'An expert-based test estimation technique that aims at making an accurate estimation using the collective wisdom of the team members.'* a), b) and d) are not correct options for the reasons given for c).

Answer 12 FL-5.1.4 Consolidation

c) is the correct option. The Wideband Delphi estimation technique is an example of the expert-based approach to test estimation. A group of experts provide estimates based on their experience.
a) is not the correct option. An Agile burndown chart tracks the actual amount of output (in terms of hours, story points, or backlog items) and does not rely on expert knowledge. The chart then provides a basis for estimating future projects of a similar nature.
b) is not the correct option. The use of ratios is an example of a metric-based estimation technique.
d) is not the correct option. Root cause analysis is a technique aimed at finding the underlying causes of defects.

Answer 13 FL-5.1.4 Consolidation

d) is the correct option. Measurements are made as early as possible in the current project to gather data. This data is then used to make the estimation. a) is not the correct option. The Wideband Delphi estimation technique is an example of the expert-based approach to test estimation. A group of experts provide estimates based on their experience.
b) is not the correct option. Heuristic evaluation is defined in the Glossary as, *'A usability review technique that evaluates a work product by using a set of heuristics.'*
Heuristic is defined as, *'A generally recognized rule of thumb that helps to achieve a goal.'*
c) is not the correct option. Agile planning poker is a consensus-based estimating technique and an example of expert-based estimation.

Answer 14 FL-5.1.4 K3

b) is the correct option. The average time spent is (6 + 14 + 16)/3 = 12 hours. a), c) and d) are not correct options for the reasons given for b).

Answer 15 FL-5.1.3 K3

b) is the correct option. 48 x 3/4 = 36 person-days. a), c) and d) are not correct options for the reason given for b).

Answer 16 FL-5.1.4 K3

a) is the correct option. The final estimate is (2 + (4 x 6) + 10) / 6 = 6 person-hours.
b), c) and d) are not correct options for the reasons given for a).

Answer 17 FL-5.1.4 K3
c) is the correct option. The final estimate is (20 + (4 x 70) + 90) / 6 = 65 person-hours.
a), b) and d) are not correct options for the reasons given for c).

Answer 18 FL-5.1.4 K3
a) is the correct option. The measurement error is (the most pessimistic estimate minus the most optimistic estimate) divided by 6, is (18 - 12) / 6 = 1.0 person-hour.
b), c) and d) are not correct options for the reasons given for a).

Answer 19 FL-5.1.4 K3
d) is the correct option. The rule agreed by the team allows for 18 to be accepted.
a) is not the correct option. Consensus was not reached as experts D and E did not agree on 18.
b) is not the correct option. Wideband Delphi is a team approach.
c) is not the correct option. Averaging all the estimates is not part of Wideband Delphi.

FL-5.1.5 (K3) Apply test case prioritization
Test case prioritization can be applied in test design, test implementation and test execution.

Prioritization can be based on several factors including:

- Availability of the appropriate software
- Frequency of use of a feature with higher use areas having higher priority
- Quality characteristics may have differing importance for the customer
- Different functionalities delivered by a system have different importance for the customer
- Complexity of individual components and system parts if more intensive testing is required
- Availability of developers
- Project or product risks and the severity of the expected damage
- Availability of testers, the test environment and test case execution time
- Release deadlines
- Need to conform to regulatory requirements or standards as the top priority

Commonly used test case prioritization strategies include:

- **Regulatory requirements** compliance where mandated is the highest priority
- **Risk-based** where the order is based on the results of risk analysis (see section FL-5.2.3). Test cases covering the most important risks are designed, implemented and executed first.
- **Coverage-based** where the order is based on coverage. Test cases achieving the highest coverage are designed, implemented and executed first. In another variant, called additional coverage prioritization, the test case achieving the highest coverage is first; each subsequent test case is the one that achieves the highest <u>additional</u> coverage for the same test technique.
- **Requirements-based** where the order is based on the priorities of the requirements. Stakeholders define the priorities of the requirements. Test cases related to the most important requirements are considered first.

FL-5.1.5 (K3) Exercises: Test Case Prioritization

FL-5.1.5 (K3) Exercise 1: Test case prioritization

You are working on a project using Agile software development. You are organizing the order of test case execution. The software schedules truck deliveries and must comply with regulatory requirements on the number of hours worked and frequency of breaks for the drivers. Regulatory requirements take precedence over non-regulatory requirements. The table below lists the test cases to be executed. Sprints are two weeks long and are numbered sequentially. Following Sprint 4 and a management review, the software is scheduled to be released.

Test Case	Regulatory Requirements	Availability
TC 1	No	Sprint 4
TC 2	No	Sprint 3
TC 3	Yes	Sprint 2
TC 4	Yes	Sprint 1
TC 5	No	Sprint 2
TC 6	Yes	Sprint 3
TC 7	Yes	Sprint 3
TC 8	Yes	Sprint 4

Given this information, what is the best execution order for the test cases?

FL-5.1.5 Exercise Answer

The following table shows the order of test cases based on prioritization of regulatory over non-regulatory requirements and availability.

Test Case	Regulatory Requirements	Availability
TC 4	Yes	Sprint 1
TC 3	Yes	Sprint 2
TC 5	No	Sprint 2
TC 6	Yes	Sprint 3
TC 7	Yes	Sprint 3
TC 2	No	Sprint 3
TC 8	Yes	Sprint 4
TC 1	No	Sprint 4

FL-5.1.5 (K3) Exercise 2: Test case prioritization based on requirements

Test cases TC-01 and TC-08 below have already been executed and the results are determined as passed. Under time pressure, you have decided to apply test case prioritization of the remaining test cases to ensure all requirements are covered at least once as early as possible.

	Test Case							
Requirement	**TC-01**	**TC-02**	**TC-03**	**TC-04**	**TC-05**	**TC-06**	**TC-07**	**TC-08**
Req-01	X							
Req-02		X						X
Req-03			X					
Req-04			X	X				
Req-05				X	X	X	X	
Req-06				X		X	X	
Req-07							X	X
Req-08				X		X		
Req-09			X		X			
Req-10		X				X		

Part 1: Which test cases should now be prioritized as high?

Part 2: A problem has arisen with TC-06 and it has to be retired. Which test case or test cases if any should become high priority for covering all requirements at least once?

FL-5.1.5 Exercise Answer

Part 1 Answer

TC-03 and TC-06 should now be prioritized as high.

Test cases TC-01 and TC-08 have covered Req-01, Req-02 and Req-07.

Req-03 needs to be covered and the only test case that will do this is TC-03 which also covers Req-04 and Req-09. This leaves requirements, Req-05, Req-06, Req-08 and Req-10 not covered. These can all be covered by TC-06.

Part 2 Answer

Retiring test case TC06, means Req-05, Req-06, Req-08 and Req-10 need to be covered.

Test case TC-02 is needed as it is the only remaining test case that covers Req-10. Test case TC-04 includes coverage of Req-05, Req-06 and Req-08.

FL-5.1.6 (K1) Recall the concepts of the test pyramid

The **test pyramid**, also called the testing pyramid, is a visual representation of the distribution of different test types across multiple levels or layers. The pyramid metaphor is used to depict the ideal proportions of each type of test, with the widest layer representing where the greatest number of tests are required. Commonly, three layers are included. These layers were originally defined as 'Unit Tests', 'Service Tests' and 'User Interface (UI) Tests' however the number and naming of the layers can differ. The higher the layer, the lower is the test isolation.

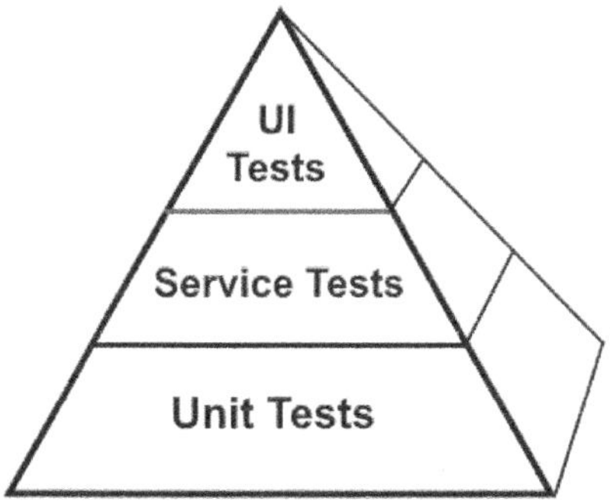

Acknowledgments: Mike Cohn and Agile Coach Journal by Roger Brown. See *References*.

The three layers of the original software test pyramid:

Bottom Layer (Unit Tests): This is the base of the pyramid and the biggest layer. Unit tests focus on testing individual components or units of code in isolation. Tests are small in scope, fast to execute and used to assess if the basic building blocks of the software work as expected. Unit tests are typically created by developers and help to uncover defects early in the development cycle.

Middle Layer (Service Tests): The middle layer of the pyramid represents Integration tests. These tests focus on verifying the interactions between different components or modules of the application. Integration tests are used to assess whether various parts of the system work together.

Top Layer (UI Tests): The top layer of the pyramid consists of UI tests. These tests focus on the user interface, for example verifying buttons, forms and menus function correctly. Typically, only a few UI tests are needed for reasonable coverage.

The test pyramid shows different tests have different levels of granularity. Granularity refers to the varying degrees of detail, precision, or scale.
Information on test priorities or relationships between different tests is not provided by the test pyramid. The test pyramid also does not reflect any coverage criteria.

An alternative test pyramid representation defines the three layers as; unit tests, integration tests and end-to-end tests. When the top level is used to represent end-to-end tests, the test pyramid shows fewer of these are needed compared to the other levels. The test pyramid may be representative of the number of tests required for each layer but does not necessarily reflect the test effort and execution time as end-to-end tests are often slower and more complex to implement and execute than tests in lower levels.

FL-5.1.7 (K2) Summarize the testing quadrants and their relationships with test levels and test types
Testing quadrants are used in the context of Agile software development to categorize different types of testing. The model provides a structured framework for organizing and understanding the various types of testing that can be performed throughout the software development lifecycle. The concept is represented as a matrix with four quadrants, each focusing on different aspects of testing.

The four quadrants of testing are shown in the diagram below.

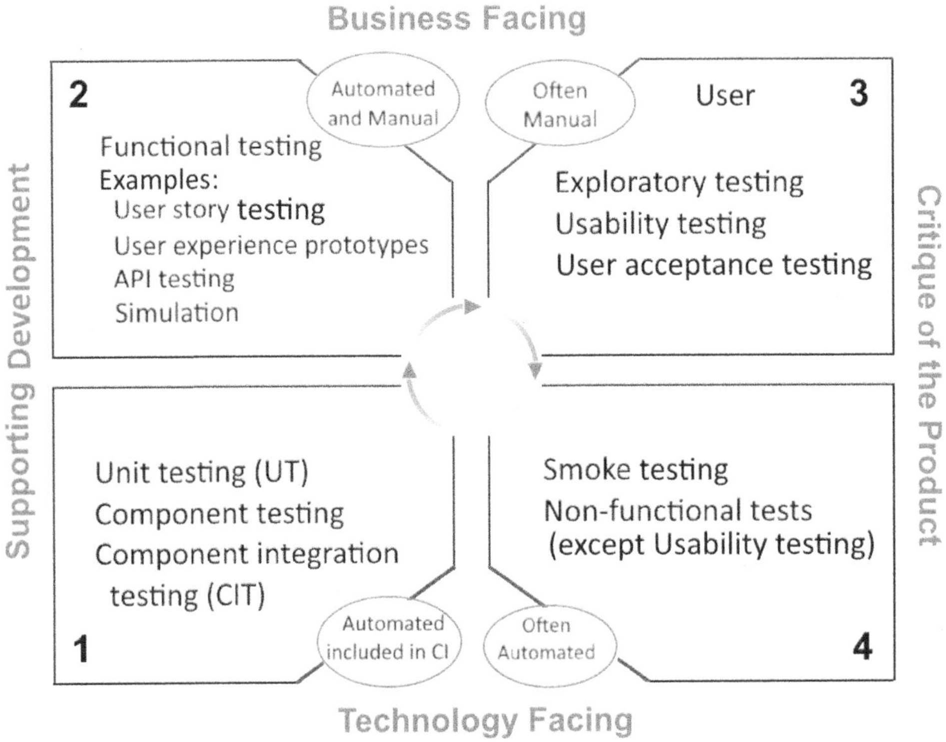

Acknowledgement: Based on the Agile testing matrix – Marick 2003. See *References*.

5.1 Questions 20 to 30 FL-5.1.5, 5.1.6, 5.1.7

Question 20 FL-5.1.5 (Consolidation) Which of the following is not considered in test case prioritization?

a) Compliance with regulatory requirements
b) User feedback and preferences
c) Random selection for testing free from bias
d) Critical areas of the application

Select ONE option

Question 21 FL-5.1.5 (Consolidation)
Prioritization based on compliance with regulatory requirements being high priority is important for the following except for which?

a) Avoiding consequences that might include lawsuits, fines or penalties
b) Ensuring all test cases pass successfully
c) Instilling customer trust and confidence
d) Opening up markets where customers prioritize regulatory compliance

Select ONE option

Question 22 FL-5.1.5 (Consolidation) What is the primary test objective of requirements-based test case prioritization where the order of test case execution is based on the priorities of the requirements traced to the test cases?

a) Maximizing the project budget
b) Minimizing the project timeline
c) Ensuring all requirements are implemented
d) Delivering the most valuable features early

Select ONE option

Question 23 FL-5.1.5 (K3) Test cases have been assigned priorities, 1 being the highest and 3 lowest.

Test Case ID	Dependency	Assessed Priority
TC01	None	3
TC02	TC03	1
TC03	TC01	3
TC04	None	3
TC05	TC03	2

Based on executing test cases with the highest priority as early as possible, which test case should be executed second?

a) TC02
b) TC05
c) TC01
d) TC03

Select ONE option

Question 24 FL-5.1.5 (K3) Agile software development lifecycle is being used. Mandatory regulatory compliance is the highest priority. The risk level is to be taken into consideration as far as possible. You have the following test cases:

Test Case	Risk Level	Regulatory Compliance	Software Availability
TC1	High	No	Sprint 2
TC2	Medium	Yes	Sprint 2
TC3	Low	Yes	Sprint 2
TC4	High	No	Sprint 1
TC5	Low	Yes	Sprint 1

Based on the given information, which of the following is the best test case execution order?

a) TC5, TC4, TC2, TC3, TC1
b) TC4, TC5, TC2, TC1, TC3
c) TC4, TC5, TC1, TC2, TC3
d) TC4, TC1, TC2, TC3, TC5

Select ONE option

Question 25 FL-5.1.6 (K1) Which of the following are true for a test pyramid?

a) Emphasizes the main focus of testing should be based on user acceptance tests
b) The higher the level, the lower the test isolation
c) The original test pyramid defines three layers, unit tests. service tests and UI tests
d) Shows different groups of tests require different coverage criteria
e) Shows there should be more integration testing than unit testing

Select TWO options

Question 26 FL-5.1.6 (K1) The test pyramid shows which of the following?

a) The relationship between different test cases
b) Distinct divisions between groups of tests
c) Information about test case priorities
d) Test focus and effort should be greatest on end-to-end testing

Select ONE option

Question 27 FL-5.1.7 (K2) Which of the following is part of Agile testing quadrant Q4: business-facing, supporting development?

a) Usability testing
b) Reliability testing
c) API testing
d) Exploratory testing

Select ONE option

Question 28 FL-5.1.7 (K2) Which of the following test categories is not in the Agile testing quadrant Q2, business facing, supporting development?

a) User acceptance testing
b) Simulations
c) User experience prototypes
d) User story testing

Select ONE option

Question 29 FL-5.1.7 (K2) Consider the following test categories (A-D) and testing quadrants (1-4):

A. User acceptance testing
B. Simulations
C. Smoke testing
D. Component testing

1. Testing quadrant Q1: Technology-facing, supporting development
2. Testing quadrant Q2: Business-facing, supporting development
3. Testing quadrant Q3: Business-facing, critique of the product
4. Testing quadrant Q4: Technology-facing, critique of the product

How do the test categories map onto the testing quadrants?

a) 1B, 2A, 3D, 4C
b) 1C, 2B, 3D, 4A
c) 1D, 2B, 3A, 4C
d) 1D, 2A, 3C, 4B

Select ONE option

Question 30 FL-5.1.7 (K2) Which of the following best describe the benefits of using the testing quadrants framework?

a) Provides a structured way to plan test activities
b) Supports communication of test ideas in a way that the rest of the team will better understand the purpose of tests
c) Is suitable for use with all projects irrespective of the software development lifecycle being used or the size of project
d) Provides detailed guidance on specific test techniques to be used
e) Supports risk-based testing with the lower quadrants having lower risk levels and higher quadrants having higher risk levels

Select TWO options

5.1 Answers and Explanations 20 to 30 FL-5.1.5, 5.1.6, 5.1.7

Answer 20 FL-5.1.5 (Consolidation)

c) is the correct option. Test case prioritization is a systematic approach, not a random approach to organizing and sequencing test cases to organizing and sequencing test cases based on specific criteria.
a), b) and d) are not correct options as compliance with regulatory requirements, user feedback and preferences and critical areas of the application can all be used to determine test case prioritization.

Answer 21 FL-5.1.5 (Consolidation)

b) is the correct option. Test case prioritization is a systematic approach with the aim that high-priority test cases are created and run before test cases with medium or low priority. All test cases for mandatory regulatory compliance should be a high priority. Test cases with low propriety may not all be executed.
a) Is not the correct option. Testing for regulatory compliance helps identify and rectify potential issues before they result in legal disputes and financial penalties.
c) is not the correct option. Compliance with regulatory requirements instills trust in customers who expect software to meet legal requirements and protect their interests.
d) is not the correct option. Regulatory compliance can be a competitive advantage, as it can open up markets and attract customers who prioritize compliance.

Answer 22 FL-5.1.5 (Consolidation)

d) is the correct option. Delivering the most valuable features early. The primary test objective of requirements-based prioritization is to identify and prioritize the most valuable requirements or features that provide the greatest business value. This approach allows for the delivery of high-priority features early in the project timeline, ensuring that the most important needs are met first.
a) and b) are not correct options. It is not solely focused on budget or timeline considerations but rather on delivering value to stakeholders. Maximizing the budget or minimizing the project timeline are not primary test objectives.
c) is not the correct option. Ensuring all requirements are implemented is not the primary test objective of requirements-based prioritization.

Answer 23 FL-5.1.5 (K3)

d) is the correct option. TC02, the highest priority should be executed as early as possible. To achieve this, TC01 should be executed first, followed by TC03 and then TC02 can be executed.

Answer 24 FL-5.1.5 K3

a) is the correct option. Sprint availability is taken into consideration as a test case cannot be executed if the software is not available Mandatory regulatory compliance is essential and test cases, where this is required, have a higher priority than those that do not have regulatory compliance specified. Test cases are then organized according to risk level, with TC2 coming before TC3.

Test Case	Risk Level	Regulatory Compliance	Software Availability
TC5	Low	Yes	Sprint 1
TC4	High	No	Sprint 1
TC2	Medium	Yes	Sprint 2
TC3	Low	Yes	Sprint 2
TC1	High	No	Sprint 2

b), c) and d) are not correct options for the reasons given for a).

Answer 25 FL-5.1.6 K1

b) and c) are the correct options. b) Test isolation is lower for higher levels.

c) Cohn (2009) defined the test pyramid with Unit, service and UI tests. See *References.*

a) is not the correct option. The broad base of the pyramid represents unit tests. The top layer represents the high-level UI tests, suggesting fewer of them are required.

d) is not a correct option. The test pyramid does not show the relationship between different tests.

e) is not a correct option. The test pyramid supports more unit testing than integration testing.

Answer 26 FL-5.1.6 K1

b) is the correct option. The test pyramid is divided into defined layers.

a) is not the correct option. The test pyramid does not show the relationship between different tests.

c) is not the correct option. The test pyramid does not include information on test case priorities.

d) is not the correct option. The base and largest layer of the pyramid is unit testing.

Answer 27 FL-5.1.7 K2

b) is the correct option. Reliability testing is a non-functional testing and part of Q4.

a) is not the correct option. Usability testing is part of Q3 where tests are user-orientated.

c) is not the correct option. API testing is part of Q2, business-facing, and supporting development.

d) is not the correct option. Exploratory testing is part of Q3 business-facing, critique of the product.

Answer 28 FL-5.1.7 K2

a) is the correct option. User acceptance testing is in Q3. b), c) and d) are not correct options. Simulations, user experience prototypes and user story testing are all in Q2.

Answer 29 FL-5.1.7 K2

c) is the correct option. 1D Component testing is in Q1. 2B Simulations is in Q2. 3A User acceptance testing is in Q3. 4C Smoke testing is in Q4.

a), b) and d) are not correct options for the reasons given for c).

Answer 30 FL-5.1.7 K2

a) and b) are the correct options. a) Testing quadrants help to ensure aspects of testing, such as unit testing, functional testing, and non-functional testing, are considered in a structured way, leading to more comprehensive test coverage. b) Testing quadrants can serve as an aid to describe the test types to other team members.

c) is not a correct option. Testing quadrants framework is most commonly used in Agile and iterative software development projects. For simple or small-scale projects with straightforward requirements and limited interactions, the testing quadrants may introduce unnecessary complexity. While some concepts from the testing quadrants can be adapted, Waterfall and traditional projects may have different test processes for which the testing quadrants framework is not always suitable.

d) is not a correct option. The testing quadrants framework provides no guidance on specific test techniques to be used. e) is not a correct option. There is no correlation between risk levels and testing quadrants.

5.2 Risk Management

Risk management is the systematic process of identifying, assessing, mitigating, and monitoring potential risks and uncertainties that could impact the success of a project, or any organizational activity. It aims to proactively address and minimize negative effects of risks while maximizing potential opportunities.

Risk assessment is the process involving the evaluation of risks in a systematic, structured way to determine their significance and impact on a project, process or objective. It aims to support informed decisions being made about risk management of a project. Risk assessment draws on the collective knowledge and experience of the project stakeholders and should be an ongoing process. As more information becomes available, risk levels may need to be changed.

Risk analysis is primarily focused on understanding and quantifying the characteristics and attributes of risks. The main purpose of risk analysis is to gain a deeper understanding of potential impacts. Risk analysis is part of a broader risk assessment process.

Risk-based testing is a test approach based on risk analysis and risk control. Test activities are selected, prioritized and managed based on the assessed risk.

Risk identification is defined in the ISTQB Glossary is, *'The process of finding, recognizing and describing risks.'* ISO25010:2023 defines risk identification as, 'The capability of the product to identify a course of events or operations that can expose life, property or environment to unacceptable risk'.

FL-5.2.1 (K1) Identify risk level by using risk likelihood and risk impact
Risk can be defined as involving exposure to a possible adverse outcome, such as loss, harm or danger. Risk level is determined using risk likelihood and risk impact.

Risk likelihood refers to the possibility that the potential risk will occur. Risk likelihood can be assigned a percentage probability value or a numerical value based on a defined scale. A commonly used scale is 1 equals high, 2 medium and 3 low risk likelihood. Typically, an exam question will be based on this three-value scale.

Determining risk likelihood can involve:

- Considering which features are used most frequently
- Seeking input from subject matter experts
- Analyzing past occurrences of similar events to determine how frequently they have occurred
- Considering environmental or external influences
- Evaluating the complexity of the product
- Assessing how the likelihood of one risk event might be influenced by the occurrence of other interconnected risks.

Risk impact refers to the size and effect of the consequences that may result from the occurrence of a specific risk event or situation. It is a measure of the potential harm, damage, loss, or negative outcomes that could affect aspects of a project, system, or organization.

A commonly used numerical scale is 1 equals High, 2 Medium and 3 Low for risk impact. Some organizations quantify risk impact by assigning a monetary value to the potential consequences and risk likelihood as a percentage. If risk impact is given as a percentage, the risk impact should be expressed as a percentage of a relevant defined metric.

Determining risk impact can involve consideration of:

- The extent to which the risk event would disrupt operations, timelines, or normal functioning
- Potential legal liabilities and financial losses
- The amount of time, effort, and resources required to recover and return to normal operations
- How the risk might affect customers, stakeholders, or end-users, such as loss of trust or satisfaction
- Consideration of longer-term impact, such as reputational damage and future lost business

Risk level is, *'The qualitative or quantitative measure of a risk defined by impact and likelihood.'* Risk level is a key concept in risk management and risk assessment. It is used to evaluate and communicate information on a particular risk. As risk level is defined by risk likelihood and risk impact, it is only known after risk likelihood and risk impact have been determined. Risk level is an output.

Risk level is calculated as:

Risk Level = Risk Likelihood x Risk Impact

Depending on the context and specific risk technique used, alternative terms may be used:

Risk Term	Alternative Names
Risk Level	Risk exposure, Risk priority, Risk Priority Number (RPN)
Risk Likelihood	Risk occurrence, Risk probability, Technical risk
Risk Impact	Risk harm, Risk effect, Business risk, Severity

Calculating risk level in this way is considered a lightweight model. Additional terms are included in calculating the risk level in some heavyweight models. These are outside the scope of the Foundation Level.

The higher the risk level the more important its treatment. A risk assessment scale may use 1 as high level and other numbers as lower risk levels, see below. In this case, the bigger the number the lower the risk level.

The risk level possibilities with three-value scales where 1 is high, 2 medium and 3 low for both risk likelihood and risk impact are:

Risk Likelihood	Risk Impact	Risk Level
High	High	1 x 1 = 1
High	Medium	1 x 2 = 2
High	Low	1 x 3 = 3
Medium	High	2 x 1 = 2
Medium	Medium	2 x 2 = 4
Medium	Low	2 x 3 = 6
Low	High	3 x 1 = 3
Low	Medium	3 x 2 = 6
Low	Low	3 x 3 = 9

If a percentage is used for risk likelihood it can be converted to a decimal equivalent by dividing by 100 and then the risk level can be calculated. For example:

Risk likelihood of occurrence = 50% and Risk impact = $600, Risk level = (0.5 x $600) = $300.

In real-world scenarios, risk level is typically only known after both risk likelihood and risk impact have been determined. However, if an exam question (ISTQB Sample Question Paper Set D, Question 30) gives the risk level and one of the inputs, risk likelihood or risk impact, it is possible to reverse calculate the other input by dividing the risk level by the known factor.

Example reverse calculation of risk impact: Risk level is \$200 and Risk likelihood 40%, Risk impact is Risk level divided by Risk likelihood, \$200 / 0.4 = \$500.

FL-5.2.2 (K2) Distinguish between project risks and product risks

Project risks relate to the management and control of a project. Project risks are where the primary effect of the potential problem is on the project's success. Project risks can be considered in four areas, technical, external, organizational (internal) and project monitoring.

Project risks include:

Technical:

- Requirements are not well-defined
- The test environment is not ready in time
- Data conversion and migration planning fall behind schedule
- Weaknesses in the development process impacting the consistency or quality of work products
- Poor defect management results in accumulated defects and technical debt
- Tools and technology problems

External:

- A third party fails to deliver a necessary product or service or goes out of business
- Contractual issues
- Regulatory requirements not met
- Competition and market forces

Organizational:

- Skills and training
- Lack of focus on testing
- Personnel issues causing conflict and problems
- Users, business staff, or subject matter experts unavailable due to other priorities
- Resources not available when required
- Budget apportioning
- Organization's priorities and project dependencies
- High change rates

Project Monitoring:

- Overall budget
- Lack of understanding of testing importance, planning, monitoring and control
- Inaccurate estimates
- Reallocation of funds to higher priority projects
- General cost-cutting across the organization that results in inadequate funding
- Developers and/or testers failing to follow up on information found in testing and reviews
- Testers not communicating their needs and/or the test results adequately
- Team size and stability
- Late changes and their approvals which result in substantial re-work

Product risks relate to the possibility that a work product fails to meet the legitimate needs of its stakeholders or end users. When product risks relate to specific quality characteristics of a product, such as functional suitability, reliability, performance efficiency, usability (interactive capability), security, compatibility, maintainability or portability (flexibility), safety, product risks are also called quality risks or product quality risks.

Examples of product risks include:

- Software does not perform its intended functions according to the specification
- System architecture does not adequately support some non-functional requirement(s)
- Complex features that may affect multiple areas, including future upgrades
- Number, type and complexity of interfaces
- A variety of platforms which include mobile and desktop not fully considered
- A particular computation that may be performed incorrectly in some circumstances
- A loop control structure that may be coded incorrectly
- Response times that may be inadequate
- Software load limitations
- Tight schedules may force developers to code hurriedly and may result in more defects*
- New or inexperienced developers may pose a greater risk to an existing product*

* Mitigation of a product risk in these particular situations is likely to be linked to a project mitigation action such as a delay in schedule or organizational change.

Product risks compared to project risks

Significant differences between product risks and project risks are:

- A product risk can, typically but not always, be mitigated by appropriate testing. This is less likely to be true for a project risk
- Product risks are one of the five primary dimensions on which test progress is monitored. Project risks are not one of the five dimensions
- Product risks are a focus of risk-based testing. A project risk is often identified as a by-product of risk-based testing
- Testers have a primary focus on finding product risks and managers typically have primary responsibility for project risks

FL-5.2.3 (K2) Explain how product risk analysis may influence the thoroughness and test scope

Product risk analysis affects the test scope by directing test efforts toward identified risks and critical areas of the software. While other areas of the software are not ignored, the primary focus is on addressing identified risks efficiently and effectively to enhance software quality and reduce potential risks to the project.

Risks can be assessed qualitatively or quantitatively. Using a three-value scale where 1 = High, 2 = Medium and 3 = Low for both risk likelihood and risk impact.
Assuming no dependencies, the priority order of risks is assessed as:

Priority Order	Risk Likelihood	Risk Impact	Risk Level
1	High	High	1 x 1 = **1**
=2	High	Medium	1 x 2 = **2**
=2	Medium	High	2 x 1 = **2**
=4	High	Low	1 x 3 = **3**
=4	Low	High	3 x 1 = **3**
6	Medium	Medium	2 x 2 = **4**
=7	Medium	Low	2 x 3 = **6**
=7	Low	Medium	3 x 2 = **6**
9	Low	Low	3 x 3 = **9**

The results of product risk analysis can be used to:

- Prioritize testing to find the high-risk defects as early as possible
- Determine the test scope to be carried out. This may then affect the test effort. A decision might be made that testing is not performed for risks with low-risk level values or the test effort for high-risk areas may need to be increased
- Determine the particular test levels and test types
- Determine the test techniques to be used and the coverage required. More formal and systematic test techniques are advisable where high risks are identified
- Determine the appropriate use of manual or automated methods
- Estimate the test effort for each task
- Determine whether any activities in addition to testing could be employed to reduce risk

Dependencies can mean the order of testing needs to be adjusted. Dependencies can include:

- A test case with a high risk level cannot be executed before a test case with a lower risk level. For example. The lower risk test case requires a data record to be added to the database. The high-priority test case is to delete the record
- The availability of software or specialist resources may influence the order of test case execution. For example, with Agile software development, an early sprint may not include the implementation of a feature to allow testing of it
- A decision by stakeholders

FL-5.2.4 (K2) Explain what measures can be taken in response to analyzed product risks
When a risk has been analyzed, several response options to risk are possible, such as risk mitigation, risk acceptance, risk transfer, or contingency planning.

Risk mitigation involves implementing the actions proposed in risk assessment to reduce the risk level, Mitigation by testing options, based on the list given in the Syllabus, include:

Select the testers with the right level of experience and skills, suitable for a given risk type

Ensure adequate time and resources for an appropriate amount of testing

Apply an appropriate level of independent testing

Perform reviews and perform static analysis

Perform vulnerability assessments and perform security testing

Apply the appropriate test techniques and coverage levels

Apply the appropriate test types addressing affected quality characteristics

Perform dynamic testing, including regression testing

Contingency planning puts in place plans to reduce the potential damage should the risk occur. This includes having contingency arrangements for the provision of resources or budget to meet or modify any of the consequences should they occur. Examples of actions that can be taken include developing a workaround that could be used should the risk occur and regular backups of the environment and data.

Transference implements a shift in accountability, responsibility or authority to a third party. The extent to which risk can be transferred may depend on the reliability and clarity of the proposed arrangements. Legal or regulatory requirements may limit, prohibit or mandate risk transference. An example of an action that can be taken is to purchase insurance.

Acceptance is making an informed decision to accept an identified risk. This may be appropriate when for example:

Cost to mitigate the risk is considered to be higher than the cost of the consequence or its effect

Risk is considered to be very low

Cost of missing a release deadline outweighs the cost of the potential damage

5.2 Questions 1 to 10 FL-5.2.1, 5.2.2, 5.2.3, 5.2.4

Question 1 FL-5.2.1 (K1) The basic level or risk is determined by which of the following?

a) Risk likelihood and risk impact
b) Risk rating and risk mitigation
c) Risk likelihood and risk mitigation
d) Risk identification and risk priority

Select ONE option

Question 2 FL-5.2.1 (K1) Which of the following statements is correct?

a) Likelihood is the risk priority; impact is the adverse risk effect if the risk occurs
b) Likelihood is the probability of the risk occurring; impact is the damage caused if the risk occurs
c) Likelihood is the risk rating; impact is the business risk if the risk occurs
d) Likelihood is the plausibility of the risk occurring; impact is the beneficial effect if the risk occurs

Select ONE option

Questions 3 FL-5.2.2 (K2) Which of the following is most likely primarily a project risk?

a) More defects may be found in the software under test than expected
b) The test environment is not available when needed
c) Specified coding standards may not have been adhered to and later result in difficulties correcting code
d) System architecture may not support the load level specified

Select ONE option

Question 4 FL-5.2.2 (K2) Which of the following is the best example of a risk that is a project risk?

a) A performance efficiency test may fail with specified response times not met
b) An issue exists with the interface between the system under test and the internet
c) Tools required for scheduled static analysis have not been purchased
d) The expected security features are not supported by the system architecture

Select ONE option

Question 5 FL-5.2.2 (K2) Which of the following is the best example of a product risk rather than a project risk?

a) The skills and training of developers
b) Late changes that are approved and result in substantial rework
c) Poor system architecture resulting in software that is difficult to maintain
d) Poor defect management resulting in accumulated unresolved defects and technical debt

Select ONE option

Question 6 FL-5.2.3 (K2) When using risk analysis and considering its influence on the thoroughness of testing, which of the following is not true?

a) When a product risk analysis uses percentage probability, a risk assessed to have a 100% probability of occurrence is no longer a risk and should be considered as a failure
b) If a product risk is assessed as having no impact, it can be discounted
c) When using risk assessment, high (1), medium (2) and low (3), a risk assessed having a high likelihood of occurrence may have a risk priority order below that of a risk assessed as having a medium likelihood of occurrence
d) Prioritizing product risks and using this to determine test case order ensures all areas of the code are covered in priority order

Select ONE option

Question 7 FL-5.2.3 (K2) Which of the following is not correct for how product risk analysis influences thoroughness and test scope?

a) Can be used for estimating the effort required for each task
b) Provides insight into areas where code complexity might be simplified and then retested
c) Guides where resources should be concentrated to address critical issues
d) Limits the activities to be employed to reduce risk to test activities
e) Has no impact on the thoroughness and test scope

Select TWO options

Question 8 FL-5.2.4 (K1) What is the primary objective of risk mitigation?

a) Identifying new defects in the software
b) Reducing the impact and likelihood of potential risks
c) Assigning responsibility for project delays
d) Automating the entire test process

Select ONE option

Question 9 FL-5.2.4 (K2) During risk analysis, before the release of the software, a risk has been identified and analyzed. The following are possible options and actions that could be taken.

1. Risk mitigation
2. Risk transference
3. Risk contingency
4. Risk acceptance

A. Plan for potential adverse outcomes
B. Apply appropriate test techniques and coverage levels
C. Put the risk on a backlog list for consideration in a future update
D. Hand the risk to a third party

Which of the following correctly links the two lists?

a) 1A, 2D, 3C, 4B
b) 1D, 2C, 3B, 4A
c) 1C, 2A, 3D, 4B
d) 1B, 2D, 3A, 4C

Select ONE option

Question 10 FL-5.2.4 (K2) Which of the following is not a mitigation action for an identified risk?

a) Meet with stakeholders to determine the potential risk level
b) Apply an appropriate level of independence in testing
c) Perform both static testing and dynamic testing
d) Apply the appropriate test techniques and coverage levels

Select ONE option

5.2 Answers and Explanations 1 to 10 FL-5.2.1, 5.2.2, 5.2.3, 5.2.4

Answer 1 FL-5.2.1 K1

a) is the correct option. Risk likelihood multiplied by risk impact is typically used to determine the overall risk level (sometimes called risk priority number).
b), c) and d) are not correct options for the reasons given for d).

Answer 2 FL-5.2.1 K1

b) is the correct option. Likelihood can be viewed as the probability of the risk occurring. It may be assessed as high (1), medium (2) or low (3) or a probability percentage. Impact is the effect if the risk occurs and can be assessed in a similar way to likelihood.
a) is not the correct option. Likelihood by itself is not the risk priority. Risk impact should also be taken into consideration for determining risk priority levels.
c) is not the correct option. The risk rating (priority or level) is likelihood x impact. Risk impact can be referred to as business risk. d) is not the correct option. Risk likelihood is best thought of as the chance of occurrence. Plausible means believable or having an appearance of truth. Risk impact is damage and is not defined as a beneficial effect.

Answer 3 FL-5.2.2 K2

b) is the correct option. The test environment being unavailable is primarily a project risk.
a), c) and d) are not correct options as they are primarily product risks.

Answer 4 FL-5.2.2 K2

c) is the correct option. The team should have purchased tools for scheduled static analysis for testing. This is a project risk.
a), b) and d) are not correct options. Software performance efficiency, access to the internet and unsupported security features are primarily product risks.

Answer 5 FL-5.2.2 K2

c) is the correct option. Poor system architecture that results in software that is difficult to maintain is a product risk.
a) is not the correct option. Poor developer skills and training can affect the product. However, this is primarily a project risk because it relates to resource management.
b) is not the correct option. Changes in project scope and requirements are a project risk as they involve potential modifications to the project's goals, which can impact the project's timeline, budget, and scope.
d) is not the correct option. Defect management primarily relates to the management and mitigation of issues and defects during the software development process and is a project risk.

Answer 6 FL-5.2.2 K2

d) is the correct option. Risks may not be evenly distributed over the entire software or system and may only be in certain areas, so it is not possible to conclude from risk-based testing that all areas of the code have been tested.

a) is not the correct option. A 100% probability of occurrence means the issue is not a risk as it will occur.

b) is not the correct option. An issue that causes no impact on any functionality or non-functional characteristic including usability and user satisfaction is not a concern.

c) is not the correct option. If a risk is assessed as high likelihood (assigned 1) and low impact (assigned 3) its priority number is 3. If a risk is assessed as medium likelihood (assigned 2) and high impact (assigned 1) its priority number is 2.

Answer 7 FL-5.2.3 K2

d) and e) are the correct options. d) Product risk analysis can determine whether any other activities in addition to testing could be employed such as contingency planning, transference of risk and other measures. e) Product risk analysis can influence the thoroughness and test scope in several ways, including as given in options a), b) and c).

a) is not a correct option. Identifying high-priority risks allows for a greater amount of the test effort to be focused on the high-risk areas.

b) is not a correct option. Identifying high-risk areas of the code can confirm code complexity in certain areas. c) is not a correct option. Risk analysis can guide resource allocation.

Answer 8 FL-5.2.4 K2

b) is the correct option. Risk level is calculated from risk likelihood and risk impact. Risk mitigation involves implementing actions to reduce risk level. a), c) and d) are not correct options for the reasons given for b).

Answer 9 FL-5.2.4 K2

d) is the correct option. 1B Test techniques and coverage levels are for risk mitigation. 2D Planning for potential outcomes is for risk contingency. 3A Handing the risk to a third party is risk transference. 4C Deferral for future consideration for the upcoming release is risk acceptance.

a), b) and c) are not correct options for the reasons given for d).

Answer 10 FL-5.2.4 K2

a) is the correct option. Risk mitigation is *'The process through which decisions are reached and protective measures are implemented for reducing or maintaining risks to specified levels.'* Assessing the potential risk level is part of risk analysis. b), c) and d) are not correct options. These are risk mitigation measures that can be taken.

5.3 Test Monitoring, Test Control and Test Completion

Test monitoring involves tracking the test process in real time and gathering information to evaluate progress against the planned schedule and objectives.

Test control uses the information from test monitoring as control directives to make adjustments and decisions as necessary to achieve the test objectives. Examples of test process control directives include:

- Adjusting resources when and where required
- Adjusting the test schedule to address a delay in the delivery of the test environment
- Re-prioritizing test cases when additional information on risks becomes available

Test completion is the point at which all planned test activities at a project milestone have been executed. A milestone can be:

- A test level is completed
- An agile iteration is finished
- A test object is completed
- A test object is cancelled
- A software system is released
- A maintenance release is completed

Test completion activities include:

- Making testware available for later use
- Leaving test environments in a satisfactory condition
- Communicating the results of testing to relevant stakeholders

FL-5.3.1 (K1) Recall metrics used for testing

Metrics in testing are measurements and indicators that help assess the quality, effectiveness, and progress of the software test process.

Metrics provide valuable insights into various aspects of testing, allowing teams to:

- Identify issues
- Continuously improve the overall software development and test process
- Use benchmarking and make comparisons
- Analyze which type of tests are providing the most value and validate the test strategy
- Analyze which test phases, levels or iterations are most effective
- Communicate in a standardized way to report test progress to stakeholders so they can make informed decisions

Common test metrics and examples of their uses include:

Type	Metrics based on	Examples of uses
Project Progress	Completion of milestones, resource usage, test effort, and project risks.	Monitoring progress and providing information for project control such as making decisions on changes to benefit progress. Reprioritization of project risks. Allocating resources and effort effectively.
Test Process Progress	Test case implementation, test environment preparation, test cases run/not run, results passed/failed, test execution time.	Gauging the efficiency of the test process.
Product Characteristics	Availability, response times, mean time between failures.	Helping stakeholders understand the stability of the software and readiness for release.
Defects	Defects found/fixed, defect density, defect detection percentage DDP.	Tracking the effectiveness of test efforts. Identifying more defect-prone areas that require additional attention.
Phase or Iteration containment	Phase or iteration in which failures are observed and phase or iteration in which defects are resolved.	Reviewing duration of iteration or phase.
Product Risks	Risks mitigated, outstanding, changes in risk levels, risk distribution, frequency.	Ongoing prioritization of test efforts on areas with higher potential for impacting the end-user experience. Information is helpful to stakeholders making business decisions based on the software.
Coverage	Requirements coverage, code coverage.	Highlighting areas of the code that have been tested and those not covered by tests, allows teams to focus on high-risk or untested portions of the software.
Cost	Costs of test effort and resources.	Assessing the cost-benefit of the test process.

Metrics are typically expressed as percentages or numbers.

Percentage metrics are derived from three elements, the Total number of items, Number of items within the total and the percentage itself.

$$\text{Percentage within the total} = \frac{\text{Number within the total}}{\text{Total}} \times 100\%$$

Having only the percentage does not show anything about the number or size and is likely to be of limited use. For example, if the percentage of test cases implemented is 50% indicates half the test cases have been implemented. However, this gives no indication of the number of test cases executed. 50% could mean five if the total is ten or 500 if the total is 1,000. When there is a change in the number of test cases implemented, for example, a further five are implemented, without knowing the total, it is not possible to give the percentage as this could in this example be 100% (ten out of ten test cases) or 50.5% (505 out of 1,000 test cases).

If you are given only one of the numbers, this does not tell you anything about the percentage. But with two out of the three elements above, it is possible to work out the third. For example, when given the percentage and the total, use the following to determine the number.

$$\text{Number within the total} = \frac{\text{Total number} \times \text{Percentage}\ _{\text{(expressed as a fraction)}}}{100}$$

The Syllabus refers to Defect Detection Percentage (DDP).

$$\text{DDP} = \frac{\text{Defects detected}}{\text{Defects present}} \times 100$$

The denominator (defects present) is approximated by counting all defects found in and after the testing activity in question. This leaves out any defects which are never identified. Such defects might matter in terms of intrinsic code quality but have not affected the software behavior.

The ISTQB Glossary includes an entry for DDP, '*The number of defects found by a test level, divided by the number found by that test level and any other means afterwards*'.

Percentages are useful for assessing what proportion of the work is completed. Numbers give a quantifiable size. Percentages used with numbers are most useful.

FL-5.3.2 (K2) Summarize the purposes, content, and audiences for test reports

A well-structured **test report** provides valuable insights to stakeholders, helping them understand the state of the testing and make informed decisions about progressing to the next phase, its release or further development. The specific contents of a test report may vary based on project requirements and the stakeholder audience. Different audiences, such as project managers, developers, test teams, business analysts, support teams, users and others, may also influence the level of formality and frequency of reporting the test process.

Test progress report, also called a test status report, is defined as, *'A type of periodic test report that includes the progress of test activities against a baseline, risks, and alternatives requiring a decision.'*

A test progress report provides updates on the ongoing testing activities during a specific phase, such as a testing cycle, sprint, iteration or a specified period such as daily, weekly, milestone etc. A test progress report is typically generated multiple times during testing. The report serves to help stakeholders understand the current state of testing, identify bottlenecks or challenges, and make informed decisions to ensure the ongoing testing progresses smoothly.

Test progress report typical contents:

Section	Details
Overview	Test period covered by the report and testing phase being reported. Test progress, such as ahead, behind schedule or deviations.
Test Activities	Summary of the testing activities performed since the last report. Overview of the progress made in terms of test tasks, defect identification, and other testing tasks since the last report.
Test Case Status	Number of test cases planned, created, executed, and remaining/pending. Test case results passed, failed. Reasons for test cases remaining/pending. Status of test case progress compared to the testing schedule.
Defect Status	Summary of defects found during testing. Breakdown of defects by severity, status, and priority.
Test Metrics	Test coverage, code coverage, and passed/failed rates, etc. Trends and changes in key metrics compared to previous reports.
Impediments for Testing	Any issues or obstacles that are hindering testing progress. Explanation of how these issues are being addressed or resolved.
Risks	Identification of any potential new or changed risks identified within the testing period.
Upcoming Activities	Overview of planned testing activities for the next reporting period. Recommended actions for any changes to be made for the next period.

Test completion report, also called a test summary report, is defined as, *'A type of test report produced at completion milestones that provides an evaluation of the corresponding test items against exit criteria.'*

The purpose of a test completion report is to provide a comprehensive overview of the entire test effort at the end of a test phase. The report serves as a record of the testing activities and outcomes. The report helps stakeholders understand the quality of the software, the coverage of testing, and any remaining risks that may need to be considered before deciding to progress to the next phase, product release or further development as appropriate.

Test completion report typical contents:

Section	**Details**
Test Summary	Overview of the testing phase that has been completed.
Deviations from Test Plan	Differences from the planned schedule, duration, effort, scope etc.
Impediments and Workarounds	Challenges or issues faced, for example with setting up and access to the test environment, availability of resources, tools and support.
Defects and Risks	Total number of defects found, categorized by risk level. Unmitigated risks, the defects not fixed
Test Metrics	Based on test progress reports, a summary of the test cases executed, passed, failed, and deferred. Overview of the test coverage achieved for different functional areas.
Lessons Learned	Review of the test process, including successes and areas for improvement. Recommendations for future testing phases or projects.
Overall Assessment	Evaluation of the testing and product quality based on the testing results, the original test plan, test objectives and exit criteria. Statement on whether the testing phase's exit criteria have been met.

FL-5.3.3 (K2) Exemplify how to communicate the status of testing

Stakeholders are typically interested in different types of information, so communication should be tailored accordingly to information that is relevant and meaningful to the audience. Graphs, tables and diagrams are useful for conveying complex information in a visual and easy-to-understand format. An appropriate level of formality for the intended audience should be used.

Communication options include:

Formal written reports that provide comprehensive information about testing activities, results, issues, and progress. These can include executive summaries for higher-level stakeholders and more technical details for the testing team.

Verbal communication with team members and other stakeholders.

Dashboards and visual aids that display data and metrics in an easily understandable format. Examples include CI/CD dashboards and task boards.*

Scheduled meetings to discuss testing progress, challenges, updates and outcomes. These can be daily stand-up meetings, weekly status meetings, or ad-hoc meetings and be held in person or online such as video or voice conferencing.

Electronic communication such as emails or chat.

Online documentation and use of collaboration tools to document and share test progress, defects, and updates. The tool may include the use of dashboards.

Recorded video updates on the test progress with a demonstration of key functionalities.

* A burndown chart is sometimes referred to as an example of a dashboard. A burndown chart shows the amount of work completed across an iteration or a project and the amount remaining to be completed. While it is commonly used in Agile project management to track the progress of development tasks in terms of hours, story points or backlog items, it does not inherently communicate the status of test efforts in detail. Its focus is primarily on overall work and may not provide specific insights into the test process or the status of individual test cases.

5.3 Questions 1 to 7 FL-5.3.1, 5.3.2, 5.3.3

Question 1 FL-5.3.1 (K1) When a code coverage metric is used, which of the following is most true?

a) High code coverage with defects uncovered and fixed means high-quality software
b) 50% code coverage means half of the optimum test effort has been achieved
c) Low code coverage may indicate there is unreachable code
d) Code coverage is always subjective

Select ONE option

Question 2 FL-5.3.1 (K1) Which of the following are metrics that can be used as part of monitoring test implementation activities?

a) Percentage of test data records loaded
b) Planned versus actual hours to create test cases
c) Number of test conditions identified
d) Percentage of test case results that are failed
e) Percentage of test cases automated

Select TWO options

Question 3 FL-5.3.2 (K2) Which of the following should not be included in a test completion report?

a) Test coverage metrics based on previous test progress reports
b) Testing impediments that affected the testing and the workarounds adopted
c) Identification of which testers submitted the most defect reports
d) Testing and product quality evaluation based on the original test plan, test objectives and exit criteria

Select ONE option

Question 4 FL-5.3.2 (K2) Which of the following statements are true for a test summary report except for which?

a) Deviations from the plan are not included as updates are made to the test plan
b) Factors that blocked test progress are included
c) Residual risks that have not been mitigated are included
d) Test metrics based on test progress reports are included

Select ONE option

Question 5 FL-5.3.2 (K2) Which of the following statements are false for a test progress report?

a) Should always be in a formal style following a set template
b) Is the same as a test summary report
c) Can include details of testing planned for the next period
d) The amount of information can be tailored depending on its audience
e) Typically produced more frequently than test completion reports

Select TWO options

Question 6 FL-5.3.3 (K2) Which of the following does not provide an example of a means of communicating the progress of test activities against a baseline, risks, and alternatives requiring a decision between milestones?

a) CI/CD dashboard
b) Test completion report
c) Test status report
d) Electronic chat channel

Select ONE option

Question 7 FL-5.3.3 (K2) Which of the following best describes an advantage of using dashboards for communicating the status of testing?

a) Dashboards provide detailed written reports for in-depth analysis
b) Dashboards offer a linear and text-based representation of data
c) Dashboards present visual data in an easily understandable format
d) Dashboards are best suited for sharing technical documents

Select ONE option

5.3 Answers and Explanations 1 to 7 FL-5.3.1, 5.3.2, 5.3.3

Answer 1 FL-5.3.1 K1

c) is the correct option. Code coverage is a measure of the degree to which the source code has been tested.

a) is not the correct option. High code coverage means more of the source code has been checked during testing, compared to code with low coverage. Code coverage focuses solely on code and does not assess other aspects of quality, such as usability, security, or performance efficiency. High code coverage does not guarantee a defect-free or high-quality software product.

b) is not the correct option. Other testing, as mentioned in a) needs to be considered.

d) is not the correct option. Code coverage is typically objective when white-box or static testing is used.

Answer 2 FL-5.3.1 K1

a) and e) are the correct options. The percentage of test data records loaded and the percentage of test cases that are automated are used in measuring test implementation activities.

b) is not a correct option. Planned versus actual hours to create test cases is a measurement for test design activities. c) is not a correct option. The number of test conditions identified is relevant for monitoring test analysis. d) is not a correct option. The percentage of test case results that are failed is relevant for monitoring test execution, not test implementation.

Answer 3 FL-5.3.2 K2

c) is the correct option. The number of defect reports submitted does not necessarily correlate to the number of defects found and fixed. Defect reports may for example be duplicates, deemed enhancement requests or on further investigation no defect found.

a), b) and d) are not correct options as they all refer to items that may be included in a test completion report. A well-structured test completion report provides valuable insights to stakeholders, helping them understand the state of the software and make informed decisions about progress to the next phase of testing or its release.

Answer 4 FL-5.3.2 K2

a) is the correct option. If there has been a deviation from the plan, this should be documented in the test summary report.

b) is not the correct option. A test summary report should include testing impediments.

c) is not the correct option. Details of residual risks may be included in the test summary report.

d) is not the correct option. Test metrics based on test progress reports may be included.

Answer 5 FL-5.3.2 K2

a) and b) are the correct options as they are false. a) Reporting on test progress to others is often informal. b) A test summary report is a synonym for a test completion report, not a test progress report.
c) is not a correct option as a test progress report, also called a test status report, typically includes details of testing planned for the next period.
d) is not a correct option. The contents of a test report should be appropriate for its audience. For example, business representatives typically require a different amount of information compared to developers. e) is not a correct option. Test progress reports are typically produced more frequently during the test process than test completion reports which are produced when a milestone is reached.

Answer 6 FL-5.3.3 K2

b) is the correct option. A test completion report is produced at completion milestones and provides an evaluation of the corresponding test items against exit criteria. Progress of test activities against a baseline, risks, and alternatives requiring a decision is covered in a test progress report.
a), c) and d) are not correct options as they are all ways test progress can be communicated.

Answer 7 FL-5.3.3 K2

c) is the correct option. Dashboards present visual data in an easily understandable format.
a), b) and d) are not correct options for the reasons given for c).

5.4 Configuration Management

Configuration management is defined as, *'A discipline applying technical and administrative direction and surveillance to identify and document the functional and physical characteristics of a configuration item, control changes to those characteristics, record and report change processing and implementation status, and verify that it complies with specified requirements.'* The *'specified requirements'* refer to identifiable and unique version naming controls and mechanisms, tracking changes and the method of recording the relationships with other configuration items.

FL-5.4.1 (K2) Summarize how configuration management supports testing

Configuration items can encompass a wide range of elements, including:

- Source code files, libraries and modules
- Documentation files, plans and reports
- Data files and test conditions
- Test conditions, test scripts, test cases, test results, test logs and test reports
- Hardware components, network and server configurations

The benefits of configuration management include:

- Supports collaboration among teams by providing a common reference for assets, reducing confusion and ensuring that everyone works with the same version
- Avoids risks that could result from unauthorized changes, inconsistencies and inadequate documentation
- Ensures the correct versions of the software configuration items are used during development, testing, and deployment
- Supports audits that are performed to verify compliance with standards, regulations, and processes
- Facilitates proper control and documentation of changes to configuration items. Changes are planned, reviewed, approved, and implemented in a controlled manner to prevent unauthorized or unplanned alterations
- Helps in understanding the evolution of a project or product by providing a historical record of changes and decisions made
- Supports efficient troubleshooting, allowing developers and engineers to refer back to specific versions and configurations to diagnose and resolve problems

For more information, see *References, ISO Standards - ISO 9001.*

5.4 Questions 1 to 6 FL-5.4.1

Question 1 FL-5.4.1 (K2) Which of the following best describes how configuration management supports testing?

a) Stores software code to ensure early versions remain available
b) Stores documentation so a record of the project is available
c) Provides a comprehensive change control system
d) Is an automated system used to configure the test environment

Select ONE option

Question 2 FL-5.4.1 (K2) Which of the following is the primary purpose of configuration management?

a) Configuring operating systems, databases, and application servers needed for the application to run
b) Planning, scheduling, estimating, reporting and controlling, test activities
c) Recognizing, recording, classifying and investigating defects
d) Controlling changes to identified fundamental components or elements of a system or product

Select ONE option

Question 3 FL-5.4.1 (K2) Which of the following, best tracks an updated test report that has been created and is to be stored in the test report repository?

a) Traceability management
b) Maintenance testing
c) Quality management
d) Configuration management

Select ONE option

Question 4 FL-5.4.1 (K2) Which of the following is not true for configuration management?

a) Automated configuration management is typically included in a DevOPs pipeline
b) Configuration items approved for testing can only be changed through a formal change control process
c) An approved configuration item can be used as a reference from which other items can be compared
d) Configuration management is the same as traceability management as they both track work products

Select ONE option

Question 5 FL-5.4.1 (K2) Which of the following best describes configuration management?

a) The practice of assigning IP addresses, setting parameters and hardware-dependent values to enable network access
b) A technique to automate test activities by managing the implementation of test tools into the test environment
c) A discipline to control changes to the software and work products
d) A practice to optimize server configurations for security and performance efficiency

Select ONE option

Question 6 FL-5.4.1 (K2) Configuration management procedures and infrastructure should be designed and set up during which test level?

a) Test planning
b) Test analysis
c) Test design
d) Test implementation

Select ONE option

5.4 Answers and Explanations 1 to 6 FL-5.4.1

Answer 1 FL-5.4.1 K2

c) is the correct option. Configuration management is defined as, *'A discipline applying technical and administrative direction and surveillance to identify and document the functional and physical characteristics of a configuration item, control changes to those characteristics, record and report change processing and implementation status, and verify that it complies with specified requirements'.* a) is not the correct option. This refers to a backup system. b) is not the correct option as this refers to a documentation repository. d) is not the correct option. Configuring an environment refers to setting up the necessary hardware, software, and network configurations to create a specific environment for development, testing, or deployment. Configuration management is a broader discipline that focuses on controlling and tracking changes to software, hardware, and documentation throughout the lifecycle. Configuration management can provide a historical record of changes and outcomes of decisions made.

Answer 2 FL-5.4.1 K2

d) is the correct option. The primary purpose of configuration management is to control changes to the functional and physical characteristics of identified fundamental components or elements within a system, product, or project, record and report change processing and implementation status, and verify that it complies with specified requirements.

a) is not the correct option. Installing and configuring software needed for the application to run is environment configuration.

b) is the not correct option. Planning, scheduling, estimating, reporting and controlling, test activities is part of test management.

c) is not the correct option. Recognizing, recording, classifying and investigating defects and is part of defect management.

Answer 3 FL-5.4.1 K2

d) is the correct option. Configuration management is a discipline for identifying, controlling and tracking software and work products. a), b) and c) are not correct options for the reasons given for d).

Answer 4 FL-5.4.1 K2

d) is the correct option as it is not true. Traceability is the relationship between two or more work products. Configuration management tracks and controls versions of the same configuration items.

a) is not the correct option. Automated configuration management is normally included when CI/CD and the associated testing are implemented as part of the DevOps pipeline.

b) is not the correct option. It is true that configuration items approved for testing can only be changed through a formal change control process. c) is not the correct option. A configuration item approved for testing is a baseline from which other items can be compared.

Answer 5 FL-5.4.1 K2

c) is the correct option. Configuration management is a discipline for identifying, controlling and tracking software and work products.

a) is not the correct option. Assigning IP addresses, setting parameters and hardware-dependent values is part of configuring a network and is not configuration management.

b) is not the correct option. Configuration management may be automated as part of an automated DevOps pipeline but does not itself automate testing activities other than identifying, controlling and tracking configuration items.

d) is not the correct option. Server configuration refers to the process of setting up and adjusting various software and hardware parameters on a server to ensure it functions correctly.

Answer 6 FL-5.4.1 K2

a) is the correct option. The purpose of configuration management is to establish and maintain the integrity of the component or system, the testware and their relationships from the start and throughout the project and product lifecycle. b), c) and d) are not correct options for the reasons given for a).

5.5 Defect Management

Defect management is a critical process in software development and testing that involves identifying, recognizing, recording, classifying, prioritizing, tracking, and resolving anomalies and defects that are found during the software development lifecycle. Defect management is a systematic approach that ensures defect reports are properly managed. This contributes to the overall quality and reliability of the software product.

FL-5.5.1 (K3) Prepare a defect report

A **defect report** is a key part of a defect management process, *'The process of recognizing, recording, classifying, investigating, resolving and disposing of defects.'* In this context, 'defect' refers to the reported anomaly or incident. On investigation, anomalies or incidents reported may or may not be determined to be actual defects. They may be found to be for example false-positive results or change requests. The template used for a defect report depends on the software development lifecycle being used.

Testers must enter complete, concise, accurate, objective, relevant and timely information in a defect report. If screenshots to illustrate the defect are included, sensitive information or confidential information should typically be removed or blurred. Some parts of a defect report, such as an identifier, may be automatically filled when using defect management tools.

The defect management process includes a workflow for handling the defect from discovery to closure of the defect reports that should be used by all stakeholders.

Document templates can be found in ISO 29119-3, see *References.*

Defect report descriptions that are unclear, ambiguous, vague, or lacking in specificity, make it difficult for the development team to understand and address the reported issue. Examples of defect report descriptions that should not be used unless they are qualified with additional specific details include:

'Software is not user-friendly'. This statement is not clear. While it conveys dissatisfaction, it does not specify what aspects of the software are considered unfriendly or how they can be improved.

'System is slow'. 'Slow' is a relative term and does not provide a clear benchmark of acceptable performance efficiency. There is also a need to specify which operations or processes are slow.

'Application does not work properly'. A general statement does not explain what functions or features are not working as expected, making it challenging to diagnose the problem.

'Screen appears strange'. This is a vague statement. Details about the screen and an explanation of what is considered normal are required.

'Search page glitch occurred'. The term 'glitch' is vague and does not explain what is happening on the product page.

'Account Problem.' This vague description does not indicate whether the issue is related to the login process, account settings, or other account-related functions.

Defect Report templates vary, but typically include the following:

Identifier	**Unique Identifier** given to the defect
Project Product version	Specific details of the software under test and version
Product	Title
Summary	A clear and concise summary with both expected result and actual result
Detailed Description	Description including the context, any recovery action needed following the failure, the data used and ease of reproducing. The test technique which revealed the problem, e.g., review, static analysis, dynamic testing, test case used
Test Steps to Reproduce	The test steps to reproduce the defect. The test case reference
Attachments	Any additional information e.g., screenshots, data dumps and logs
Test Level/ Phase/Sprint	Used to assess the effectiveness of early testing and phase containment
Probability of occurrence	Probability of the defect occurring, (all occasions, intermittent, etc.)
Defect Severity	Impact of the defect on the system and/or the product stakeholders
Defect Priority	Priority to resolve the defect (usually determined by the business impact of the failure and likelihood of occurrence)
Remarks	Notes
Reported by / Role	Name and role of the person reporting the defect
Status	The status of the defect (Open, Assigned, In progress, Confirmation, Closed, Rejected, Unconfirmed, Duplicate, Deferred)
Assigned to	The name of the person that is assigned to analyze/fix the defect
Subsystem	Subsystem or component where the defect is located. Used for cluster analysis
Resolution	Details of resolution if fixed, mitigated, accepted or other action
Conclusions	Recommendations and approvals for the action taken or not taken

When a developer has a fix for a defect the defect status report is set to confirmation. The tester then tests the fix. If the fix resolves the defect, the tester closes the defect report.

For more information on defect management and defect reports, see Software Testing Advanced Test Manager – Guide for ISTQB® certification – C. Newbould ISBN 978-0-9536056-4-4 July 2022 AiFlex Publishing.

FL-5.5.1 (K3) Exercise: Defect Reports

Consider the following entries in a defect report for an e-commerce website.

Summary: Problem with the BUYER website
Description: When attempting to complete the process of buying a product on the e-commerce website, I encountered an issue that prevented me from finalizing the purchase. The error message read: "Payment processing failed. Please try again later". In similar circumstances to the previous version, the website allowed the order to be placed, displayed a confirmation message and provided an order number.

Environment: Browser Google Chrome Operating system: Windows
Test Steps to Reproduce: Login to the website. Try to make a purchase
Severity: High **Priority**: Urgent
Notes: Please fix this issue as soon as possible.

Identify which of the defect report entries are inadequate and explain why.

FL-5.5.1 Exercise Answer

Summary: is too vague. A better summary would be, 'Checkout Process: Payment processing failure without error message'.
Version: is not specific. The latest version being tested may not be the same as that in development.

Detailed Description: does not provide a clear and concise description of the specific problem encountered, such as where the problem occurred, checkout process, product selection or other, what the product was. Why the tester believes the purchase should have been completed, such as on previous versions. Expected results are included, but without sufficient detail, such as when the error message should appear (after clicking select or confirm order or other). Why the tester believed the purchase should have been completed, such as in previous versions.

An example of a better description would be product P1442 was added to the basket. After clicking "Place Order", the website displayed an error message that read: "Payment processing failed. Please try again later". No order confirmation was received, and the purchase was not completed. In previous versions of the website, this purchase has been completed.

Environment: is not adequately detailed.
An example of better environment information would be:

Browser: Google Chrome (Version 118.0.5993.70)
Operating System: Microsoft Windows™ 11 ver 23H2
Registered User Account: [Username]
Device: Laptop company standard issue [Make and Model]

Test Steps to Reproduce: requires a step-by-step guide on how to reproduce the issue, including the specific actions taken on the website that led to the problem.

An example of test steps to reproduce might be:

Navigate to the e-commerce website URL: [website URL].
Log in with a registered user account.
Browse the product catalog and add an item to the shopping cart.
Proceed to the shopping cart and click "Checkout".
Enter shipping and payment information.
Click the 'Place Order' button to complete the purchase.

Notes: Should provide additional information or context that might be helpful, such as the tester believed the purchase should have been completed as it had done the previous version of the software.
As it has not been mentioned elsewhere, there should be comments on whether this issue is reproducible.
'Please fix this issue as soon as possible' is not helpful when urgency and priority are already included.

5.5 Questions 1 to 5 FL-5.5.1

Question 1 FL-5.5.1 (K3) A table reservation application, iTABLAR, for a restaurant is being tested. Customers can make their reservations. However, to limit issues with customers making reservations for large numbers of diners, preventing others from making bookings and then not turning up, a deposit is required for reservations for more than six diners. During testing, you have found that a user can make bookings for more than six diners without a deposit. When entering the defect report on the defect management system, the defect report identifier, date, the logged-in credentials and the default status are prefilled.

The following information has been entered in the defect report submitted.

Title: Booking for more than six diners
Software: iTABLAR v2.3. Priority: High
Description: Bookings for more than six diners can be made without needing to pay a deposit
Expected result: Six or more diners cannot be booked by one customer without a deposit
Actual result: Three out of five times when attempting to book more than six diners, a deposit was not needed

Which of the following should have been entered but has been omitted?

a) Test steps needed to create the problem
b) Defect report identifier
c) A summary of the problem
d) Probability of problem occurrence

Select ONE option

Question 2 FL-5.5.1 (K3) Availability has been identified as one of the top product risks for an application that allows users to make online purchases. You uncover a reproducible failure that results in users losing their connections to the retailer's website when checking out orders with values greater than $299 and then being unable to reconnect for between two and five minutes.

Which of the following is a good summary for a defect report for this failure that reflects the failure and its impact on stakeholders?

a) Developers have introduced a major availability defect that will cause significant impact to users when checking out large orders
b) The web server log shows Error 05556 every time test case TC04-005 is used
c) Checking out an order for more than $299 consistently results in the termination of a customer session, with a delay in availability when attempting to reconnect
d) Performance is slow and reliability poor for checking out a high-value order

Select ONE option

Question 3 FL-5.5.1 (K3) You are testing an e-retail application BUY. You are submitting the following defect report:

Title: Test Case TC17 with BUYv2.1
Summary: 'Product List' mixes currencies for the products in the product list display.
Priority: Medium
Defect Description: Clicking on 'Product List' takes the user to the product display page. Five products have their prices listed in US dollars and all other products are priced in euros. When the first product is selected by the user and added to the cart, the currency of the first product is used to set up the billing. The numeric values of subsequent products selected are then added together, regardless of currency. Users who then go to 'Checkout' to purchase the goods may be charged incorrectly if products are priced in different currencies. The problem was first observed in integration testing when the currency exchange database was added.

Which of the following have been omitted and should have been included in the report?

a) Expected results
b) Test steps to reproduce the problem
c) Actual results
d) Reference to the test case
e) Probability of occurrence

Select TWO options

Question 4 FL-5.5.1 (K3) Consider the following defect report:

Title: Expense Submission Priority: High. Date: December 1, 20XX

During the process of submitting a new expense report, an unexpected error message is displayed.

Test steps to reproduce:

1. Log in using valid credentials.
2. Click on 'Submit New Expense Report.'
3. Fill in the required details, expense category, amount, and description.
4. Attach a valid receipt image.
5. Click on the 'Submit' button.

An unexpected error message is displayed to the user instead of a confirmation message or a success notification. A screenshot of the details I entered is attached before submission. I have successfully submitted expense reports using this application before.

Which of the following has been omitted from the report?

a) Summary of anomaly
b) Expected results
c) Priority
d) Error message

Select ONE option

Question 5 FL-5.5.1 (K3) Consider the following part of a defect report that has been entered after the fields for the identifier, title, time and date anomaly observed, priority to fix, probability of occurrence and author including their role have all been completed:

Test steps to reproduce:

1. Log in to the website using a registered account
2. Add items to shopping cart
3. Proceed to 'Checkout' process
4. Fill in standard shipping for required shipping and XYZ credit card
5. Click 'Place Order' button

Expected result: After clicking 'Place Order' button, the user should be redirected to the order confirmation page, where details of the order are displayed.

Actual Result: After clicking 'Place Order' button, the user remains on the same checkout order page, and the confirmation page is not displayed.

Note: Other types of shipping required with XYZ credit card do not show this failure.

Which of the following important aspects of a good defect report are missing?

a) Summary of an anomaly being reported
b) Priority to fix
c) Test environment details
d) Use of objective tone
e) Indication if repeatable always with the same outcome

Select TWO options

5.5 Answers and Explanations 1 to 5 FL-5.5.1

Answer 1 FL-5.5.1 K3

a) is the correct option. There are no details on the test steps needed to be taken to show how more than six people can be booked without a deposit being paid or the test case used. For example, this might be in one booking at the outset, amending an existing booking, multiple bookings or depending on the number of places requested.
b) is not the correct option. The defect report identifier is filled in by the defect management software.
c) is not the correct option. The description given acts as a summary.
d) is not the correct option. The probability is indicated three out of five times.

Answer 2 FL-5.5.1 K3

c) is the correct option. The defect is summarized in an appropriate way for stakeholders.
a) is not the correct option. A defect report should focus on the failure being reported and not attribute responsibility to any person or persons. b) is not the correct option. Too much detail is included in a summary suitable for stakeholders. d) is not the correct option. The summary is too vague.

Answer 3 FL-5.5.1 K3

a) and e) are the correct options. a) Expected results should be given. For example, euros should be used at all times or the currency should be that of the user's location. e) There is no mention of whether the problem happens every time or intermittently.
b) is not the correct option. Test steps to reproduce the problem have been given.
c) is not the correct option. Actual results have been given by giving details of at least five products on the first page of the product list that have different currencies.
d) is not the correct option. Reference to the test case TC17 has been made.

Answer 4 FL-5.5.1 K3

d) is the correct option. There are no details on what the error message or error code was.
a) is not the correct option. There is a short description of the anomaly before the test steps to reproduce it are given.
b) is not the correct option. The expected results are a confirmation message or success notification.
c) is not the correct option. The priority is given as 'High'.

Answer 5 FL-5.5.1 K3

a) and c) are the correct options. a) A summary description such as 'During the checkout, with standard shipping and credit card XYZ, clicking the 'Place Order' button, does redirect the user to the order confirmation page is missing'. c) The test environment including version details is missing.
b) is not a correct option. The priority to fix is included in the part of the defect first entered. d) is not a correct option. The defect report is written with clear, unambiguous details. e) is not a correct option. Details of reproducibility are included in the part of the defect first entered.

6. TEST TOOLS

The ISTQB Exam Structures & Rules Tables v1.19 specifies two exam questions for this section. There is one K1 and one K2 level learning objective.

Keywords given in the Syllabus
test automation.

6.1 Tool Support for Testing

Tool support for software testing refers to the use of specialized software tools and applications that are designed to assist and enhance various aspects of the test process. These tools are developed to streamline testing activities, improve efficiency, and provide a structured approach to testing tasks. Tool support can cover a wide range of activities within the test process, from test planning and test case design to test execution, defect tracking, and reporting.

The Syllabus does not specifically include a mention of Artificial Intelligence, AI. AI-enabled tools are widely predicted to have an increasingly significant impact on software testing resulting in higher software quality, a quicker time to market, better optimization and cost savings. Testers are likely to encounter the use of AI-enabled tools in their work. Some exam questions may refer to the benefits and risks of AI-enabled test automation tools, so extra practice questions are included in this guide.

FL-6.1.1 (K2) Explain how different types of test tools support testing

Test tools that support and facilitate test activities can be grouped into different types depending on their purpose.

Tools based on purpose include, but are not limited to:

Type of Test Tool	Testing Support
Collaboration	Facilitates communication. Helps all involved updated with a continuous flow of project information and provides maximum transparency
Comparator	Determines the differences across data, files, databases and results
Containerization	Supports scalability and deployment standardization
Debugger	Gives insights into the software such as memory contents, data tables, file contents, and other internal program states
Design and Implementation	Facilitates the generation of test cases. Tools can work with specific requirements document models such as Unified Modeling Language, Gherkin, inputs such as classification tree etc.
Execution and Coverage	Facilitates automated test execution and coverage measurements. Automating the execution of regression testing typically provides a good return on investment
Functional	Facilitates testing functional appropriateness, functional correctness and functional completeness
Implementation	Used for test data preparation and test procedures
Management	Increases the test process efficiency and effectiveness by facilitating management of the software development lifecycle, requirements, tests, defects, configuration, and traceability. Includes configuration and version control management
Network	Facilitates evaluating the performance of various aspects of a network
Non-functional	Allows the tester to perform non-functional testing that is difficult or impossible to perform manually such as performance efficiency, load and resource utilization
Other	For example, a spreadsheet is a test tool in the context of testing, text or code editors
Static Analyzer	Supports the tester in performing reviews and code analysis without the code being executed. Can be used for some-nonfunctional testing such as portability, maintainability, some aspects of reliability, and reusability with variables reinitialized
Virtual Machine	Supports scalability and deployment standardization
AI-enabled	Leverages artificial intelligence and machine learning techniques to perform testing tasks.

6.1 Questions 1 to 5 FL-6.1.1

Question 1 FL-6.1.1 (K2) Which of the following is the most appropriate type of tool for tracking the status of a test case?

a) Test Design tool
b) Test Management tool
c) Test Execution tool
d) Test Coverage tool

Select ONE option

Question 2 FL-6.1.1 (K2) Which of the following tools can be used to enforce coding standards?

a) Collaboration
b) Test Comparator
c) Test Management
d) Static Analyzer

Select ONE option

Question 3 FL-6.1.1 (K2) What is normally a function of test management tools?

a) Reporting, controlling and completing test activities
b) Test case generation
c) Creating test procedures
d) Defining test conditions to be used

Select ONE option

Question 4 FL-6.1.1 (K2) Which of the following is not true for differentiating AI-enabled tools from other test tools?

a) AI-enabled tools can dynamically adapt test scripts, traditional test automation tools use predefined scripts
b) AI-enabled tools require less manual effort to generate test cases compared to traditional tools
c) Throughout the test process of a project, AI-enabled test tools need to be released frequently, other automation tools do not
d) AI-enabled test tools require a data set for training before the tool can provide benefits from self-learning for testing

Select ONE option

Question 5 FL-6.1.1 (K2) In which test activity is a data preparation tool used?

a) Test monitoring
b) Test analysis
c) Test implementation
d) Test execution

Select ONE option

6.1 Answers and Explanations 1 to 5 FL-6.1.1

Answer 1 FL-6.1.1 K2

b) is the correct answer. A test management tool can provide the capability for tracking the status of a test case.

a) is not the correct option. A test design tool does not track a test case through the later phases such as test execution.

c) is not the correct option. A test execution tool does not track the status of the design and creation of test cases. d) is not the correct option. A coverage tool monitors the execution of test cases and reports on how much of the statements, branches, functions and lines were run as part of the tests.

Answer 2 FL-6.1.1 K2

d) is the correct option. Static analysis tools enforce coding standards and analyze internal structures.

a) is not the correct option. A collaboration tool is used to facilitate communication. b) is not the correct option. A comparator tool determines the differences across data, files, databases and results.

c) is not the correct option. Test management tools facilitate the administration of the test process.

Answer 3 FL-6.1.1 K2

a) is the correct option. Test management is defined as, *'The process of planning, scheduling, estimating, monitoring, reporting, controlling, and completing test activities.'*

b) is not the correct option. Test case generation is part of test design and test implementation.

c) is not the correct option. Test procedure is defined as, *'A sequence of test cases in execution order, and any associated actions that may be required to set up the initial preconditions and any wrap up activities post execution.'* d) is not the correct option. Test technique is defined as, *'A procedure used to define test conditions, design test cases, and specify test data.'*

Answer 4 FL-6.1.1 K2

c) is the correct option. AI-enabled test tools have self-learning capability to allow them to adapt to change without frequent releases. a), b) and d) are not correct options as they correctly highlight differences between AI-enabled and other tools.

Answer 5 FL-6.1.1 K2

c) is the correct option. Test implementation includes creating or acquiring the testware, including that needed for execution. a), b) and d) are not correct options for the reasons given for c).

6.2 Benefits and Risks of Test Automation

While test automation does not replace manual testing, it can provide many benefits.

FL-6.2.1 (K1) Recall the benefits and risks of test automation

Benefits of using test automation tools when compared to manual testing include:

- Reduced repetitive manual testing
- Greater consistency and repeatability
- Improved objective assessment, such as for coverage
- Easy access to test information, such as producing graphs, up-to-date dashboards, aggregated data etc.
- Testing features such as a large number of (virtual) users at one time or across multiple platforms that would not be possible to do manually
- Testing time, cost and effort may be reduced, depending on the frequency of use of automation versus staff training requirements, set-up time, cost of tools and ongoing associated resources
- Faster smoke testing to determine the stability of a build
- Faster generation and preparation of data
- Reduced number of human errors, especially in complex scenarios
- Improved regression testing where the return on investment ROI is typically the greatest
- Better insights when tests fail by showing memory contents, data tables, file contents, and other internal states

Potential risks of using test automation tools include:

- Automation tools are only as good as the rules they are using
- Unrealistic expectations about the benefits
- Estimations of the time, cost and effort for the initial introduction as well as for significant and ongoing use may be under-estimated
- Over-reliance and a false sense of certainty of the level of software quality, ignoring the need for human critical thinking
- Interoperability issues between critical automation tools may be neglected, such as with requirements management tools, configuration management tools, defect management tools and tools from multiple vendors
- Using automation when manual testing is more appropriate. Automation may not fully replace human judgment, intuition, and creativity that testers bring to identify complex issues or corner cases
- Can produce false-positive results (incorrectly identifying an issue) or false-negative results (failing to identify a genuine issue)
- Tool vendors may provide a poor response for support, upgrades, and defect fixes, go out of business, retire the tool, or sell the tool to a different vendor
- Using open-source software that may be suspended with updates not available

continued ...

A new platform or technology may not be supported by the tool

Choosing an unsuitable tool that does not comply with regulatory requirements, safety or industry standards

Enhancing the test scope beyond what is required by finding defects that would not be encountered by real users and increasing the duration of the software development lifecycle

Additional potential risks of using AI-enabled tools include:

AI-enabled tools can inadvertently inherit biases present in training data, leading to biased testing results. For example, if the training data is biased towards certain user behaviors, these tools may miss critical scenarios

Can be complex to set up and configure, particularly for AI-enabled test tools. Testers might need specialized skills and knowledge to effectively use and customize these tools for their specific testing needs

May not currently be compatible with certain software environments, languages, frameworks, or architectures, limiting their usability

Use of AI-enabled tools might raise ethical considerations, for example, if AI-driven testing decisions impact user experience, behavior or privacy

Can be costly to implement, particularly AI-enabled tools

AI-enabled test tools leverage artificial intelligence and machine learning techniques to perform testing tasks. The tools can learn from historical testing data, adapt to changing software behavior, and make decisions based on patterns and insights from data. Significant advances in AI capability and machine learning suggest there is likely to be a reduction in manual testing.

Other test automation tools follow predefined scripts or test cases to automate repetitive testing tasks.

Benefits of AI-enabled test automation tools when compared to other automation tools include:

	Type of Test Automation Tools	
Capability	**AI-enabled Test Tools**	**Other Test Automation Tools**
Self-learning and adaptability	Adapt to changes in the software or system without significant manual intervention and thus improve effectiveness and accuracy.	Typically require manual script updates when the software or system changes.
Efficiency in test case generation	Speed up test case design as can automatically generate test cases based on code analysis, requirements, historical data and user behavior.	Rely on manual test case creation, which can be time-consuming and may lead to incomplete coverage.
Maintenance of test cases	Reduce the manual effort for test case maintenance by learning and adapting. Reduce the chance of human error associated with manual changes to automated scripts.	May require significant manual maintenance effort.
Test case execution and prioritization	Dynamically prioritize test cases based on risk or code changes, optimizing test execution. Execute test cases rapidly, making them particularly suitable for continuous integration and continuous delivery pipelines, CI/CD.	Execute tests in a fixed order, which may not be efficient for rapidly changing applications.
Test case coverage	Using a wide range of scenarios, including complex interactions and edge cases, results in improved test coverage.	Have some specific capabilities where defined.
Test case prioritization	Prioritize testing dynamically based on code changes, historical defect data and potential risk areas.	Have lower capability to change test case prioritization.
Natural language processing, NLP	Tools using NLP analyze natural language requirements and convert them into test cases or scenarios, bridging requirements and testing.	No NLP capabilities.
Defect prediction	Analyze historical defect data and code changes to predict areas of the application that are more likely to have defects. This helps testers focus effort effectively such as high-risk areas.	Limited defect trend prediction capability.

6.2 Questions 1 to 4 FL-6.2.1

Question 1 FL-6.2.1 (K1) Which of the following statements is true for test automation?

a) Using automation removes the risk of false-negative results during testing
b) Automation of initial testing of a new application or new features typically provides the greatest return on investment
c) Automation can simulate situations that would not be possible for manual testing to do
d) Automation always reduces overall test effort and costs

Select ONE option

Question 2 FL-6.2.1 (K1) Which of the following is not necessarily true for AI-enabled tools?

a) AI-enabled tools can dynamically adjust test strategy and test approach based on real-time feedback
b) AI-enabled tools remove the risk traditional tools may have of producing false-negative results
c) AI-enabled tools can inadvertently inherit biases present in training data, leading to biased testing results
d) AI-enabled tools can analyze historical defect data and code changes to predict high-risk areas prone to defects

Select ONE option

Question 3 FL-6.2.1 (K1) The following are benefits of using AI-enabled tools except for which?

a) Suitable for continuous integration and continuous delivery (CI/CD) pipelines
b) Reduces manual effort for test script creation when compared to other test automation tools
c) Provides immediate cost savings by speeding up testing and reducing manual effort
d) Can process some unstructured data that can then be used in test case execution

Select ONE option

Question 4 FL-6.2.1 (K1) Which of the following is not true when using automated static code testing?

a) Can produce false-positive results
b) Can produce false-negative results
c) Must be separate from the build process
d) Can provide mitigation recommendations
e) Cannot report on code optimization

Select TWO options

6.2 Answers and Explanations 1 to 4 FL-6.2.1

Answer 1 FL-6.2.1 K1

c) is the correct option. For example, test automation tools may simulate thousands of virtual users interacting with a web application to see how the application behaves under load. This is unlikely to be possible to do manually. a) is not the correct option. Automation can produce false-negative results that go unnoticed. b) is not the correct option. The greatest return is typically in regression testing and there is the least maintenance cost. d) is not the correct option. Automation can be costly to set up and may not always be cost-effective to do.

Answer 2 FL-6.2.1 K1

b) is the correct option as it is not true. Artificial Intelligence AI-enabled tools can produce false-positive results (incorrectly identifying an issue) or false-negative results (failing to identify a genuine issue), leading to inefficiencies and inaccuracies in the test process.
a) is not the correct option. AI tools can dynamically adjust test strategy and test approach based on real-time feedback, ensuring that test effort remains relevant and effective as the application evolves.
c) is not the correct option. AI tools can inadvertently inherit biases present in training data, leading to biased testing results. For example, if the training data is biased towards certain user behaviors, the AI tool might miss critical scenarios. d) is not the correct option. AI tools can analyze historical defect data and code changes to predict high-risk areas prone to defects, helping testers focus efforts effectively.

Answer 3 FL-6.2.1 K1

c) is the correct option. An initial investment in cost, training and infrastructure setup is required. AI testing tools can be complex to set up and configure. However, AI-enabled tools can lead to long-term cost savings by speeding up test processes and reducing manual effort.
a) is not the correct option. AI tools can execute tests rapidly, making them suitable for continuous integration and continuous delivery (CI/CD) pipelines and providing quick feedback to developers.
b) is not the correct option. AI tools can automatically generate test cases by analyzing requirements, code, and user behavior, reducing the manual effort required for test script creation.
d) is not the correct option. AI tools can process unstructured data such as natural language, making them valuable for testing applications with text-based input/output.

Answer 4 FL-6.2.1 K1

c) and e) are the correct options as they are not true. Static testing can and often is incorporated into the build process. e) Static test tools can identify and report on where code can be optimized based on code structures.
a) is not a correct option. A static code test tool may produce false-positive results where the tool reports a possible vulnerability that is not a concern. This can occur for example when the tool cannot be sure of the integrity and security of data as it flows through the application from input to output.
b) is not a correct option. The use of static code analysis tools can also result in false-negative results where vulnerabilities result but the tool does not report them. The tool is only as good as the rules it is based on. d) is not the correct option. Automated testing of static code can provide mitigation recommendations. For example, coding standards that should be enforced.

USING THE PRACTICE EXAMS

When you feel confident, try Practice Exam One under timed conditions.

After each Practice Exam

Before continuing, review your results. Make a review list of the questions where you did not get the correct answer. Also, make a review list of questions where your answer was correct but feel it was achieved by guesswork.

Review your lists and focus on where you do not know or incorrectly understand a term or technique. Learn the definition of terms you are unsure of. Study the techniques.

Review your lists regarding not spotting a negative word, such as a question asking for, '*Which is an untrue or incorrect answer?*' If you missed this, make a point of looking for negative words in later practice.

Review your lists where you chose the wrong option due to a word or small phrase embedded in the question which affects the answer, see previously, Chapter *About the Exam - How to Approach Exam Questions.* Add your entries to those listed in the chapter.

Keep in mind the distribution of questions. Identify and note where you may have any skills gaps, weak topics or subject areas.

For each of the questions on your review lists, look up the learning objective from the relevant Answer Grid. Work on your skills appropriately. If you need more marks from K1 level questions, make a list of terms you were not confident with. Revise these using the Glossary. If you need more marks from K2 questions, work on increasing your understanding of statements and concepts. Although it is possible to achieve a pass without answering any K3 level questions correctly, if you need more practice at K3 level go back and review the exercises and examples in this guide and look for scenarios from your work or other sources where you can practice.

Consider the time taken to answer questions, including those answered correctly. Details on the suggested time for a question are based on the K-level, see Chapter *About the Exam – Where marks can be gained or lost.* If you feel that a few questions took significantly longer than the time suggested, review why this happened and aim to improve your knowledge and skills as appropriate.

How Learning Objectives Relate to Exam Questions

An exam has 40 questions that address 40 of the 64 total learning objectives.
There are three practice exams, each with 40 questions, covering all 64 learning objectives.

Note: The order of questions in the exam has not been specified by ISTQB. Practice exam questions in this guide are ordered according to the ISTQB Exam Structures & Rules Tables v1.19. In an online exam, computer randomization results in questions, or blocks of questions, being in a different order.

The following table shows Practice Exam Questions, K-levels and learning objectives.

Q#	K level	Practice Exam One	Practice Exam Two	Practice Exam Three
1	K1	1.1.1	1.2.2	1.2.2
2	K1	1.5.2	1.5.2	1.5.2
3	K2	1.1.2	1.2.1	1.2.3
4	K2	1.3.1	1.3.1	1.3.1
5	K2	1.4.1	1.4.1	1.4.1
6	K2	1.4.3	1.4.2	1.4,4
7	K2	1.4.4	1.4.5	1.4.5
8	K2	1.5.1	1.5.3	1.5.3
9	K1	2.1.2	2.1.2	2.1.2
10	K1	2.1.3	2.1.3	2.1.3
11	K2	2.2.1	2.2.2	2.2.1
12	K2	2.2.3	2.3.1	2.2.3
13	K2	2.1.1	2.1.6	2.1.6
14	K2	2.1.4	2.1.5	2.1.4
15	K1	3.1.1	3.2.1	3.2.1
16	K1	3.2.5	3.2.3	3.2.3
17	K2	3.1.2	3.1.3	3.1.2
18	K2	3.2.2	3.2.4	3.2.2

Q#	K level	Practice Exam One	Practice Exam Two	Practice Exam Three
19	K2	4.1.1	4.1.1	4.1.1
20	K2	4.3.1	4.3.2	4.3.2
21	K2	4.3.2	4.3.3	4.3.3
22	K2	4.4.1	4.4.1	4.4.1
23	K2	4.4.3	4.4.2	4.4.2
24	K2	4.5.1	4.5.2	4.5.1
25	K3	4.2.1	4.2.1	4.2.1
26	K3	4.2.2	4.2.2	4.2.2
27	K3	4.2.3	4.2.3	4.2.3
28	K3	4.2.4	4.2.4	4.2.4
29	K3	4.5.3	4.5.3	4.5.3
*30	K1	5.1.2	5.1.6	5.2.1
31	K2	5.1.1	5.1.3	5.1.1
32	K2	5.1.7	5.1.7	5.1.7
33	K2	5.2.2	5.2.3	5.2.4
34	K2	5.3.2	5.3.2	5.3.3
35	K2	5.4.1	5.4.1	5.4.1
36	K3	5.1.4	5.1.4	5.1.4
37	K3	5.1.5	5.1.5	5.1.5
38	K3	5.5.1	5.5.1	5.5.1
39	K2	6.1.1	6.1.1	6.1.1
40	K1	6.2.1	6.2.1	6.2.1

Note: Question #30 is specified to be based on one of four learning objectives. In the three practice exam papers, three of the four learning objectives are covered. The fourth learning objective FL-5.3.1 (K1) is covered by an additional Q# 30 at the end of Practice Exam Three.

PRACTICE EXAM ONE

40 Questions
Time allowed 60 minutes
26 / 40 marks are required for a Pass

Q#1 FL-1.1.1 K1 Which of the following is a valid objective of software testing?

a) Submit as many incident reports as possible
b) Remove as many software defects in the test object as possible
c) Provide information for stakeholders' use
d) Prove all possible defects in the test object are identified

Select ONE option

Q#2 FL-1.5.2 K1 Which of the following is not an advantage of a whole team approach with business representatives, testers and developers working together?

a) The larger the team, the better the decisions made and the more successful the outcomes
b) There is a decreased reliance on test automation tools
c) More rapid delivery of a product is always achieved
d) Responsibility and accountability are removed from individual team members

Select ONE option

Q#3 FL-1.1.2 K2 When considering testing and debugging, which of the following statements is most true?

a) Debugging is uncovering failures, testing includes creating detailed documentation of the software features
b) The outcome of debugging may be an updated version of the test object, the outcome of testing is an improved understanding of the behavior of the test object
c) Debugging ensures failures identified in an iteration are resolved before the start of the next iteration, testing is the process of identifying and fixing defects as soon as possible
d) Debugging involves making code changes and typically does not require understanding of the context, data and behavior leading to the failure, whereas testing does

Select ONE option

Q#4 FL-1.3.1 K2 Which of the following are correct statements according to testing principles?

a) Early testing saves costs
b) Exhaustive testing is essential
c) Independence in testing is not possible
d) Testing does not prove the software is defect-free
e) Random testing is a good way to optimize test effort

Select TWO options

Q#5 FL-1.4.1 K2 You working on an application for booking travel tickets. Users can register and collect travel points for discounts. Non-members can book tickets but do not receive discounts.
Which of the following is part of test implementation?

a) Establishing decision tables for checking a user's entitlement to possible discounts and offers
b) Ensuring the database of members to be used in testing is anonymized
c) Estimating the test effort for integration with the payment service
d) Deciding tests should be included for transactions that are abandoned before reaching the checkout

Select ONE option

Q#6 FL-1.4.3 K2 Consider the following testware items and test activities.

1. Test case execution schedule determined
2. Test conditions determined
3. Test data requirements specified
4. Risk register set up ready

A. Test Planning
B. Test Analysis
C. Test Design
D. Test Implementation

Which of the following links the testware to the test activity where it is created?

a) 1A, 4B, 3C, 2D
b) 2A, 3B, 4C, 1D
c) 1A, 3B, 2C, 4D
d) 4A, 2B, 3C, 1D

Select ONE option

Q#7 FL-1.4.4 K2 Which of the following is an example of how traceability supports testing?

a) When impact analysis of a late change identifies requirements that may be affected, traceability between requirements, test cases and results supports the selection of test cases for regression testing
b) Traceability between the test object and the test cases helps in selecting the test metrics required for achieving the specified test coverage of the requirements
c) Traceability between test cases and test case results helps in determining the testability of requirements
d) Traceability between requirements and test case conditions helps in determining which requirements have been fully met by the software

Select ONE option

Q#8 FL-1.5.1 K2 Which of the following generic skills is least important for a tester?

a) Creating a vision of the product with its value proposition
b) Being curious and methodical
c) Being adaptable to new situations and challenges
d) Communicating objectively on failures discovered

Select ONE option

Q#9 FL-2.1.2 K1 Which of the following best describes a good testing practice?

a) Testers should be aware of which development activities in the software development lifecycle being used have a corresponding test activity and which do not
b) Testers should be involved in reviewing work products as soon as final approved documents are available
c) Testers should keep up-to-date with industry testing trends, testing tools, and best practices
d) Testers should have the same objectives for different test levels irrespective of the software development lifecycle being used to ensure efficient and consistent testing

Select ONE option

Q#10 FL-2.1.3 K1 Which of the following are true for Test-driven Development, TDD?

a) Code is produced in response to test cases
b) Tests may persist as automated test cases to ensure code quality in the future
c) Once produced, the code and test cases may not be refactored
d) The test cases created are easily understandable by stakeholders
e) An extensive system design phase is essential for directing coding

Select TWO options

Q#11 FL-2.2.1 K2 Consider the following observed test results and test levels:

1. Failures in interfaces and interactions between components
2. Failures in interfaces of the system with external services
3. Failures in demonstrating readiness for deployment due to unfulfilled user needs
4. Non-functional and functional failures in end-to-end testing

A. System testing
B. System integration testing
C. Component integration testing
D. Acceptance testing

Which best links the two lists above?

a) 1C, 2A, 3B, 4D
b) 1A, 2C, 3B, 4D
c) 1C, 2B, 3D, 4A
d) 1B, 2D, 3A, 4C

Select ONE option

Q#12 FL-2.2.3 K2 The table below shows results obtained from the first three test runs during the software development lifecycle on three consecutive versions of the software product. When a test case result is failed, a fix is applied in the next version.

	Test Case Result		
Test Case	**Execution 1**	**Execution 2**	**Execution 3**
TC01	Passed (1)	Failed (4)	Passed (7)
TC04	Passed (2)	Passed (5)	Failed (8)
TC05	Failed (3)	Failed (6)	Passed (9)

Which of the above test cases are executed as regression tests?

a) 4, 6, 8
b) 5, 7, 9
c) 7, 9
d) 4, 5, 8

Select ONE option

Q#13 FL-2.1.1 K2 How does the use of an Agile software development model impact testing?

a) Reduces the need for testing by emphasizing frequent code releases
b) Shifts testing activities to the end of the development cycle to save time
c) Promotes continuous testing throughout the software development lifecycle
d) Enforces rigid test processes to ensure consistency

Select ONE option

Q#14 FL-2.1.4 K2 Which of the following is not correct for describing an impact that DevOps has on testing?

a) Testing is integrated into automated pipelines, enabling frequent and rapid releases with fast feedback so removing the need for any manual testing
b) Infrastructure provisioning and configuration are treated as code, making validating and ensuring that the environment is consistent and accurate part of the tester's role
c) Testers are encouraged to share ownership of software quality and actively participate in the entire software development lifecycle
d) Testers can use rapid feedback to refine testing strategies and prioritize areas for improvement

Select ONE option

Q#15 FL-3.1.1 K1 Consider the following work products:

i. Requirements specification
ii. Design document
iii. Test scripts to be used in automation
iv. Contract
v. Proprietary third-party code

Which of the work products above can be examined using static testing?

a) ii, iii
b) i, ii, iv, v
c) i, ii, iii, iv
d) i, ii, iii

Select ONE option

Q#16 FL-3.2.5 K1 Which of the following best contribute to a successful review meeting?

a) Unlimited scope to ensure participants are not limited in what they can contribute
b) Scheduling a meeting time at short notice
c) Having objectives that include evaluating participants
d) Providing adequate time for participants to prepare in advance
e) Making reviews part of the organization's culture

Select TWO options

Q#17 FL-3.1.2 K2 Which of the following is not true for static testing?

a) Starts when code is available so allows for early feedback to developers
b) Can identify some security vulnerabilities
c) Leads to reduced maintenance over time
d) Identifies mismatched or incorrectly used data types in code expressions.

Select ONE option

Q#18 FL-3.2.2 K2 Which of the following tasks is undertaken during review planning?

a) Ensuring every participant has access to the work product under review
b) Making supporting information available
c) Ensuring participants understand their roles and responsibilities
d) Determining the quality characteristics to be evaluated

Select ONE option

Q#19 FL-4.1.1 K2 Which of the following statements correctly distinguishes white-box test techniques and black-box test techniques?

a) With white-box test techniques, test cases are derived from the code or internal structure of the test object, with black-box test techniques the behavior and functionality of the test object based on the requirements is evaluated
b) White-box test techniques are performed by end-users, black-box test techniques are performed by developers or testers
c) White-box test techniques focus on testing individual components of a system, black-box test techniques focus on the system as a whole
d) White-box test techniques use specification-based test techniques, black-box test techniques use structure-based test techniques

Select ONE option

Q#20 FL-4.3.1 K2 Which of the following is most true for statement testing?

a) If all the code statements are executed, every decision outcome is executed at least once
b) Low statement coverage percentage may indicate there is unreachable code
c) High percentage statement coverage ensures a high number of user scenarios have been tested
d) Percentage statement coverage provides a confidence measure of the code paths that will be most used

Select ONE option

Q#21 FL-4.3.2 K2 Consider the following control flow diagram.

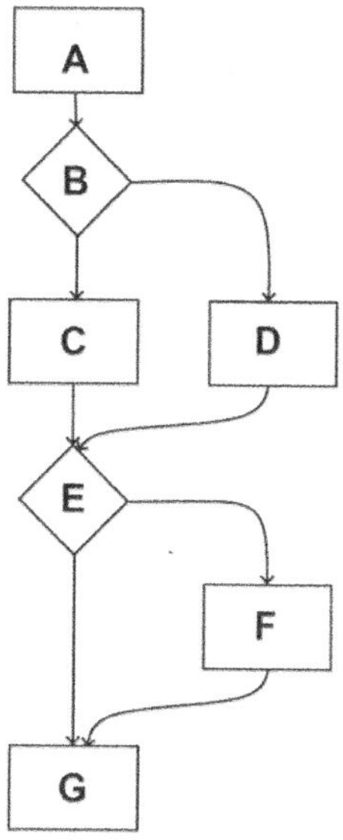

How many test cases are required for 100% branch coverage from A to G?

a) 1
b) 2
c) 3
d) 4

Select ONE option

Q#22 FL-4.4.1 K2 Which of the following is most correct for error guessing in software testing?

a) Error guessing performed by the least experienced testers is more effective than that performed by experienced testers as the least experienced testers can bring fresh perspectives
b) With situations involving intricate business logic or complex algorithms, error guessing can be particularly effective as it involves human reasoning and judgment in its approach
c) In situations where comprehensive requirements are lacking or time is limited, error guessing can help fill gaps in test coverage
d) Error guessing, when automated, is particularly effective in testing all combinations of inputs

Select ONE option

Q#23 FL-4.4.3 K2 You are testing a mobile application that allows users to access and manage their bank accounts. Stakeholders are particularly concerned about potential ad hoc security breaches. You are designing, executing and evaluating test cases against the Open Web Application Security Project (OWASP) security standard for mobile apps.
Which of the following best categorizes the test technique you are using?

a) Ad hoc testing
b) Error guessing
c) Exploratory testing
d) Checklist-based testing

Select ONE option

Q#24 FL-4.5.1 K2 Collaborative authorship of a user story requires team members to have a common understanding of the critical aspects of user stories. Which of the following is not a critical aspect of a user story that should be understood by team members?

a) Capacity
b) Card
c) Conversation
d) Confirmation

Select ONE option

Q#25 FL-4.2.1 K3 A manufacturer has a new car model that can be supplied with a choice of red, white, green, blue or black exterior paint, seat covers in grey, cream or multicolor and standard or premium alloy wheels. You are working on an application using a virtual reality headset to display any combination of the options. Using equivalence partitioning covering multiple partitions with an Each Choice (EC) approach, what is the minimum number of test cases required?

a) 15
b) 1
c) 9
d) 5

Select ONE option

Q#26 FL-4.2.2 K3 Two-Value Boundary Testing
A new income tax system deducts these payments from employees' wages:

Band	**Taxable Income**	**Tax Rate**
Personal Allowance	£1 to £11,850	0%
Basic rate	£11,851 to £46,350	20%
Middle rate	£46,351 to £150,000	40%
Higher rate	over £150,000	45%

Using two-value boundary testing, how many test cases are required to cover all given boundaries?

a) 8
b) 4
c) 10
d) 6

Select ONE option

Q#27 FL-4.2.3 K3 You are working on an application for booking e-commerce workspaces. Anyone can book a workspace. Users who have previously purchased a membership plan receive a 10% discount on all bookings. If a member does not use the facility over two months, they no longer qualify for the discount. At 15 reservations, members are offered one free booking.

	Rule							
Conditions	**R1**	**R2**	**R3**	**R4**	**R5**	**R6**	**R7**	**R8**
Membership plan purchased?	T	T	T	T	F	F	F	F
Used in last two months?	T	F	T	F	T	F	T	F
=15 reservations?	F	F	T	T	F	F	T	T
Actions								
Discount 10%	X		X					
One free booking offered			X	X			X	

Based on the information given, which of the above rules describes an impossible situation?

a) R1
b) R2
c) R5
d) R7

Select ONE option

Q#28 FL-4.2.4 K3 You are working with the following state transition diagram.

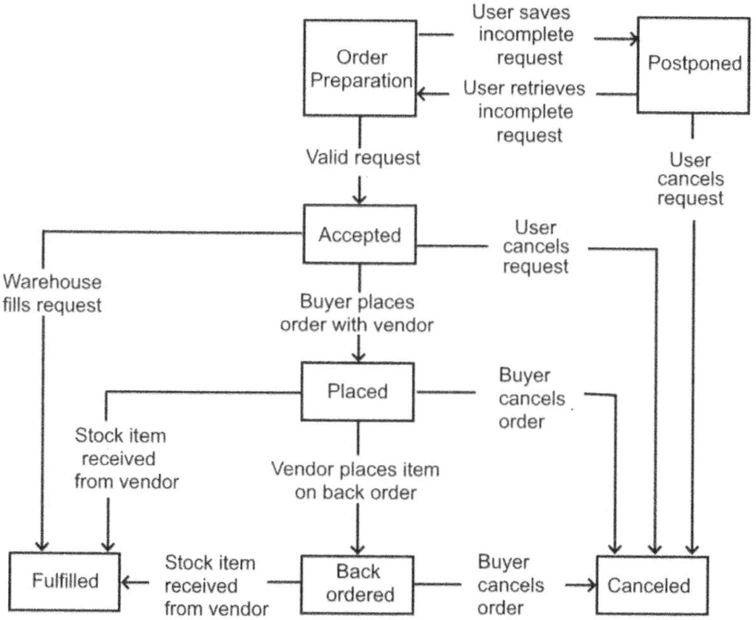

Based on this state transition diagram, how many test cases starting from 'Order Preparation' and ending at a terminal state are required for 100% all states coverage?

a) 3
b) 6
c) 2
d) 7

Select ONE option

Q#29 FL-4.5.3 K3 You have the following user story: 'As a customer, I would like to be able to track an order/package that I have placed so that I know when to expect delivery.'

Which of the following can be considered relevant acceptance test cases that can be used to guide development? The customer can:

i. Change the delivery method
ii. Enter a valid tracking number issued
iii. See the current location of the package
iv. View the status of the package 'out for delivery'
v. Apply for a return label before delivery

a) i, ii, iv
b) i, iii, iv
c) ii, iv, v
d) ii, iii, iv

Select ONE option

Q#30 FL-5.1.2 K1 Using an iterative software development lifecycle, which of the following statements is most correct for the value that testers add during release planning?

a) Testers break down user stories into testing tasks and during iteration planning testers estimate the test effort for completing the tasks within the current iteration
b) Testers estimate the effort associated with user stories and during iteration planning testers determine the test approach
c) Testers participate in project and quality risk analysis and during iteration planning testers determine the test approach
d) Testers determine the testability of user stories and during iteration planning testers identify and refine functional and non-functional aspects of the test object

Select ONE option

Q#31 FL-5.1.1 K2 Which of the following is not a purpose of a test plan?

a) To provide instructions for implementing a test case
b) To set out information that supports control of the test process
c) To describe the means and schedule for achieving the test objectives
d) To include Information that is then kept up to date throughout the test process

Select ONE option

Q#32 FL-5.1.7 K2 Consider the following testing quadrants (1-4) and test types (A-D):

1. Testing quadrant Q1: Technology-facing, supporting development
2. Testing quadrant Q2: Business-facing, supporting development
3. Testing quadrant Q3: Business-facing, critique of the product
4. Testing quadrant Q4: Technology-facing, critique of the product

A. Load testing
B. Usability testing
C. Unit testing
D. User story testing

How do the test categories best map onto the agile testing quadrants?

a) 1B, 2C, 3A, 4D
b) 1C, 2D, 3B, 4A
c) 1D, 2B, 3A, 4C
d) 1D, 2B, 3C, 4A

Select ONE option

Q#33 FL-5.2.2 K2 Which of the following is primarily a product risk rather than a project risk?

a) Unavailability of skilled developers
b) Inadequate user documentation
c) Inadequate testing of the software's core features
d) Late changes in project scope

Select ONE option

Q#34 FL-5.3.2 K2 A test summary report includes the following except for which?

a) Background information on the project
b) Information on what occurred during the test period
c) Factors that have blocked progress
d) A list of reusable testware produced

Select ONE option

Q#35 FL-5.4.1 K2 Configuration management applies technical and administrative direction with surveillance for which of the following?

a) Scope planning
b) Change control
c) Risk quantification
d) Project plan execution

Select ONE option

Q#36 FL-5.1.4 K3 You have decided to use Wideband Delphi to obtain an estimate of the test effort for a new project. You are making preparations and determining which experts should be involved. Which of the following statements are not true?

a) Wideband Delphi allows for unbiased thinking of experts as it is an unstructured technique
b) Experts who do not have the appropriate depth of knowledge of some aspects of the product or technology used, do not influence the estimate, as it is a group activity
c) If the scope is not well-defined and the project is highly innovative, the estimate may not be accurate
d) It may not be possible to achieve a consensus
e) Experts should have the opportunity to adjust their initial estimates based on the insights and perspectives of their peers

Select TWO options

Q#37 FL-5.1.5 K3 Test cases TC1 to TC8 cover requirements Req 1 to Req 8 as shown below.

	Req 1	**Req 2**	**Req 3**	**Req 4**	**Req 5**	**Req 6**	**Req 7**	**Req 8**
TC1				X		X		
TC2		X				X		X
TC3	X		X			X		X
TC4			X					
TC5			X	X	X			
TC6		X					X	
TC7						X		
TC8					X			

How many test cases should be prioritized as high for test execution so that each requirement is covered at least once as early as possible?

a) 5
b) 4
c) 3
d) 6

Select ONE option

Q#38 FL-5.5.1 K3 The following defect report has been submitted:
Title: Submitting Contact Form on Website fails with no error code
Project: AoFlex Website Version: 4.1.0 Component: Contact Form
Environment: Desktop, Windows, Chrome.
After filling out the form on 'Contact Us' page and clicking 'Submit' button, an error message is displayed, preventing successful form submission. This is high priority as it impacts users trying to contact the company. Test case TC117 was used:

1. Open the Chrome browser on the desktop
2. Navigate to the ABC Corporation website: abccorporation.com
3. Click on 'Contact Us' link in the navigation menu.
4. Fill in required fields of the contact form, including name, email, and message
5. Click 'Submit' button at the bottom of the form

Upon clicking the 'Submit' button, an error message appears, with no error code, stating, 'Error: Submission failed. Please try later.' Screenshots, showing the completed contact form and the error message are attached. The issue is reproducible and affects any user attempting to submit the contact form.

Which of the following has been omitted?

a) Specific error code
b) Expected behavior
c) Priority
d) Impact

Select ONE option

Q#39 FL-6.1.1 K2 Which type of test tool generates executable test cases from analysis of source code?

a) Debugging tool
b) Execution tool
c) Design tool
d) Requirements management tool

Select ONE option

Q#40 FL-6.2.1 K1 When test automation tools are used in the test process, the following are true except for which?

a) More objective coverage assessment can be provided than is achieved manually
b) Need for any manual testing is eliminated
c) Test cases can be performed that are not possible with manual testing
d) Test automation can result in faster smoke testing

Select ONE option

PRACTICE EXAM ONE
ANSWERS AND EXPLANATIONS

40 Answers / 40 Marks / 1 point each

Question Number	Correct Answer	Learning Objective	K-Level
1	c	FL-1.1.1	K1
2	c	FL-1.5.2	K1
3	b	FL-1.1.2	K2
*4	a, d	FL-1.3.1	K2
5	b	FL-1.4.1	K2
6	d	FL-1.4.3	K2
7	a	FL-1.4.4	K2
8	a	FL-1.5.1	K2
9	c	FL-2.1.2	K1
*10	a, b	FL-2.1.3	K1
11	c	FL-2.2.1	K2
12	d	FL-2.2.3	K2
13	c	FL-2.1.1	K2
14	a	FL-2.1.4	K2
15	c	FL-3.1.1	K1
*16	d, e	FL-3.2.5	K1
17	a	FL-3.1.2	K2
18	d	FL-3.2.2	K2
19	a	FL-4.1.1	K2
20	b	FL-4.3.1	K2

Question Number	Correct Answer	Learning Objective	K-Level
21	b	FL-4.3.2	K2
22	c	FL-4.4.1	K2
23	d	FL-4.4.3	K2
24	a	FL-4.5.1	K2
25	d	FL-4.2.1	K3
26	a	FL-4.2.2	K3
27	d	FL-4.2.3	K3
28	c	FL-4.2.4	K3
29	d	FL-4.5.3	K3
30	a	FL-5.1.2	K1
31	a	FL-5.1.1	K2
32	b	FL-5.1.7	K2
33	c	FL-5.2.2	K2
34	a	FL-5.3.2	K2
35	b	FL-5.4.1	K2
*36	a, b	FL-5.1.4	K3
37	c	FL-5.1.5	K3
38	b	FL-5.5.1	K3
39	c	FL-6.1.1	K2
40	b	FL-6.2.1	K1

* If both options selected are correct, the point assigned to the question is awarded, otherwise no point is given.

Question Number	Correct Answer	Explanation / Rationale	Learning Objective K-level
1	c	c) is the correct option. Providing information for stakeholders allows the stakeholders to make informed decisions regarding the level of quality of the test object, readiness for release, etc. a) is not the correct option. Submitting as many incident reports as possible encourages the submission of duplicate or inaccurate (false-positive) results and reports with insufficient supporting evidence. b) is not the correct option. Testing identifies failures, testing does not include fixing defects in the test object, this is done by developers. d) is not the correct option. It should not be assumed that all possible defects are identified. Testing reveals only the presence of identified failures and defects. It does not show the absence of defects.	FL-1.1.1 K1
2	c	c) is the correct option. This is because it includes 'always'. A whole team approach can reduce the time for hand-offs and resolve bottlenecks early. However, consensus-building and continual alignment of team members can delay product delivery. a) is not the correct option. A large team often requires extensive coordination and adds too much complexity for it to be useful. The level of reliance on test automation tools is not linked to the whole team approach. d) is not the correct option. All team members share some responsibility for product quality.	FL-1.5.2 K1
3	b	b) is the correct option. Debugging is the process of finding, analyzing and removing the causes of failures and can result in an updated version of the test object. a) is not the correct option. Testing triggers failures. Testers may create testware documentation, such as test plans and test cases, but this is distinct from broader documentation of software features. c) is not the correct option. Debugging takes time and effort and might require more iterations to locate and rectify issues. Testing involves uncovering failures and not fixing defects. d) is not the correct option. Analyzing a failure is likely to require an understanding of the context, data and behavior leading to the failure.	FL-1.1.2 K2
***4**	a, d	a) and d) are the correct options. The testing principles are early testing saves time and money and testing shows the presence, not the absence of defects. b) is not correct. The principle states exhaustive testing is not possible. c) and e) are not correct as neither are testing principles.	FL-1.3.1 K2
5	b	b) is the correct option. Preparing data is part of test implementation. a) is not the correct option. Establishing decision tables is part of test design. c) is not the correct option. Estimating test effort is part of test planning. d) is not the correct option. Deciding on what tests should be included is part of test analysis.	FL-1.4.1 K2

6	d	d) is the correct option. 4A - A risk register lists risks together with risk likelihood and risk impact and is created during Test Planning. The register is then updated throughout the test process as new information becomes available. 2B - Test conditions are determined during test analysis. 3C - Test data requirements are established during test design. This is then used as input to test implementation where the data is created or obtained. 1D - The test execution schedule is prepared during test implementation when the test cases have been previously created in the test design phase and are known. a), b) and c) are not correct options for the reasons given for d).	FL-1.4.3 K2
7	a	a) is the correct option. Impact analysis is, *'A software testing approach that helps define all risks associated with any change(s) made to the test object.'* Traceability between the test basis, test cases and test results helps in identifying test cases for regression testing to ensure the existing functionality of the software still works as expected. b) is not the correct option. Selecting the test metrics to collect is typically part of test planning. Traceability can be used to determine if the metrics are met. c) is not the correct option. Testability is normally determined during review of the test basis. d) is not the correct option. To determine if the requirements have been fully met in the software, traceability is needed from the requirements to the test results.	FL-1.4.4 K2
8	a	a) is the correct option. Creating a vision of the product is typically a skill for the business analyst and the business representative. b) is not the correct option. A tester should have curiosity and be thorough and methodical in their approach to identifying defects, especially for those that may be difficult to find. c) is not the correct option, Adaptability helps the tester in handling new situations and dealing with frequent software updates and new features. d) is not the correct option. A tester should communicate objectively when describing failures.	FL-1.5.1 K2
9	c	c) is the correct option. Continuous learning enhances testing skills and keeps testers informed about new challenges and solutions. a) is not the correct option. For every software development activity, there is a corresponding test activity regardless of the software development lifecycle in use. b) is not the correct option. Testers should be involved in reviewing all relevant documents as soon as draft versions are available. d) is not the correct option. Different test levels have specific and different objectives specific to that level so that testing is efficient and effective, comprehensive and avoids redundancy.	FL-2.1.2 K1
***10**	a, b	a) and b) are the correct options. a) Test-driven development is a software development technique in which the test cases are developed and then the software is developed incrementally to pass those test cases. b) Test cases can be automated and support an iterative software development lifecycle model. c) is not a correct option. After code is written to satisfy the test cases, it is necessary to refactor the test and code depending on the results and changes. d) is not a correct option. With Test-Driven Development TDD, test	FL-2.1.3 K1

<table>
<tr><td></td><td></td><td>cases are typically written by the developer in the same code language as the component or system to be developed. e) is not a correct option. TDD directs coding through test cases derived from the requirements specification and not from an extensive system design phase.</td><td></td></tr>
<tr><td>11</td><td>c</td><td>c) is the correct option. 1C - Component integration testing checks the interfaces and interactions between components. 2B - System Integration testing checks the interfaces of the system with external services. 3D - Acceptance testing looks for failures in demonstrating readiness for deployment due to unfulfilled user needs. 4A - System testing looks for non-functional and functional failures in end-to-end testing.
a), b) and d) are not correct options for the reasons given for c).</td><td>FL-2.2.1
K2</td></tr>
<tr><td>12</td><td>d</td><td>d) is the correct option. When a test case result is passed, if the test case is rerun on a later execution run it is then a part of regression testing as its purpose is to check the original defect has not returned. If it is the first time a test case is run or if the test case result on the previous execution run is failed and the test case is then repeated, it is a confirmation test.
<table>
<tr><th></th><th colspan="3">Test Case Result</th></tr>
<tr><th>Test Case</th><th>Execution 1</th><th>Execution 2</th><th>Execution 3</th></tr>
<tr><td>TC01</td><td>Passed (1)</td><td>Failed (4)</td><td>Passed (7)</td></tr>
<tr><td>TC04</td><td>Passed (2)</td><td>Passed (5)</td><td>Failed (8)</td></tr>
<tr><td>TC05</td><td>Failed (3)</td><td>Failed (6)</td><td>Passed (9)</td></tr>
</table>
a), b) and c) are not correct options for the reasons given for c).</td><td>FL-2.2.3
K2</td></tr>
<tr><td>13</td><td>c</td><td>c) is the correct option. With frequent short sprints or iterations, continuous testing is promoted.
a) is not the correct option. The frequency of releases does not reduce the need for testing and typically amplifies its importance. An aim of Agile is not just rapid development but also delivering high-quality software. b) is not the correct option. Testing is undertaken with each sprint. d) is not the correct option. Agile methodology promotes flexibility and adaptability in testing to better respond to changing requirements and project conditions.</td><td>FL-2.1.1
K2</td></tr>
<tr><td>14</td><td>a</td><td>a) is the correct option. Component tests, integration tests and regression tests can be automated to ensure consistency and repeatability. However, manual testing is still required for addressing scenarios that are challenging to automate, such as usability and scenarios requiring human judgment.
b) is not the correct option. Treating infrastructure provisioning and configuration as code allows testers to validate the infrastructure setup alongside the application code, ensuring that the environment is consistent and accurate. c) is not the correct option. DevOps supports collaboration, communication and shared ownership of software quality, between developers and testers are an important aspect of DevOps and support shared ownership of quality throughout the software development lifecycle. d) is not the correct option. Faster iterations mean testers get feedback more quickly.</td><td>FL-2.1.4
K2</td></tr>
</table>

15	c	c) is the correct option. Almost any work product can be scrutinized using static testing. Proprietary third-party code cannot be examined by static testing due to legal reasons. a), b) and d) are not correct options for reasons given for c).	FL-3.1.1 K1
***16**	d, e	d) and e) are the correct options. A successful review meeting should be part of the organization's culture. There should be adequate time allocated to prepare for review meetings. a) is not a correct option. Reviewers should focus on clear review objectives and a defined scope. b) is not a correct option. The time scheduled for the review should aim to accommodate all participants for most success. c) is not a correct option. Evaluation of participants should never be an objective of a review meeting with other participants present.	FL-3.2.5 K1
17	a	a) is the correct option. Static testing can start before the code is ready by reviewing documents such as those covering requirements, code design or architecture. b) is not the correct option. Static testing can identify some patterns of code or code constructs that could lead to security vulnerabilities. Other types of security testing should also be used. c) is not the correct option. By identifying and addressing issues early in the software development lifecycle, static testing can lead to reduced maintenance over time. d) is not the correct option. Identifying code issues early and fixing them is less costly than if they are found later in the software lifecycle.	FL-3.1.2 K2
18	d	d) is the correct option. Determining the quality characteristics to be evaluated is part of defining the scope of the review and is part of planning. a) is not the correct option. Ensuring every participant has access to the work product under review is part of review initiation. b) is not the correct option. Supporting information such as standards should be made available in the review initiation. c) is not the correct option. Ensuring participants understand their roles and responsibilities is part of review initiation.	FL-3.2.2 K2
19	a	a) is the correct option. With white-box test techniques, test cases are derived from the internal structure and processing of the test object. With black-box test techniques, test cases are based on the behavior of the test object. b) is not the correct option. White-box test techniques are based on analysis of the internal structure and code. End users typically do not have access to this or the relevant knowledge. c) is not the correct option. White-box test techniques and black-box test techniques can be used at any test level. d) is not the correct option. White-box testing uses structure-based test techniques, black-box testing uses specification-based test techniques.	FL-4.1.1 K2

20	b	b) is the correct option. A low statement coverage percentage may indicate there are parts of the code that have not been tested at all or have not been executed during testing. It is possible the code is not reachable. a) is not the correct option. Even if all statements of code are executed, this does not mean every decision outcome is executed at least once. c) is not the correct option. There is no direct correlation between a high percentage statement coverage and a high number of user scenarios tested, even though it could be true. d) is not the correct option. Statement coverage does not include branch coverage and is not a measure of the code paths that will be most used.	FL-4.3.1 K2
21	b	b) is the correct option. All branches can be tested by: TC01 A, B, C, E, G. TC02 A, B, D, E, F, G. a), c) and d) are not correct for the options given for b).	FL-4.3.2 K2
22	c	c) is the correct option. Error guessing can be used to target areas of the code that may not have been covered by other test techniques. a) is not the correct option. Error guessing is, *'A test technique in which tests are derived on the basis of the tester's knowledge of past failures, or general knowledge of failure modes'* so is most effective when performed by experienced testers. b) is not the correct option. Intricate business logic or complex algorithms may be better handled by a formal test technique. d) is not the correct option. Testing all combinations is exhaustive testing, not error guessing. Error guessing does not lend itself particularly well to automation.	FL-4.4.1 K2
23	d	d) is the correct option. The OWASP security standard is being used as a checklist. a) is not the correct option. The stakeholders are concerned about ad hoc potential security testing, but this does not mean the testing to meet these concerns is ad hoc. Ad hoc testing is not included at Foundation Level. b) is not the correct option. Error guessing does not rely heavily on documentation, such as standards. c) is not the correct option. Exploratory testing may use a test charter, identifying test objectives. This is not the same as a checklist.	FL-4.4.3 K2
24	a	a) is the correct option. Capacity is not a critical aspect of a user story. The critical aspects are card, conversation and confirmation. From the Syllabus, *Card – the medium describing a user story (e.g., an index card, an entry …). Conversation – explains how the software will be used (documented or verbal). Confirmation – the acceptance criteria.* b), c) and d) are not correct options for the reasons given for a).	FL-4.5.1 K2

<table>
<tr><td>25</td><td>d</td><td>d) is the correct option. Three partitions are required for Each Choice (EC) equivalence partitioning:
Exterior paint: 5 options | Seat covers: 3 options | Wheels: 2 options
Selecting one element from each partition and covering all elements, can be achieved with five test cases.
<table>
<tr><th>Test Case</th><th>Exterior Paint</th><th>Seat Cover</th><th>Wheels</th></tr>
<tr><td>1</td><td>Red</td><td>Grey</td><td>Standard</td></tr>
<tr><td>2</td><td>White</td><td>Multicolor</td><td>Premium alloy</td></tr>
<tr><td>3</td><td>Green</td><td>Cream</td><td>Any</td></tr>
<tr><td>4</td><td>Blue</td><td>Any</td><td>Any</td></tr>
<tr><td>5</td><td>Black</td><td>Any</td><td>Any</td></tr>
</table>
a) is not the correct option. Fifteen test cases are needed for full pairwise testing. b) is not the correct option. One test case would only result in one element from each partition being tested.
c) is not the correct option. Single partition testing, if it was possible, would require nine test cases.</td><td>FL-4.2.1
K3</td></tr>
<tr><td>26</td><td>a</td><td>a) is the correct option. There are four boundaries for the valid partitions, 8 test cases are required for 0/£1, £11,850/£11,851, £46,350/£46,351, £150,000/£151,000. No maximum boundary is specified. b), c) and d) are not correct options for the reasons given for a).</td><td>FL-4.2.2
K3</td></tr>
<tr><td>27</td><td>d</td><td>d) is the correct option. Free bookings are only available to members.
a) is not the correct option. A member who has used the facility in the last two months qualifies for the discount and if they have not made 15 reservations they do not qualify for a free booking.
b) is not the correct option. A member who has not used the facility in the last two months does not qualify for a discount and if they have not made 15 reservations they do not qualify for a free booking.
c) is not the correct option. If a user is not a member, they do not qualify for either a discount or a free booking.</td><td>FL-4.2.3
K3</td></tr>
<tr><td>28</td><td>c</td><td>c) is the correct option. There are seven states. For 100% all states coverage, the two test cases are required, for example:
TC1: Order Preparation → Accepted → Placed → Backorder → Fulfilled
TC2: Order Preparation → Postponed → Canceled
a), b) and d) are not correct options for the reasons given for c).</td><td>FL-4.2.4
K3</td></tr>
<tr><td>29</td><td>d</td><td>d) is the correct option. The focus of this user story is on tracking the order/package, making ii, iii and iv relevant acceptance test cases. i. is not appropriate as the focus of the user story is tracking an order/package already placed, not changing the delivery method. v. is not appropriate as the focus of this user story is not on an option to return the item.
a), b) and c) are not correct options for the reasons given for d).</td><td>FL-4.5.3
K3</td></tr>
</table>

30	a	a) is the correct option as both parts of the option are true, as given in the Syllabus. b) is not the correct option. Estimating the effort associated with user stories is part of iteration planning. The test approach is determined during release planning. c) is not the correct option. Release planning looks ahead to the release of the product and testers determine the test approach. Iteration planning looks ahead to the end of a single iteration. d) is not the correct option. Testers determine the testability of user stories during iteration planning.	FL-5.1.2 K1
31	a	a) is the correct option. A test script provides instructions for implementing a test case. b) is not the correct option. A test plan should provide a basis for test monitoring and test control. c) is not correct as a test plan should identify the requirements in terms of resources needed and the schedule for the test effort. d) is not correct. To be effective in providing a basis for test control and stakeholder information, the test plan should be kept updated.	FL-5.1.1 K2
32	b	b) is the correct option. 1C Unit testing is in Q1. 2D User stories testing is in Q2, business-facing. 3B Usability testing is in Q3. 4A Load testing (non-functional) is in Q4. a), c) and d) are not correct options for the reasons given for b).	FL-5.1.7 K2
33	c	c) is the correct option. Inadequate testing of the software's core features represents a product risk as it relates to potential issues or concerns regarding the quality and reliability of the software product. a) is not the correct option. The unavailability of developers is a project risk as it is part of resource management and project execution. b) is not the correct option. User documentation and communication aspects of the project, which are crucial for project management and user satisfaction, are project risks. d) is not the correct option. Changes in project scope are a project risk as it involves potential modifications to the project's goals, which can impact the project's timeline, budget and scope.	FL-5.2.2 K2
34	a	a) is the correct option. A test summary report may also be called a test completion report. Background information should have been already documented in the project plan. b), c) and d) are not correct options as they are typically included in test summary reports.	FL-5.3.2 K2
35	b	b) is the correct option. Configuration management facilitates proper control and documentation of changes to configuration items. a), c) and d) are not correct options for the reasons given for b).	FL-5.4.1 K2

<table>
<tr><td>*36</td><td>a, b</td><td>a) and b) are the correct options. a) is false as Wideband Delphi is a structured technique. b) is false as Wideband Delphi assumes expert opinions are of equal importance and relies on the experts themselves to adjust their estimates based on insights of other experts. The process is susceptible to biases.
c) is not a correct option. If the scope is not well-defined, it is open to different interpretations. If the software is highly innovative, it may be difficult for experts to reach similar estimates.
d) is not a correct option. There are many reasons why Wideband Delphi may not reach a consensus. See information for FL-5.1.4
e) is not a correct option. Experts having the opportunity to adjust their estimates is an essential part of Wideband Delphi.</td><td>FL-5.1.4
K3</td></tr>
<tr><td>37</td><td>c</td><td>c) is the correct option. Three test cases, TC3, TC5 and TC6 should be prioritized for test execution. The minimum number of test cases to cover all requirements is three.
TC3 is the only test case to cover Req 1. It also covers Reqs 3, 6 and 8.
TC6 is the only test case to cover Req 7. It also covers Req 2.
This leaves Reqs 4 and 5 not covered. TC5 will cover Req 4 and Req 5.
<table>
<tr><th></th><th>Req 1</th><th>Req 2</th><th>Req 3</th><th>Req 4</th><th>Req 5</th><th>Req 6</th><th>Req 7</th><th>Req 8</th></tr>
<tr><td>TC1</td><td></td><td></td><td></td><td>x</td><td></td><td>x</td><td></td><td></td></tr>
<tr><td>TC2</td><td></td><td>x</td><td></td><td></td><td></td><td>x</td><td></td><td>x</td></tr>
<tr><td>TC3</td><td>X</td><td></td><td>X</td><td></td><td></td><td>X</td><td></td><td>X</td></tr>
<tr><td>TC4</td><td></td><td></td><td>x</td><td></td><td></td><td></td><td></td><td></td></tr>
<tr><td>TC5</td><td></td><td></td><td>X</td><td>X</td><td>X</td><td></td><td></td><td></td></tr>
<tr><td>TC6</td><td></td><td>X</td><td></td><td></td><td></td><td></td><td>X</td><td></td></tr>
<tr><td>TC7</td><td></td><td></td><td></td><td></td><td></td><td>x</td><td></td><td></td></tr>
<tr><td>TC8</td><td></td><td></td><td></td><td></td><td>x</td><td></td><td></td><td></td></tr>
</table>
a), b) and d) are not correct options for the reasons given for c).</td><td>FL-5.1.5
K3</td></tr>
<tr><td>38</td><td>b</td><td>b) is the correct option. Expected behavior should be included. While it might be assumed from the report that successful behavior is just the successful submission of the form, this is not clear. For example, the expected behavior could be: After clicking the 'Submit' button, the contact form should be submitted successfully, and a confirmation message should be displayed indicating that the contact form has been sent or an email has been sent to the linked account indicating the outcome. Including such details means a subsequent defect report can be avoided if the results after a fix for the submission of the message are displayed. a) is not the correct option. The defect report is clear there is no specific error code to report and a screenshot is attached. b) is not the correct option. The priority is given as 'high'. d) is not the correct option. The impact is given, the issue affects all users attempting to submit the contact form.</td><td>FL-5.5.1
K3</td></tr>
</table>

39	c	c) is the correct option. Generating test cases is part of test design. a), b) and d) are not correct options for the reason given for c).	FL-6.1.1 K2
40	b	b) is the correct option. Automation does not eliminate all manual testing. Manual testing may be needed for test cases only required on a small number of occasions, exploratory testing, testing that may be difficult to automate etc. a) is not the correct option. Test automation tools produce more objective assessment compared to manual testing where there is greater potential for a subjective or incorrect input. c) is not the correct option. Automation can be used for testing scenarios with a high number of simultaneous virtual users that would not be possible manually. d) is not the correct option. Test automation can speed up smoke testing to determine if a new build is ready for the next testing phase.	FL-6.2.1 K1

PRACTICE EXAM TWO

40 Questions
Time allowed 60 minutes
26 / 40 marks are required for a Pass

Q#1 FL-1.2.2 K1 Which of the following statements is true for quality assurance and testing?

a) Quality assurance is a process-oriented, preventative approach, testing is a product-oriented, corrective approach
b) Quality assurance is a product-oriented preventative approach, testing is a process-oriented, corrective approach
c) Quality assurance is a preventative approach, testing is a corrective approach and both are product-oriented and process-oriented
d) Quality assurance and testing are interchangeable terms

Select ONE option

Q#2 FL-1.5.2 K1 Which of the following best describes the whole team approach?

a) Testers and business representatives engage in separate activities during the development and test processes, then converge at the end of the development lifecycle as a whole team for final validation
b) Testers and business representatives collaborate closely throughout the development and test processes, sharing insights, validating requirements, and jointly addressing challenges
c) Testers provide the context in which the software will be used to help business representatives and developers understand how users will interact with it
d) Testers ensure the test process remains aligned with evolving business needs and regularly communicate the status of testing to business representatives and developers

Select ONE option

Q#3 FL-1.2.1 K2 Which of the following best shows how testers may contribute to success?

a) Focus on functional testing in the early stages for early removal of defects and non-functional testing in the late stages when system and user acceptance testing are performed
b) Take responsibility for the quality of the software, giving developers more time for coding and producing fixes for identified defects
c) Provide information to stakeholders promptly to help them make informed decisions
d) Reduce the time between when the failure is reported, the defect is identified and a fix is available

Select ONE option

Q#4 FL-1.3.1 K2 Which of the following is a principle of software testing?

a) When all defects found are fixed, the software is free from defects
b) Testing should be exhaustive as defects may occur in any part of the test object
c) The approach to testing should be varied in different contexts
d) There is no beneficial outcome from continually repeating the same tests over time

Select ONE option

Q#5 FL-1.4.1 K2 Which of the following tasks are undertaken in test analysis?

a) Comparing actual test results with expected results
b) Analyzing test activities to identify lessons learned
c) Identifying testable features from the test basis
d) Identifying defects in the requirements specification
e) Analyzing failures observed in test results to identify possible causes

Select TWO options

Q#6 FL1.4.2 K2 The way testing is carried out depends on several factors. Which of the following statements is not necessarily true?

a) Test results obtained during test execution can negatively impact the test process
b) During the project, if the code doubles in size, doubling the testers is required to keep the test process on schedule
c) Those responsible for implementing the test environment should be available during test execution for maintenance and support
d) During the test process, maintaining detailed formal documentation can impact the test process

Select ONE option

Q#7 FL-1.4.5 K2 Which of the following best describes typical tasks of the tester's role and the test manager's role?

a) The tester reports the actual test results and test coverage, the test manager creates the test execution schedule
b) The tester produces the test status report on the progress of test activities compared to the test plan, the test manager identifies the test conditions
c) The tester produces the test progress report comparing actual progress with the test plan, the test manager produces the test plan
d) The tester organizes the test procedures, the test manager determines which test metrics are to be used

Select ONE option

Q#8 FL-1.5.3 K2 Which of the following is a benefit of independent testing?

a) Developers do not have responsibility for quality, so they can concentrate on code production
b) The time from when a failure is uncovered to when the defect is fixed is reduced
c) The amount of communication between testers and developers is reduced
d) Independent testers provide objective evaluation of the work product

Select ONE option

Q#9 FL-2.1.2 K1 For which software development lifecycle models is it true that for every activity, there is a corresponding test activity?

a) Iterative development and incremental development models only
b) Iterative development models only
c) Sequential development, iterative development and Incremental development models
d) Sequential development models only

Select ONE option

Q#10 FL-2.1.3 K1 Which of the following best describes Acceptance Test-Driven Development, ATDD?

a) Guides testing after development to ensure the acceptance criteria are met
b) Acceptance criteria defined by the business analyst together with the customer are used to guide development and test activities
c) Acceptance criteria are agreed through the collaboration of stakeholders and tests are automated
d) Acceptance tests are written before software is developed to satisfy the tests

Select ONE option

Q#11 FL-2.2.2 K2 Consider the four test types and the descriptions of primary focus:

1. Non-functional
2. White-box
3. Functional
4. Black-box

A. Verifying correctness directly from the code, identifying coding errors, and ensuring all possible code paths are exercised
B. Validating the software provides accurate calculated results to the required degree of precision required to meet the specified needs
C. Uncovering defects related to incorrect behavior, invalid inputs, missing features, or deviations from requirements without considering internal structure
D. Ensuring the software meets quality attributes and characteristics such as portability and reliability

Which of the following best links the two lists?

a) 1D, 2A, 3B, 4C
b) 1B, 2A, 3D, 4C
c) 1D, 2B, 3D, 4A
d) 1D, 2D, 3A, 4A

Select ONE option

Q#12 FL-2.3.1 K2 In an operational system, which of the following would most likely trigger maintenance testing?

a) Server restarts
b) Color and font changes to a user interface
c) Updates to website news articles
d) Code changes to increase load capacity and scalability
e) Database schema changes

Select TWO options

Q#13 FL-2.1.6 K2 Which of the following is a good reason to hold a retrospective?

a) Report the status of the project progress compared to the project plan
b) Recognize individual accomplishments and achievements within the team
c) Reflect on successes and challenges, with the aim of enhancing future testing
d) Unveil new organization policies and procedures for project management

Select ONE option

Q#14 FL-2.1.5 K2 Which of the following is an example of shift left?
a) Testing is made a separate activity following each development activity
b) With pressure to meet a tight project deadline, the focus moves to rapid development at the expense of thorough testing
c) Testing starts when two similar production-like test systems with rapid roll-back ability are available with moving between them when code changes are made, minimizing potential downtime
d) Non-functional testing starts with a review of the system architecture and structure design documents

Select ONE option

Q#15 FL-3.2.1 K1 Which of the following is a benefit of early and frequent feedback?
a) Limits the number of changes that a customer can make to the requirements
b) Allows for decisions to focus on areas that has the greatest impact on meeting the requirements
c) Is the only effective way the quality of changes can be measured
d) Improves the test process for future projects

Select ONE option

Q#16 FL-3.2.3 K1 In a formal review, which role is responsible for the following?

Ensuring the effective running of the review meeting
Facilitating communication and collaboration
Managing any conflicts or disagreements during the review

a) Moderator
b) Manager
c) Review leader
d) Recorder

Select ONE option

Q#17 FL-3.1.3 K2 When comparing static testing and dynamic testing, which of the following is true?

a) Dynamic testing can be used to uncover non-functional quality characteristics, static testing cannot be used to uncover non-functional quality characteristics
b) Both dynamic testing and static testing can test the requirements specification document
c) Dynamic testing typically provides better code coverage than static testing
d) Both dynamic testing and static testing can be performed manually or by test automation tools

Select ONE option

Q#18 FL-3.2.4 K2 Given the following, which type of review is most likely being used?

Motivate and enable the author to improve
Find the maximum number of defects
The author cannot act as the review leader, scribe or recorder
A review report is produced

a) Inspection
b) Technical review
c) Walkthrough
d) Informal

Select ONE option

Q#19 FL-4.1.1 K2 Which of the following best distinguishes experience-based, white-box and black-box test techniques?

a) Experience-based test techniques focus on testing from the end user's perspective, white-box test techniques evaluate the behavior of the test object, black-box test techniques rely on domain expertise
b) Experience-based test techniques rely on the tester's knowledge and experience, white-box test techniques assess the internal code, black-box test techniques assess the behavior of the test object
c) Experience-based testing is suitable for verifying code correctness, white-box test techniques are used for usability testing, black-box test techniques evaluate software based on predefined test cases
d) Experience-based test techniques are synonymous with exploratory testing, white-box test techniques emphasize requirements-based testing, black-box test techniques evaluate usability

Select ONE option

Q#20 FL-4.3.2 K2 Consider the following pseudo-code.

```
Read X
Read Y
  IF X+Y > 50 THEN Print "X+Y exceeds limit"
  ELSE Print "X+Y within range"
  ENDIF
EXIT
```

How many test cases are required for 100% branch coverage?

a) 1
b) 2
c) 3
d) 4

Select ONE option

Q#21 FL-4.3.3 K2 Which of the following best describes where white-box testing provides value?

a) The internal structure of the code needs to be thoroughly tested and analyzed
b) The focus is on testing the behavior of the test object under normal use
c) The test objective is to thoroughly assess the requirements specification
d) The test objective is to validate the correctness of user requirements and usability

Select ONE option

Q#22 FL-4.4.1 K2 Fault attack is a methodical approach in which type of test technique?

a) Exploratory testing
b) Checklist-based testing
c) Error guessing
d) Debugging

Select ONE option

Q#23 Q4.4.2 K2 Which of the following is least appropriate as a basis for exploratory testing?

a) Test charter
b) Actual results obtained during the test session
c) Results from previous projects
d) Fixed, predetermined expectations of testers

Select ONE option

Q#24 FL-4.5.2 K2 Which of the following describes how acceptance criteria can be classified as scenario-based or rule-based?

a) Scenario-based acceptance criteria are based on test conditions that should be exercised by test cases, rule-oriented acceptance criteria are based on technical details of implementation
b) Scenario-based acceptance criteria do not include references to regulations or compliance, when needed references to regulations or compliance are included in rule-oriented acceptance criteria
c) Scenario-oriented acceptance criteria can be based on 'Given/When/Then' format, rule-oriented acceptance criteria may be based on tabulated input-output mapping
d) Scenario-based acceptance criteria are based on high-level descriptions that allow for different interpretations of input conditions, rule-oriented acceptance criteria are based on well-defined and unambiguous statements that cannot be interpreted in different ways

Select ONE option

Q#25 FL-4.2.1 K3 You are working with the following equivalence partitions:

Valid Usernames:	Usernames between 5 and 10 characters long and contain only alphanumeric characters
Invalid Usernames:	Usernames that do not meet the criteria for being valid
Valid Passwords:	Passwords at least 8 characters long and must contain a combination of letters, numbers and special characters
Invalid Passwords:	Passwords that do not meet the criteria for valid passwords

You have the following test cases and inputs:

TC1: Username: Morgan.Coe	Password: Secr#t723
TC2: Username: kiran000	Password: mypassword
TC3: Username: Chris123	Password: Passw0rd!
TC4: Username: a	Password: 12345678
TC5: Username: john123	Password: Secr3t+$
TC6: Username: Kristina4242	Password: Passw0rd

You are performing a test session to execute test cases above where both inputs come from valid partitions. Which test cases should be included?

a) TC1, TC2, TC3, TC6
b) TC3, TC5
c) TC5, TC6
d) TC1, TC2, TC4, TC6

Select ONE option

Q#26 FL-4.2.2 K3

A new income tax system deducts these payments from employees' wages:

Band	Taxable Income	Tax
Personal Allowance	£1 to £11,850	0%
Basic rate	£11,851 to £45,000	20%
Middle rate	£45,001 to £140,000	40%
Higher rate	over £140,000	45%

Test cases have already been executed for income values of £11,850, £11,851, £25,001, £44,999, £45,000, £47,001, £140,000, £150,000 and £150,001. (Whole £s only).

What level of minimum coverage for three-value boundary testing of the middle rate partition has already been completed?

a) 100%
b) 66%
c) 75 %
d) 33%

Select ONE Option

Q#27 FL-4.2.3 K3 A mobile app allows a user to purchase a ticket to an event experience. The specification is: General admission tickets cost $40 for each person aged 16 years or older, otherwise the cost for up to 15 years is half the adult cost. VIP admission is available as an alternative for people 16 years and over for a payment of $80. VIP admission is not a valid option for people under 16 years. The following full decision table shows all combinations for the purchase of a ticket.

	Rule							
Conditions	**R1**	**R2**	**R3**	**R4**	**R5**	**R6**	**R7**	**R8**
General admission?	T	T	T	T	F	F	F	F
VIP admission?	T	T	F	F	T	T	F	F
Age ≥16 years?	T	F	T	F	T	F	T	F
Actions								
Payment due	$40	$20	$40	$20	$80	$40	$20	$20

From the decision table, how many columns/rules are there that result in an outcome that is both possible and correct?

a) 3
b) 4
c) 5
d) 6

Select ONE option

Q#28 FL-4.2.4 K3 You are testing an AI-enabled chatbot, modeled by the state transition diagram below.

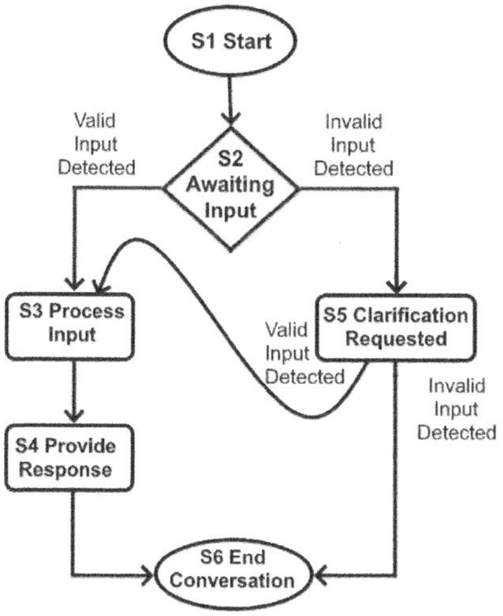

What is the minimum number of test cases starting at S1 and ending at S6 that are required to achieve coverage of all transitions shown?

a) 4
b) 2
c) 6
d) 3

Select ONE option

Q#29 FL-4.5.3 K3 You are working with the following user story:
'As a manager, I want to view current stock levels of products together with replenish lead times so that I can satisfy anticipated customer demand which can vary at different times.'

From the given information, which of the following can be considered appropriate acceptance criteria test cases for this user story?

a) Verify a stock level report on the value of stock being held can be accessed
b) Place an order for a product that is out of stock and check the date the item will be available is displayed
c) Verify products can be displayed as line items with the time to add more stock
d) Check display of the stock inventory history is clear and verify stock has been properly managed
e) Ensure the numbers of products in stock can be displayed

Select TWO options

Q#30 FL-5.1.6 K1 Which of the following is true regarding the test pyramid?

a) Provides information about test priorities and relationships between different tests
b) Supports the principle that early defect detection leads to lower costs than late detection
c) Recommends more end-to-end tests than unit tests for optimum test coverage of the application workflow
d) Provides a means to minimize resources and time by having most focus on unit tests, which are typically faster to execute than other tests

Select ONE option

Q#31 FL-5.1.3 K2 Which of the following statements concerning entry and exit criteria are true?

a) Exit criteria for a test phase can become part of entry criteria for the next test phase
b) Entry criteria for a test phase can become part of exit criteria for the next test phase
c) Exit criteria for the test process validate entry criteria for the test process are achieved
d) Entry criteria and exit criteria help to ensure smooth transitioning through the test process
e) Entry criteria focus on evaluation of the quality level reached in the phase for which the entry criteria apply

Select TWO options

Q#32 FL-5.1.7 K2 Consider testing quadrants (1-4) and the test types that can be performed (A-D):

1. Testing quadrant Q1: Technology-facing, supporting development
2. Testing quadrant Q2: Business-facing, supporting development
3. Testing quadrant Q3: Business-facing, critique of the product
4. Testing quadrant Q4: Technology-facing, critique of the product

A. Acceptance criteria and can be manual or automated
B. Smoke testing and most non-functional testing are often automated
C. Component integration
D. API testing

Which of the following best links the two lists?

a) 1D, 2C, 3B, 4A
b) 1B, 2A, 3D, 4C
c) 1C, 2D, 3A, 4B
d) 1D, 2A, 3B, 4C

Select ONE option

Q#33 FL-5.2.3 K2 The following are examples of how product risk analysis influences thoroughness and test scope except for which?

a) Product risk analysis is first performed after initial testing has been completed so the scope of risk-based testing can be determined more accurately
b) Results of product risk analysis can determine the particular test levels and test types to be performed
c) Results of product risk analysis determine the particular test techniques to be used
d) Product risk analysis enables prioritization of testing to find the critical defects as early as possible

Select ONE option

Q#34 FL-5.3.2 K2 Which of the following is typically not included in a test progress report?

a) Impediments affecting testing and workarounds
b) Assessment of the technologies used to develop the software
c) Status of test case execution and defect identification
d) Identification of potential new risks and their impact

Select ONE option

Q#35 FL-5.4.1 K2 Which of the following is not a benefit of configuration management?

a) Optimization of resources to achieve desired outcomes while balancing project constraints and priorities
b) Ensuring correct versions of the software and relevant documentation are delivered at release time
c) Support of audits performed to verify compliance with standards, regulations and processes
d) Aids in understanding the evolution of a project or product

Select ONE option

Q#36 FL-5.1.4 K3 In the previous project, the development effort was 750 person-days. Two testers contributed 60 days each and a third tester contributed 30 days. For the newt project, the development effort has been estimated as 600 person days. Only two testers are available and will share the test effort equally. Using ratio-based estimation, which of the following is the estimate for the number of person-hours each tester will need to contribute to the new project?

a) 120
b) 60
c) 50
d) 90

Select ONE option

Q#37 FL-5.1.5 K3 You have the following showing the test cases, their dependencies and priorities (1 = highest, 3 = lowest). The dependencies are shown by the arrows, for example, TC03 and TC04 are both dependent on TC01. (There are no dependencies on TC02).

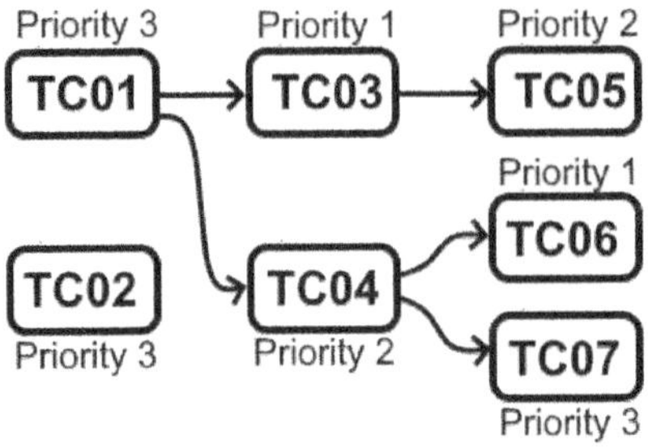

For priority order testing using the given information, what is the correct test execution order?

a) TC01, TC03, TC04, TC06, TC05, TC02, TC07
b) TC03, TC06, TC04, TC05, TC01, TC02, TC07
c) TC01, TC03, TC05, TC04, TC06, TC07, TC02
d) TC02, TC05, TC03, TC01, TC06, TC04, TC07

Select ONE option

Q#38 FL-5.5.1 K3 You are testing a website set up to provide an interface for searching academic papers across distributed university depositories. Most searches result in documents being retrieved but in a few cases Error 404 is unexpectedly returned.

You are submitting a defect report with the following:

Title: Document retrieval Error 404, document not found
Degree of risk: Medium
Priority: High
Details: Three unexpected incidents of Error 404 have occurred when using the Administrator's username. Network access has been thoroughly checked and verified as operating correctly. The Administrator username authorization for access to the papers has been verified but permissions checks may not have been implemented correctly.
The Administrator username can access other depositories.
Expected result: An authorized user should be able to access academic papers.

Valuable information that has been omitted and should be in the report, includes the following except for which?

a) Test steps needed to create the problem
b) Ideas for improving the test case
c) Website and browser versions
d) Report identifier

Select ONE option

Q#39 FL-6.1.1 K2 When comparing AI-enabled test tools with traditional test tools without AI capability, which of the following statements correctly differentiates the two types of tools?

a) AI-enabled tools often require less manual effort for test script creation compared to traditional tools
b) Traditional tools excel in simulating real user interactions, AI-enabled tools struggle in this aspect
c) AI-enabled tools are straightforward to set up and configure, traditional tools may be complicated to set up and configure
d) AI-enabled tools can use structured or unstructured data, traditional tools require data to be more structured
e) AI-enabled tools are not able to handle the complex scenarios and edge cases that traditional tools can

Select TWO options

Q#40 FL-6.2.1 K1 Which of the following is most true in describing a benefit of test automation tools?

a) Tools can automate all manual tests and perform tasks such as large data validation that would be impossible to run manually due to the amount of data involved
b) Test automation tools cannot improve on test coverage that can be achieved manually
c) Return on investment for test automation execution tools is highest when testing the functionality of new features of an application
d) Test automation tools can reduce test implementation and test execution times to provide faster feedback and help in meeting deadlines

Select ONE option

PRACTICE EXAM TWO ANSWERS AND EXPLANATIONS

40 Answers / 40 Marks / 1 point each

Question Number	Correct Answer	Learning Objective	K-Level
1	a	FL-1.2.2	K2
2	b	FL-1.5.2	K1
3	c	FL-1.2.1	K2
4	c	FL-1.3.1	K2
*5	c, d	FL-1.4.1	K2
6	b	FL-1.4.2	K2
7	d	FL-1.4.5	K2
8	d	FL-1.5.3	K2
9	c	FL-2.1.2	K1
10	d	FL-2.1.3	K1
11	a	FL-2.2.2	K2
*12	d, e	FL-2.3.1	K2
13	c	FL-2.1.6	K2
14	d	FL-2.1.5	K2
15	b	FL-3.2.1	K1
16	a	FL-3.2.3	K1
17	d	FL-3.1.3	K2
18	a	FL-3.2.4	K2
19	b	FL-4.1.1	K2
20	b	FL-4.3.2	K2

Question Number	Correct Answer	Learning Objective	K-Level
21	a	FL-4.3.3	K2
22	c	FL-4.4.1	K2
23	d	FL-4.4.2	K2
24	c	FL-4.5.2	K2
25	b	FL-4.2.1	K3
26	d	FL-4.2.2	K3
27	a	FL-4.2.3	K3
28	d	FL-4.2.4	K3
*29	c, e	FL-4.5.3	K3
30	b	FL-5.1.6	K1
*31	a, d	FL-5.1.3	K2
32	c	FL-5.1.7	K2
33	a	FL-5.2.3	K2
34	b	FL-5.3.2	K2
35	a	FL-5.4.1	K2
36	b	FL-5.1.4	K3
37	a	FL-5.1.5	K3
38	b	FL-5.5.1	K3
*39	a, d	FL-6.1.1	K2
40	d	FL-6.2.1	K1

* If both options selected are correct, the point assigned to the question is awarded, otherwise no point is given.

Question Number	Answer	Explanation / Rationale	Learning Objective K-level
1	a	a) is the correct option. Quality assurance is '*activities focused on providing confidence that quality requirements will be fulfilled*'. refers to the process of planning how testing and monitoring are organized and implemented. Testing is '*the process within the software development lifecycle that evaluates the quality of a component or system and related work products*'. b), c) and d) are not correct options for the reasons given for a).	FL-1.2.2 K1
2	b	b) is the correct option. Business representatives, testers and developers work together in interlinking ways throughout the project. a) is not the correct option. The whole team approach aims to adopt this approach throughout the development lifecycle. c) is not the correct option. Business representatives should help testers understand how the software will be used. d) is not the correct option. The whole team approach involves collaboration among team members, not just one-way communication.	FL-1.5.2 K1
3	c	c) is the correct option. Providing information to stakeholders so they can make informed decisions, such as when to release the software, is a way testers contribute to success. a) is not the correct option. Testing, of both functionality and non-functionality, should be undertaken at the earliest opportunity. This reduces time and costs that might otherwise be encountered at late stages. For example, usability testing can start when there is a minimum viable product. It may be appropriate to start performance efficiency testing of a component before integration testing. Late discovery of non-functional defects can be extremely costly to the success of a project. b) is not the correct option. For the project to be successful, the responsibility for quality should be shared by all members of the project team. d) is not the correct option. Developers analyze the failures to identify defects and provide fixes, which contributes to the time between the failure being reported and the fix being provided.	FL-1.2.1 K2
4	c	c) is the correct option. There is no single universally acceptable approach to testing. The context should be taken into account. a) is not the correct option. It is a misconception to expect that fixing all defects found ensures there are no remaining undiscovered defects. b) is not the correct option. A principle of software testing is that testing cannot be exhaustive to the point where all possible defects have been remedied. d) is not the correct option. Although tests in the same area may, over time, fail to find new effects (pesticide paradox), regression testing involves rerunning tests to ensure the latest version of the test object continues to work as expected.	FL-1.3.1 K2

***5**	c, d	c) and d) are the correct options. Test analysis is the activity that identifies test conditions by analyzing the test basis. c) Identifying testable features is required for establishing test conditions. d) The requirements specification is part of the test basis, the body of knowledge used as the basis for test analysis and design. a) is not a correct option. Comparing actual test results with expected results is part of test execution. b) is not a correct option. Test activities to identify lessons learned improvement is part of test completion. e) is not a correct option. Analyzing failures observed in test results to identify possible causes is part of test execution and development debugging.	FL-1.4.1 K2
6	b	b) is the correct option. Increasing the code size increases the project size. Increasing the test team increases the amount of coordination and management required. Adding testers is likely to require time for the new testers to familiarize themselves with the software and the project status. a) is not the correct option. The test results themselves can have an impact on the test effort and test process. Having high-quality software at the start of test execution and quick, solid defect fixes provided prevents delays in the test execution process. If a defect, once identified, has to undergo multiple cycles of fix/retest/re-open, this can affect the schedule and budget. c) is not the correct option. During test execution, executing test cases may compromise the test system. To avoid delay in the test process, those responsible for implementing the test environment should be available during test execution for maintenance and support. Testing may show some aspects of the test environment may need adjustment. d) is not the correct option. Although good project documentation can be a positive factor, producing detailed formal documentation throughout the test process, such as carefully specified test cases, requires more effort and can result in delays.	FL-1.4.2 K2
7	d	d) is the correct option. Organizing test procedures is a task of the tester. A test procedure is defined as, *'A sequence of test cases in execution order, and any associated actions that may be required to set up the initial preconditions and any wrap-up activities after execution'.* Determining the test metrics, part of planning test monitoring and test control, is a main focus area for a test manager. a) is not the correct option. The tester creates the test execution schedule during test implementation and reports actual test results and test coverage during the test execution activity. b) is not the correct option. The tester identifies the test conditions as part of test analysis and the test manager reports the progress of the test activities compared to the test plan, c) is not the correct option. The test manager produces the test plan and produces the test progress report.	FL-1.4.5 K2

8	d	d) is the correct option. Independent testers challenge assumptions in an unbiased way and provide an objective evaluation of the work product. a) is not the correct option. Responsibility for quality is shared. b) is not the correct option. Independent testing may take more time than having a developer or tester on the development team test the code and fix defects. c) is not the correct option. Communication between testers and developers is still required.	FL-1.5.3 K2
9	c	c) is the correct option. The rule, 'for every activity there is a corresponding test activity' that is independent of the software development lifecycle model being used. a), b) and d) are not correct options for the reasons given for c).	FL-2.1.2 K1
10	d	d) is the correct option. ATDD is a test-driven development approach. a) is not the correct option. ATDD is an integral part of the development stage. b) is not the correct option. Defining the acceptance criteria should involve stakeholders, not just business analysts and customers. c) is not the correct option. Acceptance criteria may be automated as acceptance tests, but it is not always necessary or cost-effective to do so.	FL-2.1.3 K1
11	a	a) is the correct option. Black-box testing can encompass both functional and non-functional aspects of the software's behavior. Black-box testing could be linked with B, C or D. However, it cannot be linked as 4A as it does not have access to the code. This eliminates options c) and d). Non-functional testing ensures that the software meets quality attributes and characteristics such as portability and reliability 1D. Non-functional testing cannot be linked as 1B. This eliminates b) as the correct option. White-box testing's primary focus is on directly detecting coding issues related to functionality. However, it can also indirectly uncover some non-functional defects by evaluating how the code implementation adheres to non-functional requirements. With 1D already linked, and D not being the primary focus, white-box should be linked as 2A, this eliminates options c) and d). b), c) and d) are not correct options for the reasons given for a).	FL-2.2.2 K2
12*	d, e	d) and e) are the correct options. d) if there are changes made for different load and scalability requirements, maintenance testing should be performed to ensure that the system can handle the anticipated traffic. e) Modifications to the database schema, such as adding or modifying tables or fields, should trigger maintenance testing to ensure that data integrity and functionality are preserved. a) is not the correct option. Simply restarting a server does not require maintenance testing. b) is not a correct option. Minor changes to the user interface, such as adjustments to colors and fonts may not always trigger a requirement for maintenance testing if they don't affect the underlying functionality of the system. c) is not a correct option. For non-critical content such as news articles on a website might not necessarily warrant maintenance testing unless it's linked to underlying system changes.	FL-2.3.1 K2

13	c	c) is the correct option. Retrospectives are important for continual improvement of testing. a) is not the correct option. There are other opportunities to report the status of project progress, such as sprint reviews or daily stand-ups. b) is not the correct option. Recognizing individual achievements may be relevant in other contexts but is not the primary focus of a retrospective. d) is not the correct option. New organization policies and procedures could be communicated using various channels and this is not the primary objective of a retrospective, which focuses on identifying improvement opportunities.	FL-2.1.6 K2
14	d	d) is the correct option. Shift left involves performing testing and quality assurance activities as early as possible in the software development lifecycle. Although non-functional testing is typically associated with assessing how well the system performs under various conditions, it can start with system architecture and structure design documents, and in some cases, it is beneficial to do so. a) is not the correct option. When testers are not involved early in the development process, or when they are treated as a separate activity, it hinders shift left. Effective collaboration between developers and testers is a key aspect of shift left. b) is not the correct option. Intense pressure to meet tight project deadlines can lead to a focus on rapid development at the expense of thorough testing. This can undermine shift left. c) is not the correct option. Some testing, such as static testing, can be done before production-like systems are available.	FL-2.1.5 K2
15	b	b) is the correct option. Providing early information allows for appropriate and timely decisions to be made. a) is not the correct option. A customer may make change requests according to a pre-agreed procedure. c) is not the correct option. There are many ways the quality of changes can be measured. d) is not the correct option. Early feedback on test results on a project can improve the test process but if the aim is to improve future projects, the feedback is not needed early or frequently.	FL-3.2.1 K1
16	a	a) is the correct option. The moderator ensures the effective running of review meetings, including mediation, time management, and a safe review environment in which everyone can speak freely. b) is not the correct option. The manager is responsible for deciding what is to be reviewed and providing resources. c) is not the correct option. The review leader takes overall responsibility for the review. d) is not the correct option. The recorder documents the review information.	FL-3.2.3 K1

17	d	d) is the correct option. Dynamic testing and static testing techniques can be performed manually or by using test automation tools. a) is not the correct option. Static testing can be used to test some non-functional quality characteristics when the code is not running. For example, maintainability and ease of making adjustments to the code or identifying code patterns that may result in poor performance efficiency. b) is not the correct option. Static testing can test the format of the requirements specification document. However, dynamic testing is performed with software running. c) is not the correct option. Static testing can typically provide better code coverage than dynamic testing may.	FL-3.1.3 K2
18	a	a) is the correct option. The author not acting as the review leader, scribe or recorder applies to inspections. b) is not the correct option. Finding defects is a purpose of all reviews, but technical reviews also focus on discussing technical problems that may extend to design or other aspects. c) is not the correct option. An author typically acts as a review leader for a walkthrough review. d) is not the correct option. Reports can be produced for all types of reviews, but typically not for informal reviews.	FL-3.2.4 K2
19	b	b) is the correct option. Experience-based test techniques use the knowledge and experience of testers. White-box test techniques are based on analysis of the internal structure or code of the test object. Black-box test techniques are based on an analysis of the specified behavior of the test object without reference to its internal structure. a) is not the correct option. Exploratory testing is not limited to testing from the end user's perspective. White-box test techniques derive test cases from the internal structure or code of the test object, not expected behavior. Black-box test techniques are based on the requirements specification. c) is not the correct option. Exploratory testing can be wide-ranging and include testing for behavior, functional and non-functional characteristics. White-box test techniques are not focused on usability testing. Having predefined test cases is not limited to black-box test techniques. d) is not the correct option. Exploratory testing is one type of experience-based test technique. White-box test techniques are not based on requirements. Black-box test techniques include more than just usability testing.	FL-4.1.1 K2
20	b	b) is the correct option. All branches are tested with two test cases. For example: Test case ONE: with inputs such as X = 40, Y = 20 prints 'X+Y exceeds limit'. Test case TWO: with inputs such as X = 10, Y = 15 prints 'Within range'. (See the example of branch testing in section FL-4.3.2). a), c) and d) are not correct options for the reasons given for b).	FL-4.3.2 K2

21	a	a) is the correct option. White-box testing is based on the internal structure of the software. b) is not the correct option. White-box testing is based on the code or internal structure of the test object. c) is not the correct option. White-box testing is not based on the requirements specification. d) is not the correct option. White-box testing is not based on user requirements or usability specifications.	FL-4.3.3 K2
22	c	c) is the correct option. Fault attack testing is concerned with assessing system resilience by deliberately introducing faults. The Syllabus states, *'Fault attacks are a methodical approach to the implementation of error guessing. It involves the tester creating or acquiring a list of possible errors, defects and failures, and then designing tests that will identify defects associated with the errors, expose the defects, or cause the failures.'* a) is not the correct option. With exploratory testing, tests are simultaneously designed, executed and evaluated. b) is not the correct option. Checklist-based testing is focused on systematically verifying that specific requirements or criteria have been met. d) is not the correct option. Debugging is not a test technique. It is the process of finding, analyzing and removing the causes of failures in a component or system.	FL-4.4.1 K2
23	d	d) is the correct option. Exploratory testing does not involve having predetermined expectations about the outcomes. Testers remain open to discovering new issues or uncovering unknown aspects of the software. a) is not the correct option. Exploratory testing can be based on a test charter, which is defined as, *'A mission statement that guides an exploratory test session*. b) is not the correct option. Exploratory testing is an approach where testers dynamically design, execute and evaluate tests. c) is not the correct option. Exploratory testing is an approach based on testers using their experience and knowledge gained from previous projects.	FL-4.4.2 K2
24	c	c) is the correct option. Given/When/Then format is a way to write scenario-oriented acceptance criteria. Using a tabulated form of input-output mapping is a way to write a form of rule-based acceptance criteria. a) is not the correct option. Scenario-based acceptance and rule-oriented acceptance criteria are based on test conditions that should be exercised by test cases. Acceptance criteria are not based on technical details of implementation. b) is not the correct option. Regulations and compliance should be considered if relevant in acceptance criteria, regardless of their classification, although rule-oriented is likely to be more suited to comprehensive coverage of regulations. d) is not the correct option. Both scenario-oriented and rule-oriented acceptance criteria should be well-defined and unambiguous.	FL-4.5.2 K2

25	b	b) is the correct option. Test cases TC3 and TC5 use input values both from the valid partitions. TC1: Username: Morgan.Coe (invalid) Password: Secr#t723 (valid) TC2: Username: kiran000 (valid) Password: mypassword (invalid) TC3: Username: Chris123 (valid) Password: Passw0rd! (valid) TC4: Username: a (invalid) Password: 12345678 (invalid) TC5: Username: john123 (valid) Password: Secr3t+$ (valid) TC6: Username: Kristina4242 (invalid) Password: Passw0rd (invalid) a), c) and d) are not correct options for the reasons given for b).	FL-4.2.1 K3
26	d	d) is the correct option. **Band** / **Taxable Income** / **Tax** / **3-value Lower Boundary** / **3-value Upper Boundary** Middle Rate / £45,001 to £140,000 / 40% / £45,000/£45,001/£45,002 / £139,999/£140,000/£140,001 With three-value boundary testing, six values are needed to test the two boundaries. £45,000 and £140,000 have already been tested. This is 2/6, equal to 33% minimum coverage. a), b) and c) are not correct options for the reasons given for d).	FL-4.2.2 K3
27	a	a) is the correct option. R3, R4, and R5 are valid rules. R1 and R2 are not possible as either a general admission ticket or a VIP ticket is available, not both and the payment does not reflect the price of two tickets being purchased. R6 is not correct as a VIP ticket is not available to a person less than 16 years old. R7 and R8 are not valid as there is a payment but no ticket, so there should be no payment due, as VIP admission is not available for anyone under 16 years of age.	FL-4.2.3 K3
28	d	d) is the correct option. The following test cases are required: Test case One: S1, S2, S3, S4, S6 Test case Two: S1, S5, S3, S4, S6 Test case Three: S1, S5, S6 a), b) and c) are not correct options for the reasons given for d).	FL-4.2.4 K3
***29**	c, e	c) and e) are the correct options. c) is required to show the replenishment lead time of a particular product. e) is required to show the quantity of each product. c) and e) could be on the same display page. a) is not a correct option. The user story does not include a requirement to report the value of the stock. b) is not a correct option. A customer would place an order and the user story is for what a manager needs. d) is not a correct option. As the user story does not specify inventory history is required, this is not a relevant test case. Although history may be useful, there are reasons why this may not be needed such as these are new or different products or customer buying patterns are known to have been different in the past.	FL-4.5.3 K3

Table for question 26:

Band	Taxable Income	Tax	3-value Lower Boundary	3-value Upper Boundary
Middle Rate	£45,001 to £140,000	40%	£45,000/£45,001/£45,002	£139,999/£140,000/£140,001

30	b	b) is the correct option. The test pyramid emphasizes having a broad base of unit or component tests which allow for early defect detection. a) is not the correct option. The test pyramid does not provide information about test priorities and relationships between different tests. c) is not the correct option. Test pyramid recommends fewer end-to-end tests, which means there may be gaps in test coverage for the complete application workflow. d) is not the correct option. The test pyramid does not provide information on resources or time. While unit tests are typically faster to execute than end-to-end tests, setting up a comprehensive suite of unit tests can be time-consuming. Maintaining a large number of unit tests can become challenging as the codebase grows.	FL-5.1.6 K1
***31**	a, d	a) and d) are the correct options. a) Exit criteria for a test phase such as the test implementation could for example require 90% of the test cases to have been implemented and ready for execution. This could also be part of the entry criteria for test execution to start. d) Entry criteria and exit criteria are used to help ensure smooth transitioning between phases of the test process. b) is not a correct option. Entry criteria for a particular test phase do not become exit criteria for the subsequent phase. c) is not a correct option. Entry criteria should have been validated for the test phase to start. Exit criteria are validated at the end of the test phase. e) is not a correct option. Exit criteria focus on the evaluation of the work done.	FL-5.1.3 K2
32	c	c) is the correct option. 1C, 2D, 3A, 4B 1C - Q1 includes unit and component testing, this is where automated testing can be effective. 2D - Q2 includes API testing. Testing can be manual or automated. 3A - Q3 includes acceptance criteria which can be manual or automated. 4B - Q4 includes smoke and non-functional testing such as performance efficiency, where testing is often but not always suitable for automating.	FL-5.1.7 K2
33	a	a) is the correct option as it is not true. Product risk analysis should be performed at the earliest possible time and before testing starts. Risk analysis should then be an ongoing activity throughout the software development lifecycle as more information becomes known. and can determine whether any other activities in addition to testing might be employed. b), c) and d) are not correct options as they are all ways product risk analysis can influence the scope and thoroughness of testing.	FL-5.2.3 K2

34	b	b) is the correct option. Test progress reports should provide insights into the progress of testing activities, such as test case execution, defect identification, and coverage. Including an assessment of the technologies could divert attention from the main purpose of the report and or confuse stakeholders. a), c) and d) are not correct options as they are relevant in a test progress report. Test progress reports are typically focused on communicating the status of testing activities, results and identification of new or emerging risks to stakeholders.	FL-5.3.2 K2
35	a	a) is the correct option. Resource allocation is the process of optimizing the use of resources. While configuration management can support resource use by providing a common reference for teams to work from and thus avoid unnecessary work on different incorrect versions, it does not consider project constraints and priorities. b) is not the correct option. Configuration management ensures that the right versions of configuration items are used during development, testing, and deployment. c) is not the correct option. Audits ensure that configurations match documented requirements and practices. d) is not the correct option. Configuration management can provide a historical record of changes and outcomes of decisions made about configuration items.	FL-5.4.1 K2
36	b	b) is the correct option. Previous project: Development test effort = 750 days, Total test effort = (60 x 2) +30 = 150 person days, Ratio is 5:1. For the new project: development test effort = 600 days, so based on the ratio 5:1, Test effort = 600 x 1/5 = 120 person-hours. This equates to 60 hours per tester. a), c) and d) are not correct options for the reason given for b).	FL-5.1.4 K3
37	a	a) is the correct option. The order TC1, TC3, TC4,TC6, TC5,TC2. TC7 shows dependency and priority are correctly used. b) is not the correct option. TC3, TC6, TC4, TC5, TC1, TC2, TC7 order is based on priority but does not consider dependency. c) is not the correct option. TC1, TC3, TC5, TC4, TC6, TC7, TC2 order is based on starting with TC1 and working across without considering dependency. d) is not the correct option. TC02, TC5, TC3, TC1, TC6, TC4, TC7 order is based on incorrect reading of the direction of arrows.	FL-5.1.5 K3
38	b	b) is the correct option. Ideas for improving the test case are not typically a requirement for submitting a defect report. a) Is not the correct option. There are no details of which link(s) were being tested This should have been included. c) is not correct. The website and browser versions are not given. These details should have been included. d) is not the correct option. The defect report should have a unique identifier.	FL-5.5.1 K3

***39**	a, d	a) and d) are the correct options. a) By automatically generating test cases from analyzing requirements, code, and user behavior, AI-enabled tools can reduce the manual effort required for test script creation, when compared to that required when using traditional tools. This reduces the chance of human error associated with traditional automation scripts. d) AI-enabled tools can process unstructured data such as natural language, making them valuable for testing applications with text-based input/output and other similar characteristics. Traditional tools require structured data. b) is not a correct option. AI-enabled tools can simulate real user interactions, enabling comprehensive usability and user experience testing on a larger scale than is possible using traditional tools. c) is not a correct option. AI-enabled testing tools can be complex to set up and configure. e) is not a correct option. AI-enabled tools used with a wide range of scenarios, including complex interactions and edge cases, result in improved test coverage compared to manually defined test cases. An edge case is a problem or situation that occurs only at an extreme (max. or min.) operating parameter.	FL-6.1.1 K2
40	d	d) is the correct option. Tools can reduce the time for data preparation during test implementation and reduce the time for test execution of large numbers of test cases, detecting defects (test tools for static testing) and failures (tools for dynamic testing) earlier. a) is not the best option. It is not correct to assume tools can automate <u>all</u> manual tests. Human judgment may be required. b) is not the correct option. Test automation tools can improve/extend test coverage in some situations by executing more tests than may be possible with manual testing. c) is not the best option. The return on investment for automation execution tools is usually highest when using these tools for regression testing because of low-level maintenance with expected and repeated execution.	FL-6.2.1 K1

PRACTICE EXAM THREE

40 Questions
Time allowed 60 minutes
26 / 40 marks are required for a Pass

Q#1 FL-1.2.2 K1 Which of the following relating to quality assurance and testing is false?

a) Quality assurance can enhance the requirements gathering process, testing confirms the product works as expected
b) Quality assurance focuses on preventative and proactive measures, testing focuses on product corrective measures
c) Quality assurance activities involve validation of the product against predefined quality criteria, testing establishes the quality standards
d) Quality assurance activities may include auditing the test process, testing activities include inspection of the product under test to identify issues

Select ONE option

Q#2 FL-1.5.2 K1 Which of the following statements is most true for the whole team approach?

a) Testers work with business representatives to create appropriate acceptance tests
b) Testers help business representatives define the test strategy
c) The team at the beginning of the project remains as the team until completion.
d) To maximize team efficiency, testers take on responsibility for software quality to allow developers to focus on coding

Select ONE option

Q#3 FL-1.2.3 K2 Which of the following statements is most correct?

a) Defects are code mistakes, errors are failures in the software and root causes are issues in the development process
b) Defects are issues in the development process, errors are code faults and root causes are failures in the software
c) Defects are failures in the work products, errors are issues in the development process and root causes are defects in the software
d) Defects are faults in work products, errors are human mistakes, failures are deviations from expected behavior and root causes are fundamental reasons for the occurrence of a problem

Select ONE option

Q#4 FL-1.3.1 K2 Which of the following is always true?

a) A test team should be thorough and test everything
b) There will be no undiscovered defects after effective testing
c) The cost of quality does not depend on when testing finds defects
d) There is no universally applicable approach to testing

Select ONE option

Q#5 FL-1.4.1 K2 Which of the following are not part of the test execution activity?

a) Adding details of any unresolved defects to a backlog of product items
b) Reporting anomalies based on failures observed
c) Analyzing anomalies to identify likely or possible causes
d) Comparing actual test results with expected results
e) Setting up the test environment

Select TWO options

Q#6 FL-1.4.4 K2 The following describe the value of maintaining traceability during the test process except for which?

a) Provides information to assess product quality, test process capability and project progress
b) Provides the sequence of test cases in execution order linked with any associated actions required to set up the pre-conditions
c) Facilitates test audits and helps meet IT governance criteria
d) Assists in communicating the technical aspects of testing to stakeholders in an understandable manner

Select ONE option

Q#7 FL-1.4.5 K2 Which of the following tasks belong primarily to the tester's role?

a) Designing solutions to new requirements
b) Identifying test conditions
c) Organizing test cases into test procedures
d) Creating the test plan
e) Deciding on the test metrics to be collected

Select TWO options

Q#8 FL-1.5.3 K2 Which of the following is the best example of an advantage of independent testing?

a) Independent testers can spend more time on testing activities as they do not have to spend as much time communicating with software developers
b) Developers may abdicate their responsibility for quality and focus on the quantity of code they can produce
c) Independent testers question assumptions behind the requirements, design and implementation that may have been missed by developers
d) Independent testers have better domain-specific knowledge than software developers

Select ONE option

Q#9 FL-2.1.2 K1 The following are good testing practices, independent of the chosen software development lifecycle, except for which?

a) For every development activity, there should be a corresponding test activity
b) Testers should be involved in reviewing work products as soon as drafts are available
c) Test analysis and test design for a given test level should begin during the corresponding development phase
d) One set of test objectives should be used throughout to ensure consistency, irrespective of the test level

Select ONE option

Q#10 FL-2.1.3 K1 Which of the following is a test-first approach to development?

a) Prototyping
b) Behavior-driven Development
c) Domain-driven Design
d) Feature-driven Development

Select ONE option

Q#11 FL-2.2.1 K2 Which of the following best describes the primary focus of integration testing?

a) Interface mismatches
b) Procedure failures
c) Design defects
d) Code logic defects

Select ONE option

Q#12 FL-2.2.3 K2 Which of the following correctly distinguishes confirmation testing from regression testing?

a) Confirmation testing ensures code changes made to fix a defect do not affect existing functionality or behavior, regression testing validates defect fixes
b) Confirmation testing is performed by developers, regression testing is performed by testers
c) Confirmation testing focuses on verifying that a fix for a defect works as intended, regression testing checks that existing functionality and behavior are unaffected
d) Confirmation testing is automated, and regression testing is performed manually

Select ONE option

Q#13 FL-2.1.6 K2 Which of the following are most true for retrospectives?

a) If the team believes there is nothing to improve, the retrospective should be canceled and the time saved allocated to other activities
b) If more time is needed to accomplish the current sprint or iteration objectives, retrospectives can be canceled to help meet goals or deadlines
c) To be effective, a retrospective should follow the same agenda and format as a previously successful retrospective
d) Retrospectives are important for the successful implementation of testing with Continuous Improvement CI
e) Participants in retrospectives can include testers, developers, architects, the product owner and business analyst

Select TWO options

Q#14 FL-2.1.4 K2 Which of the following statements best describes DevOps?

a) A collection of methodologies for providing fast software delivery and infrastructure changes
b) Shift left with developers taking responsibility for all operations tasks
c) Collaboration and communication of developers, testers and operations staff to achieve a set of common objectives
d) Automation of the process of software delivery and removal of the need for manual testing

Select ONE option

Q#15 FL-3.2.1 K1 Why is early and frequent testing feedback to stakeholders beneficial?

a) Allows developers to focus on those features that deliver the most value
b) Minimizes overall collaboration and communication among stakeholders
c) Provides stakeholders with information to make business decisions
d) Reduces the need for project documentation
e) Limits the potential for project scope adjustments

Select TWO options

Q#16 FL-3.2.3 K1 Consider the roles and responsibilities below:

1. Manager
2. Review leader
3. Moderator
4. Reviewer

A. Decides what is to be reviewed
B. Ensures effective running of the review meeting
C. Performs the actual review
D. Has overall responsibility for the review, deciding who should be involved

Which option links the roles and responsibilities in reviews?

a) 1D, 2A, 3C, 4B
b) 1A, 2D, 3B, 4C
c) 1D, 2B, 3A, 4C
d) 1B, 2C, 3A, 4D

Select ONE option

Q#17 FL-3.1.2 K2 Which of the following is a capability of static code testing?

a) Forcing failures in the software to locate defects
b) Identifying data dependencies or data changes that occur during execution
c) Determining memory usage when running with different loads
d) Finding code constructs that could negatively impact performance efficiency

Select ONE option

Q#18 FL-3.2.2 K2 Which of the following best summarizes the activities of a review process?

a) Static testing in which a work product or process is evaluated by one or more individuals to detect defects or to provide improvements
b) A regular event in which team members discuss results, review their practices and identify ways to improve
c) A meeting of a cross-functional team of stakeholders to manage reported defects from initial detection to ultimate
d) Dynamic testing, where a work product or process is evaluated by one or more individuals to detect defects or to provide improvements

Select ONE option

Q#19 FL-4.1.1 K2 Which of the following statements best distinguishes white-box and black-box testing?

a) White-box test techniques are performed only manually, black-box test techniques are performed manually or automated
b) White-box test techniques are primarily used for functional testing, black-box test techniques are primarily used for performance efficiency and usability testing
c) When the implementation of the code changes, white-box test cases may need to be changed, black-box test cases may not need changing
d) White-box test techniques are performed without the code running, black-box test techniques are performed with the code running
e) White-box test cases can be derived from the code or the code design documents, black-box test cases can be derived from the requirements specification

Select TWO options

Q#20 FL-4.3.2 K2 Which of the following statements about branch testing is correct?

a) If the code includes only unconditional branches, 100% branch coverage can be achieved without executing a test case
b) If the code includes only unconditional statements, the number of test cases required for branch testing is the same as for statement testing
c) Branch testing tests the outcomes of conditional statements and does not include testing unconditional statements
d) Branch testing is particularly useful for ensuring all combinations of conditions are tested when short-circuiting programming is being used

Select ONE option

Q#21 FL-4.3.3 K2 Which of the following describes a potential benefit of white-box testing?

a) Verifies the correctness of user requirements and functionalities
b) Ensures the software is user-friendly and intuitive
c) Can ensure all functional requirements are met
d) Can ensure the entire code is considered

Select ONE option

Q#22 FL-4.4.1 K2 Which of the following is true for an error guessing approach to testing?

a) Involves performing formal in-depth analysis of system requirements to identify potential areas of concern
b) Focuses on achieving specific coverage metrics to identify areas where errors made by developers are likely to occur
c) Involves systematic test case creation based on specific inputs, expected results, or coverage criteria
d) Can fill gaps in situations where the requirements specification is lacking or inadequate

Select ONE option

Q#23 FL-4.4.2 K2 For which of the following is exploratory testing the least appropriate approach?

a) Regression testing is an ongoing requirement
b) Requirements and specifications are out of date
c) Restricted amount of time to undertake testing
d) Limited knowledge of the software product

Select ONE option

Q#24 FL-4.5.1 K2 The following can be used in collaborative authorship of user stories, except for which?

a) Mind mapping
b) Knowledge silo
c) Brainstorming
d) Whiteboarding

Select ONE option

Q#25 FL-4.2.1 K3 You are testing an application intended to calculate income tax, based on whole GB pound values. There is an allowance of £15,000 before income tax is payable. A basic rate of tax then applies to the next £29,999 of income. An intermediate rate of tax applies to income above the basic rate and up to a total income of £60,000. A higher rate applies to any additional income.

Using equivalence partitioning, which of the following options has all of its values in different partitions for the various tax bands?

a) £10,000, £15,000, £30,000, £60,000
b) £10,000, £20,000, £45,000, £75,000
c) £900, £16,000, £51,000, £61,000
d) £9,000, £30,000, £45,000, £60,000

Select ONE option

Q#26 FL-4.2.2 K3 You are testing a system that calculates home energy efficiency ratings. Points are allocated based on the energy efficiency measures adopted.

1 - 21 points	Very weak
22 - 39 points	Weak
40 - 55 points	Fair
56 - 69 points	Satisfactory
70 - 81 points	Good
82 - 90 points	Very good
91 - 100 points	Excellent

Test cases have been executed with the following input values for points: 69, 21, 39, 70, 82, 55, 91,101. What is the two-value boundary value analysis percentage coverage achieved with the test cases already performed?

a) More than 50% but less than 100%
b) Less than 50%
c) 100%
d) 50%

Select ONE option

Q#27 FL-4.2.3 K3 You are working on an application that manages the loan of equipment from a store. If the equipment is specialized, the borrower must have the necessary specialist skills otherwise the request is rejected. If the request has not been rejected and the equipment is already out on hire, the request is put on the waitlist until the equipment becomes available.

	Rule							
Conditions	**R1**	**R2**	**R3**	**R4**	**R5**	**R6**	**R7**	**R8**
Equipment available?	T	T	T	T	F	F	F	F
Specialist item?	T	F	T	F	F	T	T	F
Requestor has specialist skills?	F	F	T	T	F	T	F	T
Actions								
Reject request	X						X	
Dispatch equipment		X	X	X		X		
Waitlist request					X			X

From the information given, which of the rules above includes an error?

a) R2
b) R8
c) R6
d) R4

Select ONE option

Q#28 FL-4.2.4 K3 You are using state transition testing for an application that has four states S1, S2, S3 and S4. The valid 0-switch transitions are: S1, to either S2 or S3, both directions between S2 and S3, S2 to S4 and S3 to S4. There is no return transition from S4.

Starting at S1 and ending at S4, which of the following correctly describes the number of test cases needed to achieve 100% all states coverage and 100% valid transitions coverage required?

a) One test case for all states coverage, two test cases for valid transitions coverage
b) Two test cases for all states coverage, two test cases for valid transitions coverage
c) Two test cases for all states coverage, three test cases for valid transitions coverage
d) One test case for all states coverage, three test cases for valid transitions coverage

Select ONE option

Q#29 FL-4.5.3 K3 You have the following acceptance criteria:
A user with a valid email address should be able to reset their password using a trusted password reset link sent by email. After five minutes, the issued link should expire.

How many of the following test cases can be derived from the given acceptance criteria?

TC01 Verification of the user's ability to log in after resetting their password
TC02 Testing the email confirmation link's functionality
TC03 Verification of the password reset link expiring within two minutes
TC04 Testing the software's response to an invalid password link entered
TC05 Verification the administrator can unlock an account blocked due to the old password being used

a) 5
b) 4
c) 3
d) 2

Select ONE option

Q#30 FL-5.2.1 K1 When determining risk level, which of the following statements is correct?

a) Likelihood is the assessed risk level; impact is the assessed adverse effect if the risk occurs
b) Likelihood is the assessed chance of the risk occurring; impact is the assessed effect if the risk occurs
c) Likelihood is the risk rating; risk impact is the business risk if the risk occurs
d) Likelihood is the qualitative assessment of the risk; risk impact is the qualitative assessment

Select ONE option

Q#31 FL-5.1.1 K2 Consider the following from a test plan:
'Integration points with the inventory management system and customer database will be tested to ensure data consistency and accurate product information.'

Which part of the test plan does this belong to?

a) Context of testing
b) Test approach
c) Test scope
d) Test deliverables

Select ONE option

Q#32 FL-5.1.7 K2 Consider testing quadrants (1-4) and the testing that can be performed (A-D).

1. Testing quadrant Q1: Technology-facing, supporting development
2. Testing quadrant Q2: Business-facing, supporting development
3. Testing quadrant Q3: Business-facing, critique of the product
4. Testing quadrant Q4: Technology-facing, critique of the product

A. User story testing
B. Component integration testing
C. Exploratory testing
D. Portability testing

Which of the following best links the two lists?

a) 1B, 2A, 3C, 4D
b) 1C, 2D, 3A, 4B
c) 1A, 2B, 3D, 4C
d) 1D, 2C, 3B, 4A

Select ONE option

Q#33 FL-5.2.4 K2 Consider the following tasks and product risk control options:

1. Perform reviews and perform static analysis to detect defects early
2. Make regular back-ups of the test environment in case the environment is compromised during testing
3. Work with stakeholders to identify very low risks, and given the currently available resources, are not to be resolved
4. Purchase insurance coverage to protect against financial loss if specific risks occur

A. Acceptance
B. Mitigation
C. Transference
D. Contingency

Which of the following links the two lists?

a) 1B, 2D, 3A, 4C
b) 1A, 2B, 3C, 4D
c) 1B, 2A, 3D, 4C
d) 1B, 2C, 3A, 4D

Select ONE option

Q#34 FL-5.3.3 K2 Which of the following can provide the status and progress of the current test process being undertaken?

a) Regular communication between stakeholders
b) Details of a previous project
c) A software dashboard with real-time updates
d) Vacation schedule of testers
e) Test summary report

Select TWO options

Q#35 FL-5.4.1 K2 In the context of software testing, which of the following best describes an activity in configuration management?

a) Optimizing hardware resources such as processor and memory
b) Defining user access permissions and security settings
c) Setting up network routers and switches
d) Managing version control for testware

Select ONE option

Q#36 FL-5.1.4 K3 Using three-point estimation to estimate test effort for a new feature added to an application feature, the following estimates have been made:

Most optimistic estimation	3 person-hours
Most likely estimation	4.5 person-hours
Most pessimistic estimation	9 person-hours

What is the final estimate of test effort with its measurement error?

a) 5 ± 1.5 person-hours
b) 5 ± 1 person-hours
c) 4.5 ± 1 person-hours
d) 4.5 ± 4.5 person-hours

Select ONE option

Q#37 FL-5.1.5 K3 The following test cases are testing an application for an online flight booking system. The test cases have been prioritized by stakeholders as shown, with 1 the highest priority, and 3 the lowest priority.

Test Case ID	Test Condition covered	Dependency	Assessed Priority
TC01	Select Flight	None	2
TC02	Book hold luggage	TC01	3
TC03	Enter passenger details	TC01	2
TC04	Choose seat	TC05	2
TC05	Book Flight	TC03	1

Which test case should be executed as the third test case?

a) TC02
b) TC05
c) TC01
d) TC03

Select ONE option

Q#38 FL-5.5.1 K3 Consider the following defect report:
Project: ABC App v4.0 Priority: High
Description: Failure encountered while trying to log in to the ABC App account with a valid account code and two-factor authentication 2FA inputs. Login process failed, displaying an error message but an authentication code was still sent to the linked 2FA device. The authentication code should not be sent when login fails. The login process failure prevents users from accessing their accounts despite having an authentication code.
Attachments: Screenshots showing the login process error message.

For how many of the six items below has information been completely omitted in the defect report?

Expected result
Error message text
Test environment details
Is the failure reproducible
Priority
Impact

a) 4
b) 2
c) 3
d) 5

Select ONE option

Q#39 FL-6.1.1 K2 Which of the following best describe main purposes of a test execution tool?

a) Runs automated test scripts to evaluate the test object
b) Tracks the status of test cases throughout the software development lifecycle
c) Facilitates establishing test suites from test cases for execution
d) Facilitates efficient scheduling of the execution of test cases
e) Anonymizes the required data for security reasons

Select TWO options

Q#40 FL-6.2.1 K1 When considering the benefits and risks of the use of AI-enabled tools, which of the following is least correct?

a) AI-enabled tools lead to unbiased testing while traditional tools requiring human intervention may lead to biased testing
b) AI-enabled tools are suitable for continuous integration and continuous delivery (CI/CD) pipelines, providing quick feedback to developers
c) AI-enabled tools can dynamically prioritize testing based on code changes, defect data, and potential risk areas
d) In some scenarios, AI-enabled tools provide better test coverage than traditional tools can

Select ONE option

ADDITIONAL Question #30 FL-5.3.1 K1 (Target time to answer 1 minute)

The ISTQB Exam Structures & Rules Tables v1.19 specify one question should be on one of four learning objectives, FL-5.1.2, 5.1.6, 5.2.1 or 5.3.1. In the practice exams, all Questions #30 are based on the first three learning objectives. This additional question provides an exam question on FL-5.3.1. Note: There are other practice questions on FL-5.3.1 in the 5.3 Questions section.

Q#30 FL-5.3.1 K1 Categories of test metrics include:

1.	Product quality metrics	A.	Number of test cases executed/not executed
2.	Project progress metrics	B.	Percentage of code tested
3.	Test process progress metrics	C.	User interface (UI) response times
4.	Cost metrics	D.	Amount of resources used
5.	Coverage metrics	E.	Task completion figures

Which of the following best links the two lists?

a) 1C, 2D, 3A, 4B, 5E
b) 1B, 2D, 3E, 4A, 5C
c) 1D, 2E, 3A, 4C, 5B
d) 1C, 2E, 3A, 4D, 5B

Select ONE option

PRACTICE EXAM THREE ANSWERS AND EXPLANATIONS

40 Answers / 40 Marks / 1 point each

Question Number	Correct Answer	Learning Objective	K-Level
1	c	FL-1.2.2	K1
2	a	FL-1.5.2	K1
3	d	FL-1.2.3	K2
4	d	FL-1.3.1	K2
*5	a, e	FL-1.4.1	K2
6	b	FL-1.4.4	K2
*7	b, c	FL-1.4.5	K2
8	c	FL-1.5.3	K2
9	d	FL-2.1.2	K1
10	b	FL-2.1.3	K1
11	a	FL-2.2.1	K2
12	c	FL-2.2.3	K2
*13	d, e	FL-2.1.6	K2
14	c	FL-2.1.4	K2
*15	a, c	FL-3.2.1	K1
16	b	FL-3.2.3	K1
17	d	FL-3.1.2	K2
18	a	FL-3.2.2	K2
*19	c, e	FL-4.1.1	K2
20	b	FL-4.3.2	K2

Question Number	Correct Answer	Learning Objective	K-Level
21	d	FL-4.3.3	K2
22	d	FL-4.4.1	K2
23	a	FL-4.4.2	K2
24	b	FL-4.5.1	K2
25	c	FL-4.2.1	K3
26	d	FL-4.2.2	K3
27	c	FL-4.2.3	K3
28	a	FL-4.2.4	K3
29	c	FL-4.5.3	K3
30	b	FL-5.2.1	K1
31	c	FL-5.1.1	K2
32	a	FL-5.1.7	K2
33	a	FL-5.2.4	K2
*34	a, c	FL-5.3.3	K2
35	d	FL-5.4.1	K2
36	b	FL-5.1.4	K3
37	b	FL-5.1.5	K3
38	b	FL-5.5.1	K3
*39	a, d	FL-6.1.1	K2
40	a	FL-6.2.1	K1

* If both options selected are correct, the point assigned to the question is awarded, otherwise no point is given.

Question Number	Correct Answer	Explanation / Rationale	Learning Objective K-level
1	c	c) is the correct option as it is not true. Quality assurance focuses on processes, not products. Testing focuses on products working correctly. a) is not the correct option for the reasons given for c). b) is not the correct option. Quality assurance focuses on preventative measures and proactive measures to provide confidence that quality requirements will be met. Testing focuses on corrective and reactive measures to improve product quality. d) is not the correct option. All team members have some responsibility for quality.	FL-1.2.2 K1
2	a	a) is the correct option. In a whole-team approach, any team member with the necessary knowledge and skills can be part of performing any task. Business representatives should know the acceptance criteria, and testers will be validating them. b) is not the correct option. Testers work with developers to agree on the test strategy. Testers collaborate with business representatives to help create suitable acceptance tests. c) is not the correct option. The whole-team approach relies on collaboration among team members, not on the team composition remaining unchanged throughout the project. d) is not the correct option. In the whole team approach, all team members are responsible for quality.	FL-1.5.2 K1
3	d	d) is the correct option. The ISTQB Glossary defines a defect as *'an imperfection or deficiency in a work product where it does not meet its requirements or specifications or impairs its intended use'*. Synonyms are *'bug, fault, flaw'*. An error is *'a human action that results in a defect.* Synonym *'mistake'*. A failure is *'an event in which a component or system does not meet its requirements within specified limits during its execution'*. Synonym *'malfunction'*. A root cause is *'a source of a defect such that if it is removed, the occurrence of the defect type is decreased or removed'*. A root cause arises from systemic process deficiencies, such as poorly defined requirements, inadequate peer review or a lack of edge-case testing, which allowed the mistake to happen. a), b) and c) are not correct options. They contain one or more incorrect definitions or usage of defect, error, failure and root cause.	FL-1.2.3 K2

4	d	d) is the correct option. There is no universally applicable approach to testing. The test approach should take into account the context. a) is not correct. Exhaustive testing is not possible except in trivial small situations. b) is not the correct option. Testing shows the presence of defects, not the absence of them. c) is not the correct option. Early testing saves time and money so the cost of quality is reduced since fewer failures will occur later in the software life cycle when they are more costly to address.	FL-1.3.1 K2
***5**	a, e	a) and e) are the correct options. a) Creating or adding to a product backlog of unresolved defects for product backlog items is part of test completion. e) Setting up the test environment is part of test implementation the test environment is part of test implementation. b), c) and d) are not correct options as the tasks are all part of test execution.	FL-1.4.1 K2
6	b	b) is the correct option. Test procedure (not traceability) is defined as, *'The sequence of test cases in execution order linked with any associated actions required to set up the pre-conditions.'* a, c) and d) are not correct options. These are benefits of traceability.	FL-1.4.4 K2
***7**	b, c	b) and c) are the correct options. b) The tester's role is mainly focused on test analysis, test design, test implementation and test execution. Identifying test conditions is part of test analysis. c) Organizing test cases into test procedures is part of test implementation. A test procedure is defined as, *'A sequence of test cases in execution order, and any associated actions that may be required to set up the initial preconditions and any wrap up activities post execution.'* a) is not a correct option. Developers design the solutions to new requirements. d) is not a correct option. Creating the test plan is test planning. The test manager is responsible for creating the test plan. e) is not the correct option. The test manager's role includes test monitoring and test control. To do this effectively, the test manager determines which test metrics should be collected.	FL-1.4.5 K2
8	c	c) is the correct option. Independent testers typically operate with an unbiased perspective. a) is not good practice. Communication is essential. b) is not the correct option, as developers abdicating their responsibility for quality is not an advantage. d) is not the correct option. Testers may not always have better domain-specific knowledge than developers.	FL-1.5.3 K2

9	d	d) is the correct option. Having one set of test objectives throughout is not good testing practice. Different test levels have specific and different test objectives. This allows for testing to be appropriately comprehensive and avoid redundancy. a) is not the correct option. For every development activity, there should be a corresponding test activity, so that development activities are subject to quality control. b) is not the correct option. Testers reviewing work products as soon as drafts are available supports shift left. c) is not the correct option. Test analysis and design for a given test level begins during the corresponding development phase.	FL-2.1.2 K1
10	b	b) is the correct option. BDD is a test-first development approach. a) is not the correct option. Prototyping is a development approach in which a prototype is built, then repeatedly tested and reworked until an acceptable product is achieved. c) is not the correct option. Domain-driven design DDD is not inherently a test-first approach. It focuses on the core domain and domain logic. d) is not the correct option. FDD is not typically considered a test-first approach as it does not adhere to the strict 'test-first' philosophy. It is primarily a software development process that focuses on delivering features in a systematic and planned manner.	FL-2.1.3 K1
11	a	a) is the correct option. Integration testing looks for mismatches in interfaces and failures in interactions between integrated test objects. b) is not the correct option. Integration testing is not focused on finding procedure failures. c) is not the correct option. Any failure might be the result of a design defect, however, uncovering design defects is not a primary focus of integration testing. d) is not the correct option. Component testing looks for code logic defects.	FL-2.2.1 K2
12	c	c) is the correct option. Confirmation testing is, '*A type of change-related testing performed after fixing a defect to confirm that a failure caused by that defect does not reoccur.*' Regression testing is, '*A type of change-related testing to detect whether defects have been introduced or uncovered in unchanged areas of the software.'* a) is not the correct option for the reasons given for c). b) is not the correct option. Confirmation testing and regression testing are not distinguished by who performs the testing. d) is not the correct option. Both confirmation testing and regression testing can be either manual or automated.	FL-2.2.3 K2
***13**	d, e	d) and e) are the correct options. d) The benefits of a retrospective include increasing test effectiveness and efficacy of any test process. e) The benefits of a retrospective include team bonding and team members learning from each other. a) is not a correct option. There is no perfect process or product, there is always something to improve, so a retrospective should not be canceled for this reason. b) is not a correct option. Cancelling retrospectives to achieve goals and deadlines removes the opportunity to identify improvements. If the	FL-2.1.6 K2

		team repeatedly does not meet the deadlines, it should review what is happening here and retrospectives are required. c) is not a correct option. Retrospectives should encourage creativity and ideas for improvement. Keeping to the same format and agenda is not conducive to this aim.	
14	c	c) is the correct option. DevOps promotes team autonomy. a) is not the correct option. DevOps is an organizational approach and not a collection of methodologies. b) is not the correct option. While DevOps requires shift left within an organization, it does not involve developers taking responsibility for all operations tasks. d) is not the correct option. DevOps does not remove the need for some manual testing. For example, manual testing from the user's perspective is typically required.	FL-2.1.4 K2
***15**	a, c	a) and c) are the correct options. a) Information provided early to developers allows them to focus on areas of most value to stakeholders. c) Given early information, stakeholders can update decisions such as release dates, features to be included and more. b) is not a correct option. Early stakeholder feedback often requires increased communication and documentation to ensure alignment and address concerns. d) is not the correct option. Early stakeholder feedback often requires increased documentation to ensure alignment and address concerns. e) is not a correct option. Early feedback can lead to adjustments in project scope based on evolving requirements and user feedback, which can be beneficial for delivering a successful product.	FL-3.2.1 K1
16	b	b) is the correct option. 1A - The manager decides what is to be reviewed. 2D - The review leader has overall responsibility for the review, deciding who should be involved. 3B - The moderator ensures the effective running of the review meeting. 4C - A reviewer performs the actual review. a), c) and d) are not correct options for the reasons given for b).	FL-3.2.3 K1
17	d	d) is the correct option. Static testing can identify code constructs that could lead to performance bottlenecks, such as inefficient algorithms or resource leaks. a) is not the correct option. Static testing identifies and locates defects. Dynamic testing triggers failures. b) is not the correct option. Dynamic testing is performed when the software is being executed. c) is not the correct option. As the software is running with data loads, static testing is not used.	FL-3.1.2 K2
18	a	a) is the correct option. The ISTQB Glossary defines a review as, *'A type of static testing in which a work product or process is evaluated by one or more individuals to detect defects or to provide improvements.'* b) is not the correct option. It defines a retrospective, which focuses on practices. c) is not the correct option. It refers to a defect triage meeting. d) is not the correct option due to the inclusion of 'dynamic'.	FL-3.2.2 K2

*19	c, e	c) and e) are the correct options. c) White-box test techniques are structure-based techniques that derive test cases from the system's implementation or internal structure. If the implementation changes, white-box test cases may need to be changed. Black-box test cases need to change only if the system's behavior changes. a) is not a correct option. White-box testing can be manual or automated for example, to detect certain code standards. b) is not a correct option. Black-box testing checks functional and non-functional behaviors. d) is not a correct option. The distinction between code running or not running refers to dynamic testing and static testing.	FL-4.4.1 K2
20	b	b) is the correct option. If the code includes only unconditional statements, the number of test cases required for branch testing is the same as for statement testing. a) is not the correct option. At least one test case is required to execute the branches. c) is not the correct option. Branch testing includes testing unconditional statements. d) is not the correct option. Branch testing is not useful when the code includes short-circuiting. Short-circuiting programming is a concept in which the compiler skips the execution or evaluation of some sub-expressions in a logical expression.	FL-4.3.2 K2
21	d	d) is the correct option. White-box testing provides coverage metrics that show the amount of code that has been covered by testing. White-box testing can then identify additional tests to increase code coverage. a), b) and c) are not correct options. White-box testing is based on the internal structure of the software and not on the requirements or usability specifications.	FL-4.3.3 K2
22	d	d) is the correct option. Error guessing does not rely heavily on formal documentation or specifications to identify potential errors. Testers may draw from their past experiences, similar systems, or general knowledge of common software issues to guess where errors might exist. a) is not the correct option. Error guessing involves guesswork rather than in-depth analysis. b) is not the correct option. Error guessing does not focus on achieving specific coverage metrics, such as statement coverage or branch coverage. Instead, it relies on the tester's intuition and experience to identify areas where errors made by developers are likely to occur. c) is not the correct option. Error guessing involves guesswork based on the tester's intuition and experience.	FL-4.4.1 K2
23	a	a) is the correct option. Exploratory testing can lack consistency and so is not as appropriate for regression testing as other test approaches. b) is not the correct option. Exploratory testing is a useful test technique to use when specifications are few or inadequate. c) is not the correct option. Exploratory testing is a useful test technique to use when time is restricted. d) is not the correct option. Exploratory testing can help the tester gain knowledge of the test object.	FL-4.4.2 K2

<table>
<tr><td>24</td><td>b</td><td>b) is the correct option. A knowledge silo refers to a person who has information or skills that are not shared.
a) is not the correct option. Mind mapping is a way of showing the connections between key ideas using images, lines and links.
c) is not the correct option. Brainstorming is a group problem-solving method that involves the contribution of creative ideas and solutions from group members. d) is not the correct option. Whiteboarding refers to the practice of using a whiteboard or similar tool to visually represent and develop ideas collaboratively.</td><td>FL-4.5.1
K2</td></tr>
<tr><td>25</td><td>c</td><td>c) is the correct option. The partitions are as shown:

Allowance | Basic | Intermediate | Higher
1 £15,000 | £15,001 £45,000 | £45,001 £60,000 | £60,001 and above

a) is not the correct option. Two values, £10,000 and £15,000 in the 'Allowance' partition.
b) is not the correct option. Two values, £20,000 and £45,000 are in the 'Basic' partition.
d) is not the correct option. Two values, £30,000 and £45,000 are in the 'Basic' partition.</td><td>FL-4.2.1
K3</td></tr>
<tr><td>26</td><td>d</td><td>d) is the correct option. There are eight boundaries to check with 16 input values required. These are 0/1, 21/22, 39/40, 55/56, 69/70, 81/82, 90/91, 100/101. Eight of these are checked with the given eight inputs. a), b) and c) are not correct options for the reasons given for d).</td><td>FL-4.2.2
K3</td></tr>
<tr><td>27</td><td>c</td><td>c) is the correct option. R6 indicates the equipment is <u>not</u> available and can be dispatched. It should indicate the request is on the waitlist.
a) is not the correct option. The equipment is available and not specialist so can be dispatched.
b) is not the correct option. The equipment is not immediately available and is not specialist so the request can be added to the waitlist irrespective of the requestor having specialist skills. d) is not the correct option. The equipment is available and not specialist so can be dispatched.</td><td>FL-4.2.3
K3</td></tr>
<tr><td>28</td><td>a</td><td>a) is the correct option as shown by the diagram.
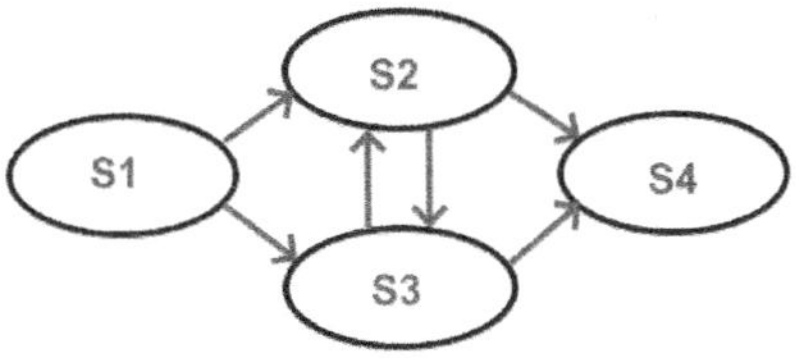

All states coverage TC1: S1 to S2 to S3 to S4
All valid transitions TC2: S1 to S2 to S3 to S4
TC3: S1 to S3 to S2 to S4
b), c) and d) are not correct options for the reason given for a).</td><td>FL-4.2.4
K3</td></tr>
</table>

29	c	c) is the correct option. Three of the test cases are derived correctly from the given acceptance criteria. These are: TC01 Verifies the user can log in with the reset password shows the reset process has been successful. TC02 Covers an aspect of the password reset process that may not be explicitly outlined in the acceptance criteria (email confirmation link's functionality) but is essential for overall functionality. TC04 Testing the software's response to an invalid password link entered is essential to ensure the password is not reset if an invalid password link is entered. Test cases should confirm positive and negative behavior. Two of the test cases are not correctly derived from the given acceptance criteria. These are: TC03 The acceptance criteria specifies five minutes, not two for the reset link to expire. TC05 The acceptance criteria refers to a user wanting to reset a password and not unblocking accounts. a), b) and d) are not correct options for the reasons given for c).	FL-4.5.3 K3
30	b	b) is the correct option. Likelihood can be viewed as the probability of the risk occurring. It may be assessed as high (1), medium (2) or low (3) or a probability percentage. Impact is the effect if the risk occurs and is assessed in a similar way to likelihood. The risk level/rating/priority number/exposure is risk likelihood x risk impact. a) is not the correct option. Risk likelihood by itself is not the risk level. Risk impact should also be taken into consideration for the risk level. c) is not the correct option. The risk rating is risk likelihood x risk impact. Risk impact can be referred to as business risk. d) is not the correct option. Risk likelihood can be assessed qualitatively or quantitatively or by a combination of both and cases assigned a value. Risk impact can be similarly assessed.	FL-5.2.1 K1
31	c	c) is the correct option. Test scope defines what is included and excluded from testing. a) is not the correct option. The context of testing includes details of the hardware, software, and network configurations required for testing as well as information about any tools, testing frameworks, and testing environments to be used. b) is not the correct option. The test approach covers the methodologies and techniques to be used, for example, the amount of manual testing and automated testing. d) is not the correct option. The test deliverables part of a test plan lists testware that will be produced as a result of testing and details of how these deliverables will be organized and managed.	FL-5.1.1 K2

32	a	a) is the correct option. 1B API testing is in Q2. 2A Component integration testing is in Q1. 3C Exploratory testing is in Q3. 4D. Portability testing (non-functional testing) is in Q4. b), c) and d) are not correct options for the reasons given for a).	FL-5.1.7 K2
33	a	a) is the correct option. 1B Undertaking test activities such as performing reviews and static testing, is risk mitigation by testing. 2D Making backups is a risk contingency measure. 3A Deciding not to take any action is risk acceptance. 4C Purchasing insurance is a transference measure. b), c) and d) are not correct options for the reasons given for a).	FL-5.2.4 K2
***34**	a, c	a) and c) are the correct options. a) Regular communication between stakeholders is a means of communicating the status and progress of the test process. c) A dashboard can display real-time data and metrics on the status and progress of the test process in a visual and easily understood format. b) is not the correct option. Details of the previous project do not communicate the status of the current test process. d) is not a correct option. The vacation schedule of the testers does not indicate the status of the current test process. e) is not the correct option. A test summary report, also called a test completion report, is produced at completion milestones and provides an evaluation of the corresponding test items against exit criteria.	FL-5.3.3 K2
35	d	d) is the correct option. Configuration management includes, '*...applying technical and administrative direction and surveillance to identify and document the functional and physical characteristics of a configuration item and control changes to those characteristics....*' a) is not the correct option. Optimizing hardware is an operations test task that focuses on improving the performance efficiency of physical hardware components. b) is not the correct option. Setting up user access permissions and security settings is a specific aspect of system administration focused on controlling and managing user interactions within a system or application. c) is not the correct option. Setting up network routers and switches is limited to network settings and parameters and does not address broader concerns such as version control or documentation management.	FL-5.4.1 K2
36	b	b) is the correct option. The estimate is $(3 + (4 \times 4.5) + 9) / 6 = 5$. The measurement error is (the most pessimistic estimate minus the most optimistic estimate) divided by 6, $(9 - 3) / 6 = 1$ person-hour. The measurement error is ±1 hour. a), c) and d) are not correct options for the reasons given for b).	FL-5.1.4 K3
37	b	b) is the correct option TC05 is the highest priority. However, TC05 cannot be executed until TC03 has been executed and TCO3 needs TC01 to have been executed. a), c) and d) are not correct options for the reasons given for b).	FL-5.1.5 K3

38	b	b) is the correct option. Two items are completely omitted. No information on the test environment such as the input device used or the linked device for the authentication code. The test environment is defined as the '*environment containing hardware, instrumentation, simulators, software tools, and other support elements needed to perform a test*'. There is also no indication the failure can be reproduced. The other items have not been completely omitted. The expected result is given as the authentication code should not be sent if the login fails. The error message text is included in the screenshot attachment. The impact is given as the login failure prevents users from accessing their accounts despite having an authentication code. The priority is given as high. a), c) and d) are not correct options for the reasons given for b).	FL-5.5.1 K3
***39**	a, d	a) and d) are the correct options. a) Executing automated test scripts is the main purpose of a test execution tool. d) With test execution tools, test cases can be scheduled to be run at any predetermined time, including out-of-hours. b) is not a correct option. Tracking the status of test cases throughout the software development lifecycle is a test management tool. c) is not a correct option. Test cases are organized into test suites during test implementation. e) is not a correct option. A test data implementation tool is used to prepare anonymized data.	FL-6.1.1 K2
40	a	a) is the correct option as it is the least correct. AI-enabled tools can inherit biases present in training data sets, leading to biased testing results. b) is not the correct option. AI-enabled tools can execute tests rapidly, making them suitable for continuous integration and continuous delivery (CI/CD) pipelines, providing quick feedback to developers. c) is not the correct option. AI-enabled tools adapt and learn so can dynamically prioritize testing based on code changes, historical defect data, and potential risk areas. d) is not the correct option. AI-enabled tools can be used in a wide range of scenarios, including complex interactions and intricate data flows and this leads to improved test coverage compared to manually defined test cases.	FL-6.2.1 K1
30	d	d) is the correct option. The correct links are: 1C User Interface (UI) response times – Product quality metrics. 2E Task completion - Project progress metrics. 3A Number of test cases executed/not executed - Test process progress metrics. 4D Amount of resources used - Cost metrics. 5B Percentage of code tested - Coverage metrics. a), b) and c) are not correct options for the reasons given for d).	FL-5.3.1 K1

BOOKING THE EXAM

You are ready to book the exam when you feel you meet the requirements of the learning objectives.

There is variation in the content between the exams of different exam Boards. The ISTQB statement from the ISTQB Sample Exam Introduction states the sample questions, '*should serve as guidance for question writers .... these sample questions should offer many ideas for the individual Member Boards on how to create good questions and appropriate answer sets for their examinations.*' As a result, exam questions can differ between Member Boards. ISTQB publish exam rules, structure and question formats that should provide consistency between the different Member Boards.

Exams may be taken at approved test centers or online. The ISTQB® General Assembly voted in May 2022 to permit exam delivery using a remote proctor as a permanent option for candidates taking certification exams that are part of the ISTQB® Certified Tester scheme. This allows candidates greater flexibility in their choice of Exam Member Board, which may be in a different country from the one where they reside, see Chapter *Booking the Exam.*

Online exams are available from ASTQB®, the American Software Testing Qualifications Board Inc., which accepts worldwide bookings. The exam can be scheduled at a convenient local time. From the ASTQB website, astqb.org, *'ASTQB's ISTQB exams are built by the American Board to be user-friendly and must meet the following criteria:*

1. *Each question for ASTQB's ISTQB exam is written by a person who has successfully completed an examination writing course and holds at least one Advanced level certification.*
2. *Each question is also reviewed and approved by at least two other examination writers.*
3. *ASTQB's ISTQB exam question performance is carefully monitored via psychometric analysis to ensure:*
    The question is performing correctly (the right proportion of people are getting it right).
    The question is fair with no misleading or easily mistaken wording.
    Each distractor (wrong answer) is fair and clear.
    The question is a valid test of the examinee's knowledge and is matched to the material in the syllabus and the learning objective.
    The correct answer is indisputable (not based on opinion).
4. *Each ASTQB's ISTQB exam question is matched to the specific learning objective in the syllabus.*
5. *Questions are balanced among the learning objectives of the syllabus.'*

The ASTQB® and their exam provider AT*SQA can add candidates who have passed, to both the Official U.S. List of Software Testers™ and the ISTQB® Successful Candidate Registry. With testing jobs now available remotely, offshore and in different time zones to provide faster feedback to developers, there are advantages to being on both these registers. The ASTQB® contact team are responsive and helpful to enquiries.

Online exams are now also available from other providers. When choosing to take an online exam, check first you have an environment that meets the requirements. Also, check you can complete the set-up requirements and that you understand the role of the proctor in monitoring the exam. Refer to the appropriate exam provider's website for details.

The exam may be booked independently through many channels:

ASTQB® The American Software Testing Qualifications Board Inc. - astqb.org

iSQI® The International Software Quality Institute Inc. - isqi.org/en/

GASQ® The Global Association for Software Quality - gasq.org/en/home.html

Some providers from the ISTQB® list of exam providers - www.istqb.org

Some Member Boards by Country - istqb.org/istqb-where-you-are/your-local-member-board.html

Extra time of 25% can be given for non-native language candidates and those with certain special needs. Extra time must be agreed upon in advance with the test provider and officially documented. Check the time required to complete a request to the relevant exam board well in advance of the exam date.

The total price of the exam (fee and applicable tax) can vary between different providers. Promotion codes and offers may be available through some channels. Terms, limitations and conditions may apply. If you have attended a training course, you may have the exam fee included in the price you paid for the course. This may include two attempts at the exam. Your instructor or exam provider will give details.

Good luck with the exam.

REFERENCES

This guide has referenced the versions of ISTQB® documents available at the time of publication from the ISTQB® website, www.istqb.org, further details are given below.

Copyright of ISTQB® referenced publications
The author acknowledges that this guide relies on the ISTQB® Certified Tester Foundation Level Syllabus (CTFL), Standard Glossary of Terms, Sample Exam Questions and Answers and other published materials. These are used in accordance with the statement in Section 0.1 of the ISTQB® Foundation Syllabus v4.0.1.
The author acknowledges the following named contributors from the ISTQB Syllabus v4.0.1.

ISTQB Glossary Documents
The Online Glossary is updated from time to time and should be used as the official reference. This guide uses the (updated) online version which is currently based on Glossary v4.8 with updates made to November 2026.

ISTQB® Standard Glossary of Terms used in Software Testing, version 4.8 (2026).
Web page: https://glossary.istqb.org/

About the ISTQB® Glossary: https://glossary.istqb.org/en_US/help/about

ISTQB® Glossary App (Official)
Google Play™ play.google.com/store/apps/details?id=org.istqb.istqbglossary
Apple Store™ apps.apple.com/gb/app/istqb-glossary-official/id1263653021

ISTQB Publications

News / Press Releases

ISTQB® News May 9, 2023 Release of Certified Tester Foundation Level v4.0 (CTFL) Syllabus.
ISTQB® NEWS, May 13, 2022 Remote proctor exams now a permanent delivery option.
ISTQB® NEWS, July 9, 2021 New version of the Official ISTQB® Glossary App released.

Syllabus

ISTQB® Foundation Level (CTFL) Syllabus 2024 v4.0.1 15th Sept 2024
istqb.org/certifications/certified-tester-foundation-level

ISTQB® Foundation Level (CTFL) Syllabus 2018 v3.1.1 1st July 2021 (sunset May 2024)
istqb.org/certifications/certified-tester-foundation-level-v3-1

Sample Exam Questions and Answers

ISTQB® CTFL - Sample Exam A Questions v1.7 (April 2025)
ISTQB® CTFL - Sample Exam A Answers v1.7 (April 2025)
ISTQB® CTFL - Sample Exam B Questions v1.7 (April 2025)
ISTQB® CTFL - Sample Exam B Answers v1.7 (April 2025)
ISTQB® CTFL - Sample Exam C Questions v1.6 (March 2025)
ISTQB® CTFL - Sample Exam C Answers v1.6 (March 2025)
ISTQB® CTFL - Sample Exam D Questions v1.5 (May 2025)
ISTQB® CTFL - Sample Exam D Answers v1.5 (May 2025)

Exam Information

ISTQB® Exam Structures and Rules v1.2 May 2025
ISTQB® Exam Structures & Rules Tables v1.19 August 2026

Registers of Successful Candidates

ISTQB® Successful Candidate Register - scr.istqb.org
Official U.S. List of Software Testers™ - atsqa.org/certified-testers

Other ISTQB Documents

ISTQB® Certified Tester Usability Testing (CT-UT)
istqb.org/certifications/certified-tester-usability-testing-ct-ut/
Select CT-UT Syllabus v1.0

ISTQB® Certified Tester Advanced Level Test Analyst (CTAL-TA)
istqb.org/certifications/certified-tester-advanced-level-test-analyst/
Select CTAL-TA Syllabus v4

ISTQB® Certified Foundation Level Agile Tester (CTFL-AT)
istqb.org/certifications/certified-tester-foundation-level-agile-tester-ctfl-at/
Select CTFL-AT Syllabus v1.0

ISO/IEC Standards

[ISO 25010] ISO/IEC 25010:2011 Systems and software engineering - Systems and software Quality Requirements and Evaluation (SQuaRE) System and software quality models (Chapter 4).

[ISO 25010] ISO/IEC 25010:2023 Systems and software engineering - Systems and software Quality Requirements and Evaluation (SQuaRE) - Product quality model.

[ISO 26515] ISO/IEC 26515:2018] Systems and software engineering - Developing information for users in an Agile environment.

[ISO 29119-1] ISO/IEC/IEEE 29119-1:2022 Software and systems engineering - Software testing - Part 1: General concepts.

[ISO 29119-2] ISO/IEC/IEEE 29119-2:2021 Software and systems engineering - Software testing - Part 2: Test processes.

[ISO 29119-3] ISO/IEC/IEEE 29119-3:2021 Software and systems engineering - Software testing - Part 3: Test documentation.

[ISO 29119-4] ISO/IEC/IEEE 29119-4:2021 Software and systems engineering - Software testing - Part 4: Test techniques.

[ISO 9241-210:2019] Ergonomics of human-system interaction - Part 210: Human-centred design for interactive systems.

[ISO 20246] ISO/IEC 20246:2017 Software and systems engineering - Work product reviews.

[ISO 25000] ISO/IEC 25000:2014 Software engineering - Software product quality requirements.

[ISO 12207] ISO 12207:2017 Systems and software engineering, Software life cycle processes.

[ISO 14764] ISO/IEC/IEEE 14764:2026 Software engineering - Software life cycle processes – maintenance

[ISO 24765] ISO/IEC/IEEE 24765:2026 Systems and software engineering - vocabulary.

ISO 9000:2026 Quality management systems – Fundamentals and vocabulary

ISO 9001:2026 Quality management systems – Requirements

Other Sources

American Software Testing Qualifications Board ASTQB® - www.astqb.org

Object Management Group® OMG-DMN™ Decision Model and Notation - omg.org/spec/DMN
omg.org/spec/DMN/1.3/PDF publication March 2021
omg.org/spec/DMN/1.4/Beta1/PDF publication March 2022
omg.org/spec/DMN/1.7/Beta1/PDF publication September 2026

Object Management Group® Unified Modeling Language™ - omg.org/spec/UML/2.5.1/PDF Dec 2017

Agile Agile Alliance® - agilealliance.org/the-alliance/
Agile Glossary – agilealliance.org/agile101/agile-glossary/ 'Agile pyramid'

Test Pyramid - Mike Cohn - mountaingoatsoftware.com/blog/the-forgotten-layer-of-the-test-automation-pyramid Roger Brown - agilecoachjournal.com/2014-01-28/the-agile-testing-pyramid

Testing Quadrants based on original work by Brian Marick (2003) defining the testing matrix.
exampler.com/old-blog/2003/08/22/#agile-testing-project-2
Exploration through Example Marick, B. (2003) exampler.com/old-blog/2003/08/21.1.html#agile-testing-project-1

Partitions - Introduction to Software Testing 2nd Edn. Ch 6.2-6.2 - Ammann and Offutt Cambridge University Press 2016.

Hawthorne Studies - oxfordreference.com

Hawthorne Effect - en.wikipedia.org/wiki/Hawthorne_effect

Deming Institute - Red bead experiment deming.org/lessons-from-the-red-bead-experiment-with-dr-deming

Software Testing Techniques, 2nd. Edition. Boris Beizer. Van Nostrand Reinhold, Boston MA. 1990.
Black-box Testing Techniques for Functional Testing of Software and Systems. Boris Beizer, Wiley 1995 and 2008.

Checklists - Software Engineering Notes - Reference dl.acm.org/doi/pdf/10.1145/308769.308798
A Survey of Software Inspection Checklists - Bill Brykczynski Institute for Defense Analyses VA. USA.

Pairwise Testing - www.pairwise.org
Process Specification, Dr Dario Landa-Silva University of Nottingham School of Computer Science.
www.cs.nott.ac.uk/~pszjds/teaching/archive/G52LSSLecture17.pdf

Oxford English Dictionary - www.oed.com

Bloom's Taxonomy of Educational Objectives: A Forty-year Retrospective (National Society for the Study of Education Yearbooks) Lorin W. Anderson (Editor), Lauren A. Sosniak (Editor) 1994.

Testing Principles

1. Testing shows the presence, not the absence of defects.
Buxton, J.N. and Randell B., eds (1970), Software Engineering Techniques. Report on a conference sponsored by the NATO Science Committee, Rome, Italy. 27–31 October 1969, p. 16.

2. Exhaustive testing is impossible.
Manna, Z., Waldinger, R. (1978) "The logic of computer programming," *IEEE Transactions on Software Engineering 4(3), pp. 199-229.*

3. Early testing saves time and money.
Boehm, B. (1981) Software Engineering Economics, Prentice Hall, Englewood Cliffs, NJ.

4. Defects cluster together.
Endres, A. (1975) "An Analysis of Errors and Their Causes in System Programs," *IEEE Transactions on Software Engineering 1(2), pp. 140-149.*

Manna, Z., Waldinger, R. (1978) "The logic of computer programming," *IEEE Transactions on Software Engineering 4(3).*

5. Tests wear out.
Beizer, B. (1990) Software Testing Techniques (2e), Van Nostrand Reinhold: Boston MA.

6. Testing is context dependent.
Kaner, C., Bach, J., and Pettichord, B. (2011) Lessons Learned in Software Testing: A Context-Driven Approach, 1st ed., Wiley.

7. Absence-of-defects fallacy.
Boehm, B. (1981) Software Engineering Economics, Prentice Hall, Englewood Cliffs, NJ.

APPENDIX A
ABBREVIATIONS AND ACRONYMS

AI	Artificial Intelligence
API	Application Programming Interface
AR	Augmented Reality
ASTQB®	American Software Testing Qualifications Board®
ATDD	Acceptance Test-Driven Development
BDD	Behavior-Driven Development
BVA	Boundary Value Analysis
BVT	Build Verification Test
CD	Continuous Delivery
CI	Continuous Integration
CIO	Chief Information Officer
CIT	Component Integration Testing
COTS	Commercial off-the-shelf Software
CRM	Customer Relationship Management
DDD	Domain-driven design
DDE	Defect Detection Effectiveness
DDP	Defect Detection Percentage - Test levels or iterations where defects are found/fixed
DMN™	OMG® – Decision Model and Notation™
DoD	Definition of Done
DoR	Definition of Ready
DRD	Decision Requirements Diagram (OMG-DMN)
DevOps	Set of practices that combines software development and IT operations
EC	Each Choice – a combinatorial technique
EP	Equivalence Partitioning
FDD	Feature-Driven Development
GNU™	Free software, not Unix but upward compatible with Unix
GUI	Graphical User Interface
HTML	Hypertext Markup Language
IEC	International Electrotechnical Commission
IEEE	Institute of Electrical and Electronics Engineers
INVEST	Independent, Negotiable, Valuable, Estimable, Small, Testable (ref User Story)
IoT	Internet of Things
ISO	International Organization for Standardization
ISTQB®	International Software Testing Qualifications Board®
MBT	Model-based testing
NLP	Natural Language Processing
OAT	Operational Acceptance Testing

OMG®	Object Management Group®
OWASP®	Open Worldwide Application Security Project®
QA	Quality Assurance
QC	Quality Control
ROI	Return on Investment
RPN	Risk Priority Number
RAD	Rapid Application Development
RUP	Rational Unified Process
SDLC	Software Development Lifecycle
SLC	System Lifecycle
SIT	System Integration Testing
SUS	System Usability Scale
SUT	System Under Test
TA	Test Analyst (ISTQB)
TDD	Test-Driven Development
TM	Test Manager (ISTQB)
TTA	Technical Test Analyst (ISTQB)
UAT	User Acceptance Testing
UI	User Interface
UML™	OMG® – Unified Modeling Language™
UT	Unit Testing
UX	User Experience
VR	Virtual Reality
XML	Extensible Markup Language
XP	Extreme Programming

APPENDIX B
PAIRWISE AND N-WISE TESTING

Pairwise Testing

Pairwise testing is a combinatorial technique and is defined as *'A black-box test technique in which test cases are designed to exercise pairs of parameter-value pairs.'* There is no ISTQB Foundation Level learning objective for pairwise testing. However, an understanding may be required when considering multiple equivalence partitioning, see below ISTQB® Sample Exam Set A v1.0 2023-04-21 Question #20.

Pairwise testing aims to uncover defects that arise from comprehensive coverage of those feasible to test combinations of two parameters. The assumption is that defects can occur from the interaction of two parameter-values from different parameters or equivalence partitions. The technique involves a systematic approach where all possible pairs are identified and then invalid combinations are removed, leaving testable combinations.

Example 1: For two parameter values, one having two options, one having three parameter values, there are 3 x 2 pairs and 2 x 3 = 6 test cases. For example, for a house:

Window frame color: White, Grey, Brown

Front door color: Blue, Red

Test Case	Window	Door
TC1	White	Blue
TC2	White	Red
TC3	Grey	Blue
TC4	Grey	Red
TC5	Brown	Blue
TC6	Brown	Red

Example 2: For three parameter values, two having two values, one having three parameter values can also be covered by 3 x 2 = 6 test cases. For example, a fence is added to the above. The fence can be Green or Brown. For three parameter values, two having two values, one having three parameter values, there are 2 x (3 x 2) + (2 x 2) = 16 pairs. Note the duplicate pairs in the table below.

Test Case	Window	Door	Fence	Pairs Tested
TC1	White	Blue	Green	White window/Blue door, White window/Green fence **Blue door/Green fence**
TC2	White	Red	Brown	White window/Red door, White window/Brown fence Red door/Brown fence
TC3	Grey	Blue	Green	Grey window/Blue door, Grey window/Green fence (Blue door/Green fence covered in TC1)
TC4	Grey	Red	Green	Grey window/Red door, Grey window/Green fence **Red door/Green fence**
TC5	Brown	Blue	Brown	Brown window/Blue door, Brown window/Brown fence Blue door/Brown fence
TC6	Brown	Red	Green	Brown window/Red door, Brown window/Green fence (Red door/Green fence covered in TC4)

There are ways to work out in advance the number of test cases needed. This can be complex, particularly when there are a large number of parameters and/or each parameter has a large number of values and is outside the scope of Foundation Level.

Pairwise testing is explained in more detail in Software Testing Advanced Test Analyst Complete Guide for ISTQB® Exam, C. Newbould, see *References*.

ISTQB® Sample Exam Set A v1.0 2023-04-21 Question #20
Although there is no learning objective specified for pairwise testing at Foundation Level, a basic understanding may be required, such as for ISTQB® Sample Exam question Set A v1.2 2023-11-06 Question #20.

'Question #20 (1 Point) You are testing a simplified apartment search form which has only two search criteria:

- *floor (with three possible options: ground floor; first floor; second or higher floor)*
- *garden type (with three possible options: no garden; small garden; large garden)*

Only apartments on the ground floor have gardens. The form has a built-in validation mechanism that will not allow you to use the search criteria which violate this rule.

Each test has two input values: floor and garden type. You want to apply equivalence partitioning (EP) to cover each floor and each garden type in your tests.

What is the minimal number of test cases to achieve 100% EP coverage?

a) 3
b) 4
c) 5
d) 6

Select ONE option'

Answer #20
ISTQB® Sample Exam Set A v1.2 Answers gives b) as the correct option.

A systematic pairwise approach, as follows, can be used to define all pair combinations and then remove invalid ones. In this scenario, with only two parameters, garden and floor, pairwise testing is the same as all combinations testing.

There are two parameters (or equivalence partitions), the garden (no, small, large) and floor (ground, first, second or higher), each parameter having three possible values. This requires 3 x 3 = 9 test cases for all pairs coverage.

Test Case	Garden	Floor	Comment
TC1	None	Ground	May or may not be valid
TC2	None	First	
TC3	None	Second / higher	
TC4	Small	Ground	
TC5	Small	First	Not Valid
TC6	Small	Second / higher	Not Valid
TC7	Large	Ground	
TC8	Large	First	Not Valid
TC9	Large	Second / higher	Not Valid

The built-in validation mechanism means four of the possible pairs (first floor and second or higher floors can be assumed not to have gardens) are not feasible, so these can be removed from the table.

N-wise Testing

It is possible defects may occur as a result of the interaction of three or more parameter-values from different parameters. This is much less common compared to finding defects occurring from the interaction between two parameter-values.

Given any number of parameters, if every n combination of parameter-values of n parameters must be covered in at least one test case, N-wise testing can be used. For example, 3-wise coverage requires every triple set of inputs from three parameters to be covered in at least one test case. Pairwise coverage can be considered to be a special case of N-wise coverage, where n is 2.

As with the use of any testing technique, consideration needs to be given to the test effort required and its effectiveness. The number of test cases increases with higher N-wise pattern sets. For example, with three parameters each having three parameter-values (3 x 3 x 3) = 27 test cases are required compared to (3 x 3) = 9 test cases for pairwise testing. If a project's schedule permits, higher order N-wise pattern sets can be tested to reduce the risk of missing subtle corner-case defects (problems or situations that occur with combinations of inputs that are outside normal operating parameters). It may also be appropriate in certain scenarios where for example safety is critical in all situations. However, it may not be practical or useful to cover all combinations in most scenarios.

N-wise testing is equal to all combinations testing when n is equal to the total number of parameters. For example, for a system with four parameters, performing 4-wise testing tests all possible combinations of these parameters.

APPENDIX C
DECISION TABLES OMG-DMN

Object Management Group® Decision Model Notation™, OMG-DMN™ is a standard for describing and modeling decision logic. DMN™ is designed to be readable and understandable by users in business and IT. It enables different groups to easily and effectively collaborate.

Although not in the Foundation Syllabus, Decision Model Notation™, and specifically OMG-DMN™, is commonly used in the workplace, replacing 'classic' full decision table notation. It is now used in the ISTQB Advanced Test Analyst Syllabus. The Object Management Group®, OMG®, is an open membership, not-for-profit, technology standards consortium. See *References*.

OMG-DMN™ is not limited by the number of values a condition may have. It also has several other advantages over classic full decision tables, including improved readability. OMG-DMN™ tables can be in different orientations.

Examples below show DMN™ notation being used as difficult to read. OMG-DMN™ notation is used with input expressions to show its readability.

For more details on OMG-DMN™, how to create decision tables based on this notation and the added benefits, see the book Software Testing Advanced Test Analyst Complete Guide for ISTQB Exam by C. Newbould ISBN 978-0-9536056-3-7.

Example 1: Simple DMN™ Decision Table

An organization has a shipping policy based on the weight and destination of the package. The destination is validated and then the weights are considered. The shipping rules for valid weights (greater than 0 kg and less than or equal to Max. kg) are as follows:

1. If the weight of the package is less than or equal to 1 kg and the destination is within the country, the shipping cost is $5.
2. If the weight of the package is more than 1 kg and less than or equal to 3 kg and the destination is within the country, the shipping cost is $10.
3. If the weight of the package is greater than 3 kg or the destination is International, the shipping cost is $25.

OMG-DMN decision table

Destination	Weight kg	Shipping Cost $	Test Case
Within Country	>0 weight ≤ 1	5	1
	1 < weight ≤ 3	10	2
	3 > weight ≤ Max.	25	3
International	≤ Max.	25	4

Example 2: OMG-DMN™ notation, three orientations and a full classic decision table for comparison. An online retail company wishes to reward its customers with loyalty cards. For orders with a loyalty card and an order value > £150 a 5% discount applies and free next-day delivery. For orders with a loyalty card and an order of £50 to £150, a 3% discount applies and free 3-5 day delivery. For orders with a loyalty card less than £50, the discount is 1%.

Vertical Orientation - Example 2				
Customer	Loyalty card			No Loyalty card
Order Value £	>150	[50–150]	<50	–
Discount %	5	3	1	0
Delivery	Free next-day	Free 3–5 days	3–5 days chargeable	3–5 days chargeable
Hit = U	1	2	3	4

Horizontal Orientation - Example 2				
Hit = U	Customer	Order Value £	Discount %	Delivery
1	Loyalty card	>150	5	Free next-day
2		[50 – 150]	3	Free 3–5 days
3		<50	1	3–5 days chargeable
4	No Loyalty card	–	0	3–5 days chargeable

<table>
<tr><th colspan="4">OMG–DMN™ Crosstab Orientation - Example 2</th></tr>
<tr><td colspan="2" rowspan="2">Discount %
Delivery</td><td colspan="2">Customer</td></tr>
<tr><td>Loyalty Card</td><td>No Loyalty Card</td></tr>
<tr><td rowspan="3">Order Value £</td><td>>150</td><td>5%
Free next-day delivery</td><td rowspan="3">0%
3–5 days chargeable</td></tr>
<tr><td>[50–150]</td><td>3%
Free 3–5 days</td></tr>
<tr><td><50</td><td>1%
3–5 days chargeable</td></tr>
</table>

Note: A crosstab output cell may have more than one output entry.

Classic Full Decision table: To simplify the table, there is no condition row for orders equal to £50 or equal to £150. This condition is assigned to columns 4 and 8 where 'Order > £150' and 'Order < £50' are both False.

	Rule							
Condition	**1**	**2**	**3**	**4**	**5**	**6**	**7**	**8**
Loyalty Card?	T	T	T	T	F	F	F	F
Order > £150	T	T	F	F	T	T	F	F
Order < £50	T	F	T	F	T	F	T	F
Action								
5% discount	X	X						
3% discount				X				
1% discount	X		X					
Free next-day delivery	X	X						
Free 3-5 days delivery			X					
Chargeable 3-5 days delivery			X		X	X	X	X

Columns 1 and 5 describe impossible situations, a single order cannot be greater than £150 and less than £50 at the same time.

Example 3: OMG-DMN™ Decision Table

Customers can apply for loans. Inputs are customer type, risk score and credit score. The output is an assignment of recommended category which the loan company can then use to make a final decision on whether to grant the loan.

OMG–DMN™ Loan Application - Example 3			
Customer	**Risk Score**	**Credit Score**	**Recommended Category**
Existing	< 110	< 550	High
		[550 … 580]	Medium
		> 580	Low
	[110 … 125]	< 570	High
		[570 … 600]	Medium
		> 600	Low
	> 125	-	Extra Low
Non-existing	≤ 100	< 540	High
		[540 … 560]	Medium
		> 560	Low
	> 100	< 550	High
		[550 … 575]	Medium
		> 575	Low

In this scenario, it would be more difficult to use a single classic full decision table. If using classic full decision tables, a hierarchy of classic full decision tables would be advisable.

APPENDIX D
SYLLABUS V4.0

ISTQB® Certified Tester Foundation Level (CTFL) v4.0 is an updated and significantly changed version of Syllabus v3.1.1 2018. The 2023 Syllabus aims to reflect changes in software development and testing. The Syllabus introduces some content from the ISTQB Foundation Level Agile Tester (CTFL-AT) certification and there is greater alignment with Agile methodologies.

The main changes to the Syllabus are:

Whole team (K1) and collaboration-based test approaches have been added with two new learning objectives (K2) on user stories and acceptance criteria with a further new learning objective (K3) on acceptance test-driven development (ATDD) (K3).

Existing content on test levels and reviews is reduced. Integration testing is now split into two separate test levels, component integration testing and system integration testing.

New content is included in test first development approaches (K1), DevOps (K2), shift left (K2), and retrospectives (K2).

Black-box techniques are updated. Each Choice (EC) coverage, a combinatorial technique, is included with equivalence partitioning. Use case testing is removed. Minimizing a full decision table is now identified as being outside the scope of the Syllabus. An additional explanation of state transition coverage metrics is added.

White-box decision testing and coverage are replaced with the more commonly used white-box branch testing and coverage (K3).

'Managing the Test Activities' section is significantly rewritten with more Agile concepts, including the test pyramid (K1), testing quadrants (K2) and communicating testing (K2). Some details on test strategy and factors influencing the test process are removed.

Expanded content on estimation (K2) for ratios, extrapolation, three-point and Wideband Delphi.

An additional learning objective (K2) on measures that can be taken in response to analyzed product risks has been added to the existing three learning objectives.

Independence of testing has moved from 'Managing the Test Activities' to the 'Fundamentals of Testing' section.

The Test Tools section has been simplified with reduced emphasis on tool types (K2) and a focus on the benefits and risks of test automation (K1).

Learning Objectives: The number of Syllabus v3.1 and v4.0 learning objectives and K-level distributions are shown in the table below.

Syllabus v3.1.1				
Section	**Number of Learning Objectives**			
	K1	**K2**	**K3**	**Total**
Fundamentals of Testing	2	11	0	**13**
Testing throughout the SDLC	2	6	0	**8**
Static Testing	2	5	1	**8**
Test Techniques	0	8	4	**12**
Test Management	4	9	2	**15**
Tools Support for Testing	5	1	0	**6**
Total	**15**	**40**	**7**	**62**

Syllabus v4.0 / v4.01				
Section	**Number of Learning Objectives**			
	K1	**K2**	**K3**	**Total**
Fundamentals of Testing	3	11	0	**14**
Testing Throughout the SDLC	2	8	0	**10**
Static Testing	4	4	0	**8**
Test Analysis and Design	0	9	5	**14**
Managing the Test Activities	4	9	3	**16**
Test Tools	1	1	0	**2**
Total	**14**	**42**	**8**	**64**

Questions: The number of Syllabus v3.1 and v4.0 questions and K-level distributions are shown in the table below.

Syllabus v3.1.1				
Section	**Number of Questions**			
	K1	**K2**	**K3**	**Total**
Fundamentals of Testing	2	6	0	**8**
Testing throughout the SDLC	1	4	0	**5**
Static Testing	1	3	1	**5**
Test Techniques	1	5	5	**11**
Test Management	2	5	2	**9**
Tools Support for Testing	1	1	0	**2**
Total	**8**	**24**	**8**	**40**

Syllabus v4.0 / v4.01				
Section	**Number of Questions**			
	K1	**K2**	**K3**	**Total**
Fundamentals of Testing	2	6	0	**8**
Testing Throughout the SDLC	2	4	0	**6**
Static Testing	2	2	0	**4**
Test Analysis and Design	0	6	5	**11**
Managing the Test Activities	1	5	3	**9**
Test Tools	1	1	0	**2**
Total	**8**	**24**	**8**	**40**

APPENDIX E
ISO/IEC 25010:2023

ISO/IEC 25010:2023 - Published 2023/11 '... document was prepared by Joint Technical Committee ISO/IEC JTC 1, Information technology, Subcommittee SC 7, Software and systems engineering. This second edition of ISO/IEC 25010, together with the first edition of ISO/IEC 25002 and the first edition of ISO/IEC 25019, cancels and replaces ISO/IEC 25010:2011.

Changes include:

Characteristic / Subcharacteristic	**Details of change**
Interaction capability	Replaces 'Usability'
User engagement	Replaces 'User interface aesthetics'
Inclusivity	Comes from 'Accessibility' being divided into two
User assistance	Comes from 'Accessibility' being divided into two
Self-descriptiveness	Added as a subcharacteristic of 'Interaction capability'
Flexibility	Replaces 'Portability'
Scalability	Added as a subcharacteristic of 'Flexibility'
Safety	Added as a new 'Quality' characteristic
Operational constraint	Added as a subcharacteristic of 'Safety'
Risk identification	Added as a subcharacteristic of 'Safety'
Fail safe	Added as a subcharacteristic of 'Safety'
Hazard warning	Added as a subcharacteristic of 'Safety'
Safe integration	Added as a subcharacteristic of 'Safety'
Faultlessness	Subcharacteristic of 'Reliability', replaces 'Maturity'
Resistance	Added as a subcharacteristic of 'Security'

Several terms have been given more accurate definitions. For example:

'Learnability' (ISO) is now defined as, 'The capability of a product to have specified users learn to use specified product functions within a specified amount of time.'

ISTQB Glossary uses an earlier definition of 'learnability' as, *'The degree to which specified users can learn to use a component or system within a defined period.'*

'Risk identification' (ISO) is now defined as, 'The capability of a product to identify a course of events or operations that can expose life, property or environment to unacceptable risk.'

ISTQB Glossary uses an earlier definition of 'risk identification' as, *'The process of finding, recognizing and describing risks.'*

'Operational constraint' (ISO) now refers to 'The capability of the product to constrain its operation to within safe parameters or states when encountering operational hazard.'

ISO/IEC 25010:2023 Quality Characteristics Model (published 11/2023).

ISO/IEC 25010:2023 Quality Characteristics Model

Functional suitability	Performance efficiency	Compatibility	Interaction capability	Reliability	Security	Maintainability	Flexibility	Safety
Functional correctness	Time-behavior	Co-existence	Appropriateness recognizability	Faultlessness	Confidentiality	Modularity	Adaptability	Operational constraint
Functional appropriateness	Resource utilization	Interoperability	Learnability	Availability	Integrity	Reusability	Scalability	Risk identification
Functional completeness	Capacity		Operability	Fault tolerance	Non-repudiation	Analyzability	Installability	Fail safe
			User error protection	Recoverability	Accountability	Modifiability	Replaceability	Hazard warning
			User engagement		Authenticity	Testability		Safe integration
			Inclusivity		Resistance			
			User assistance					
			Self-descriptiveness					

Index

Feedback

Your feedback is important. Please send feedback, comments and questions to: contact@revisionary.co.uk

Check for updates at: revisionary.co.uk

Publisher

AiFlex Publishing UK publish@aiflex.com

Other Books on Software Testing by C. Newbould

See the website **revisionary.co.uk** for more information, sample pages and comparisons as well as updates and details of books on software testing.

Software Testing Foundation Level – Guide for ISTQB® certification – C. Newbould
Syllabus v4 ISBN 978-0-9536056-6-8 November 2023 373pp AiFlex Publishing, (updated 2026).
"This Guide covers all necessary topics to help establish, build, and extend knowledge of the software testing foundation level for ISTQB® certification. Updated to Syllabus v4.0.1, the book shows what is required to achieve the ISTQB® Foundation Level CTFL qualification. The book supports self-study, classroom learning, and reference. It includes three complete practice exams and over 200 original practice questions aligned to all learning objectives, together with answers and detailed explanations that follow the specified exam structure and question format."

Software Testing AI Testing CT-AI – Exam Preparation for ISTQB® certification – C. Newbould
Syllabus v2.0 ISBN 978-0-9536056-9-9 October 2026 148pp AiFlex Publishing.
"This book covers essential topics to help build knowledge of software testing for the ISTQB® Certified Tester AI Testing CTAL-AI qualification. Based on the updated ISTQB AI Testing Syllabus v2.0 (April 2026), the book clearly explains exam techniques required to achieve certification. The book supports self-study and complements training courses. It includes three complete practice exams with over 120 original questions and answers. The questions are aligned with and cover all learning objectives, together with detailed explanations following the specified exam structure and formats."

Software Testing Test Management – Guide for ISTQB® certification – C. Newbould
Syllabus v3.0 ISBN 978-0-9536056-8-2 April 2026 440pp AiFlex Publishing.
"This Guide covers essential topics to help build and extend knowledge of software test management for the ISTQB® Advanced Level for Test Management CTAL-TM qualification. Based on Syllabus v3.0, the book clearly explains what is required to achieve the certification. The book will be helpful for self-study, as an aid in learning and training settings and as a reference. It includes two complete practice exams and over 280 original practice questions throughout the sections, all with answers and explanations. Examples are aligned with and cover all learning objectives, together with answers and detailed explanations following the specified exam structure and question format."

Software Testing Technical Test Analyst – Guide for ISTQB® certification – C. Newbould
Syllabus v4.0 ISBN 978-0-9536056-7-5 June 2025 470pp AiFlex Publishing.
"This Guide covers essential topics to help build and extend knowledge of software testing for the ISTQB® Advanced Level for Technical Test Analyst CTAL-TTA qualification. Based on Syllabus v4.0, the book clearly explains what is required to achieve the certification. The book will help with self-study, learning and training, and as a reference. It includes two complete practice exams and over 290 original practice questions throughout the sections, with answers. Examples are aligned with and cover all learning objectives, together with answers and detailed explanations following the specified exam structure and question format."